D1178043

VOLUME

Silver Spoon

HIROMU ARAKAWA

STORY & CHARACTERS

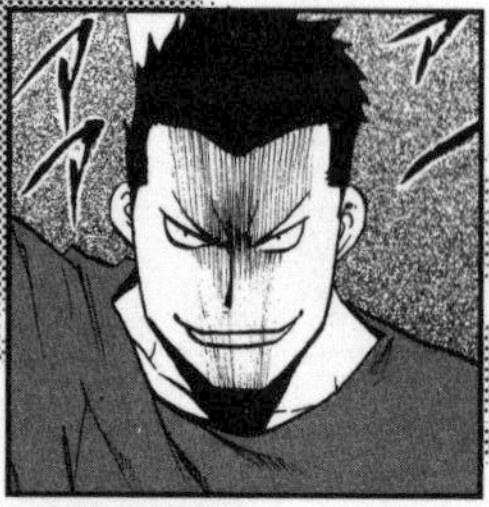

ICHIROU KOMABA

A first-year student at Ooezo Agricultural High School, enrolled in the Dairy Science Program. Pitcher for the baseball team with the potential to be their next ace player. Plans on taking over the family farm after graduation.

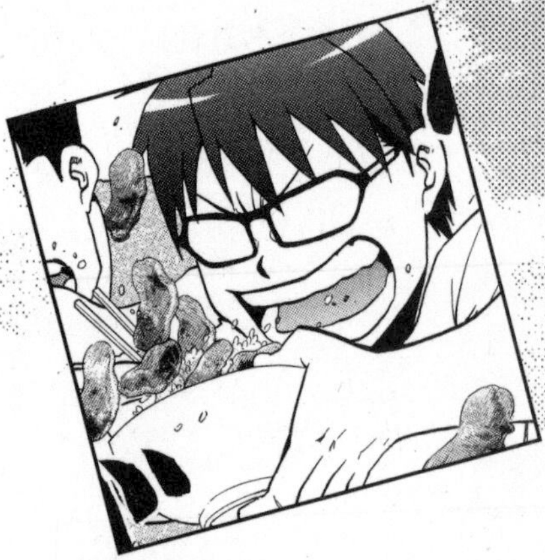

YUUGO HACHIKEN

A first-year student at Ooezo Agricultural High School, enrolled in the Dairy Science Program. A city kid from Sapporo who got in through the general entrance exam. Now he's vice president of Equestrian Club.

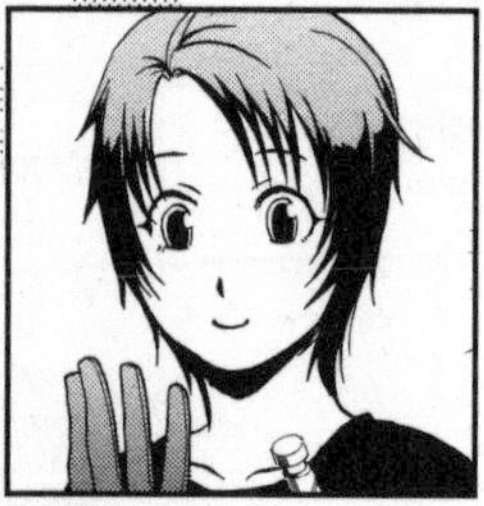

AKI MIKAGE

A first-year student at Ooezo Agricultural High School, enrolled in the Dairy Science Program. Her family keeps cows and horses, and she's expected to carry on the family business. Deep down, though, she wants to work with horses...

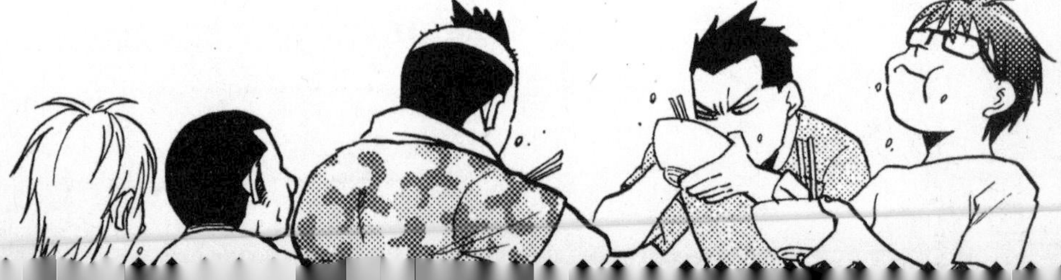

TAMAKO INADA

A first-year student at Ooezo Agricultural High School, enrolled in the Dairy Science Program. Her family runs a megafarm. A complete enigma.

The Story Thus Far:

Pork Bowl is sent to the slaughterhouse, and Hachiken buys all of his meat for ¥25,296, using the money he earned working on Mikage Ranch. With instruction from Inada-senpai, Hachiken processes Pork Bowl's meat into bacon all by himself. Then, joined by his friends and fellow students at Ezo AG, he eats it. And it's delicious. Hachiken's earnestness sits in his stomach... And the season changes from summer to autumn...
Hachiken becomes vice president of the Equestrian Club, and Komaba shines as a pitcher on the baseball team. But for some reason, Aki has been crying...

SHINNOSUKE AIKAWA

A first-year student at Ooezo Agricultural High School, enrolled in the Dairy Science Program. His dream is to become a veterinarian.

KEIJI TOKIWA

A first-year student at Ooezo Agricultural High School, enrolled in the Dairy Science Program. Son of chicken farmers. Awful at academics.

CONTENTS

Silver Spoon

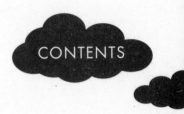

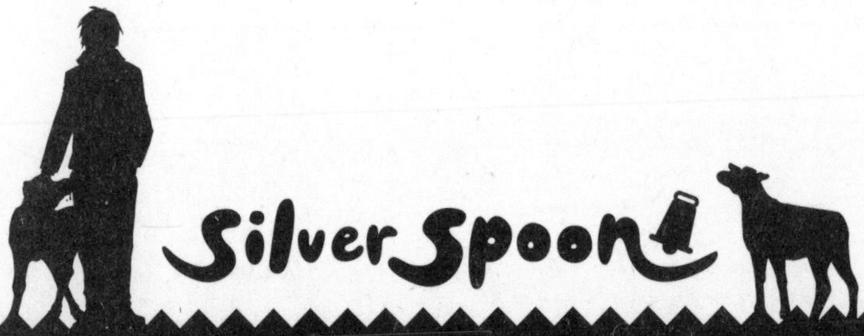

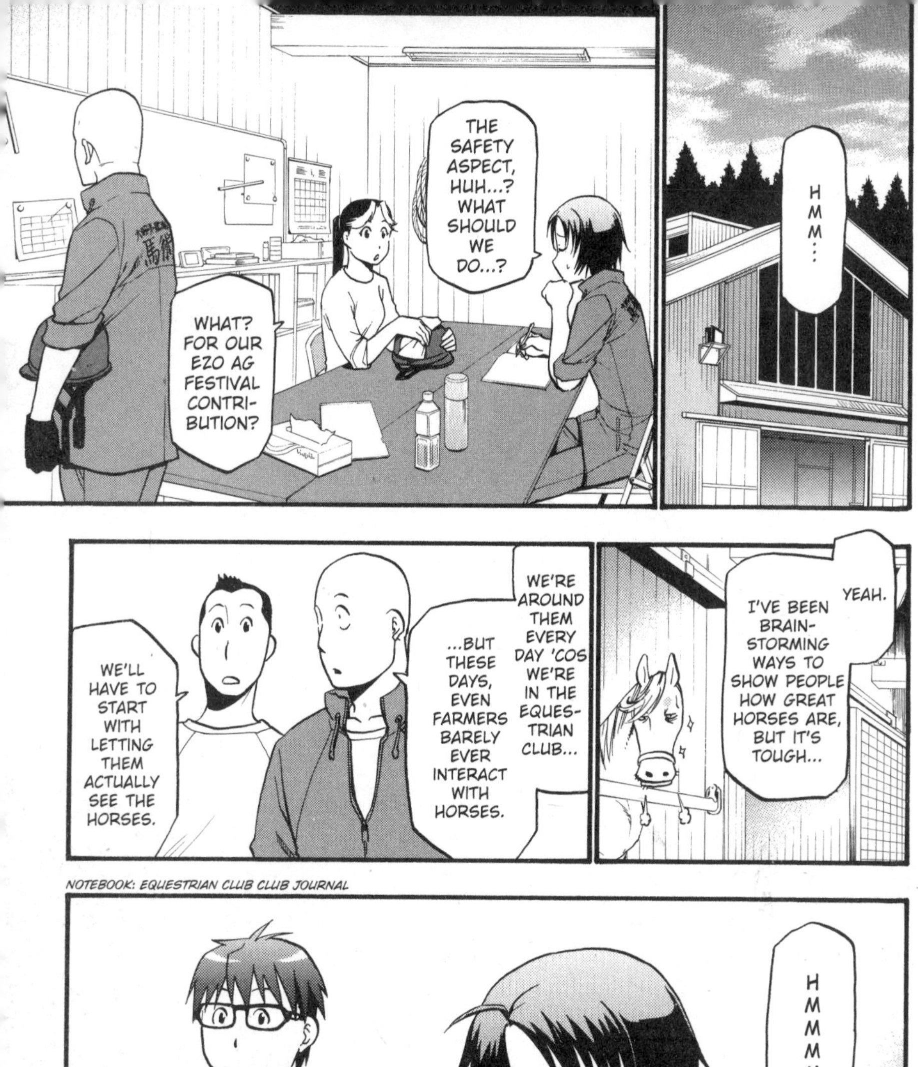
HMM...
THE SAFETY ASPECT, HUH...? WHAT SHOULD WE DO...?
WHAT? FOR OUR EZO AG FESTIVAL CONTRIBUTION?
YEAH.
I'VE BEEN BRAIN-STORMING WAYS TO SHOW PEOPLE HOW GREAT HORSES ARE, BUT IT'S TOUGH...
WE'RE AROUND THEM EVERY DAY 'COS WE'RE IN THE EQUES-TRIAN CLUB...
...BUT THESE DAYS, EVEN FARMERS BARELY EVER INTERACT WITH HORSES.
WE'LL HAVE TO START WITH LETTING THEM ACTUALLY SEE THE HORSES.

NOTEBOOK: EQUESTRIAN CLUB CLUB JOURNAL

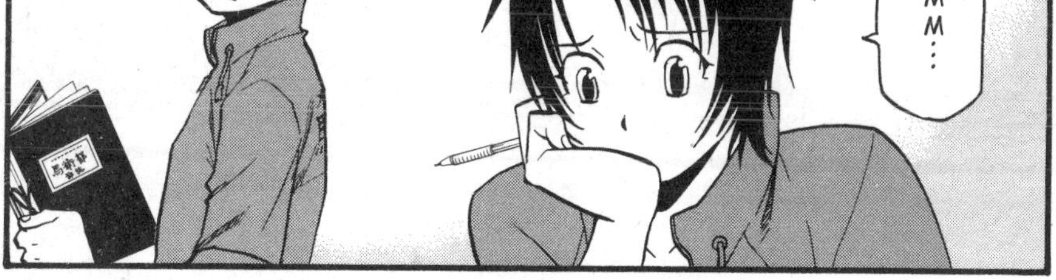
HMMMMM...

Chapter 36:
Tale of Autumn ⑤

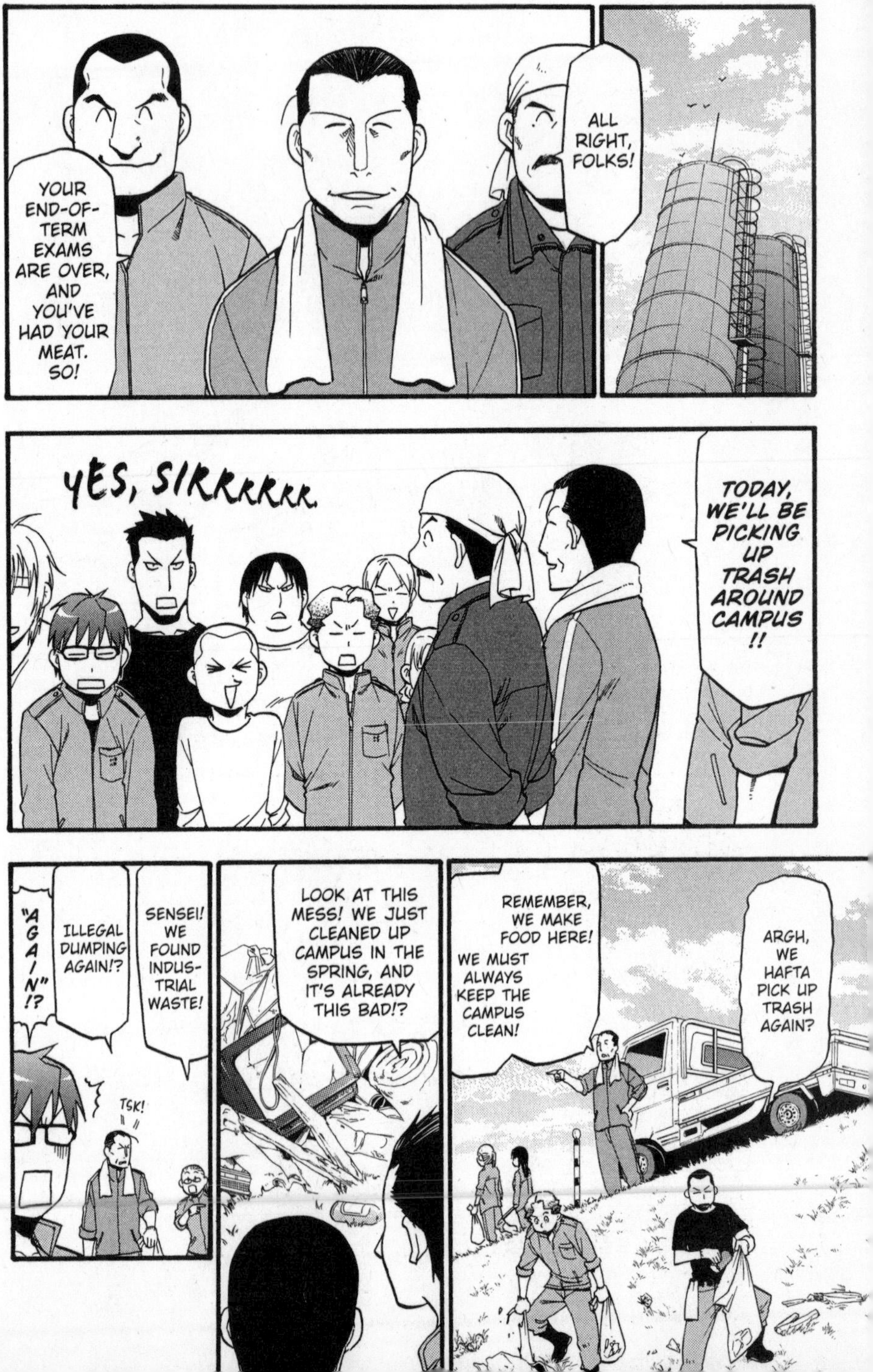

ALL RIGHT, FOLKS!
YOUR END-OF-TERM EXAMS ARE OVER, AND YOU'VE HAD YOUR MEAT. SO!
TODAY, WE'LL BE PICKING UP TRASH AROUND CAMPUS!!
YES, SIRRRRRR.
ARGH, WE HAFTA PICK UP TRASH AGAIN?
REMEMBER, WE MAKE FOOD HERE!
WE MUST ALWAYS KEEP THE CAMPUS CLEAN!
LOOK AT THIS MESS! WE JUST CLEANED UP CAMPUS IN THE SPRING, AND IT'S ALREADY THIS BAD!?
SENSEI! WE FOUND INDUS-TRIAL WASTE!
ILLEGAL DUMPING AGAIN!?
"AGAIN"!?
TSK!

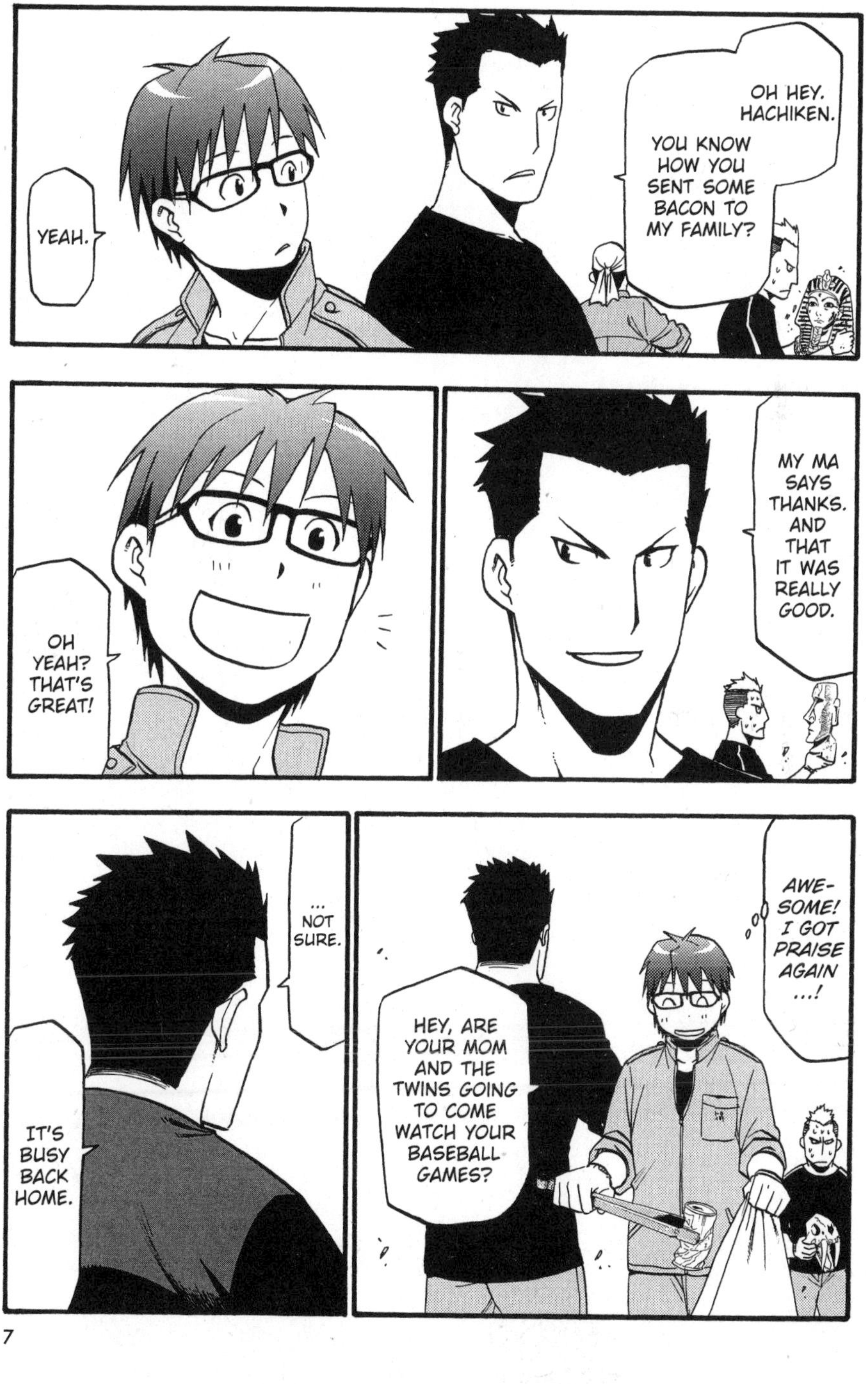
OH HEY. HACHIKEN.
YOU KNOW HOW YOU SENT SOME BACON TO MY FAMILY?
YEAH.
MY MA SAYS THANKS. AND THAT IT WAS REALLY GOOD.
OH YEAH? THAT'S GREAT!
AWE-SOME! I GOT PRAISE AGAIN ...!
HEY, ARE YOUR MOM AND THE TWINS GOING TO COME WATCH YOUR BASEBALL GAMES?
... NOT SURE.
IT'S BUSY BACK HOME.

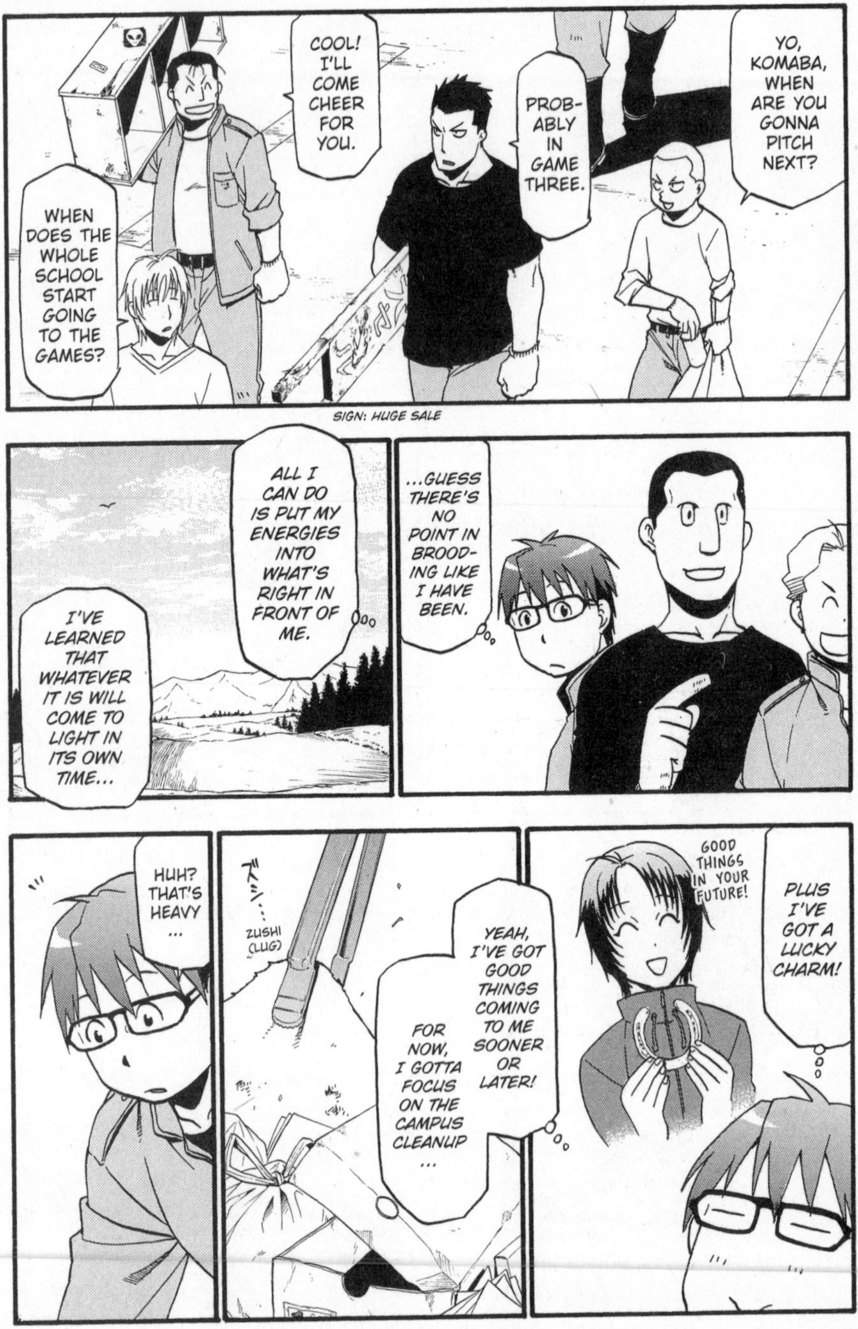
YO, KOMABA, WHEN ARE YOU GONNA PITCH NEXT?
PROBABLY IN GAME THREE.
COOL! I'LL COME CHEER FOR YOU.
WHEN DOES THE WHOLE SCHOOL START GOING TO THE GAMES?
...GUESS THERE'S NO POINT IN BROODING LIKE I HAVE BEEN.
ALL I CAN DO IS PUT MY ENERGIES INTO WHAT'S RIGHT IN FRONT OF ME.
I'VE LEARNED THAT WHATEVER IT IS WILL COME TO LIGHT IN ITS OWN TIME...
PLUS I'VE GOT A LUCKY CHARM!
GOOD THINGS IN YOUR FUTURE!
YEAH, I'VE GOT GOOD THINGS COMING TO ME SOONER OR LATER!
FOR NOW, I GOTTA FOCUS ON THE CAMPUS CLEANUP...
ZUSHI (LUG)
HUH? THAT'S HEAVY...

SIGN: HUGE SALE

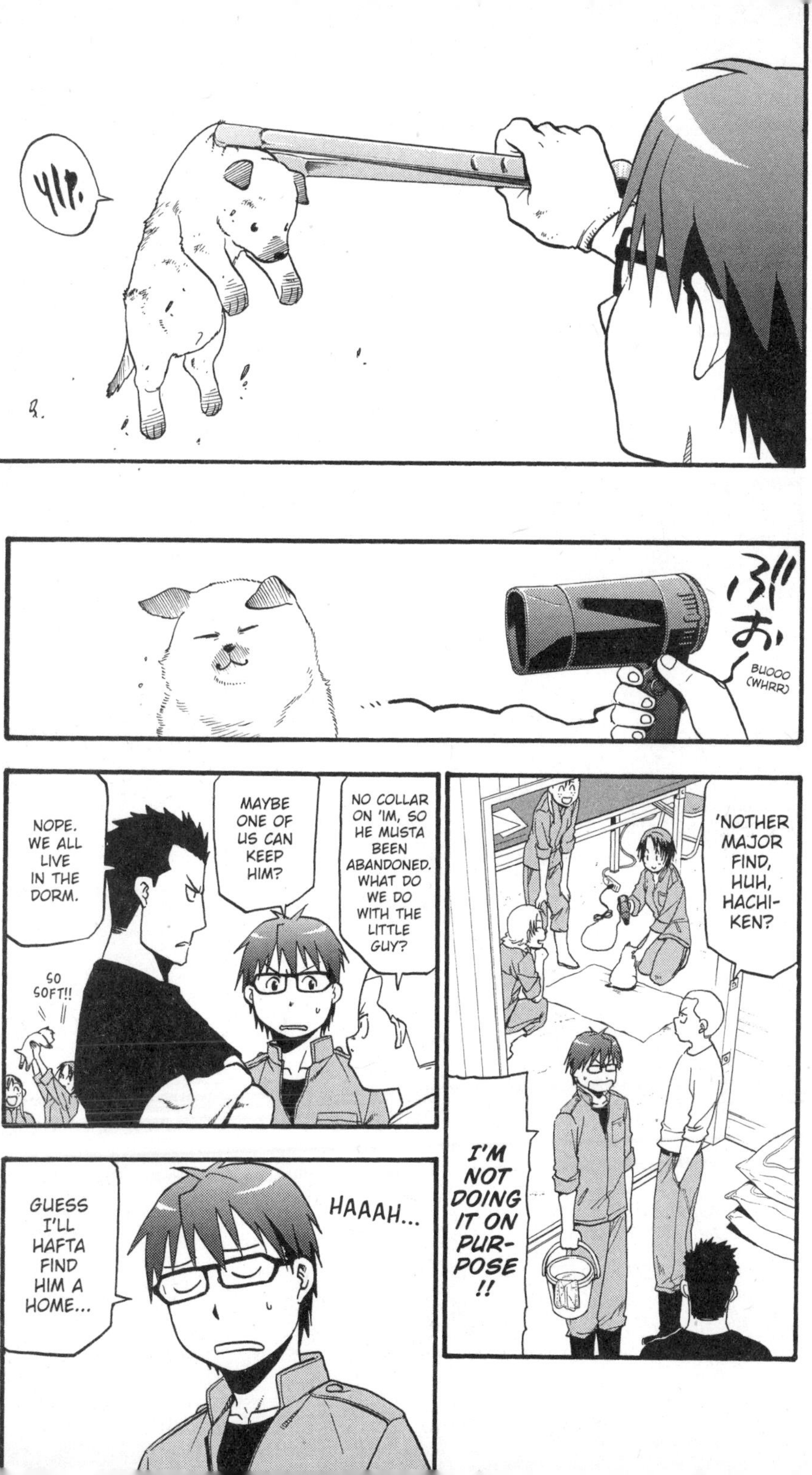
YIP.
ぶおー
BUOOO (WHRR)
'NOTHER MAJOR FIND, HUH, HACHIKEN?
I'M NOT DOING IT ON PURPOSE!!
NO COLLAR ON 'IM, SO HE MUSTA BEEN ABANDONED. WHAT DO WE DO WITH THE LITTLE GUY?
MAYBE ONE OF US CAN KEEP HIM?
NOPE. WE ALL LIVE IN THE DORM.
SO SOFT!!
HAAAH...
GUESS I'LL HAFTA FIND HIM A HOME...

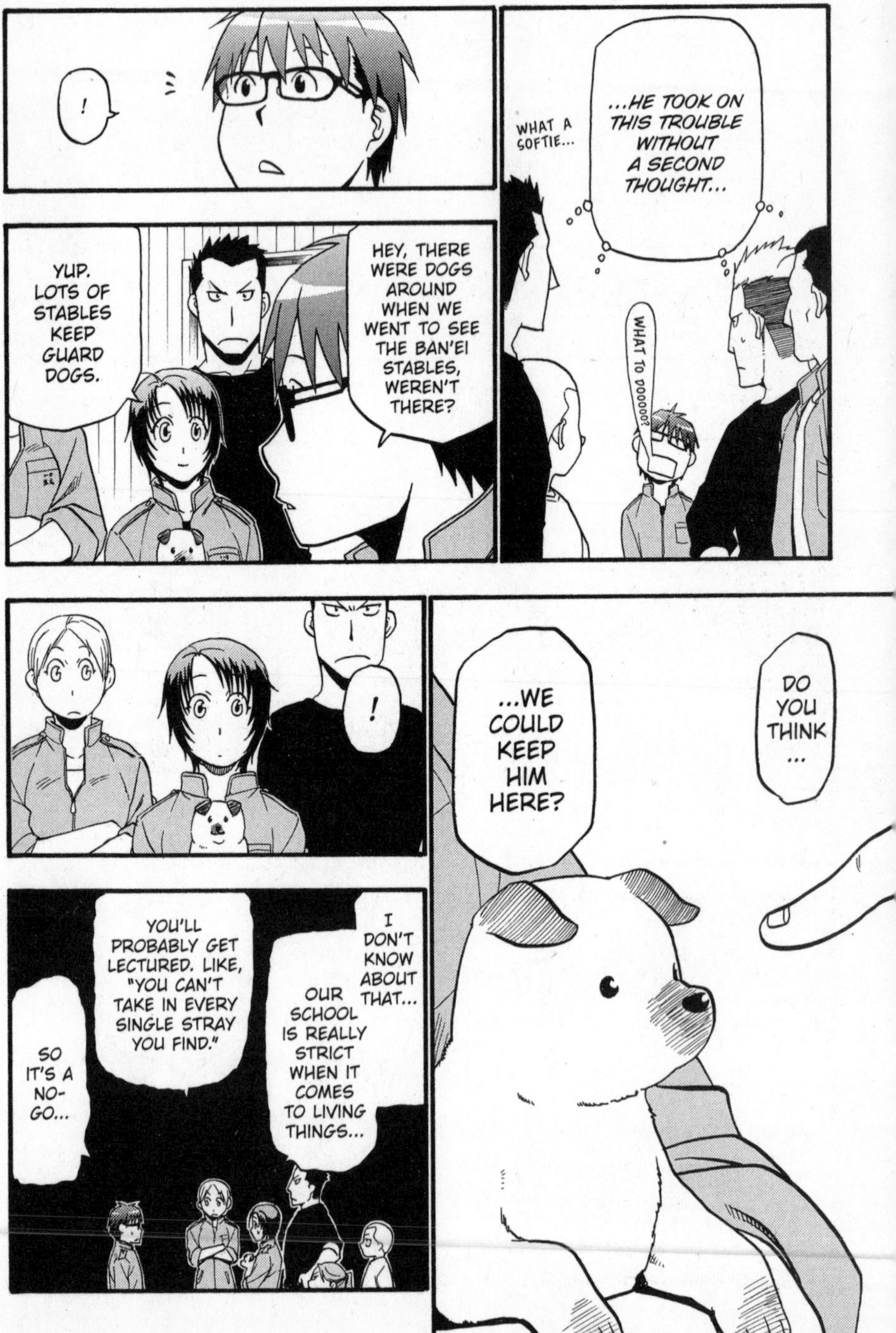
...HE TOOK ON THIS TROUBLE WITHOUT A SECOND THOUGHT...
WHAT A SOFTIE...
WHAT TO DOOOO?
!
HEY, THERE WERE DOGS AROUND WHEN WE WENT TO SEE THE BAN'EI STABLES, WEREN'T THERE?
YUP. LOTS OF STABLES KEEP GUARD DOGS.
DO YOU THINK ...
...WE COULD KEEP HIM HERE?
!
I DON'T KNOW ABOUT THAT...
OUR SCHOOL IS REALLY STRICT WHEN IT COMES TO LIVING THINGS...
YOU'LL PROBABLY GET LECTURED. LIKE, "YOU CAN'T TAKE IN EVERY SINGLE STRAY YOU FIND."
SO IT'S A NO-GO...

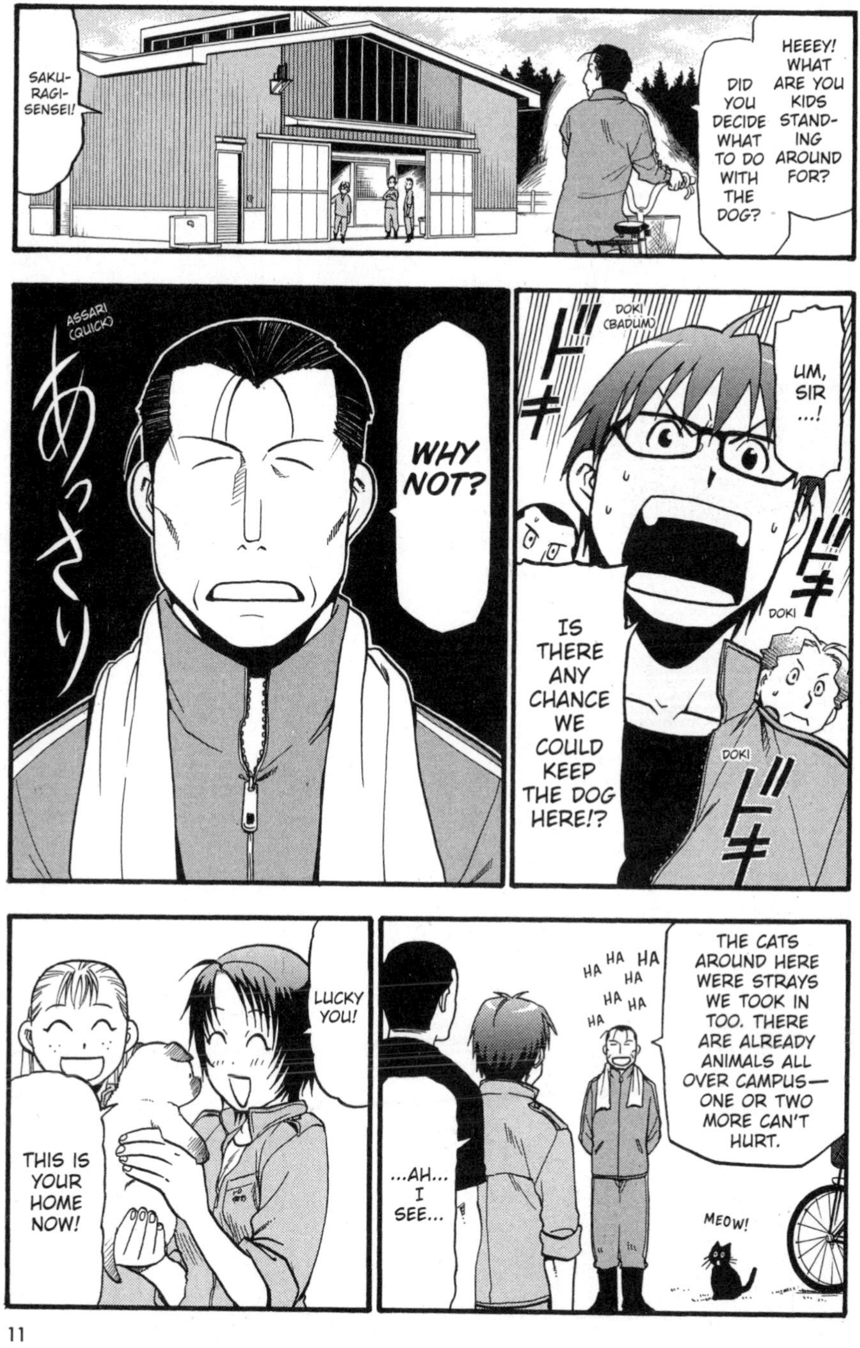
HEEEY! WHAT ARE YOU KIDS STANDING AROUND FOR?
DID YOU DECIDE WHAT TO DO WITH THE DOG?
SAKURAGI-SENSEI!
DOKI (BADUM)
UM, SIR...!
IS THERE ANY CHANCE WE COULD KEEP THE DOG HERE!?
DOKI
DOKI
WHY NOT?
ASSARI (QUICK)
THE CATS AROUND HERE WERE STRAYS WE TOOK IN TOO. THERE ARE ALREADY ANIMALS ALL OVER CAMPUS—ONE OR TWO MORE CAN'T HURT.
HA HA HA HA HA HA HA
...AH... I SEE...
MEOW!
LUCKY YOU!
THIS IS YOUR HOME NOW!

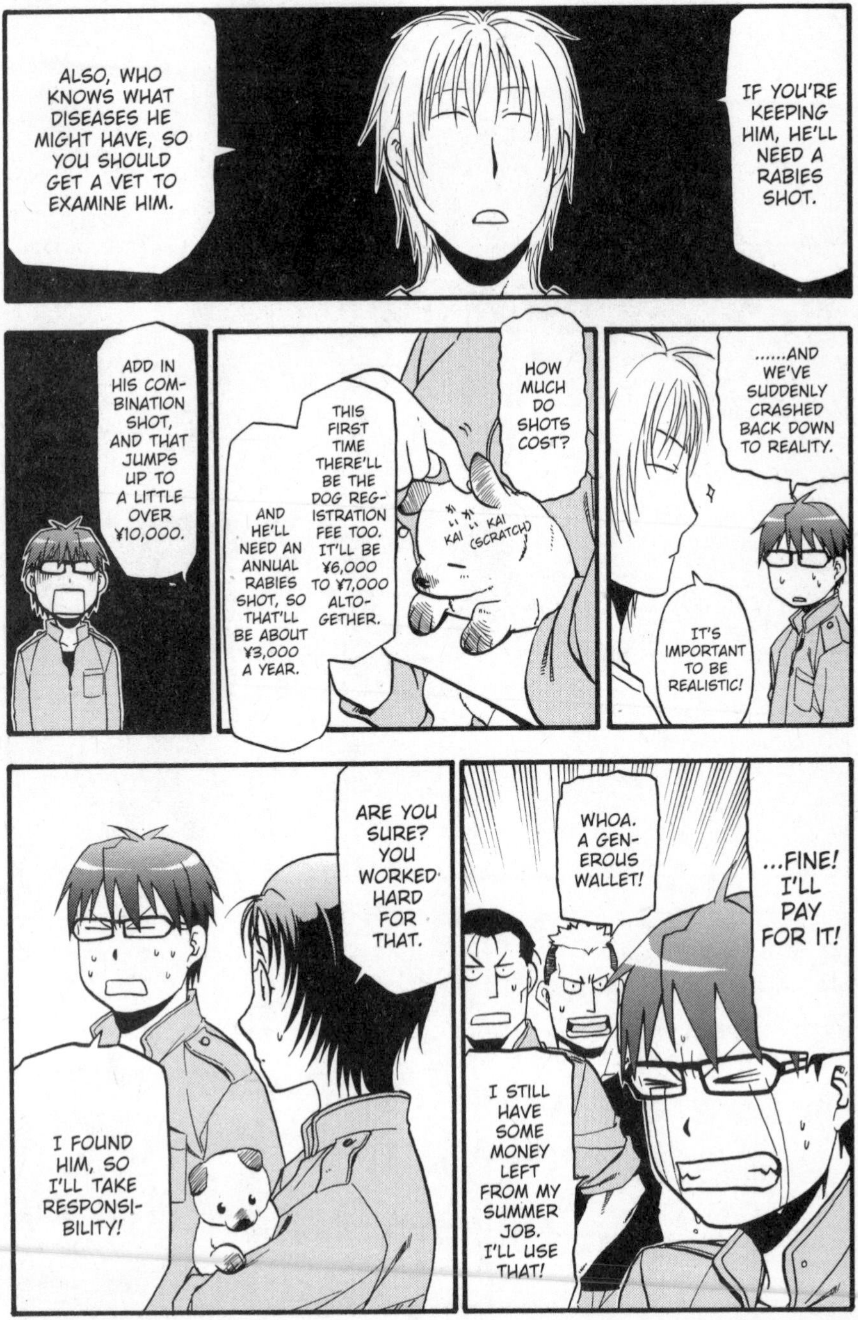
IF YOU'RE KEEPING HIM, HE'LL NEED A RABIES SHOT.
ALSO, WHO KNOWS WHAT DISEASES HE MIGHT HAVE, SO YOU SHOULD GET A VET TO EXAMINE HIM.
......AND WE'VE SUDDENLY CRASHED BACK DOWN TO REALITY.
IT'S IMPORTANT TO BE REALISTIC!
HOW MUCH DO SHOTS COST?
KAI KAI (SCRATCH)
THIS FIRST TIME THERE'LL BE THE DOG REGISTRATION FEE TOO. IT'LL BE ¥6,000 TO ¥7,000 ALTOGETHER.
AND HE'LL NEED AN ANNUAL RABIES SHOT, SO THAT'LL BE ABOUT ¥3,000 A YEAR.
ADD IN HIS COMBINATION SHOT, AND THAT JUMPS UP TO A LITTLE OVER ¥10,000.
...FINE! I'LL PAY FOR IT!
WHOA. A GENEROUS WALLET!
I STILL HAVE SOME MONEY LEFT FROM MY SUMMER JOB. I'LL USE THAT!
ARE YOU SURE? YOU WORKED HARD FOR THAT.
I FOUND HIM, SO I'LL TAKE RESPONSIBILITY!

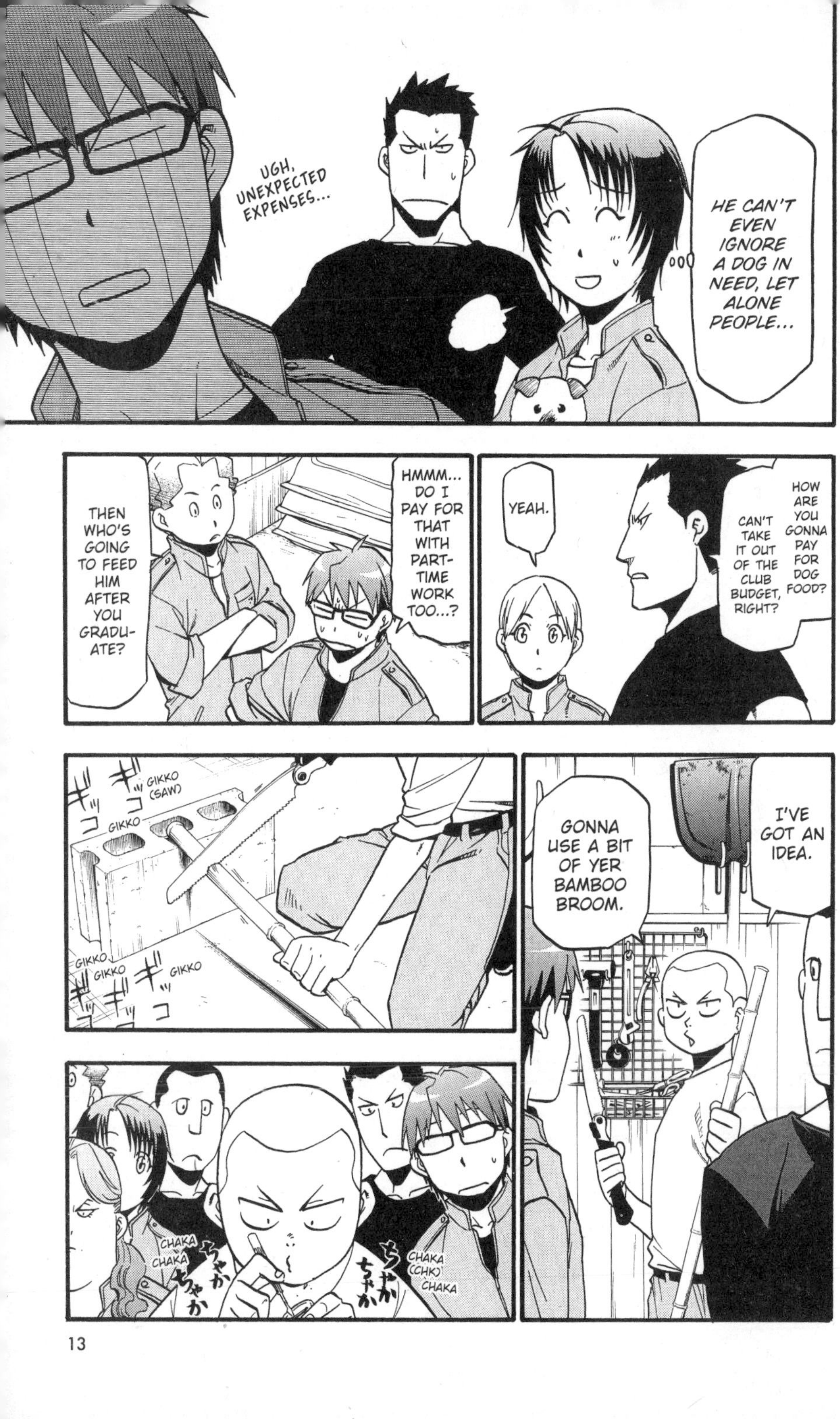
HE CAN'T EVEN IGNORE A DOG IN NEED, LET ALONE PEOPLE...
UGH, UNEXPECTED EXPENSES...
HOW ARE YOU GONNA PAY FOR DOG FOOD?
CAN'T TAKE IT OUT OF THE CLUB BUDGET, RIGHT?
YEAH.
HMMM... DO I PAY FOR THAT WITH PART-TIME WORK TOO...?
THEN WHO'S GOING TO FEED HIM AFTER YOU GRADUATE?
I'VE GOT AN IDEA.
GONNA USE A BIT OF YER BAMBOO BROOM.
ギッコ GIKKO (SAW)
GIKKO
ギッコ ギッコ GIKKO GIKKO GIKKO
ちゃか ちゃか CHAKA (CHK) CHAKA
ちゃか ちゃか CHAKA CHAKA

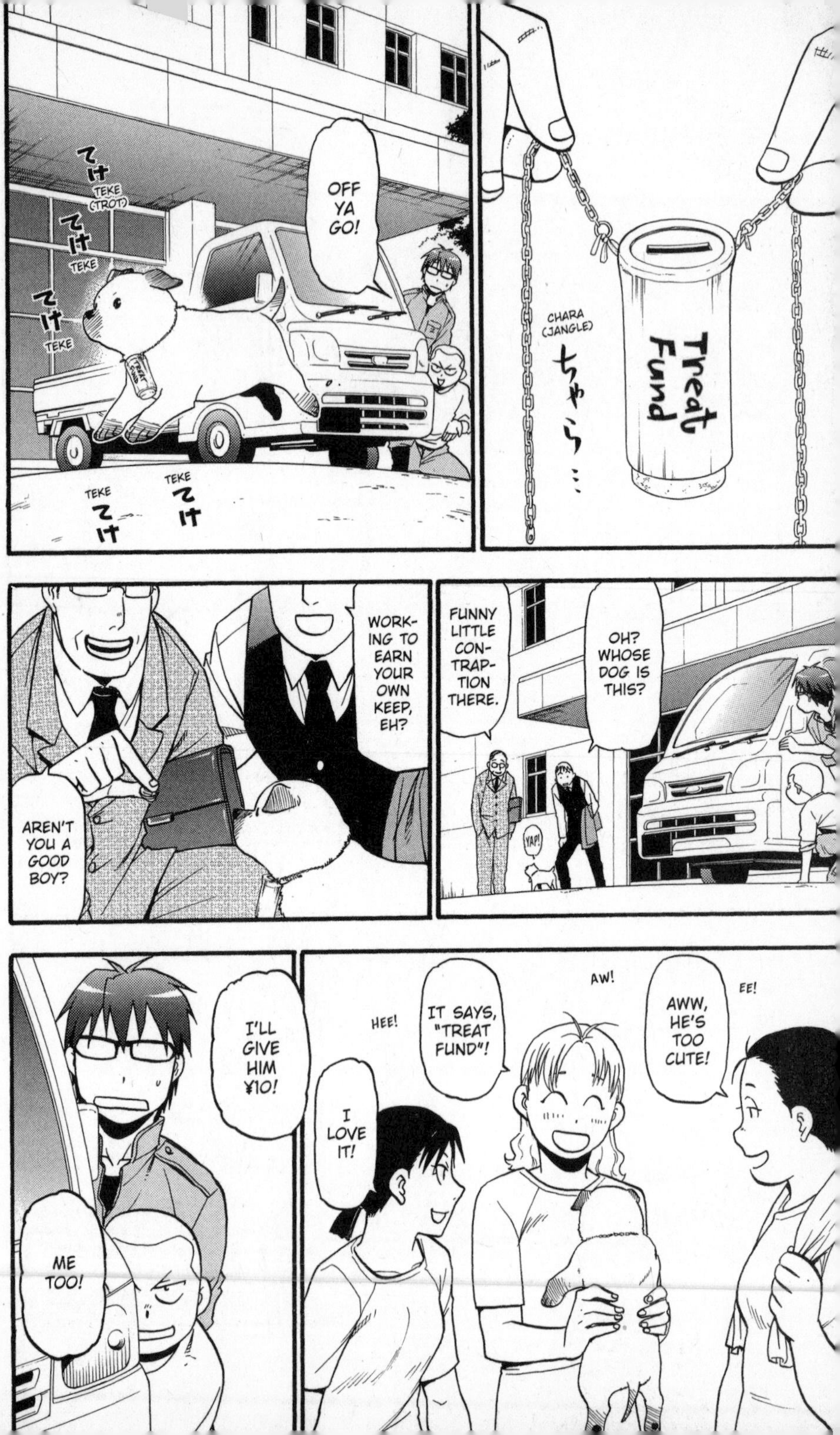
Treat Fund
ちゃら…
CHARA (JANGLE)
てけ
TEKE (TROT)
てけ
TEKE
てけ
TEKE
OFF YA GO!
てけ
TEKE
てけ
TEKE
OH? WHOSE DOG IS THIS?
FUNNY LITTLE CONTRAPTION THERE.
YAP!
WORKING TO EARN YOUR OWN KEEP, EH?
AREN'T YOU A GOOD BOY?
AWW, HE'S TOO CUTE!
EE!
AW!
IT SAYS, "TREAT FUND"!
HEE!
I LOVE IT!
I'LL GIVE HIM ¥10!
ME TOO!

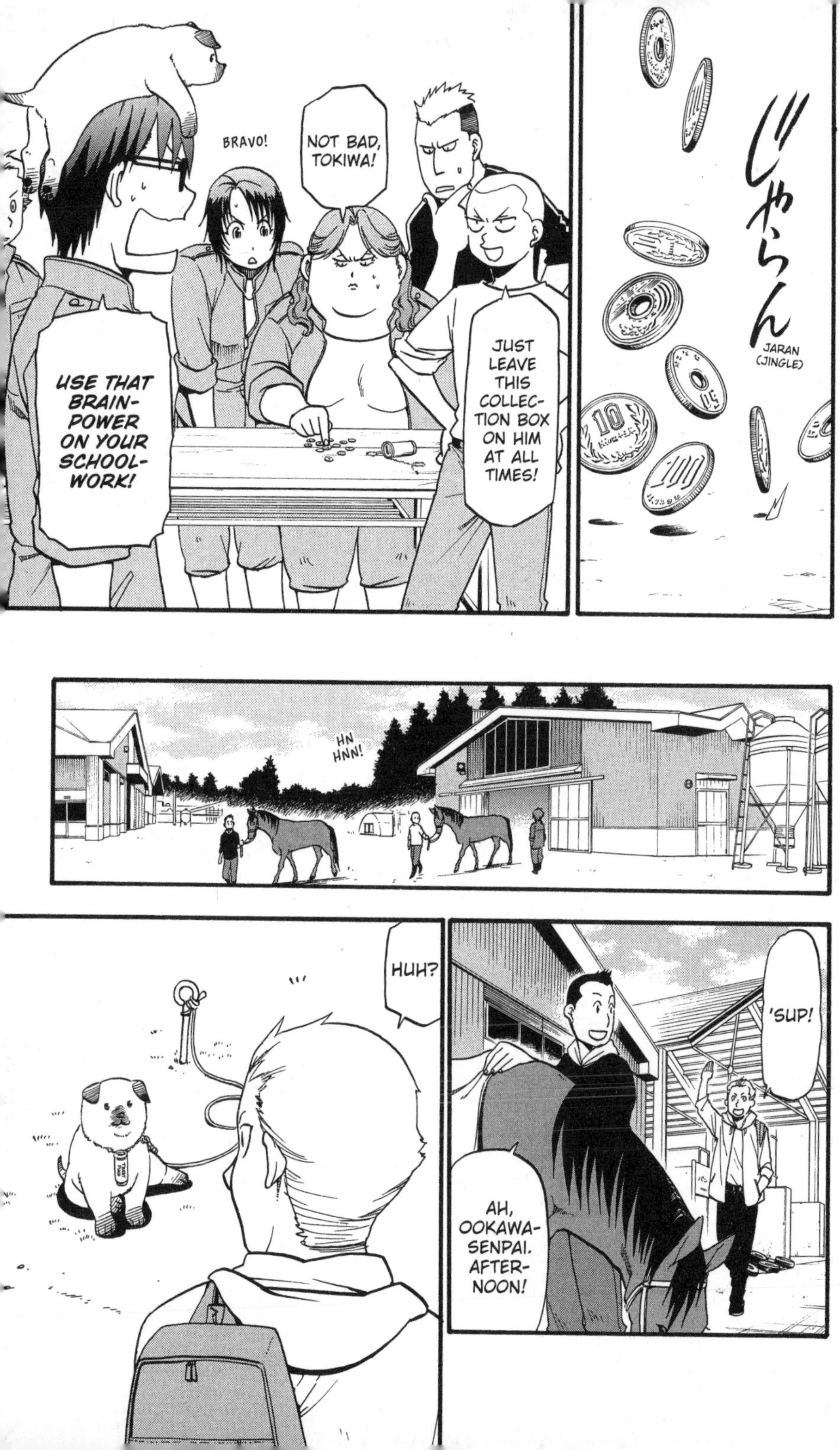

じゃらん
JARAN (JINGLE)
NOT BAD, TOKIWA!
BRAVO!
JUST LEAVE THIS COLLECTION BOX ON HIM AT ALL TIMES!
USE THAT BRAIN-POWER ON YOUR SCHOOL-WORK!
HN HNN!
'SUP!
AH, OOKAWA-SENPAI. AFTER-NOON!
HUH?

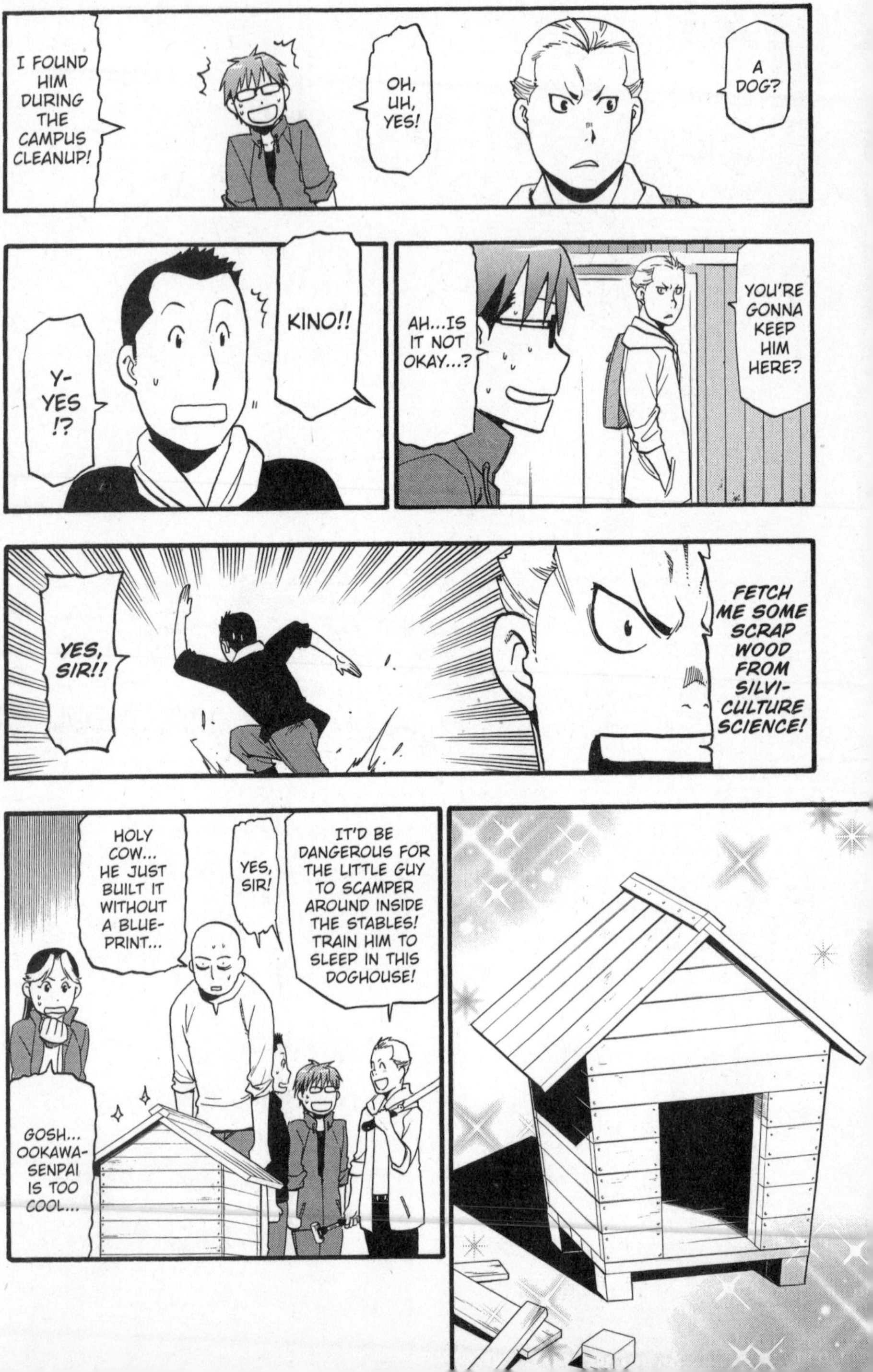
A DOG?
OH, UH, YES!
I FOUND HIM DURING THE CAMPUS CLEANUP!
YOU'RE GONNA KEEP HIM HERE?
AH...IS IT NOT OKAY...?
KINO!!
Y-YES!?
FETCH ME SOME SCRAP WOOD FROM SILVI-CULTURE SCIENCE!
YES, SIR!!
IT'D BE DANGEROUS FOR THE LITTLE GUY TO SCAMPER AROUND INSIDE THE STABLES! TRAIN HIM TO SLEEP IN THIS DOGHOUSE!
YES, SIR!
HOLY COW... HE JUST BUILT IT WITHOUT A BLUE-PRINT...
GOSH... OOKAWA-SENPAI IS TOO COOL...

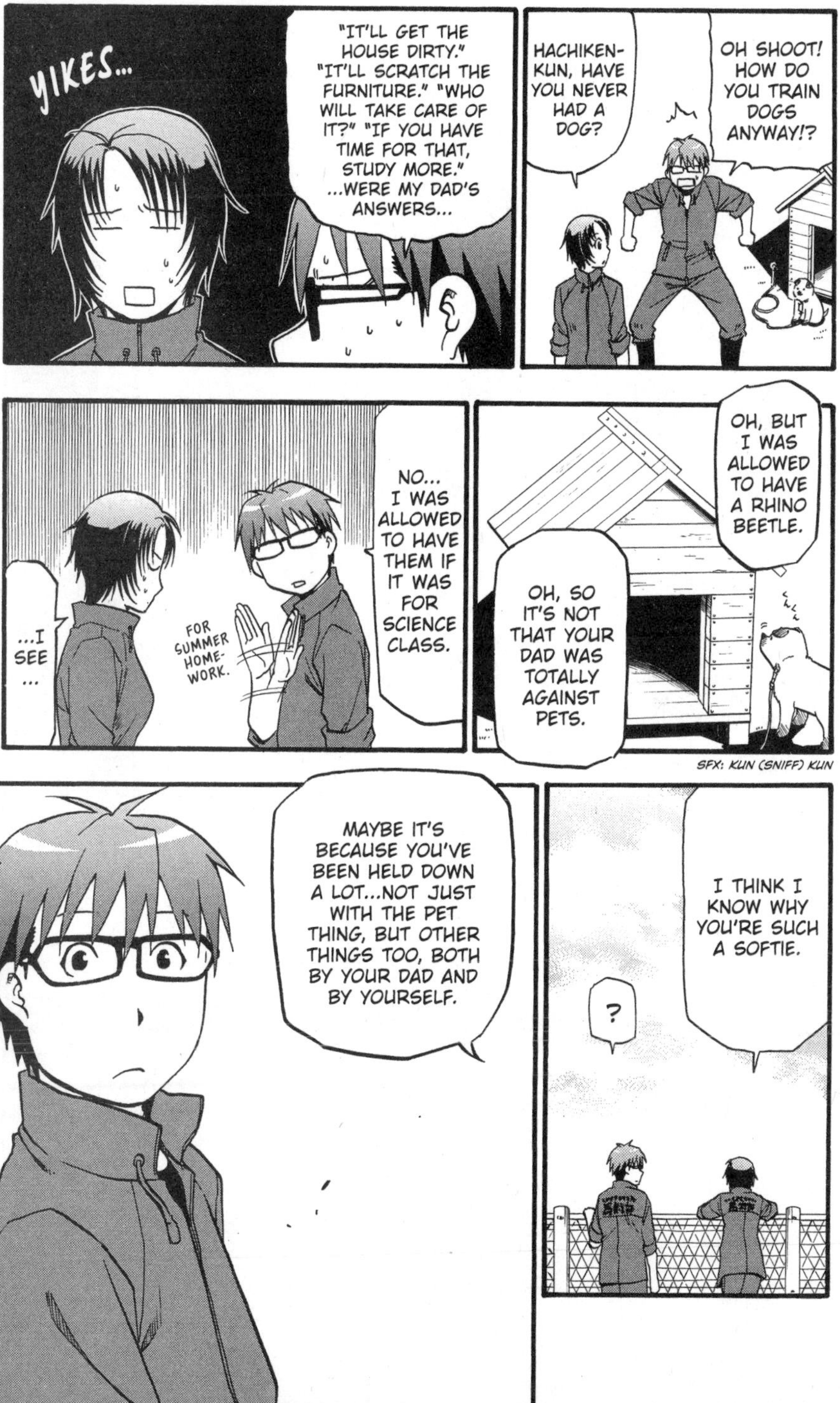
OH SHOOT! HOW DO YOU TRAIN DOGS ANYWAY!?
HACHIKEN-KUN, HAVE YOU NEVER HAD A DOG?
"IT'LL GET THE HOUSE DIRTY." "IT'LL SCRATCH THE FURNITURE." "WHO WILL TAKE CARE OF IT?" "IF YOU HAVE TIME FOR THAT, STUDY MORE." ...WERE MY DAD'S ANSWERS...
YIKES...
OH, BUT I WAS ALLOWED TO HAVE A RHINO BEETLE.
OH, SO IT'S NOT THAT YOUR DAD WAS TOTALLY AGAINST PETS.
NO... I WAS ALLOWED TO HAVE THEM IF IT WAS FOR SCIENCE CLASS.
FOR SUMMER HOMEWORK.
...I SEE...
I THINK I KNOW WHY YOU'RE SUCH A SOFTIE.
?
MAYBE IT'S BECAUSE YOU'VE BEEN HELD DOWN A LOT...NOT JUST WITH THE PET THING, BUT OTHER THINGS TOO, BOTH BY YOUR DAD AND BY YOURSELF.
SFX: KUN (SNIFF) KUN

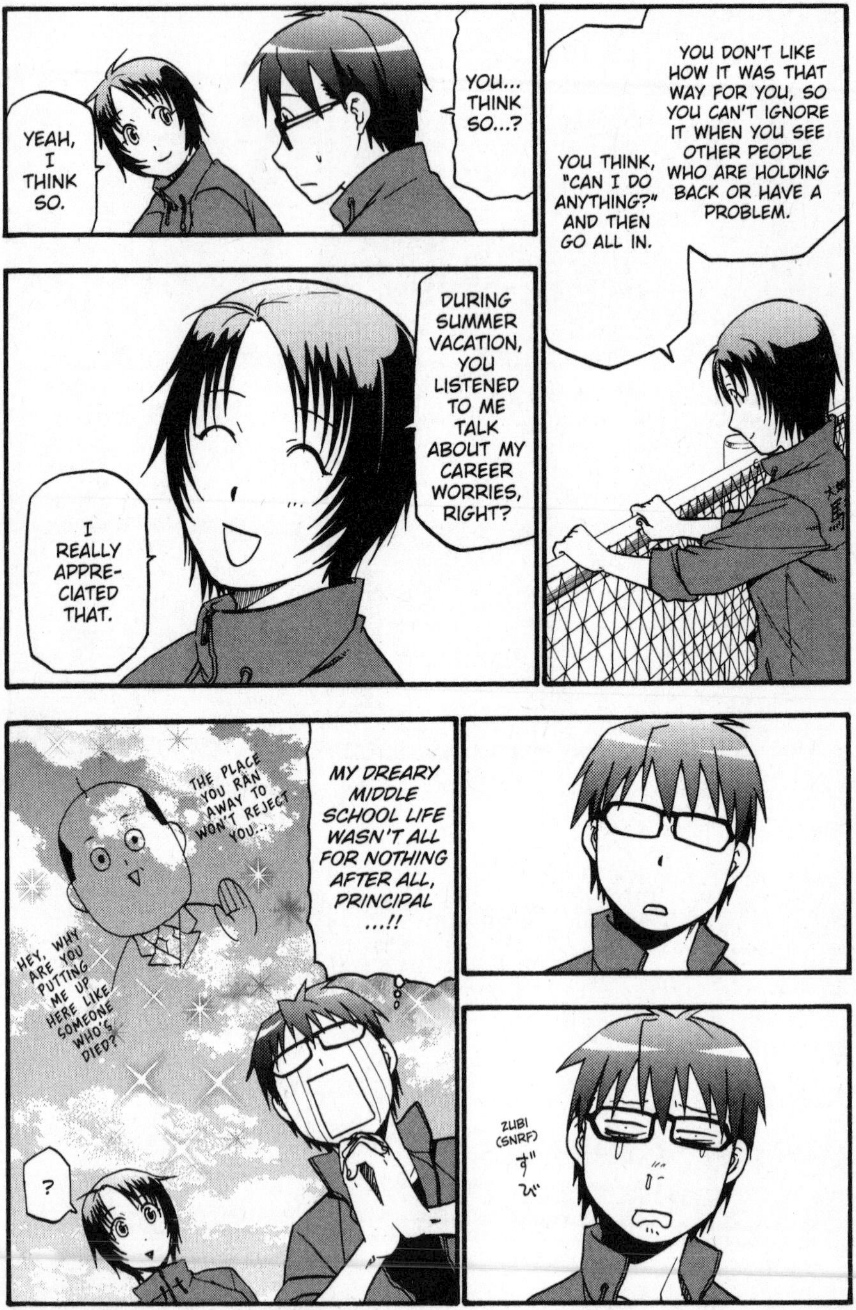
YOU DON'T LIKE HOW IT WAS THAT WAY FOR YOU, SO YOU CAN'T IGNORE IT WHEN YOU SEE OTHER PEOPLE WHO ARE HOLDING BACK OR HAVE A PROBLEM.
YOU THINK, "CAN I DO ANYTHING?" AND THEN GO ALL IN.
YOU... THINK SO...?
YEAH, I THINK SO.
DURING SUMMER VACATION, YOU LISTENED TO ME TALK ABOUT MY CAREER WORRIES, RIGHT?
I REALLY APPRECIATED THAT.
ZUBI (SNRF)
ずび
MY DREARY MIDDLE SCHOOL LIFE WASN'T ALL FOR NOTHING AFTER ALL, PRINCIPAL...!!
THE PLACE YOU RAN AWAY TO WON'T REJECT YOU...
HEY, WHY ARE YOU PUTTING ME UP HERE LIKE SOMEONE WHO'S DIED?
?

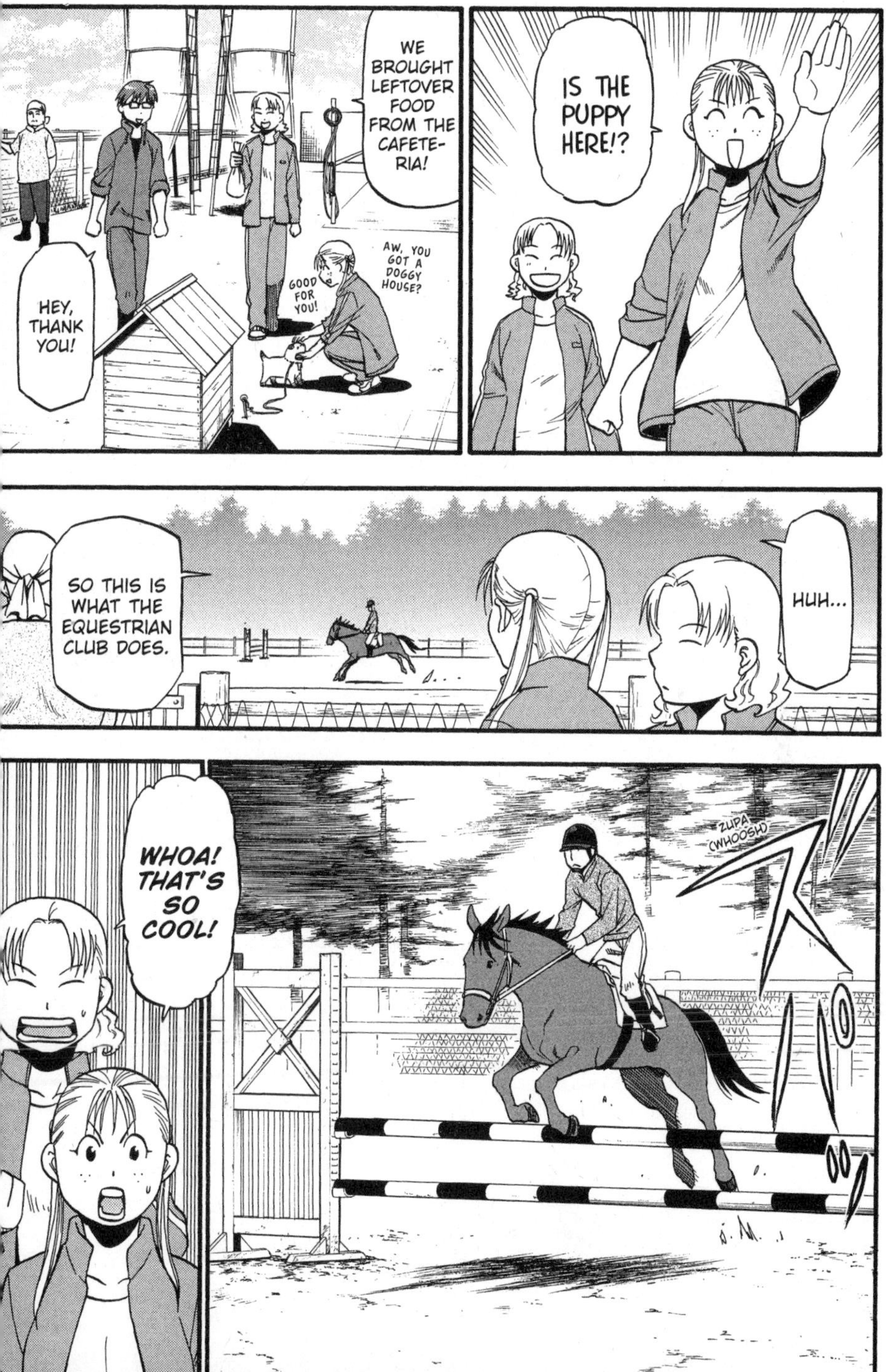
IS THE PUPPY HERE!?
WE BROUGHT LEFTOVER FOOD FROM THE CAFETERIA!
AW, YOU GOT A DOGGY HOUSE?
GOOD FOR YOU!
HEY, THANK YOU!
HUH...
SO THIS IS WHAT THE EQUESTRIAN CLUB DOES.
ZUPA (WHOOSH)
WHOA! THAT'S SO COOL!

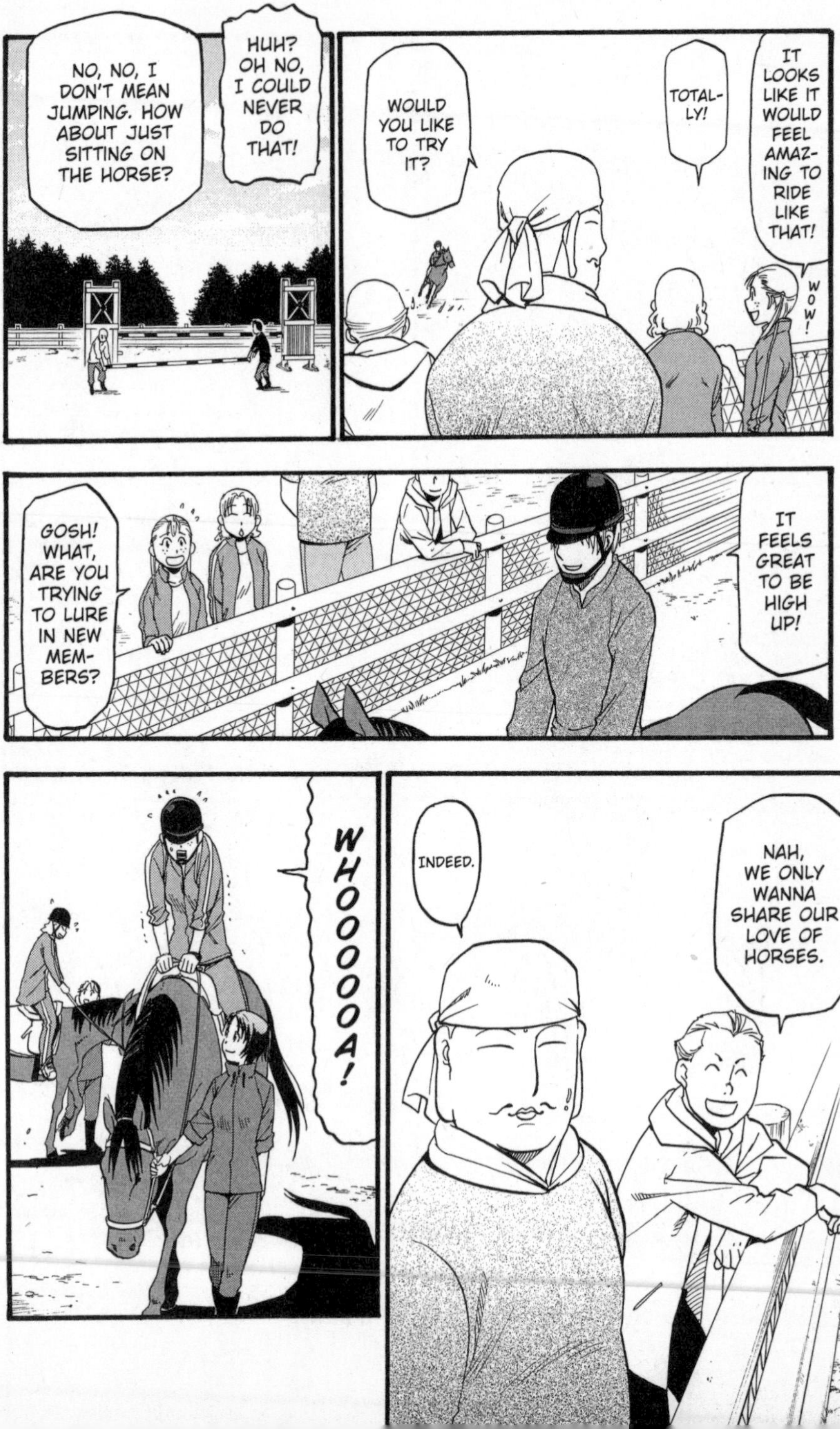
IT LOOKS LIKE IT WOULD FEEL AMAZING TO RIDE LIKE THAT!
WOW!
TOTALLY!
WOULD YOU LIKE TO TRY IT?
HUH? OH NO, I COULD NEVER DO THAT!
NO, NO, I DON'T MEAN JUMPING. HOW ABOUT JUST SITTING ON THE HORSE?
IT FEELS GREAT TO BE HIGH UP!
GOSH! WHAT, ARE YOU TRYING TO LURE IN NEW MEMBERS?
NAH, WE ONLY WANNA SHARE OUR LOVE OF HORSES.
INDEED.
WHOOOOOOA!

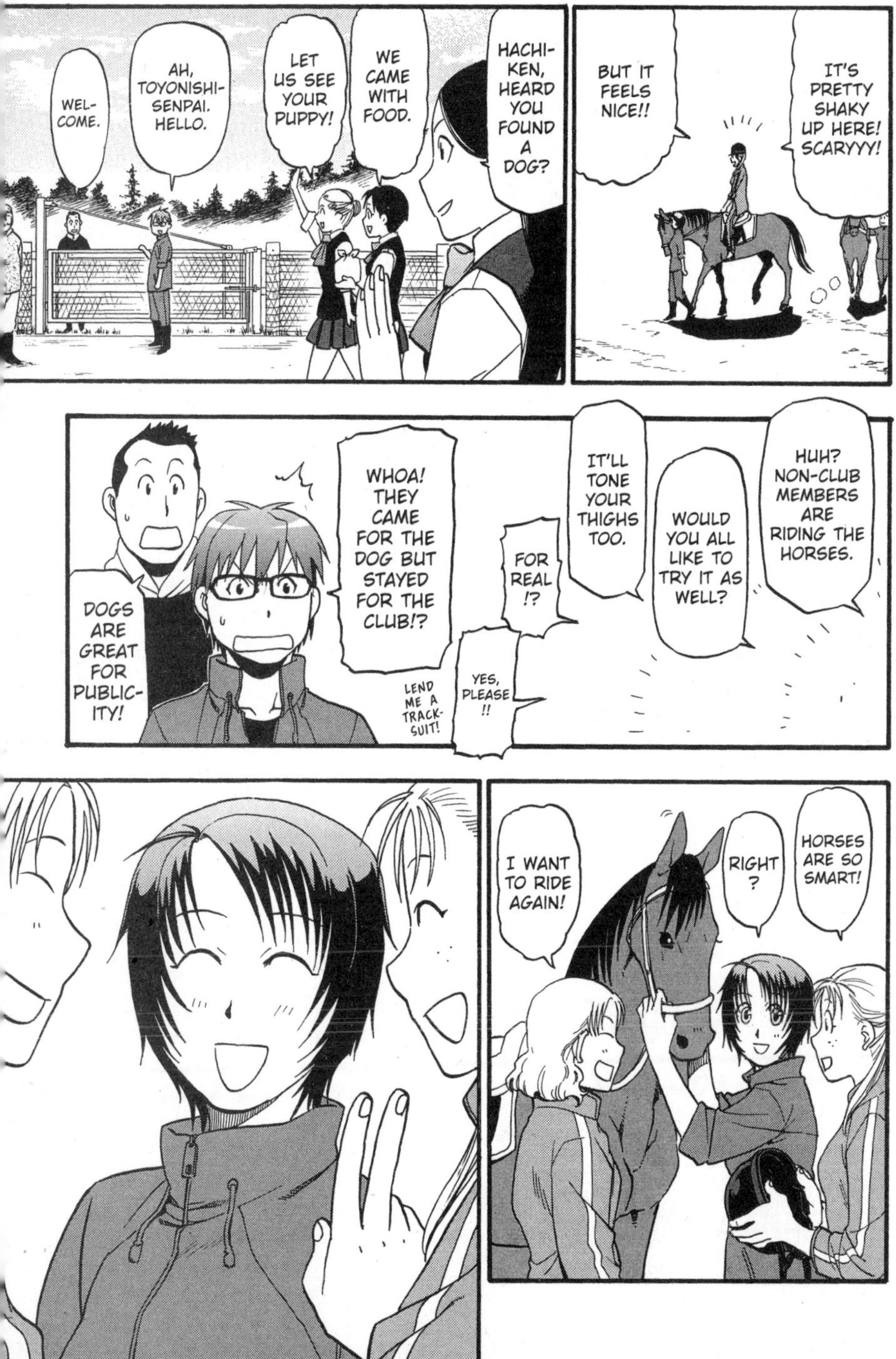
IT'S PRETTY SHAKY UP HERE! SCARYYY!
BUT IT FEELS NICE!!
HACHI-KEN, HEARD YOU FOUND A DOG?
WE CAME WITH FOOD.
LET US SEE YOUR PUPPY!
AH, TOYONISHI-SENPAI. HELLO.
WEL-COME.
HUH? NON-CLUB MEMBERS ARE RIDING THE HORSES.
WOULD YOU ALL LIKE TO TRY IT AS WELL?
IT'LL TONE YOUR THIGHS TOO.
FOR REAL!?
YES, PLEASE!!
LEND ME A TRACK-SUIT!
WHOA! THEY CAME FOR THE DOG BUT STAYED FOR THE CLUB!?
DOGS ARE GREAT FOR PUBLIC-ITY!
HORSES ARE SO SMART!
RIGHT?
I WANT TO RIDE AGAIN!

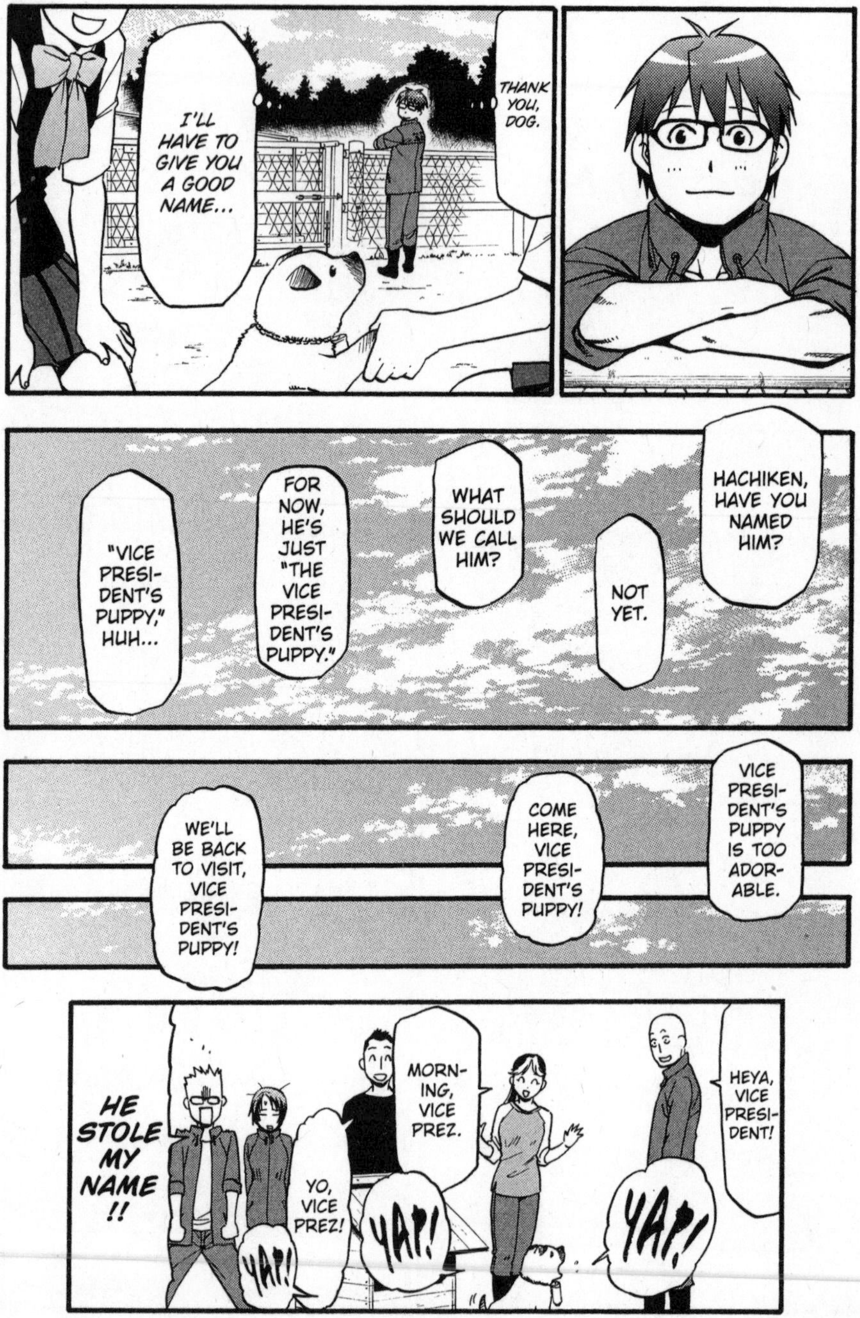
THANK YOU, DOG.
I'LL HAVE TO GIVE YOU A GOOD NAME...
HACHIKEN, HAVE YOU NAMED HIM?
NOT YET.
WHAT SHOULD WE CALL HIM?
FOR NOW, HE'S JUST "THE VICE PRESIDENT'S PUPPY."
"VICE PRESIDENT'S PUPPY," HUH...
VICE PRESIDENT'S PUPPY IS TOO ADORABLE.
COME HERE, VICE PRESIDENT'S PUPPY!
WE'LL BE BACK TO VISIT, VICE PRESIDENT'S PUPPY!
HEYA, VICE PRESIDENT!
YAP!
MORNING, VICE PREZ.
YAP!
YO, VICE PREZ!
YAP!
HE STOLE MY NAME!!

Chapter 37:

Tale of Autumn ⑥

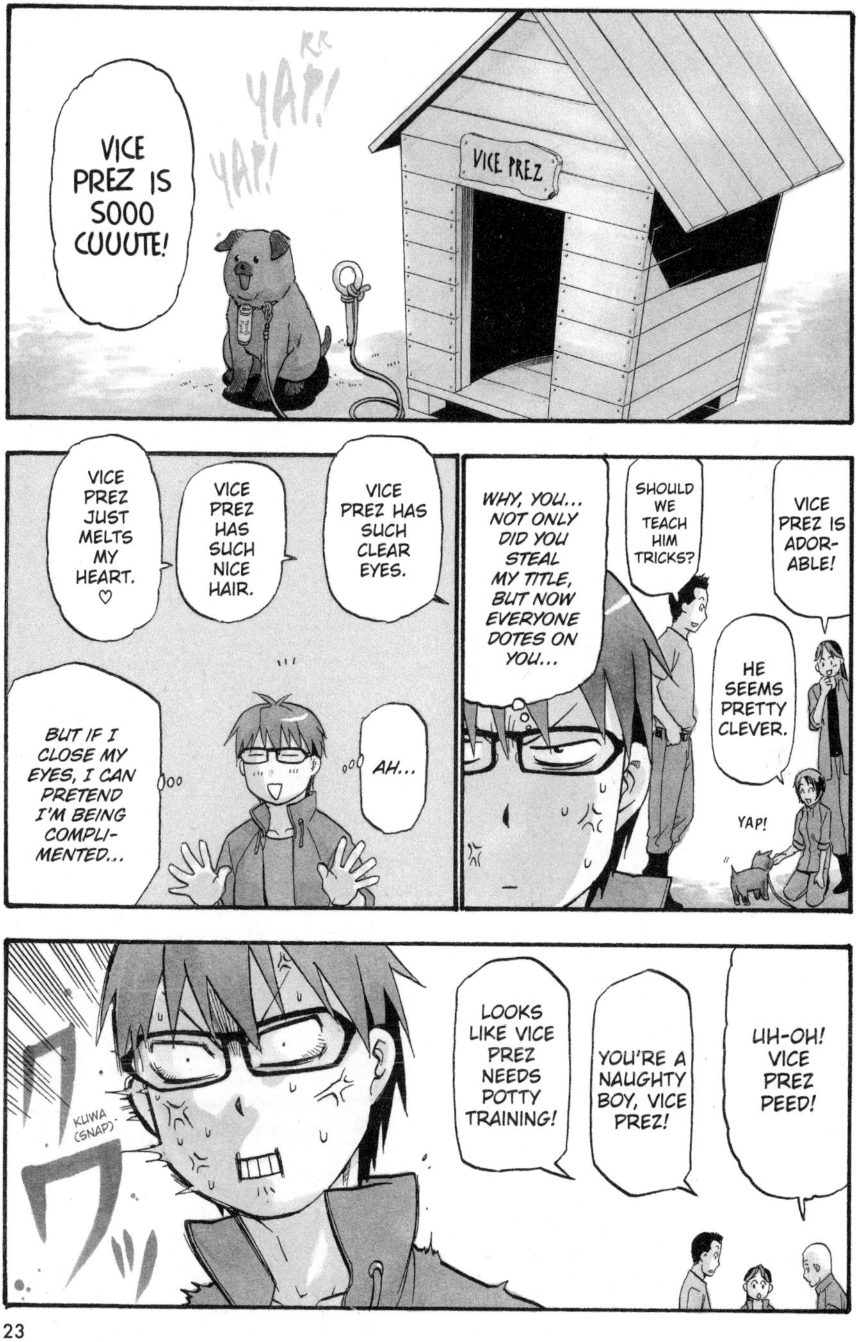
VICE PREZ
YAP! YAP!
VICE PREZ IS SOOO CUUUTE!
VICE PREZ IS ADORABLE!
SHOULD WE TEACH HIM TRICKS?
WHY, YOU... NOT ONLY DID YOU STEAL MY TITLE, BUT NOW EVERYONE DOTES ON YOU...
HE SEEMS PRETTY CLEVER.
YAP!
VICE PREZ HAS SUCH CLEAR EYES.
VICE PREZ HAS SUCH NICE HAIR.
VICE PREZ JUST MELTS MY HEART. ♡
AH...
BUT IF I CLOSE MY EYES, I CAN PRETEND I'M BEING COMPLIMENTED...
UH-OH! VICE PREZ PEED!
YOU'RE A NAUGHTY BOY, VICE PREZ!
LOOKS LIKE VICE PREZ NEEDS POTTY TRAINING!
KUWA (SNAP)

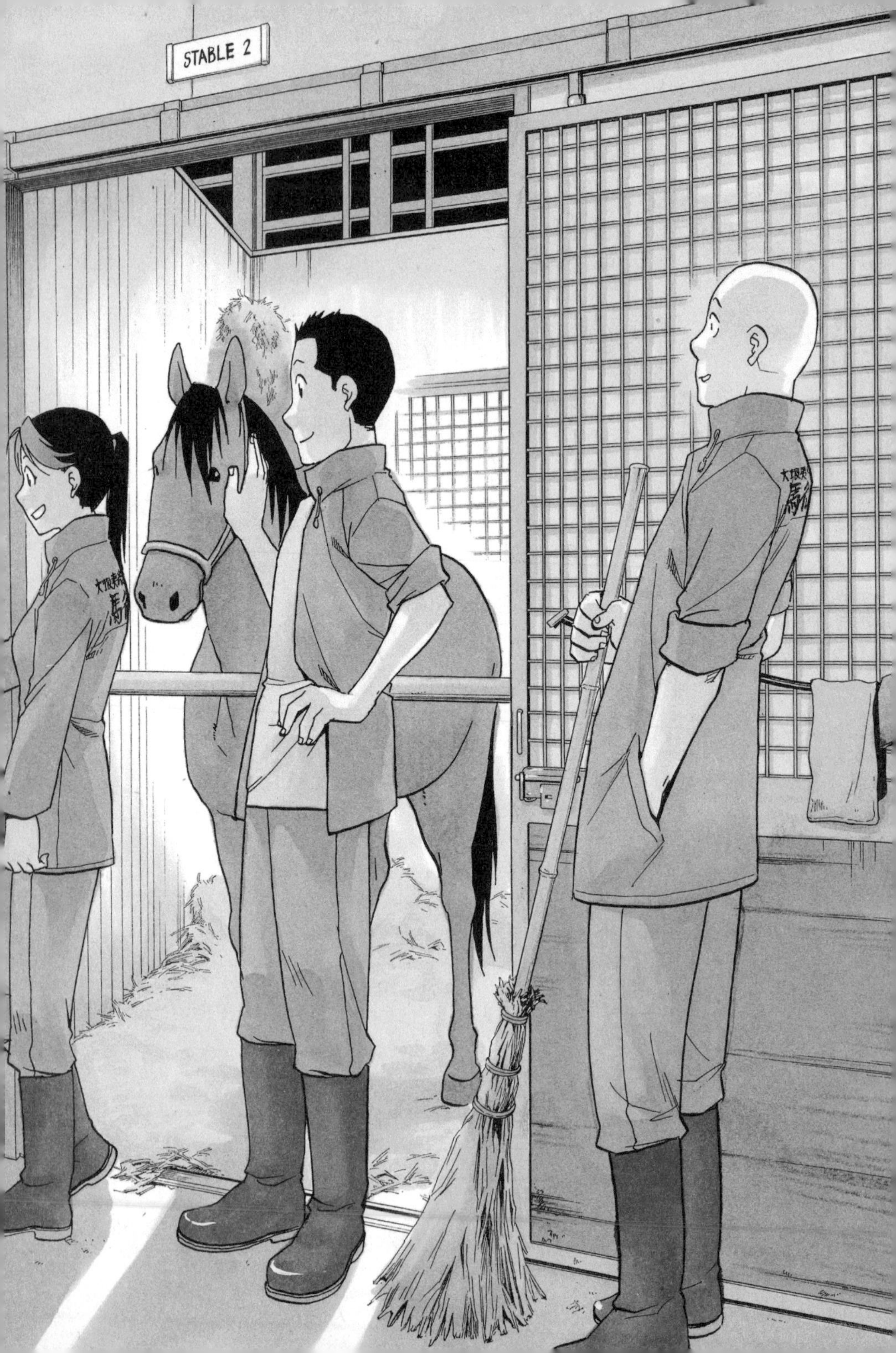
STABLE 2

Chapter 37:
Tale of Autumn ⑥

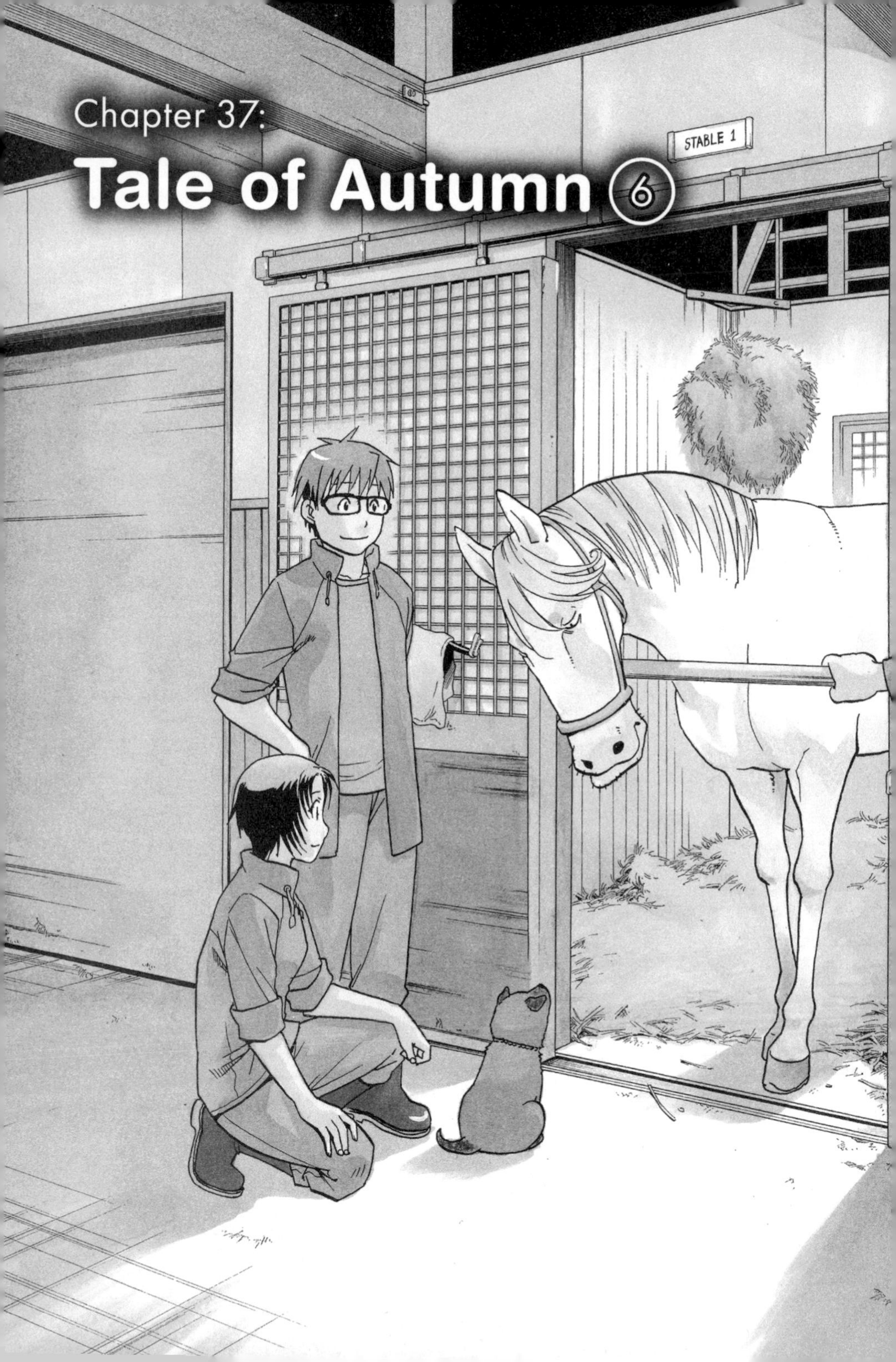
STABLE 1

EQUESTRIAN CLUB

MIKA TOYONISHI

FOOD SCIENCE PROGRAM, YEAR 3

OBIHIRO TAISHOU MIDDLE SCHOOL

COLLEGE BOUND

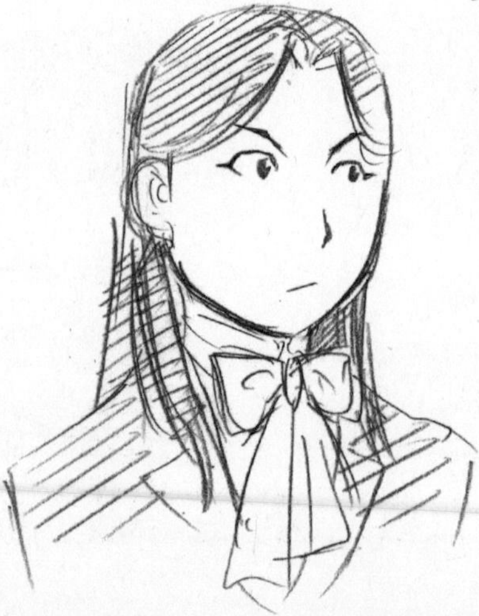

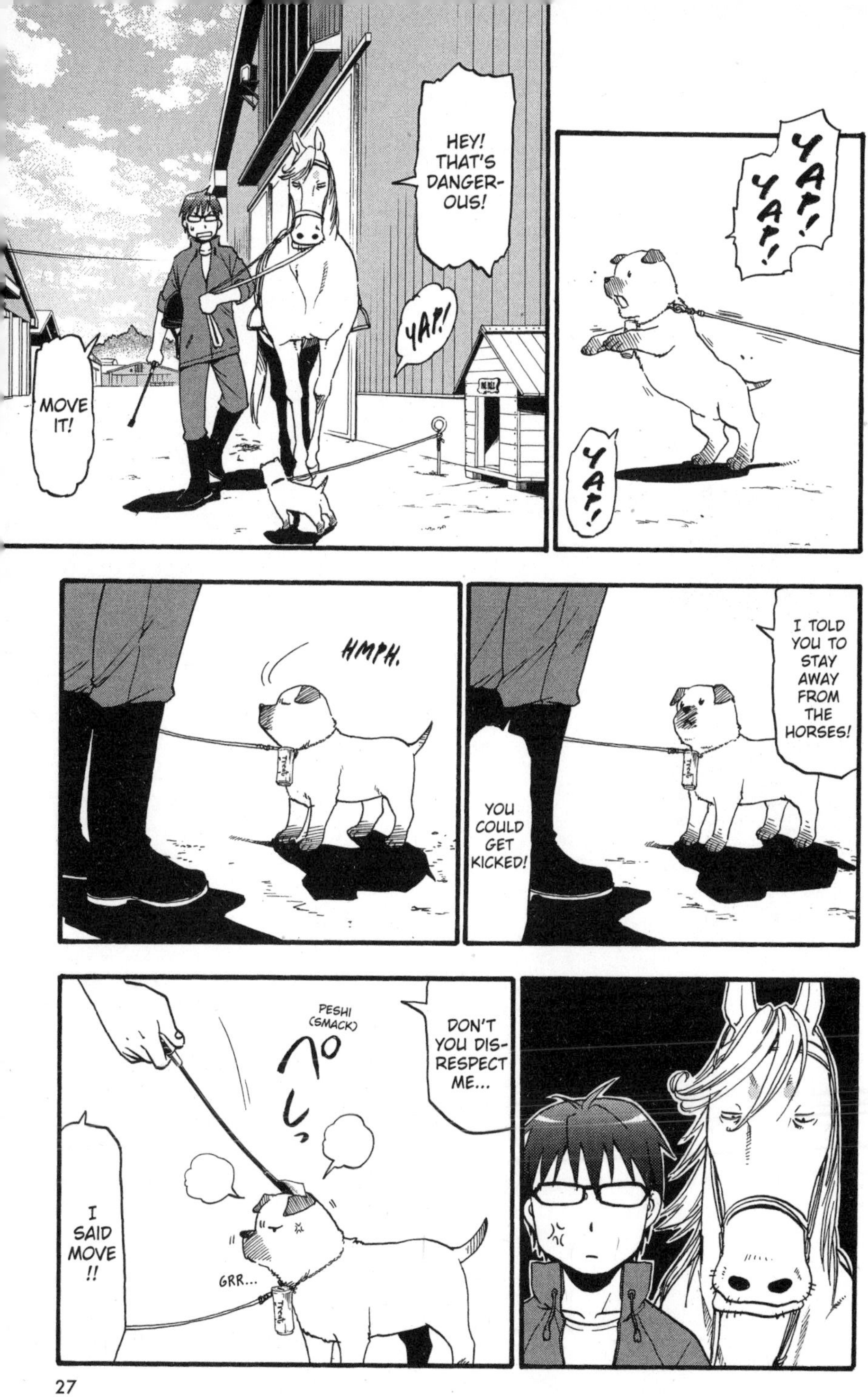
YAP! YAP!
YAP!
HEY! THAT'S DANGER-OUS!
YAP!
MOVE IT!
I TOLD YOU TO STAY AWAY FROM THE HORSES!
YOU COULD GET KICKED!
HMPH.
DON'T YOU DIS-RESPECT ME...
PESHI (SMACK)
I SAID MOVE !!
GRR...

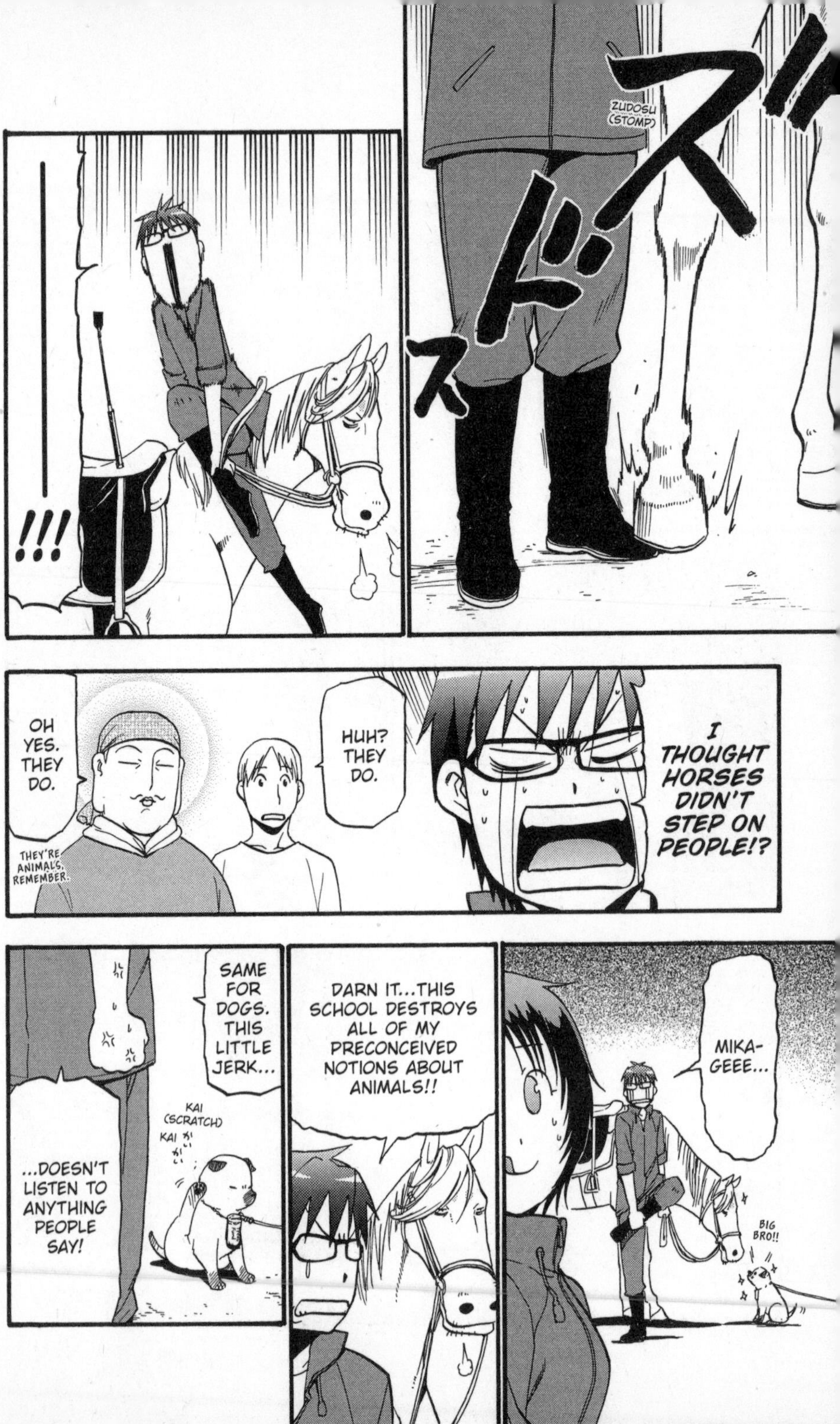
ZUDOSU (STOMP)
——
!!!
I THOUGHT HORSES DIDN'T STEP ON PEOPLE!?
HUH? THEY DO.
OH YES. THEY DO.
THEY'RE ANIMALS, REMEMBER.
MIKA-GEEE...
BIG BRO!!
DARN IT...THIS SCHOOL DESTROYS ALL OF MY PRECONCEIVED NOTIONS ABOUT ANIMALS!!
SAME FOR DOGS. THIS LITTLE JERK...
KAI (SCRATCH)
KAI
...DOESN'T LISTEN TO ANYTHING PEOPLE SAY!

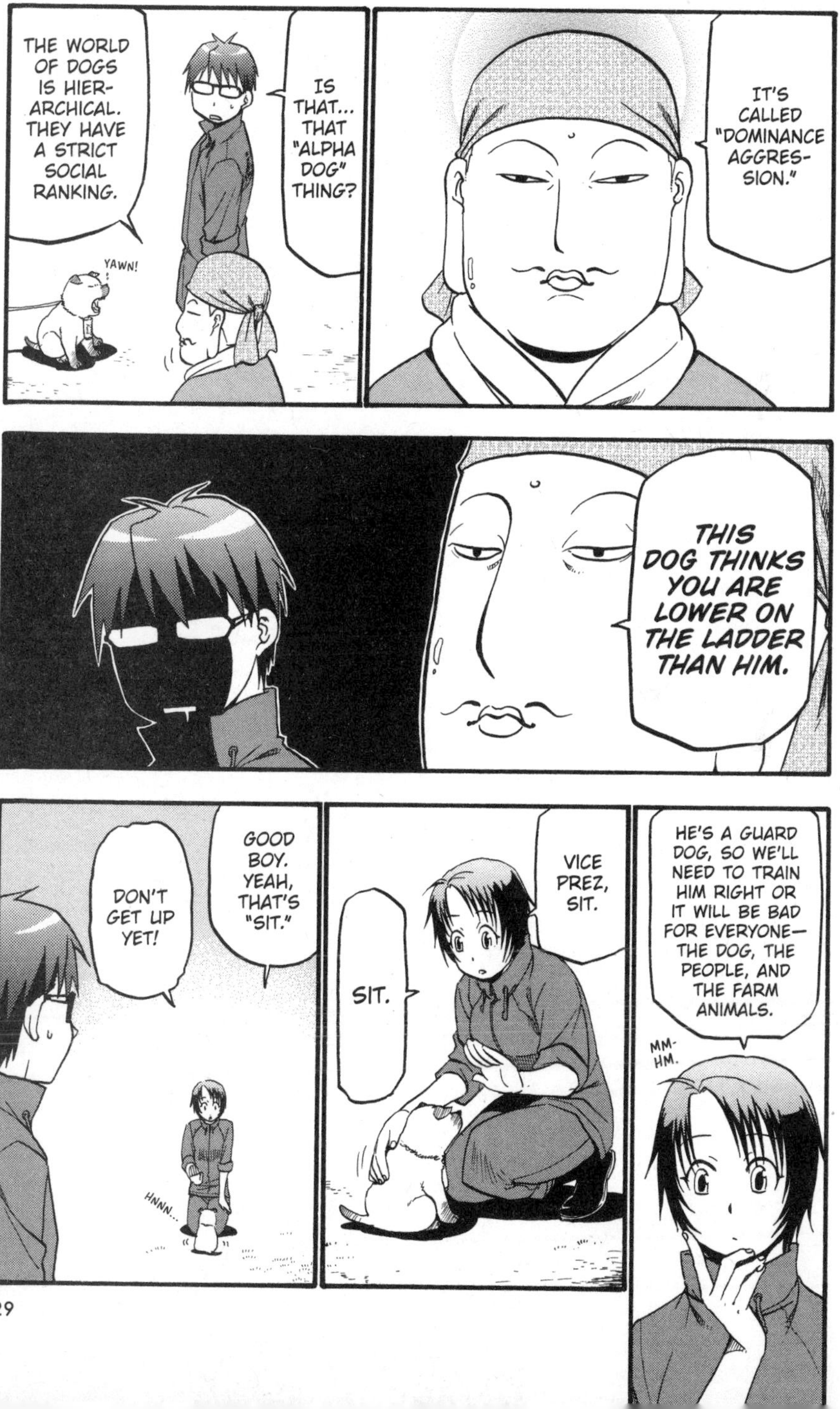
IT'S CALLED "DOMINANCE AGGRES-SION."
IS THAT... THAT "ALPHA DOG" THING?
THE WORLD OF DOGS IS HIER-ARCHICAL. THEY HAVE A STRICT SOCIAL RANKING.
YAWN!
THIS DOG THINKS YOU ARE LOWER ON THE LADDER THAN HIM.
HE'S A GUARD DOG, SO WE'LL NEED TO TRAIN HIM RIGHT OR IT WILL BE BAD FOR EVERYONE— THE DOG, THE PEOPLE, AND THE FARM ANIMALS.
MM-HM.
VICE PREZ, SIT.
SIT.
GOOD BOY. YEAH, THAT'S "SIT."
DON'T GET UP YET!
HNNN...

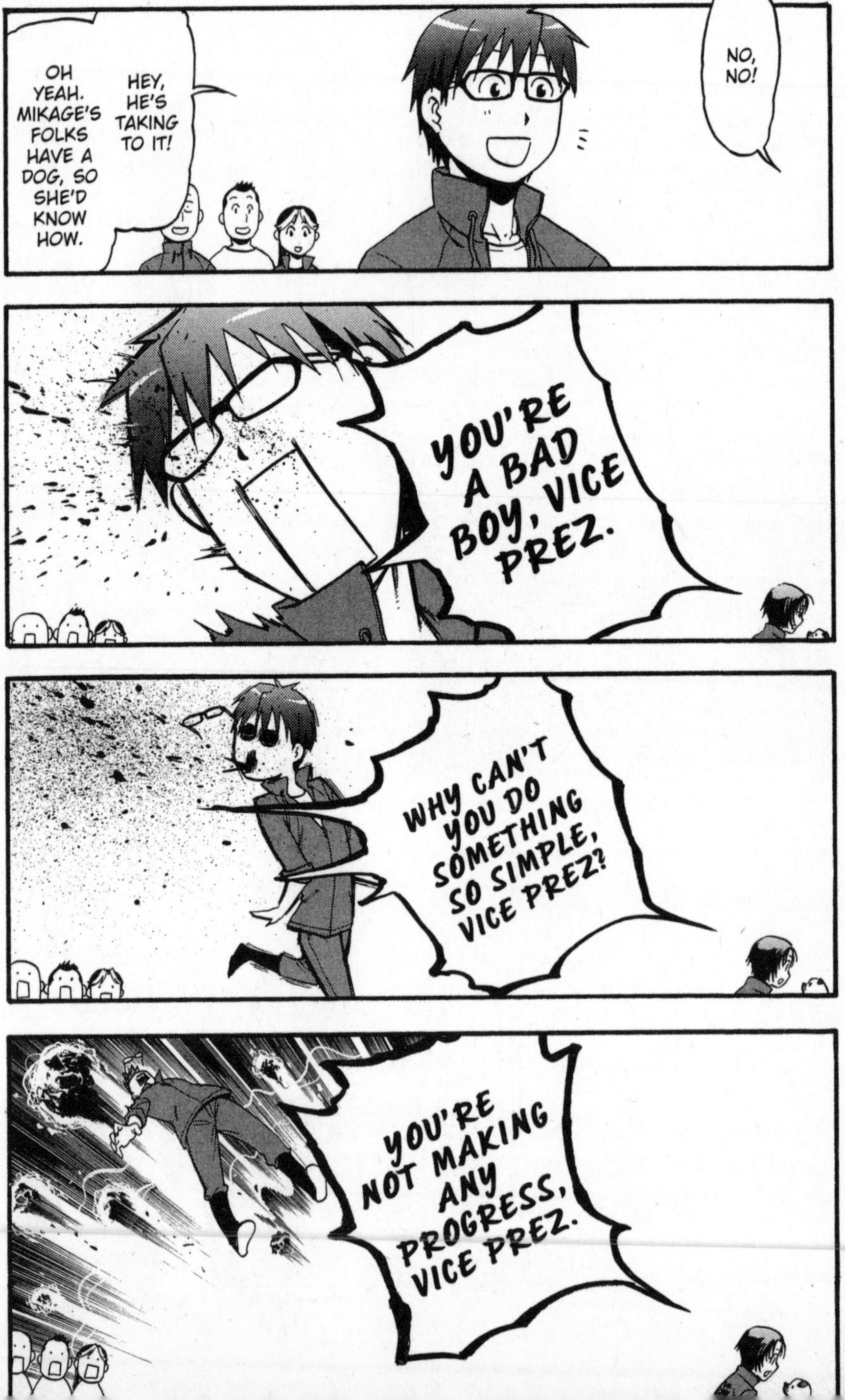
NO, NO!
HEY, HE'S TAKING TO IT!
OH YEAH. MIKAGE'S FOLKS HAVE A DOG, SO SHE'D KNOW HOW.
YOU'RE A BAD BOY, VICE PREZ.
WHY CAN'T YOU DO SOMETHING SO SIMPLE, VICE PREZ?
YOU'RE NOT MAKING ANY PROGRESS, VICE PREZ.

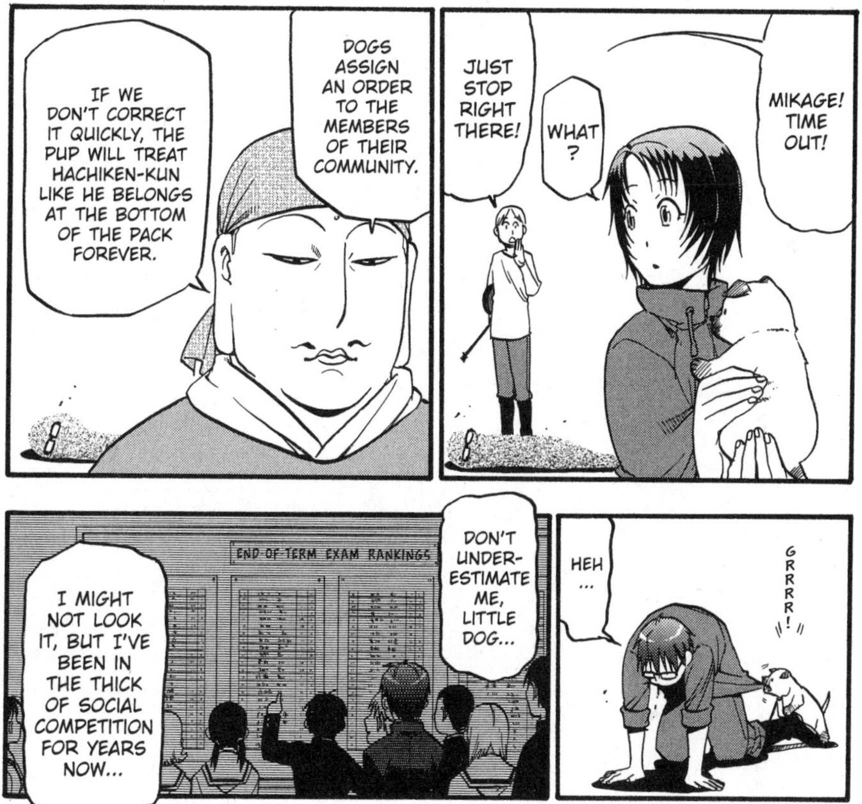
MIKAGE! TIME OUT!
WHAT?
JUST STOP RIGHT THERE!
DOGS ASSIGN AN ORDER TO THE MEMBERS OF THEIR COMMUNITY.
IF WE DON'T CORRECT IT QUICKLY, THE PUP WILL TREAT HACHIKEN-KUN LIKE HE BELONGS AT THE BOTTOM OF THE PACK FOREVER.
HEH...
GRRRR!
DON'T UNDER-ESTIMATE ME, LITTLE DOG...
END OF TERM EXAM RANKINGS
I MIGHT NOT LOOK IT, BUT I'VE BEEN IN THE THICK OF SOCIAL COMPETITION FOR YEARS NOW...

BOOKS: MAN'S BEST FRIEND, UNDERSTANDING DOG BEHAVIOR, PICTURE ENCYCLOPEDIA OF DOGS, TRAINING DOGS, MY FIRST TIME: LIVING WITH A DOG

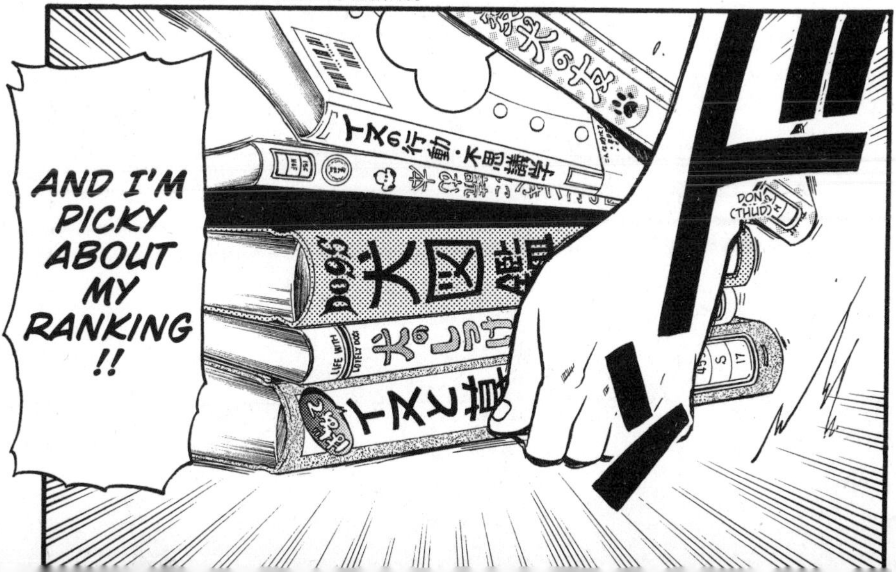
AND I'M PICKY ABOUT MY RANKING!!
DON (THUD)

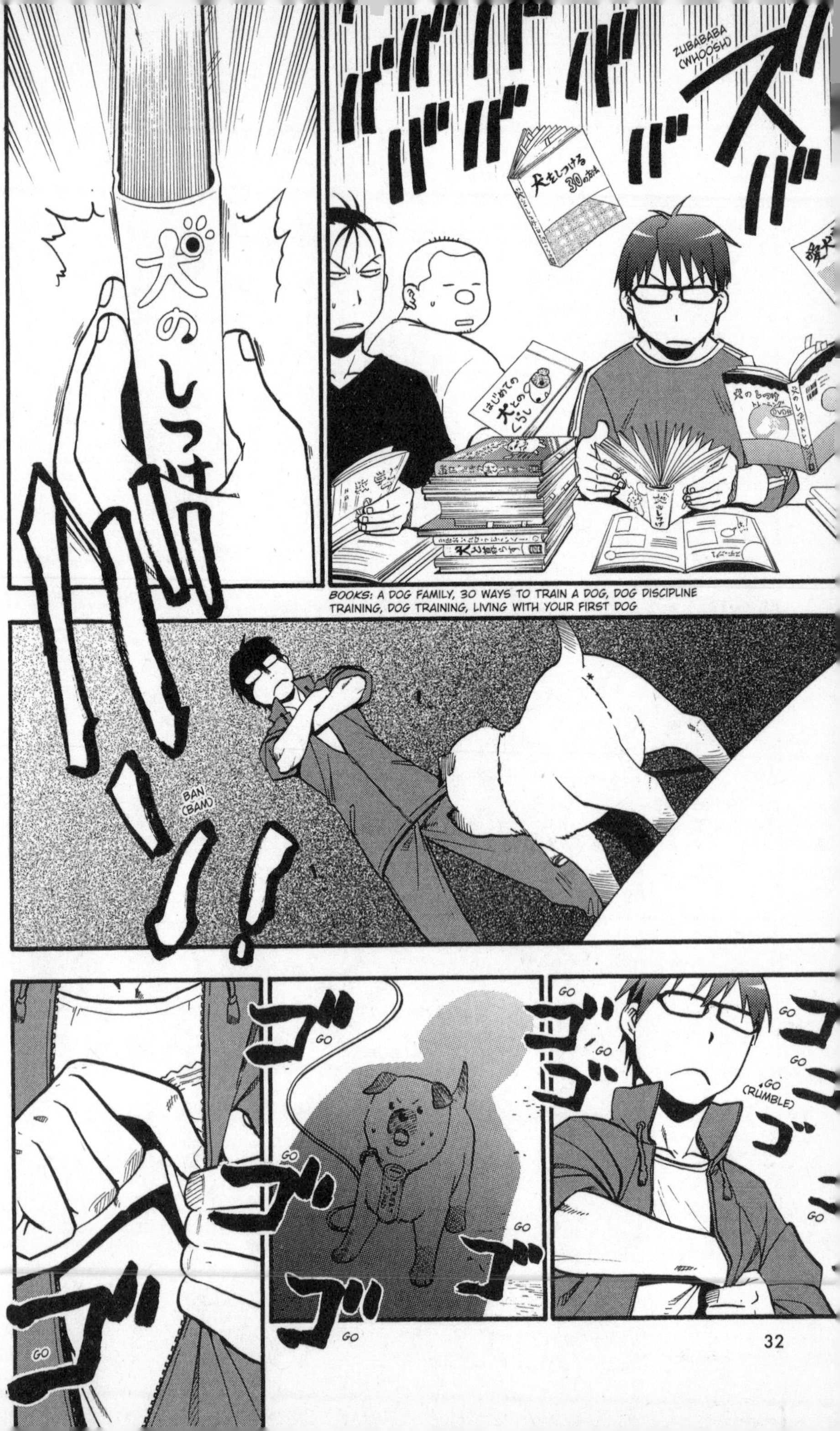
ZUBABABA (WHOOSH)
犬をしつける 30の方法
はじめての犬とのくらし
BOOKS: A DOG FAMILY, 30 WAYS TO TRAIN A DOG, DOG DISCIPLINE TRAINING, DOG TRAINING, LIVING WITH YOUR FIRST DOG
犬のしつけ
BAN (BAM)
GO
GO
GO
GO
GO (RUMBLE)
GO
GO
GO
GO
GO
GO

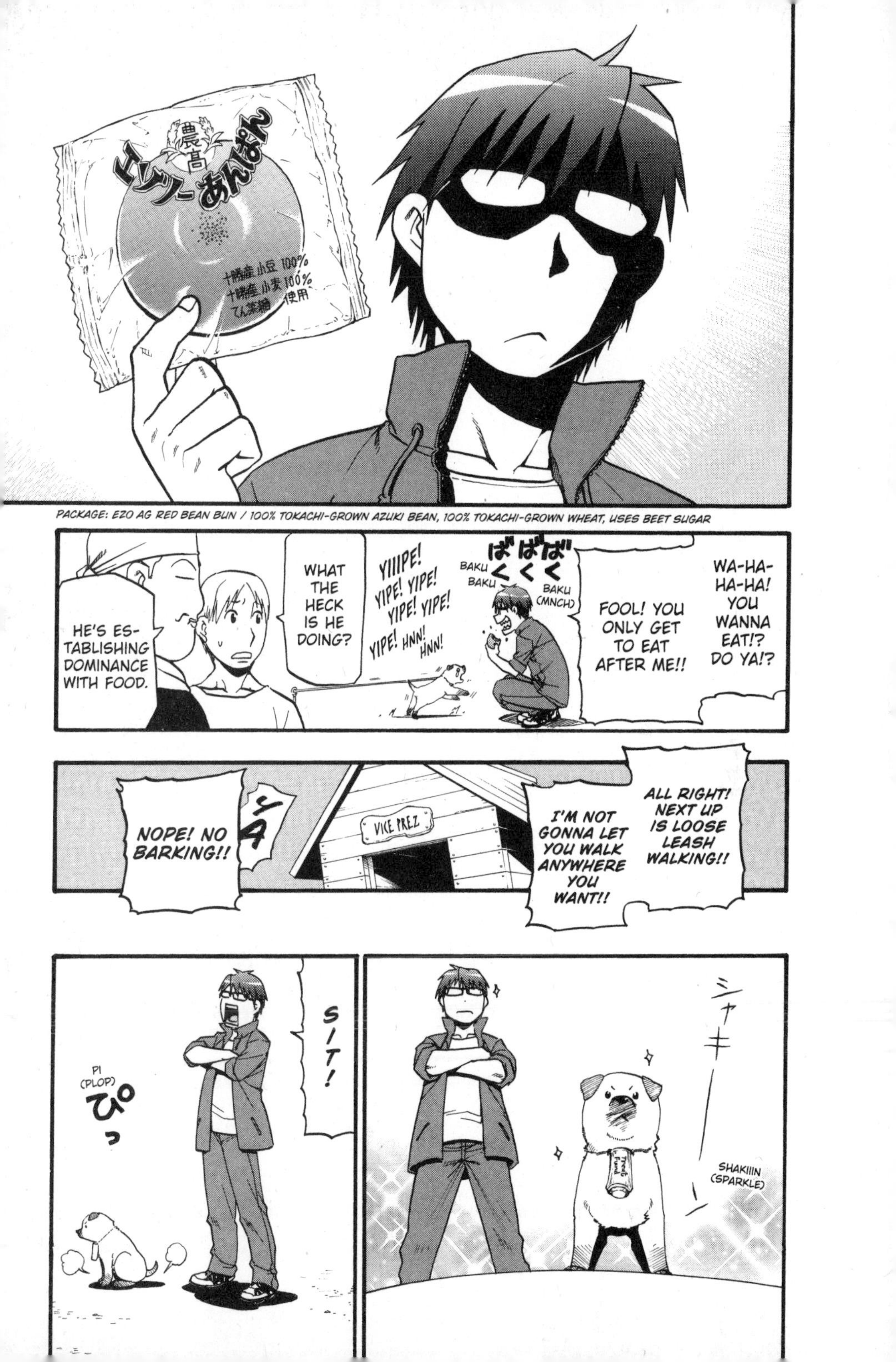
農高
エゾノー あんぱん
十勝産 小豆 100%
十勝産 小麦 100%
てん菜糖 使用
PACKAGE: EZO AG RED BEAN BUN / 100% TOKACHI-GROWN AZUKI BEAN, 100% TOKACHI-GROWN WHEAT, USES BEET SUGAR
WA-HA-HA! YOU WANNA EAT!? DO YA!?
FOOL! YOU ONLY GET TO EAT AFTER ME!!
ばばば
くくく
BAKU BAKU BAKU (MNCH)
YIIIPE! YIPE! YIPE! YIPE! YIPE! YIPE! HNN! HNN!
WHAT THE HECK IS HE DOING?
HE'S ESTABLISHING DOMINANCE WITH FOOD.
ALL RIGHT! NEXT UP IS LOOSE LEASH WALKING!!
I'M NOT GONNA LET YOU WALK ANYWHERE YOU WANT!!
VICE PREZ
NOPE! NO BARKING!!
シャキーン
SHAKIIIN (SPARKLE)
Treats Food
SIT!
PI (PLOP)
ぴっ

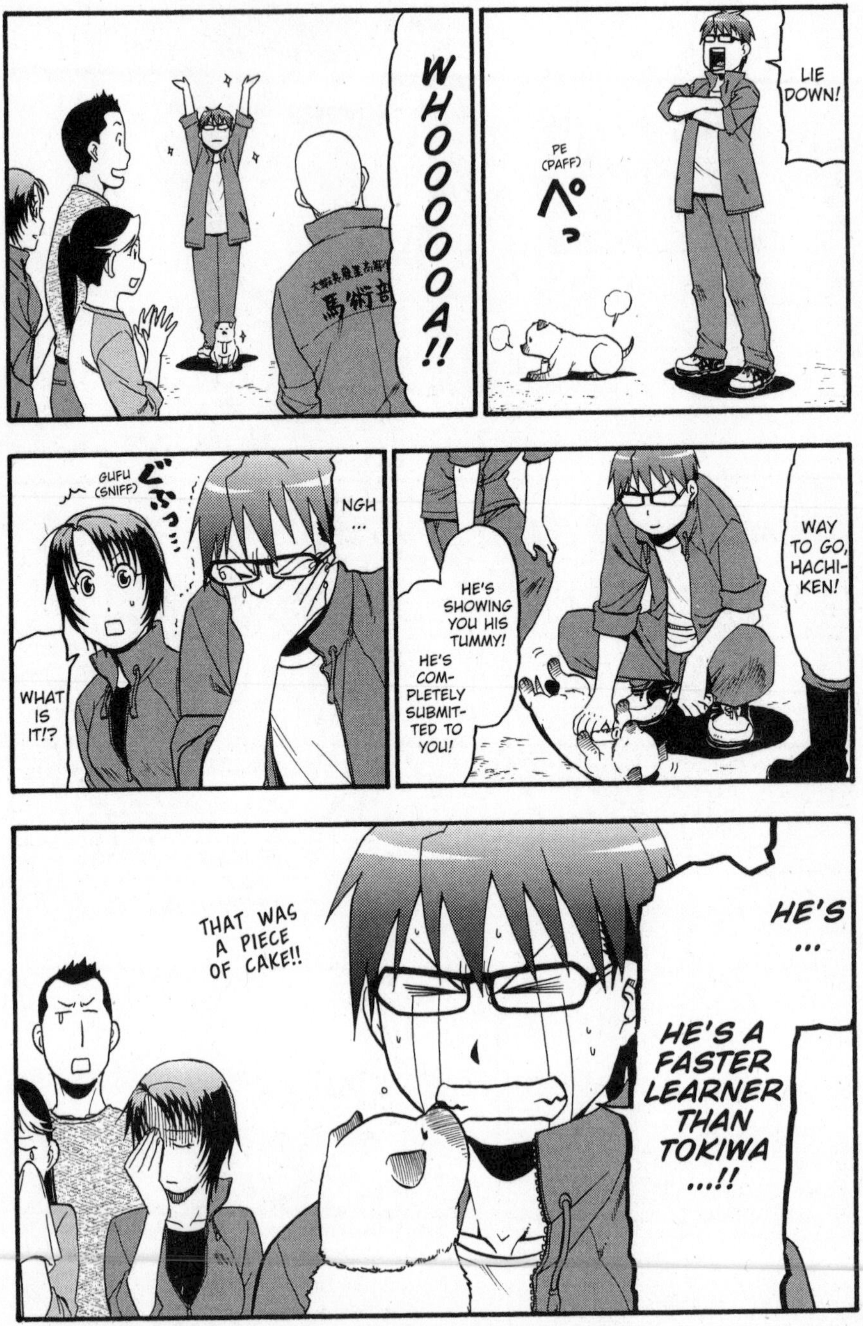
LIE DOWN!
PE (PAFF)
ぺっ
WHOOOOOOA!!
馬術部
WAY TO GO, HACHIKEN!
HE'S SHOWING YOU HIS TUMMY!
HE'S COMPLETELY SUBMITTED TO YOU!
NGH ...
GUFU (SNIFF)
ぐふっ
WHAT IS IT!?
HE'S ...
HE'S A FASTER LEARNER THAN TOKIWA ...!!
THAT WAS A PIECE OF CAKE!!

BUILDING: OOEZO AGRICULTURAL HIGH SCHOOL STUDENT DORMS

SCREEN: TOKACHI PRELIMS ROUND 2

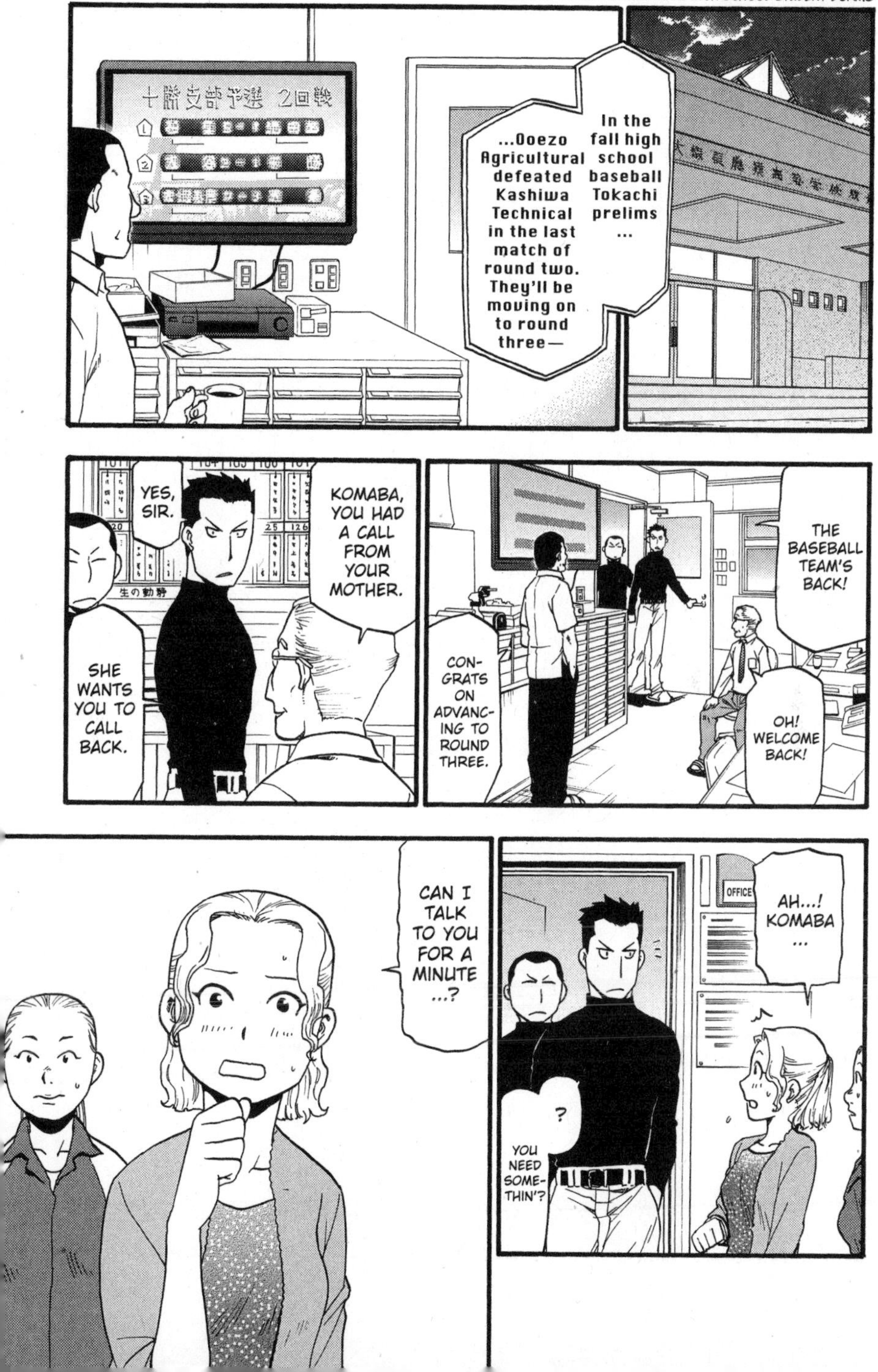
In the fall high school baseball Tokachi prelims ...
...Ooezo Agricultural defeated Kashiwa Technical in the last match of round two. They'll be moving on to round three—
THE BASEBALL TEAM'S BACK!
OH! WELCOME BACK!
CON-GRATS ON ADVANC-ING TO ROUND THREE.
KOMABA, YOU HAD A CALL FROM YOUR MOTHER.
YES, SIR.
SHE WANTS YOU TO CALL BACK.
AH...! KOMABA ...
?
YOU NEED SOME-THIN'?
CAN I TALK TO YOU FOR A MINUTE ...?

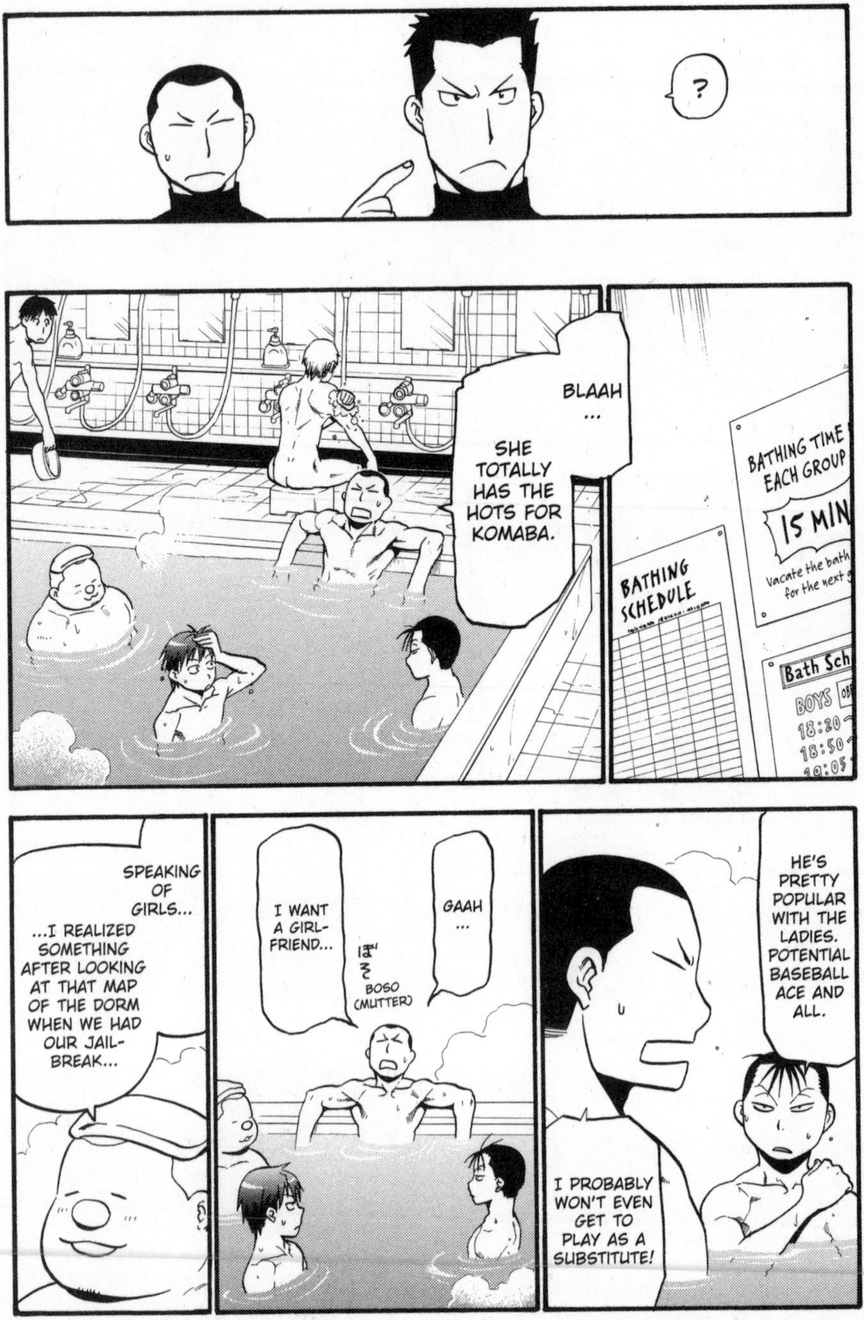
?
BATHING SCHEDULE
BATHING TIME
EACH GROUP
15 MIN
BOYS
18:20
18:50
BLAAH...
SHE TOTALLY HAS THE HOTS FOR KOMABA.
HE'S PRETTY POPULAR WITH THE LADIES. POTENTIAL BASEBALL ACE AND ALL.
I PROBABLY WON'T EVEN GET TO PLAY AS A SUBSTITUTE!
GAAH...
I WANT A GIRLFRIEND...
ぼそ
BOSO (MUTTER)
SPEAKING OF GIRLS...
...I REALIZED SOMETHING AFTER LOOKING AT THAT MAP OF THE DORM WHEN WE HAD OUR JAILBREAK...

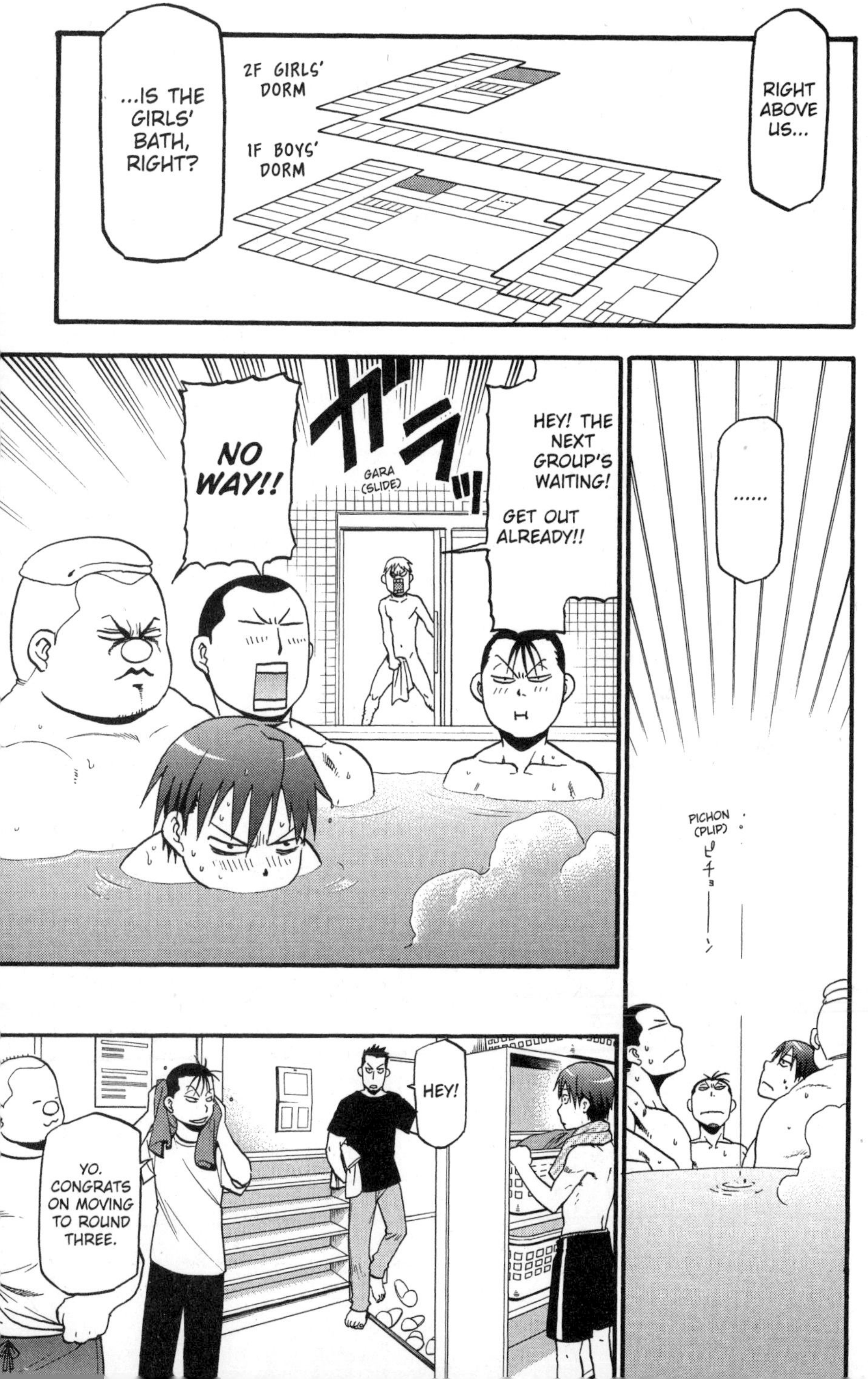
RIGHT ABOVE US...
2F GIRLS' DORM
1F BOYS' DORM
...IS THE GIRLS' BATH, RIGHT?
......
PICHON (PLIP)
ピチョーン
HEY! THE NEXT GROUP'S WAITING!
GET OUT ALREADY!!
ガラッ
GARA (SLIDE)
NO WAY!!
HEY!
YO. CONGRATS ON MOVING TO ROUND THREE.

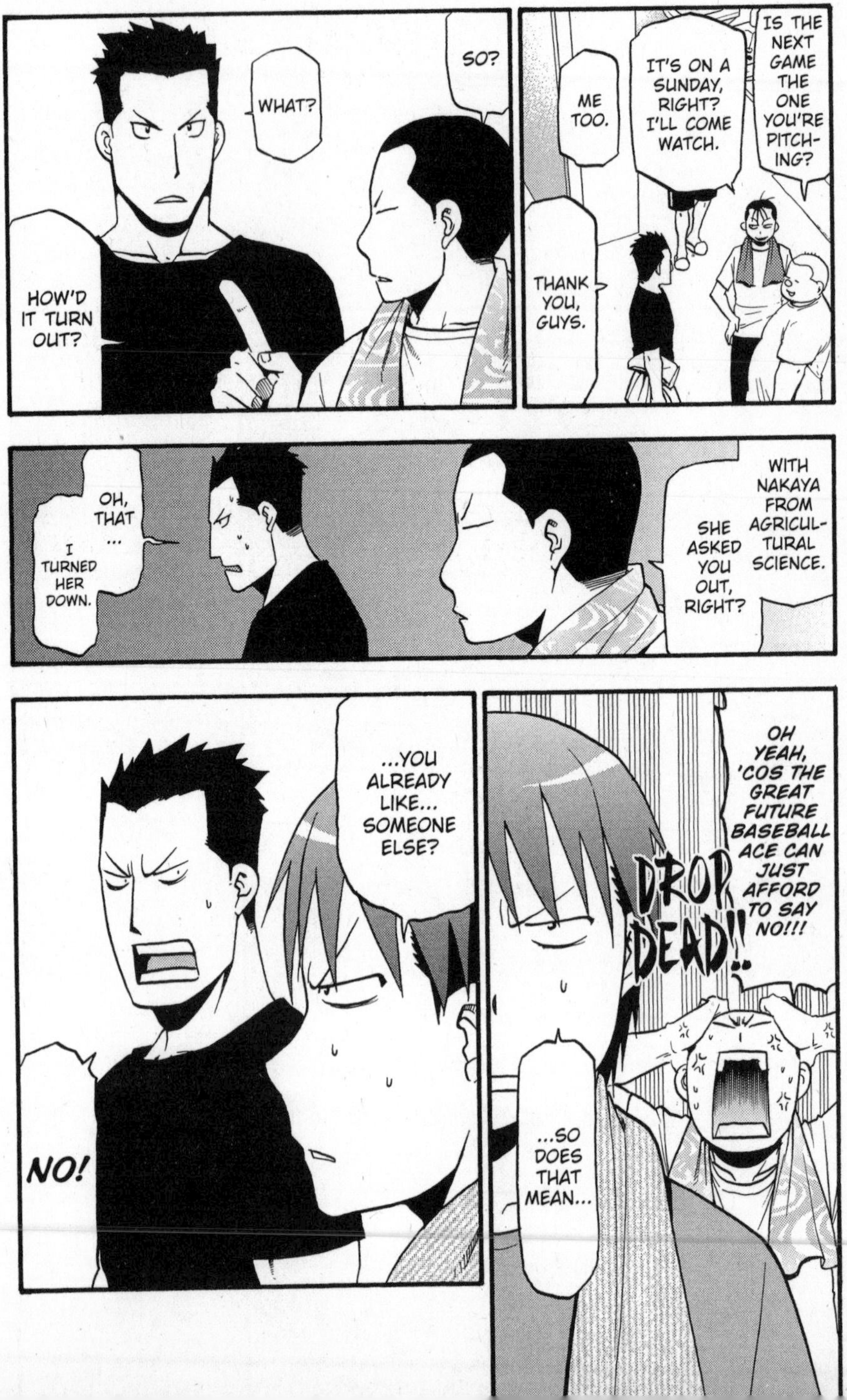

IS THE NEXT GAME THE ONE YOU'RE PITCHING?
IT'S ON A SUNDAY, RIGHT? I'LL COME WATCH.
ME TOO.
THANK YOU, GUYS.
SO?
WHAT?
HOW'D IT TURN OUT?
WITH NAKAYA FROM AGRICULTURAL SCIENCE.
SHE ASKED YOU OUT, RIGHT?
OH, THAT...
I TURNED HER DOWN.
OH YEAH, 'COS THE GREAT FUTURE BASEBALL ACE CAN JUST AFFORD TO SAY NO!!!
DROP DEAD!!
...SO DOES THAT MEAN...
...YOU ALREADY LIKE... SOMEONE ELSE?
NO!

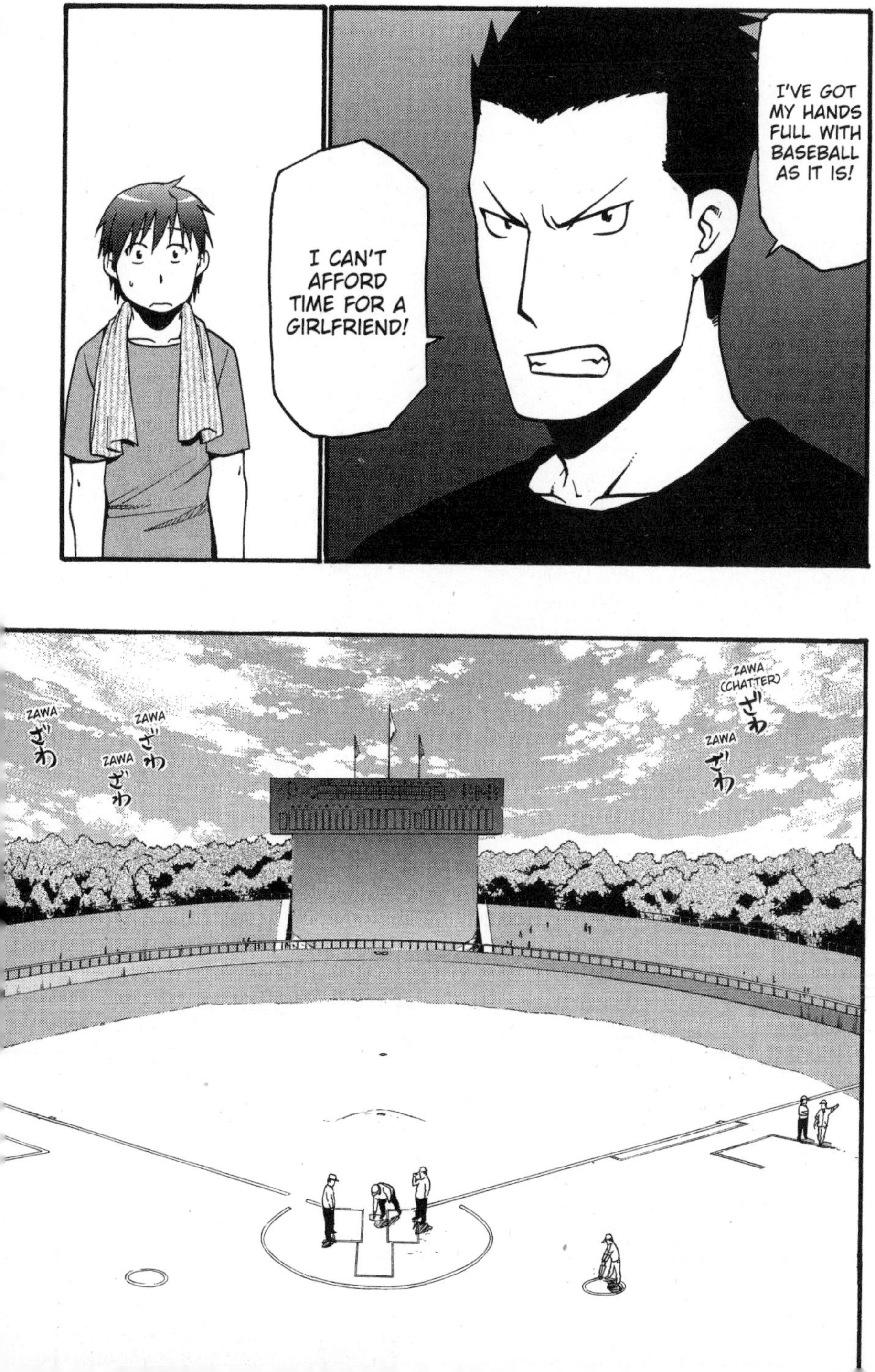
I'VE GOT MY HANDS FULL WITH BASEBALL AS IT IS!
I CAN'T AFFORD TIME FOR A GIRLFRIEND!
ZAWA (CHATTER) ざわ
ZAWA ざわ
ZAWA ざわ
ZAWA ざわ
ZAWA ざわ

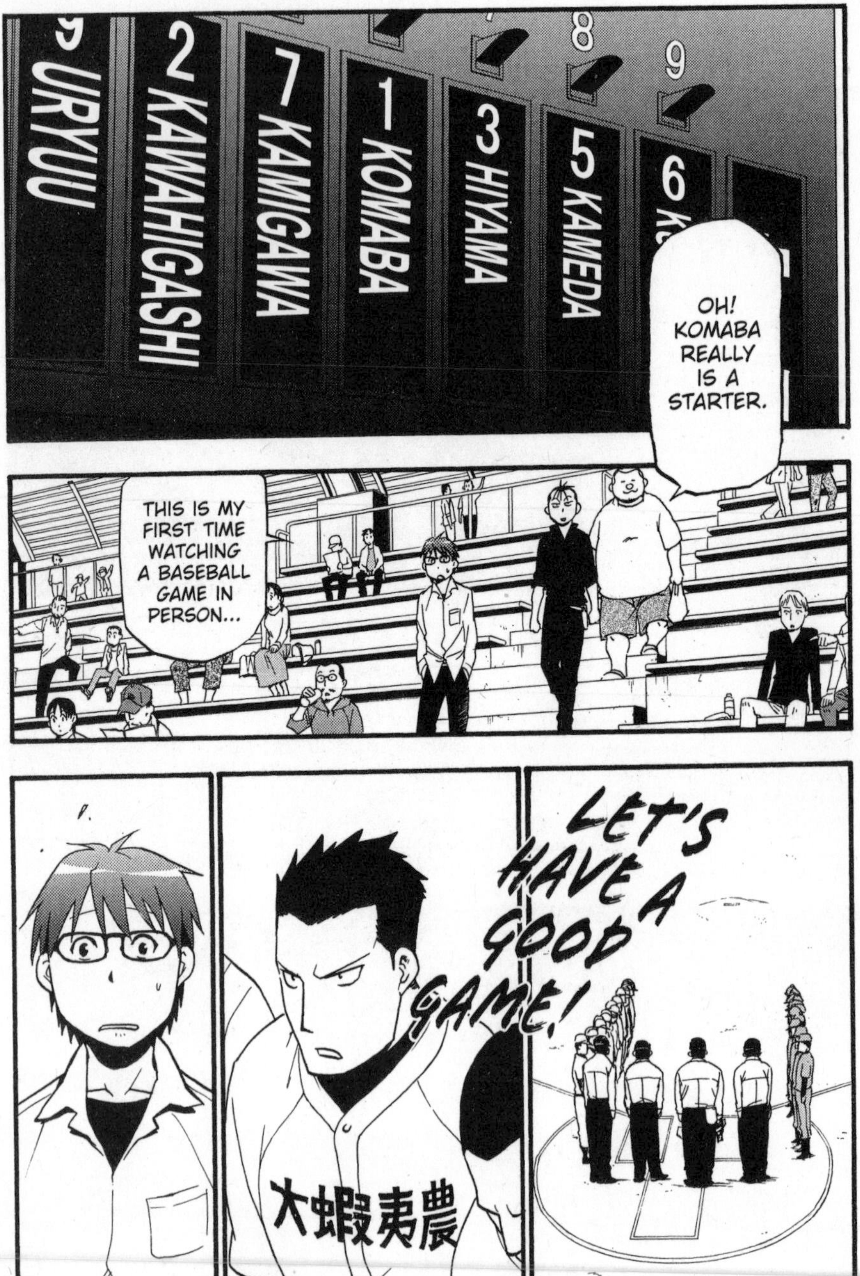
9 URYUU
2 KAWAHIGASHI
7 KAMIGAWA
1 KOMABA
3 HIYAMA
5 KAMEDA
OH! KOMABA REALLY IS A STARTER.
THIS IS MY FIRST TIME WATCHING A BASEBALL GAME IN PERSON...
LET'S HAVE A GOOD GAME!
大蝦夷農

SHIRT: OOEZO AG

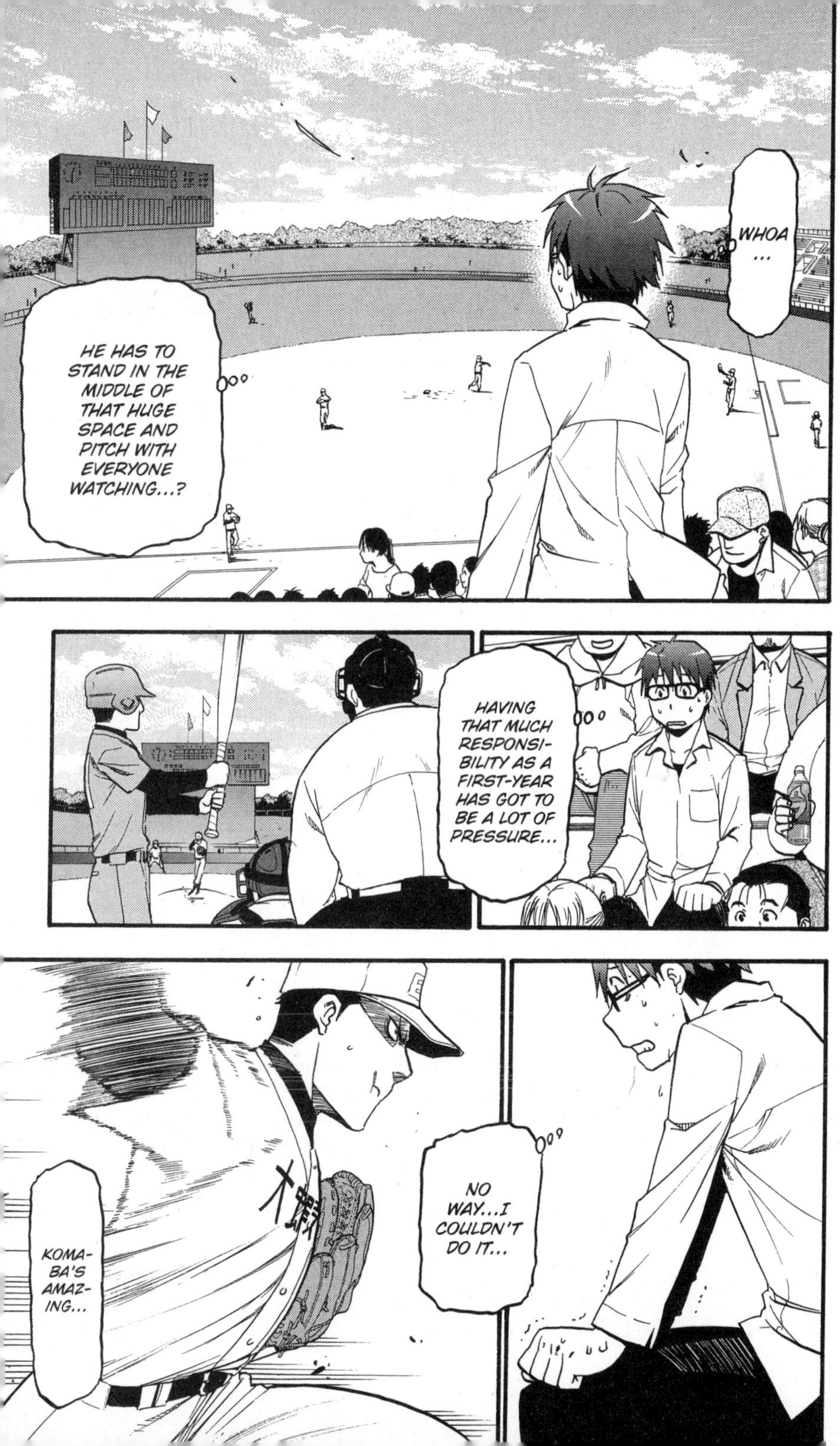
WHOA ...
HE HAS TO STAND IN THE MIDDLE OF THAT HUGE SPACE AND PITCH WITH EVERYONE WATCHING...?
HAVING THAT MUCH RESPONSI-BILITY AS A FIRST-YEAR HAS GOT TO BE A LOT OF PRESSURE...
NO WAY...I COULDN'T DO IT...
KOMA-BA'S AMAZ-ING...

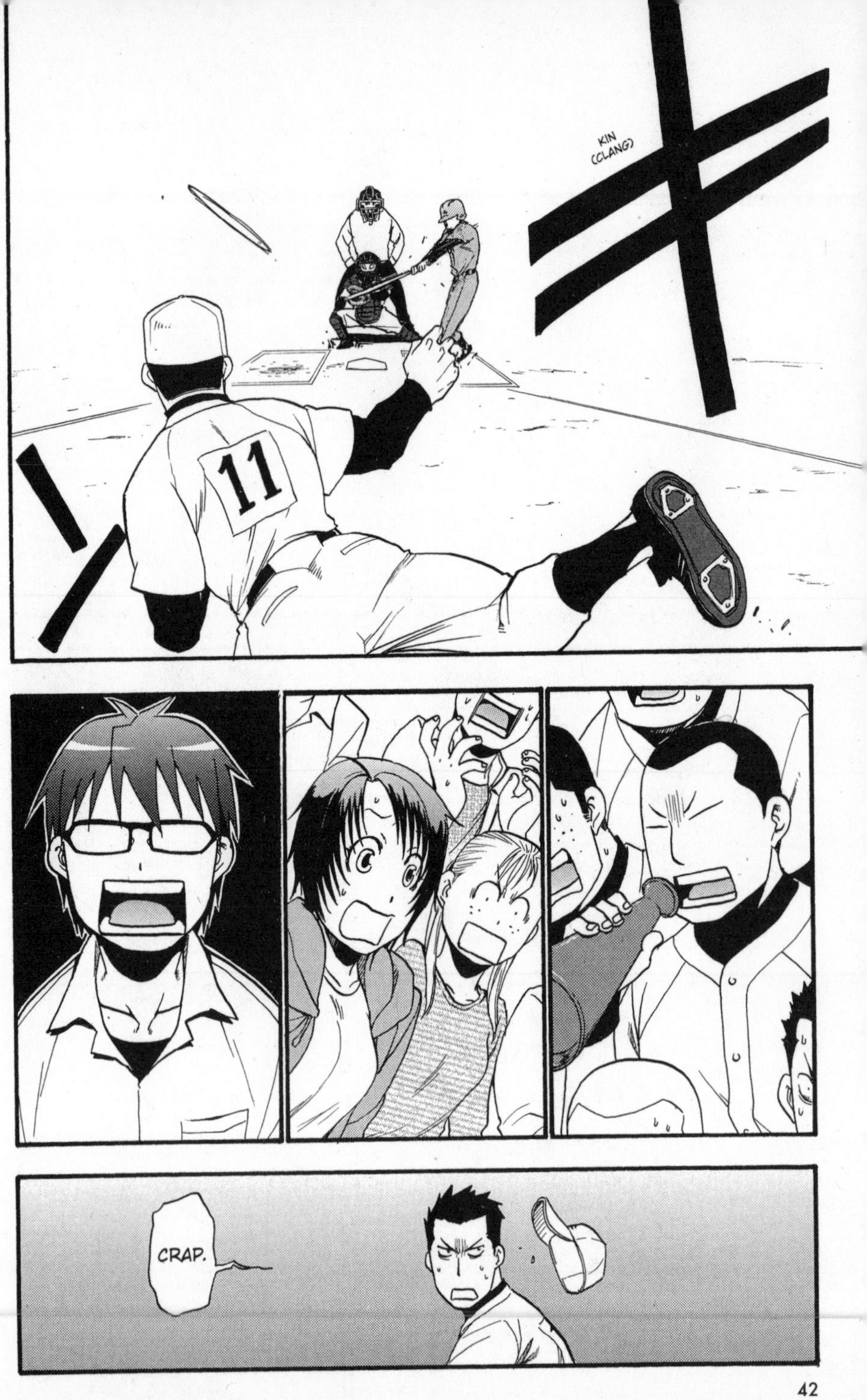
KIN (CLANG)
CRAP.

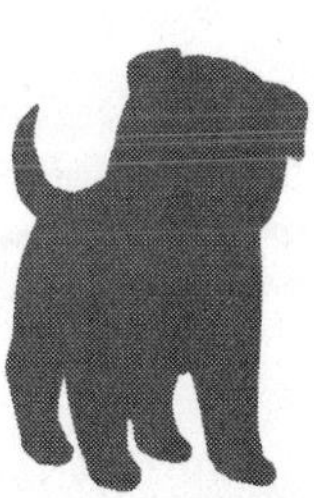

Silver Spoon

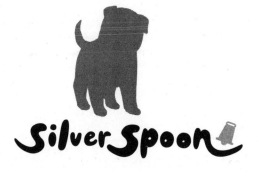

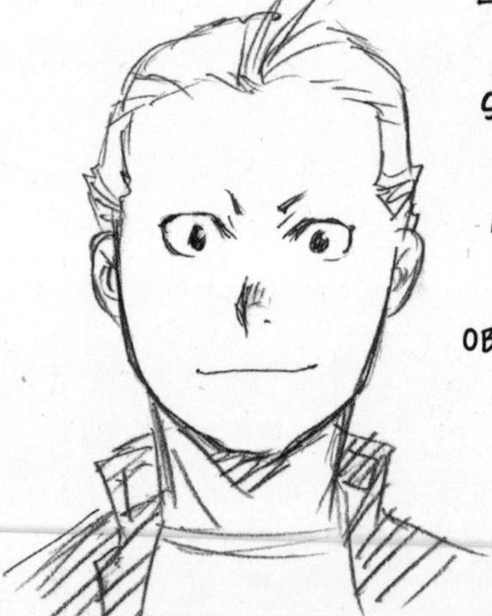

EQUESTRIAN CLUB

SHINEI OOKAWA

AGRICULTURAL ENGINEERING, YEAR 3

OBIHIRO OOZORA NORTH MIDDLE SCHOOL

JOB HUNTING

Chapter 38:
Tale of Autumn ⑦

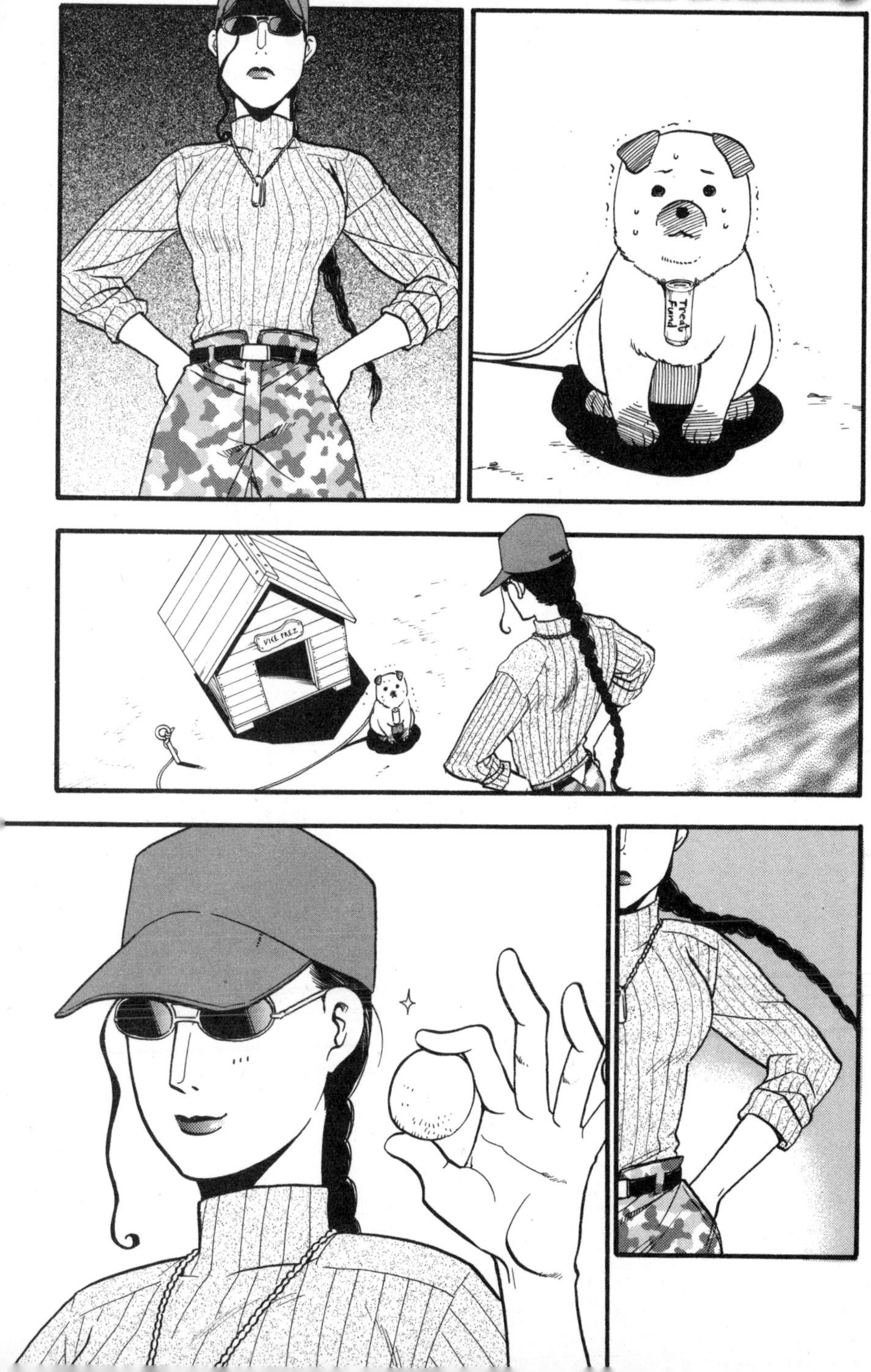

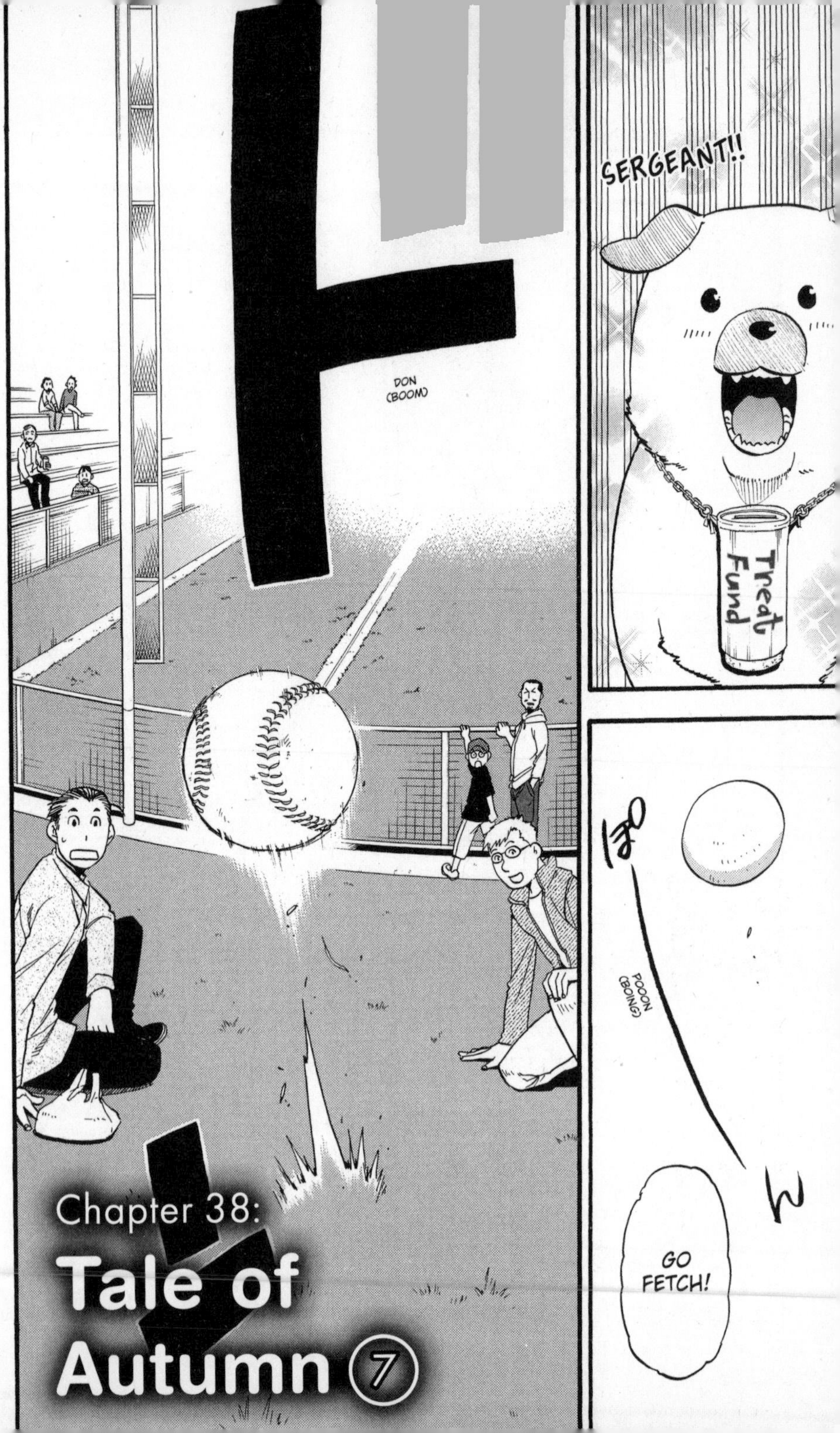
SERGEANT!!
Treat Fund
POOON (BOING)
GO FETCH!
DON (BOOM)
Chapter 38:
Tale of Autumn 7

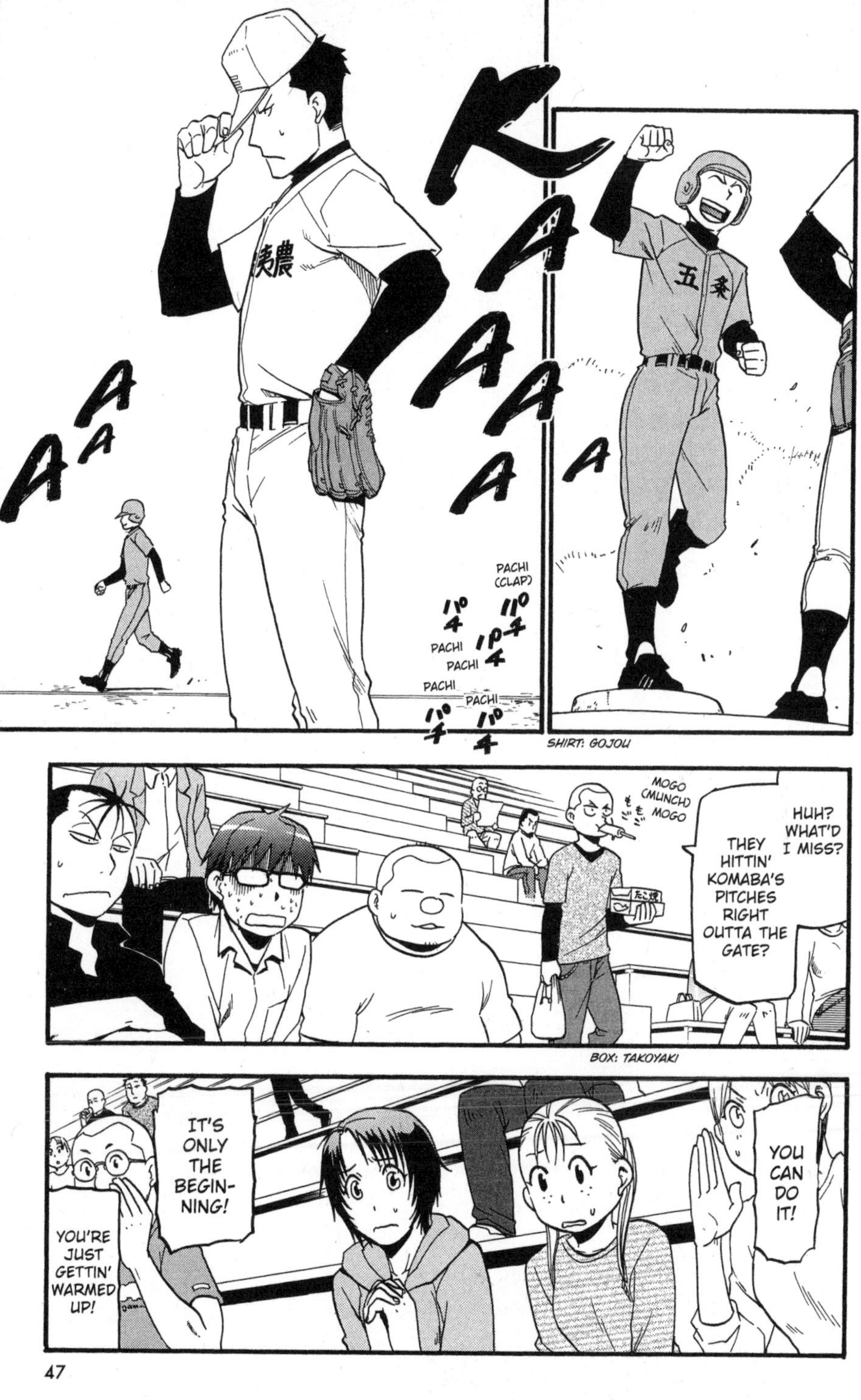
A
KAAAAA
AAA
PACHI (CLAP)
PACHI
PACHI
PACHI
PACHI
SHIRT: GOJOU
HUH? WHAT'D I MISS?
THEY HITTIN' KOMABA'S PITCHES RIGHT OUTTA THE GATE?
MOGO (MUNCH) MOGO
BOX: TAKOYAKI
YOU CAN DO IT!
IT'S ONLY THE BEGIN-NING!
YOU'RE JUST GETTIN' WARMED UP!

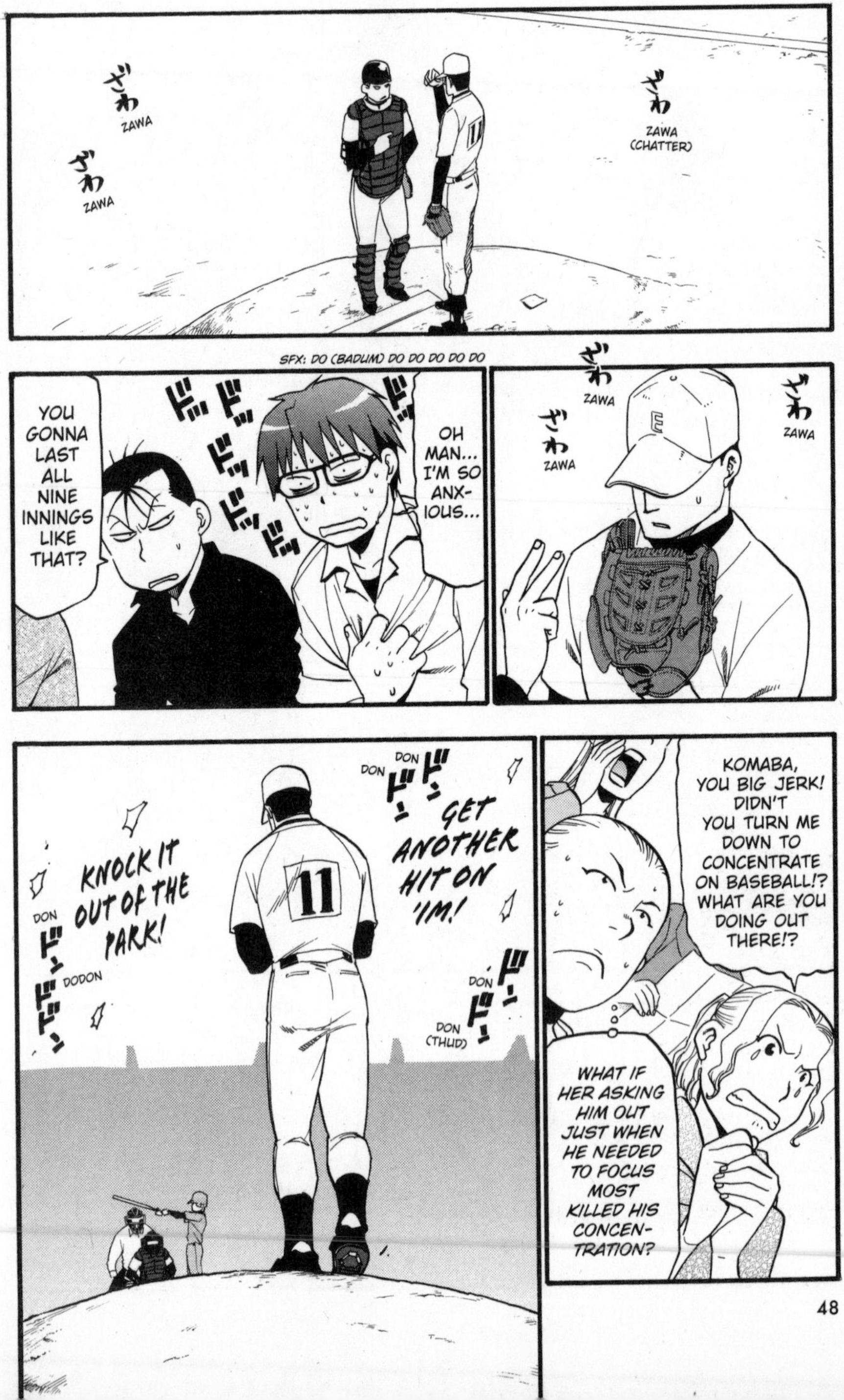
ざわ
ZAWA (CHATTER)
ざわ
ZAWA
ざわ
ZAWA
SFX: DO (BADUM) DO DO DO DO DO
ざわ
ZAWA
ざわ
ZAWA
ざわ
ZAWA
OH MAN... I'M SO ANX-IOUS...
YOU GONNA LAST ALL NINE INNINGS LIKE THAT?
KOMABA, YOU BIG JERK! DIDN'T YOU TURN ME DOWN TO CONCENTRATE ON BASEBALL!? WHAT ARE YOU DOING OUT THERE!?
WHAT IF HER ASKING HIM OUT JUST WHEN HE NEEDED TO FOCUS MOST KILLED HIS CONCEN-TRATION?
DON DON
GET ANOTHER HIT ON 'IM!
DON (THUD) DON
KNOCK IT OUT OF THE PARK!
DON DODON

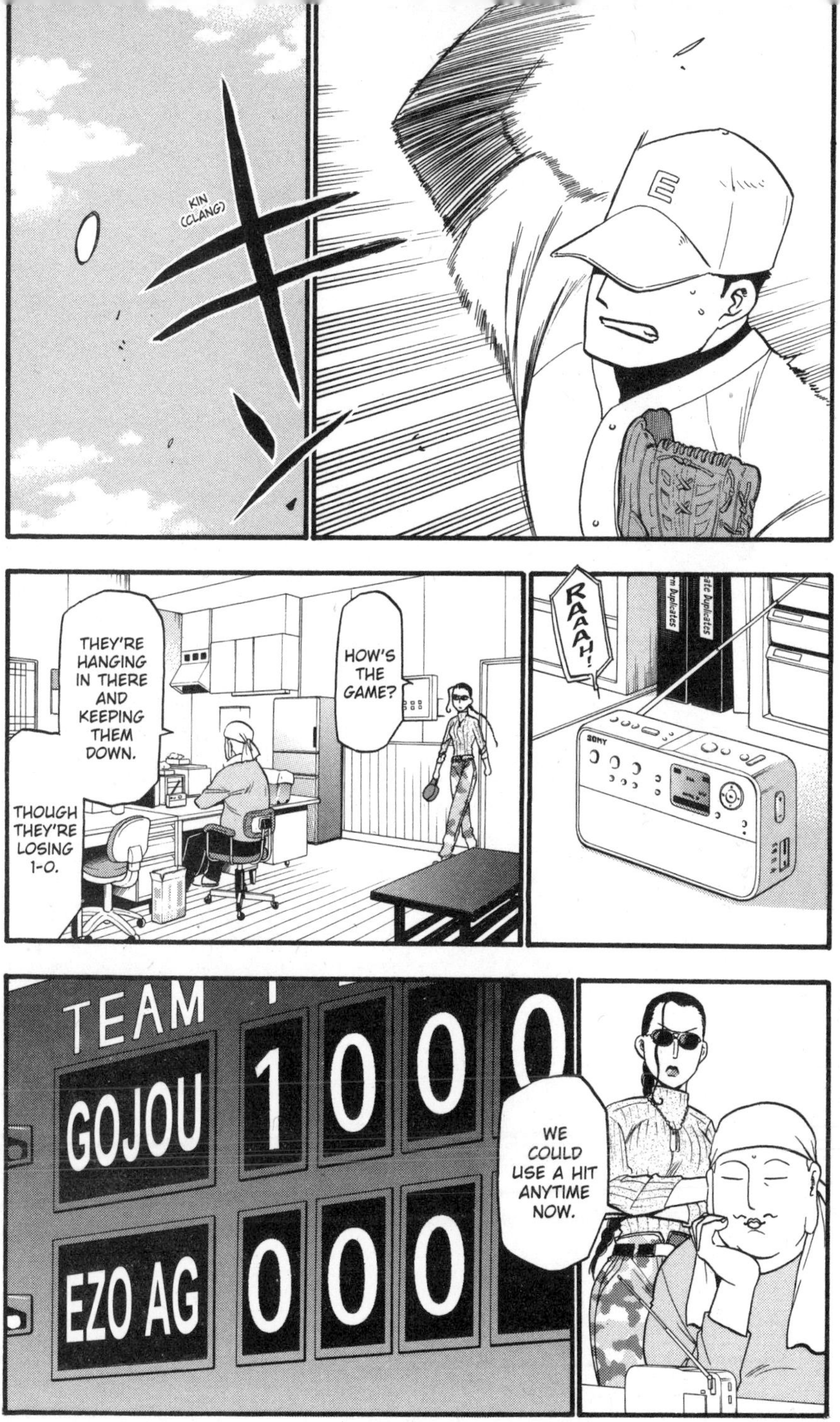
KIN (CLANG)
RAAAH!
SONY
HOW'S THE GAME?
THEY'RE HANGING IN THERE AND KEEPING THEM DOWN.
THOUGH THEY'RE LOSING 1-0.
WE COULD USE A HIT ANYTIME NOW.
TEAM
GOJOU 1 0 0 0
EZO AG 0 0 0

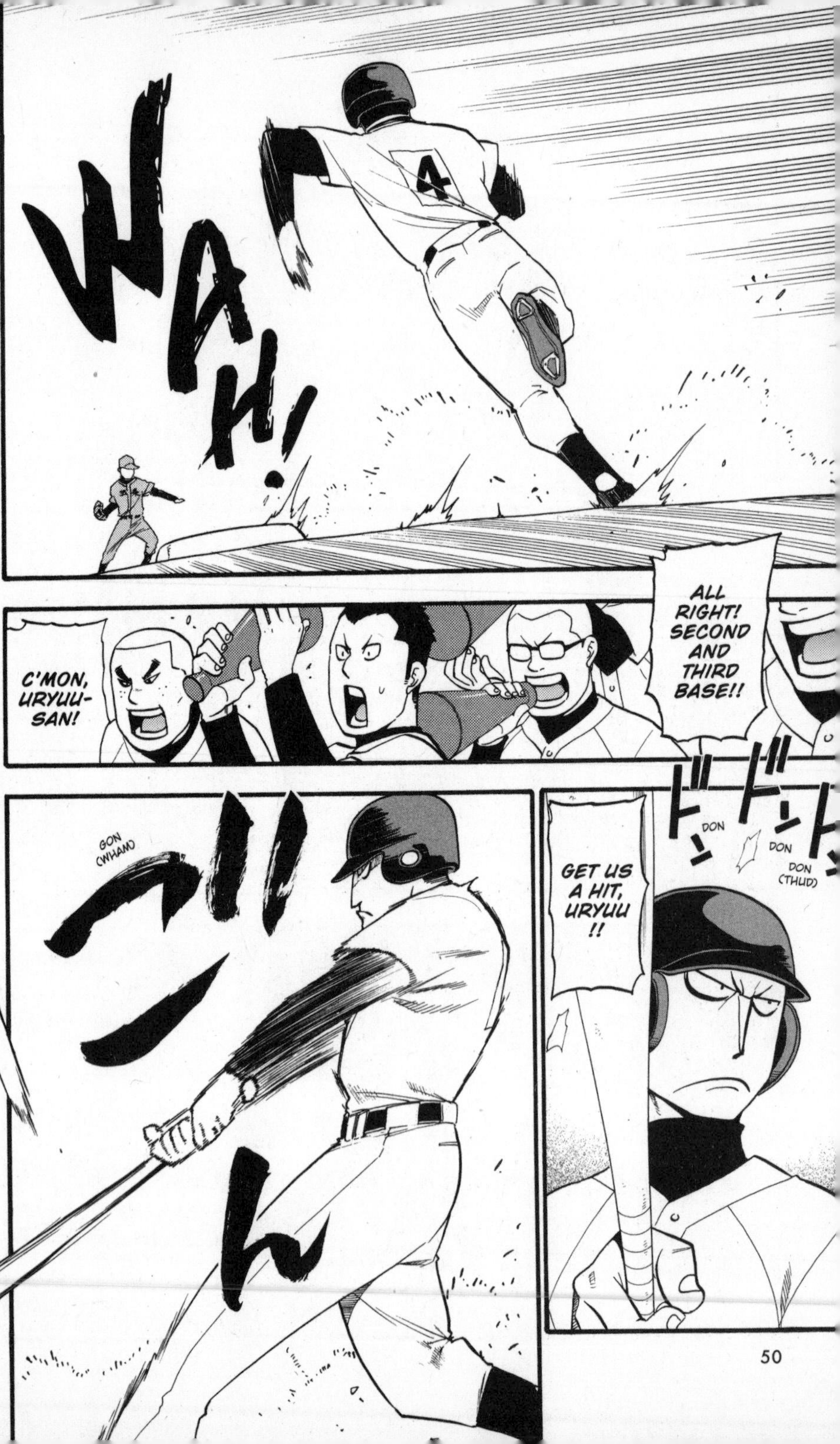
WAAH!
ALL RIGHT! SECOND AND THIRD BASE!!
C'MON, URYUU-SAN!
DON
DON
DON (THUD)
GET US A HIT, URYUU!!
GON (WHAM)

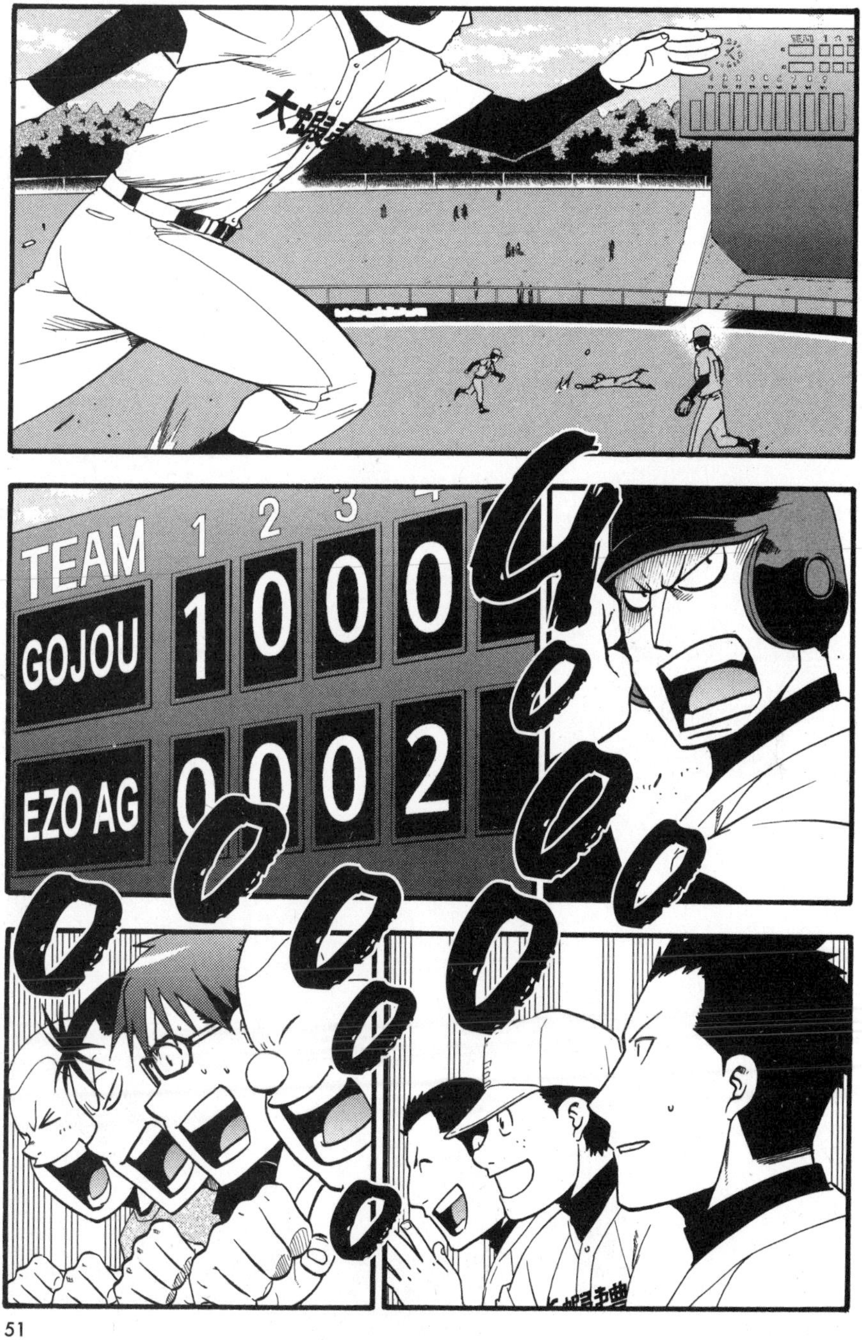
TEAM 1 2 3 4
GOJOU 1 0 0 0
EZO AG 0 0 0 2

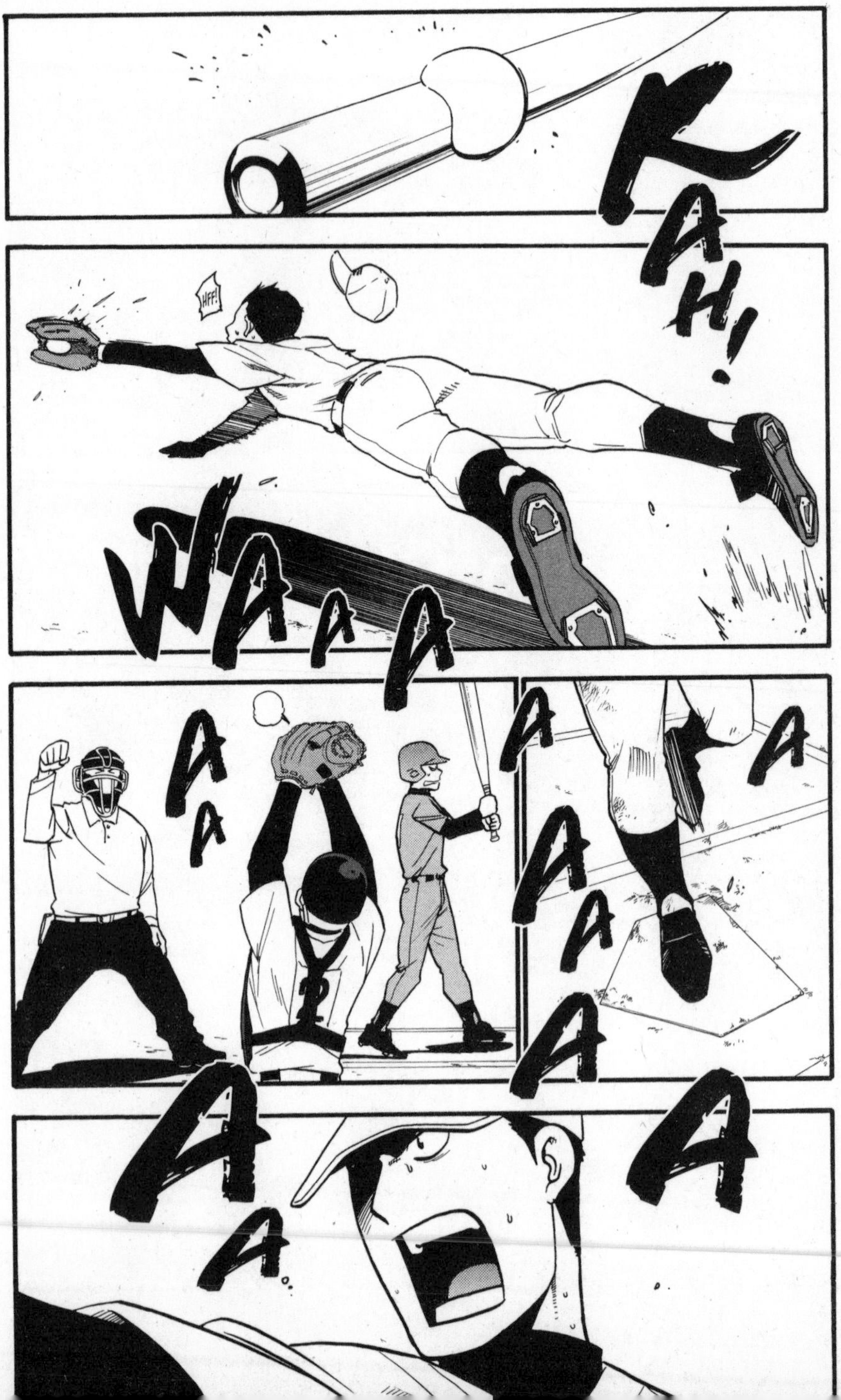

KAH!
HFF!
WAAAAAAAAAAAAAAAAAAA...

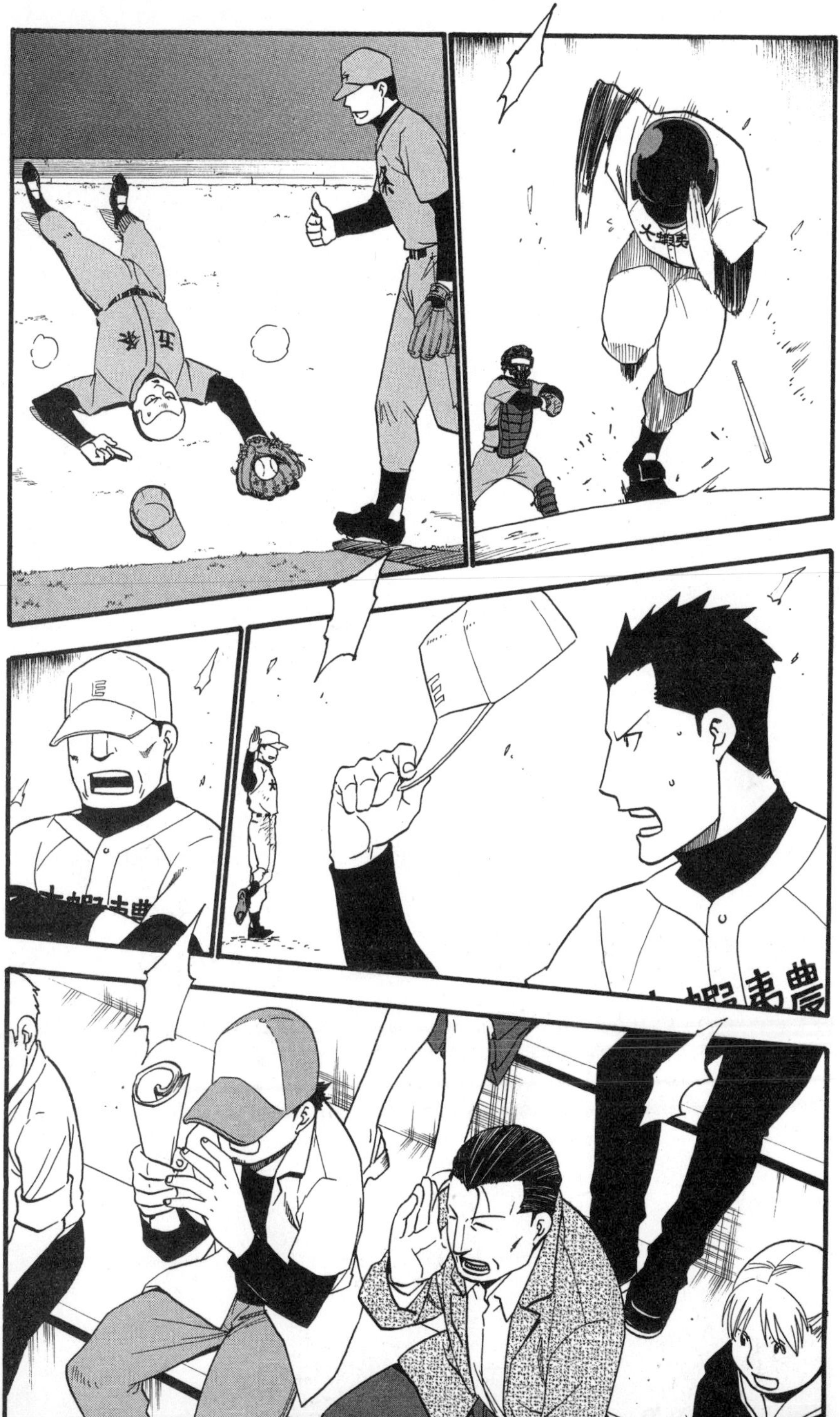

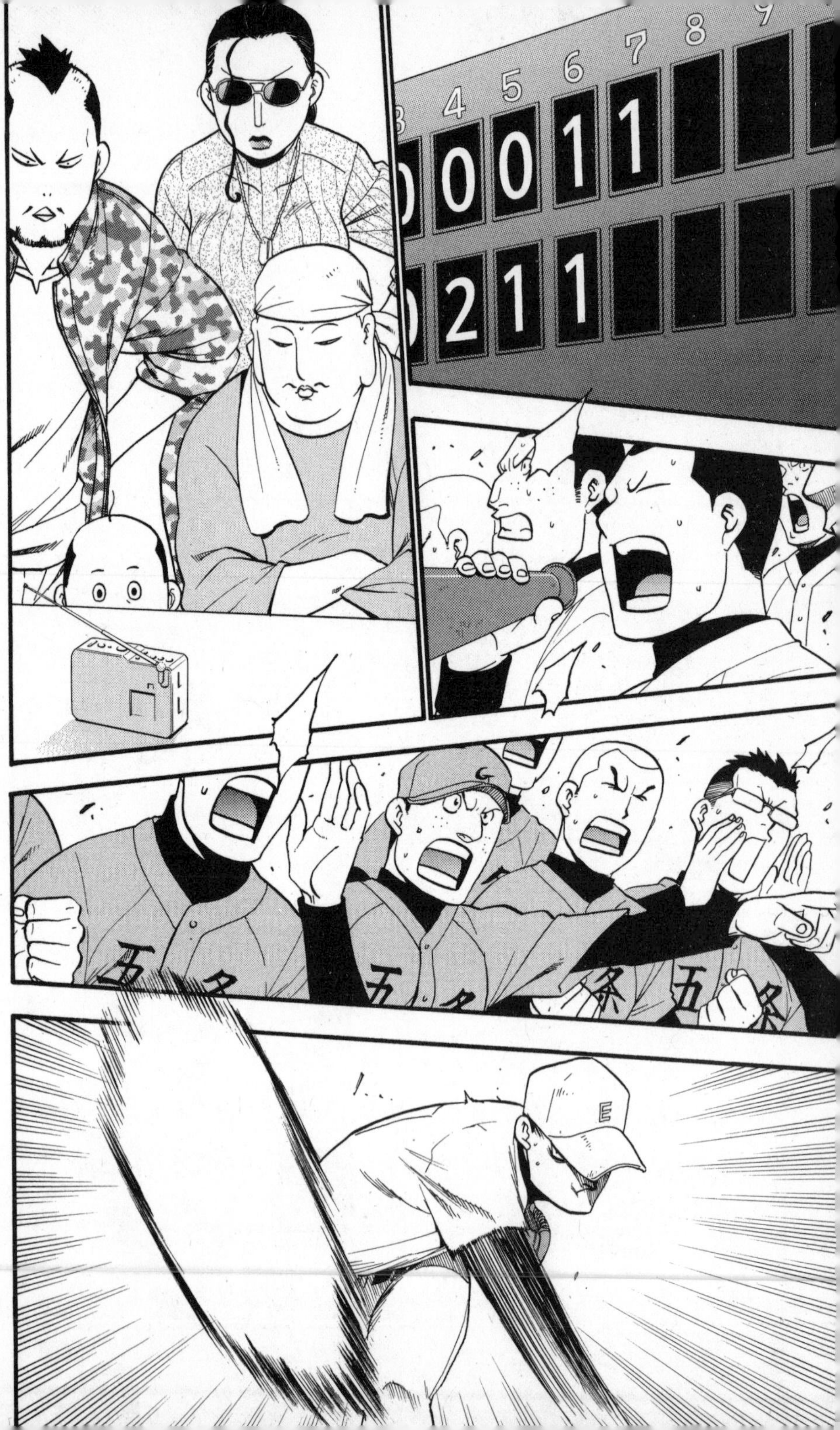

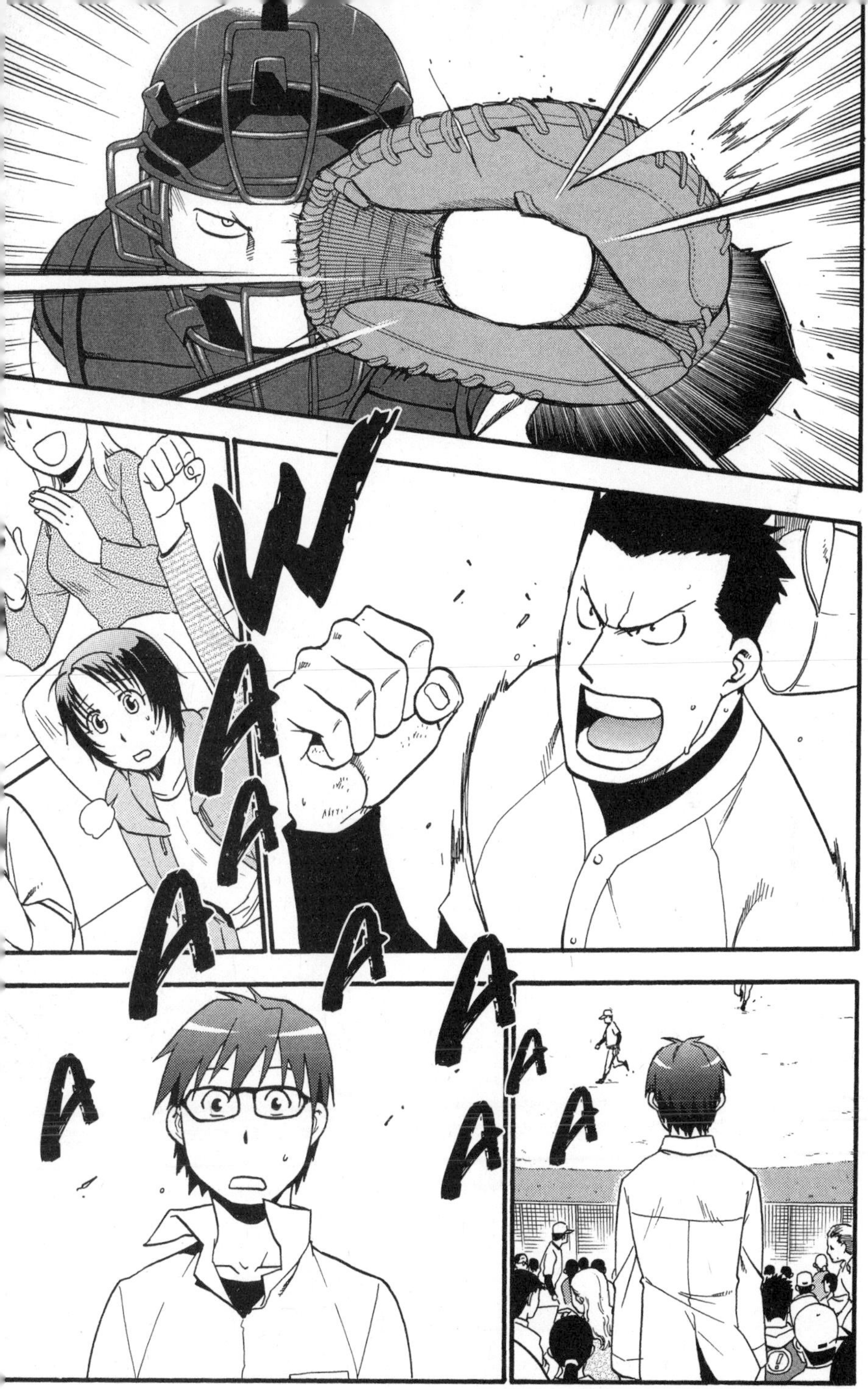
WAAAAAAAAA

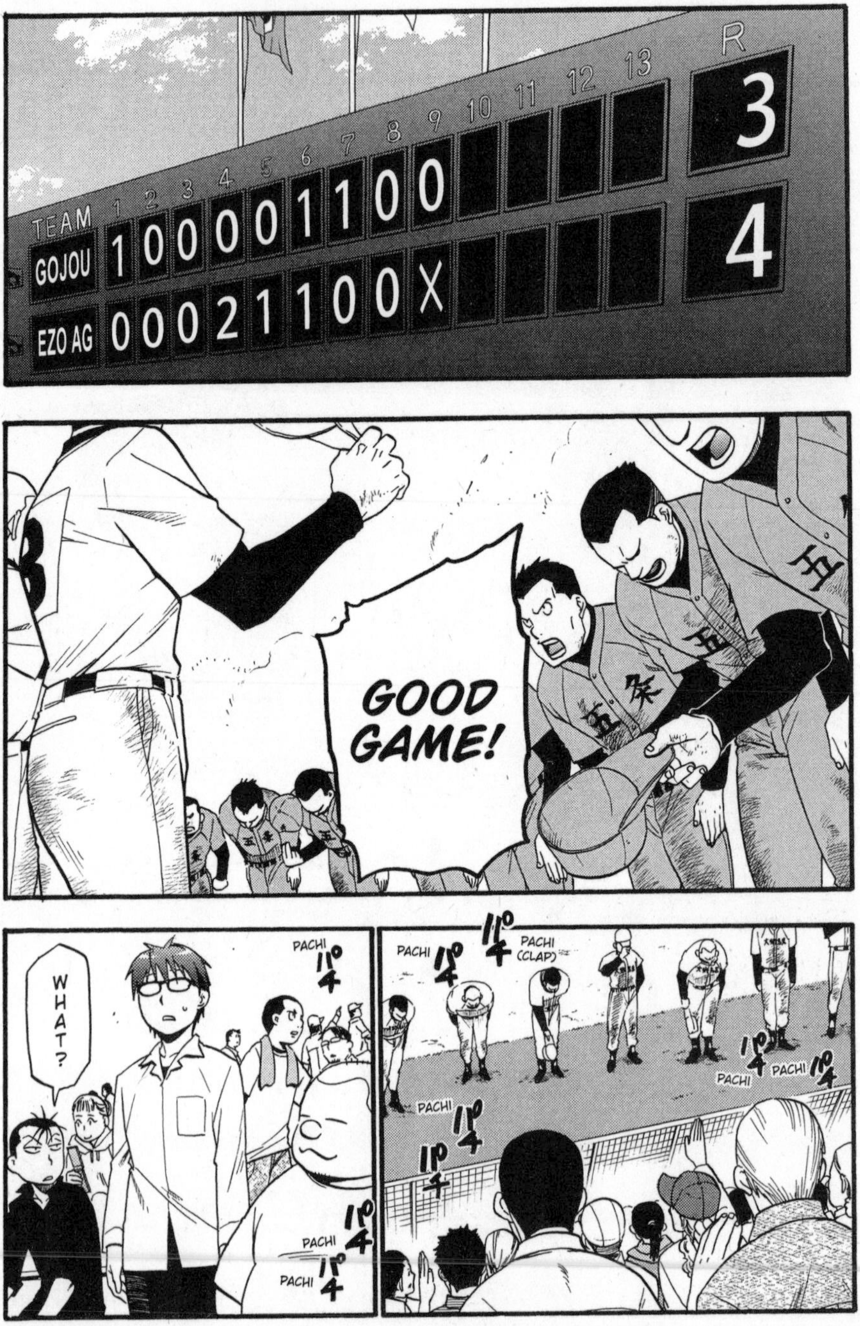
TEAM 1 2 3 4 5 6 7 8 9 10 11 12 13 R
GOJOU 1 0 0 0 0 1 1 0 0 3
EZO AG 0 0 0 2 1 1 0 0 X 4
GOOD GAME!
PACHI (CLAP)
PACHI
PACHI
PACHI
PACHI
PACHI
WHAT?
PACHI
PACHI

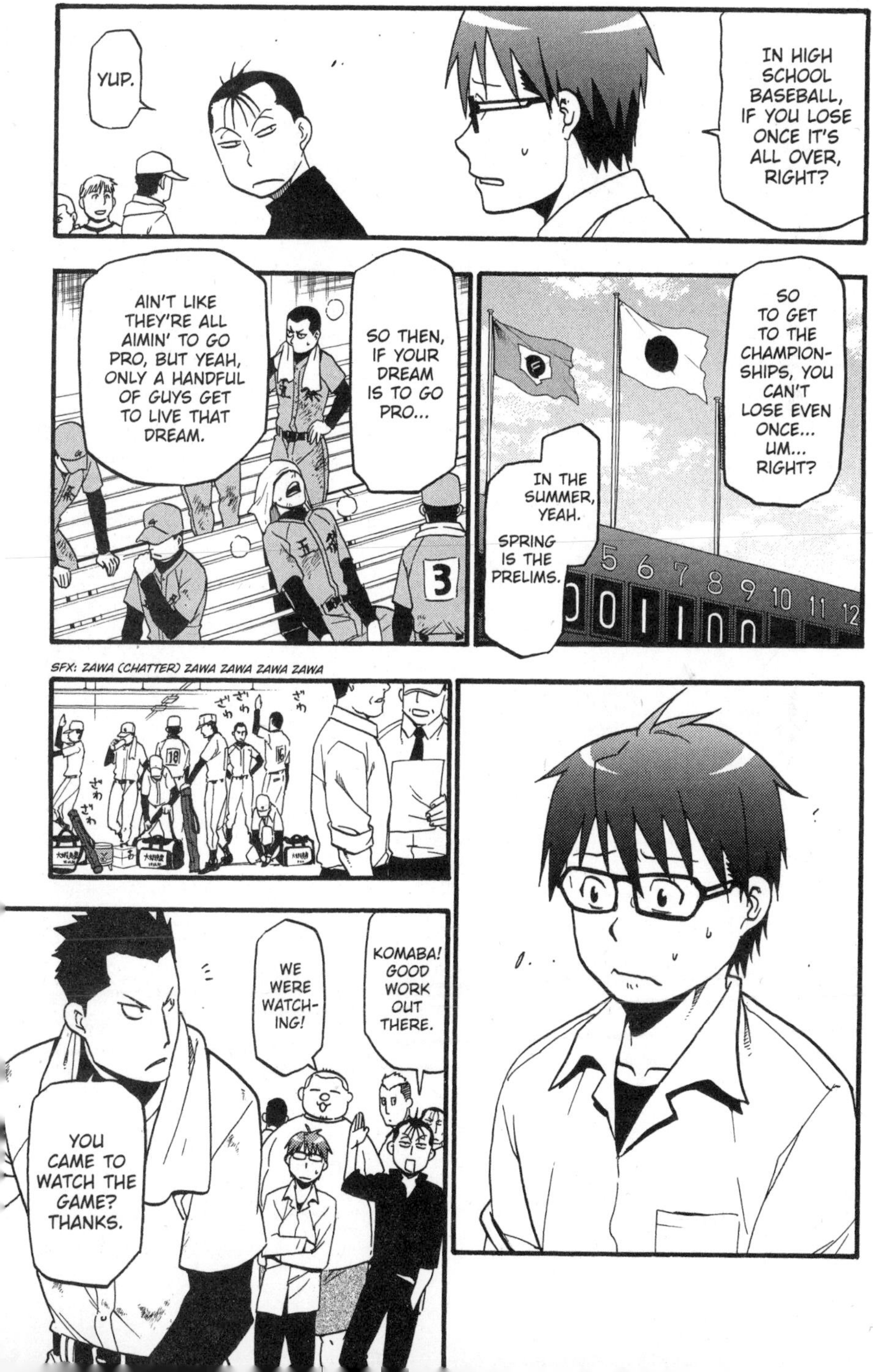
IN HIGH SCHOOL BASEBALL, IF YOU LOSE ONCE IT'S ALL OVER, RIGHT?
YUP.
SO TO GET TO THE CHAMPIONSHIPS, YOU CAN'T LOSE EVEN ONCE... UM... RIGHT?
IN THE SUMMER, YEAH.
SPRING IS THE PRELIMS.
SO THEN, IF YOUR DREAM IS TO GO PRO...
AIN'T LIKE THEY'RE ALL AIMIN' TO GO PRO, BUT YEAH, ONLY A HANDFUL OF GUYS GET TO LIVE THAT DREAM.
SFX: ZAWA (CHATTER) ZAWA ZAWA ZAWA ZAWA
KOMABA! GOOD WORK OUT THERE.
WE WERE WATCHING!
YOU CAME TO WATCH THE GAME? THANKS.

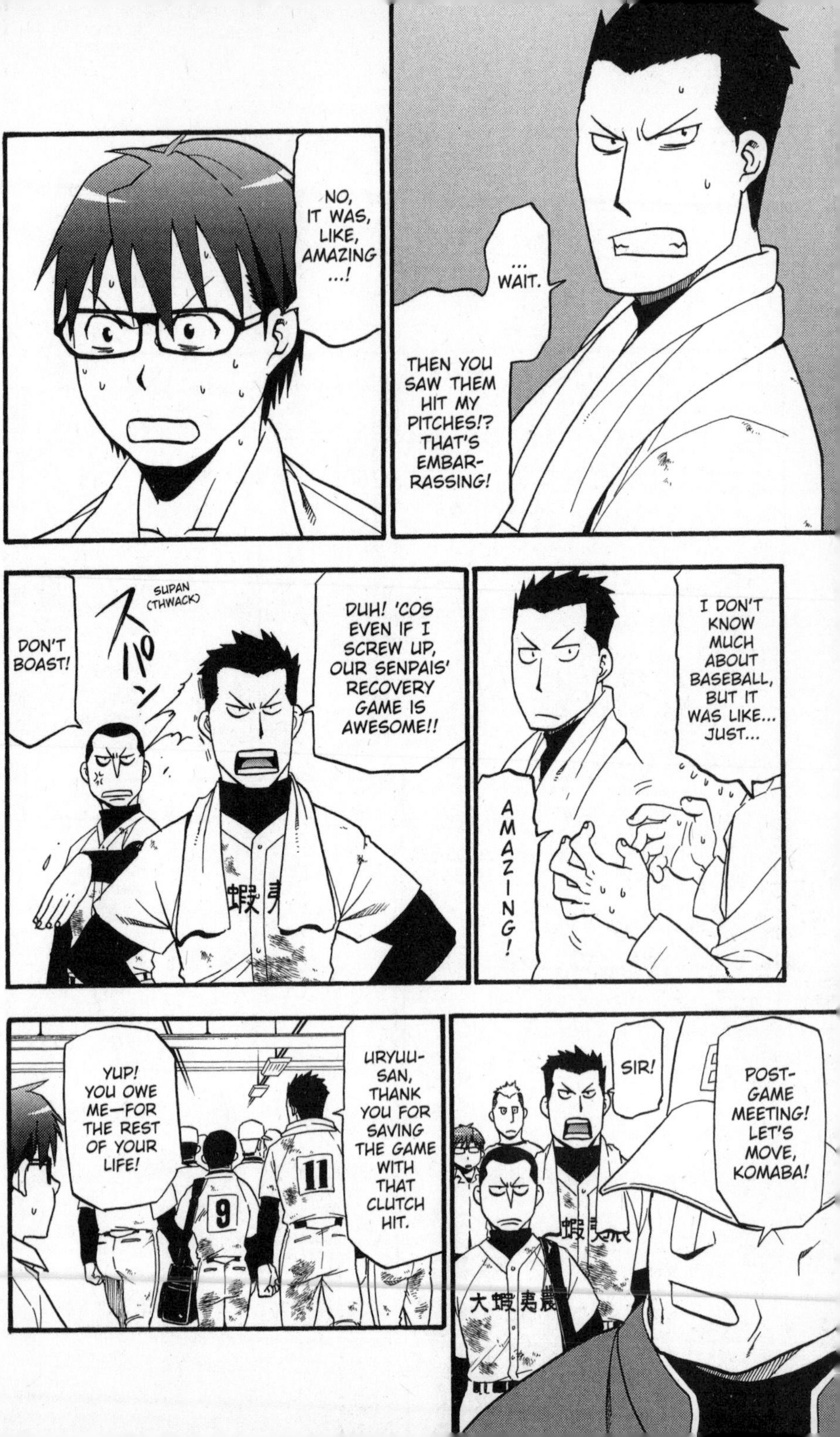
...WAIT.
THEN YOU SAW THEM HIT MY PITCHES!? THAT'S EMBARRASSING!
NO, IT WAS, LIKE, AMAZING ...!
I DON'T KNOW MUCH ABOUT BASEBALL, BUT IT WAS LIKE... JUST...
AMAZING!
DUH! 'COS EVEN IF I SCREW UP, OUR SENPAIS' RECOVERY GAME IS AWESOME!!
スパン
SUPAN (THWACK)
DON'T BOAST!
POST-GAME MEETING! LET'S MOVE, KOMABA!
SIR!
URYUU-SAN, THANK YOU FOR SAVING THE GAME WITH THAT CLUTCH HIT.
YUP! YOU OWE ME—FOR THE REST OF YOUR LIFE!

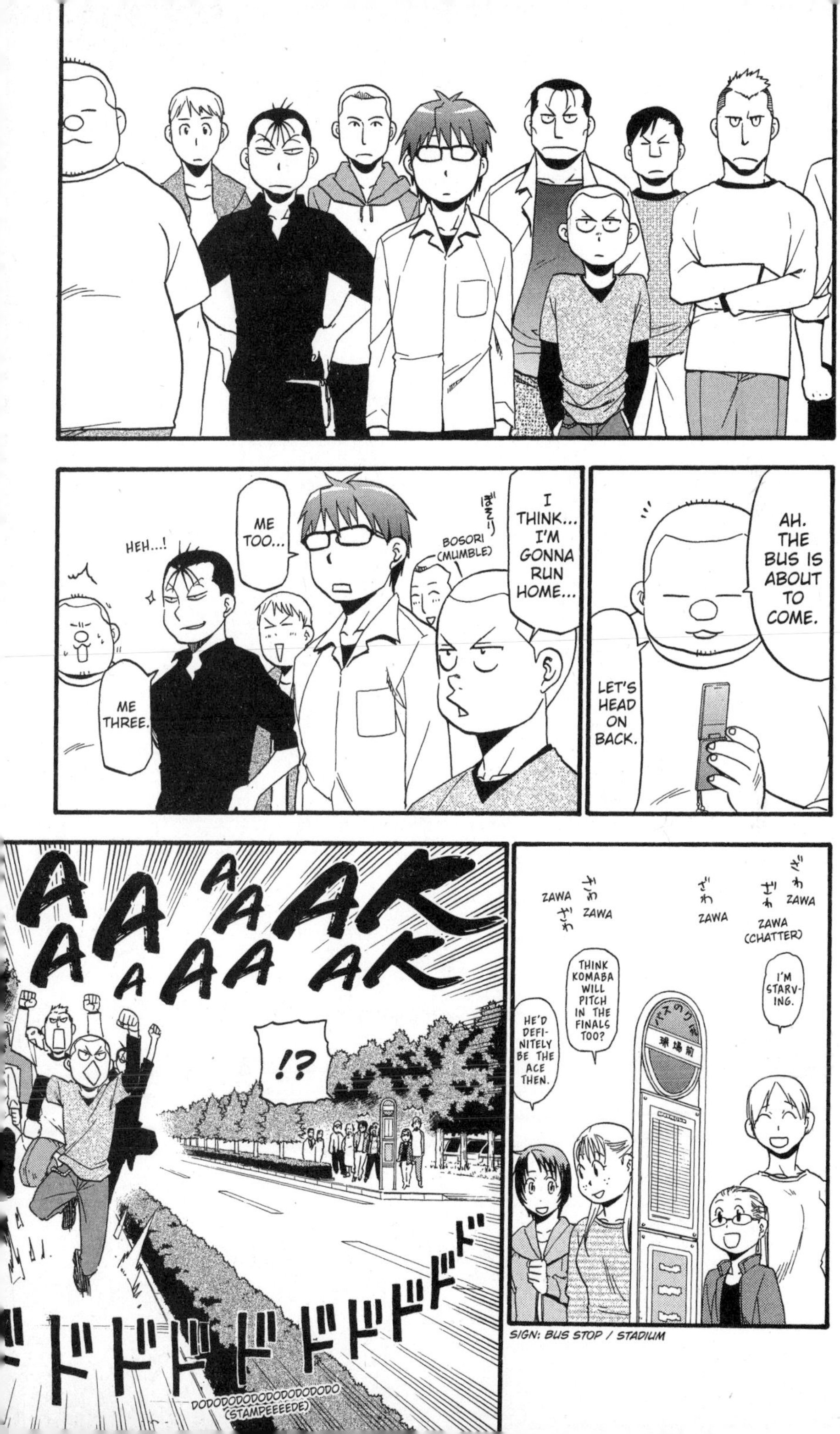
AH. THE BUS IS ABOUT TO COME.
LET'S HEAD ON BACK.
I THINK... I'M GONNA RUN HOME...
ぼそり
BOSORI (MUMBLE)
ME TOO...
HEH...!
ME THREE.
ざわ ざわ
ZAWA ZAWA
ZAWA (CHATTER)
ざわ
ZAWA
ざわ ざわ
ZAWA ZAWA
I'M STARV-ING.
THINK KOMABA WILL PITCH IN THE FINALS TOO?
HE'D DEFI-NITELY BE THE ACE THEN.
SIGN: BUS STOP / STADIUM
AAAAK
AAAAAR
!?
ドドドドドドドドド
DODODODODODODODODO (STAMPEEEEDE)

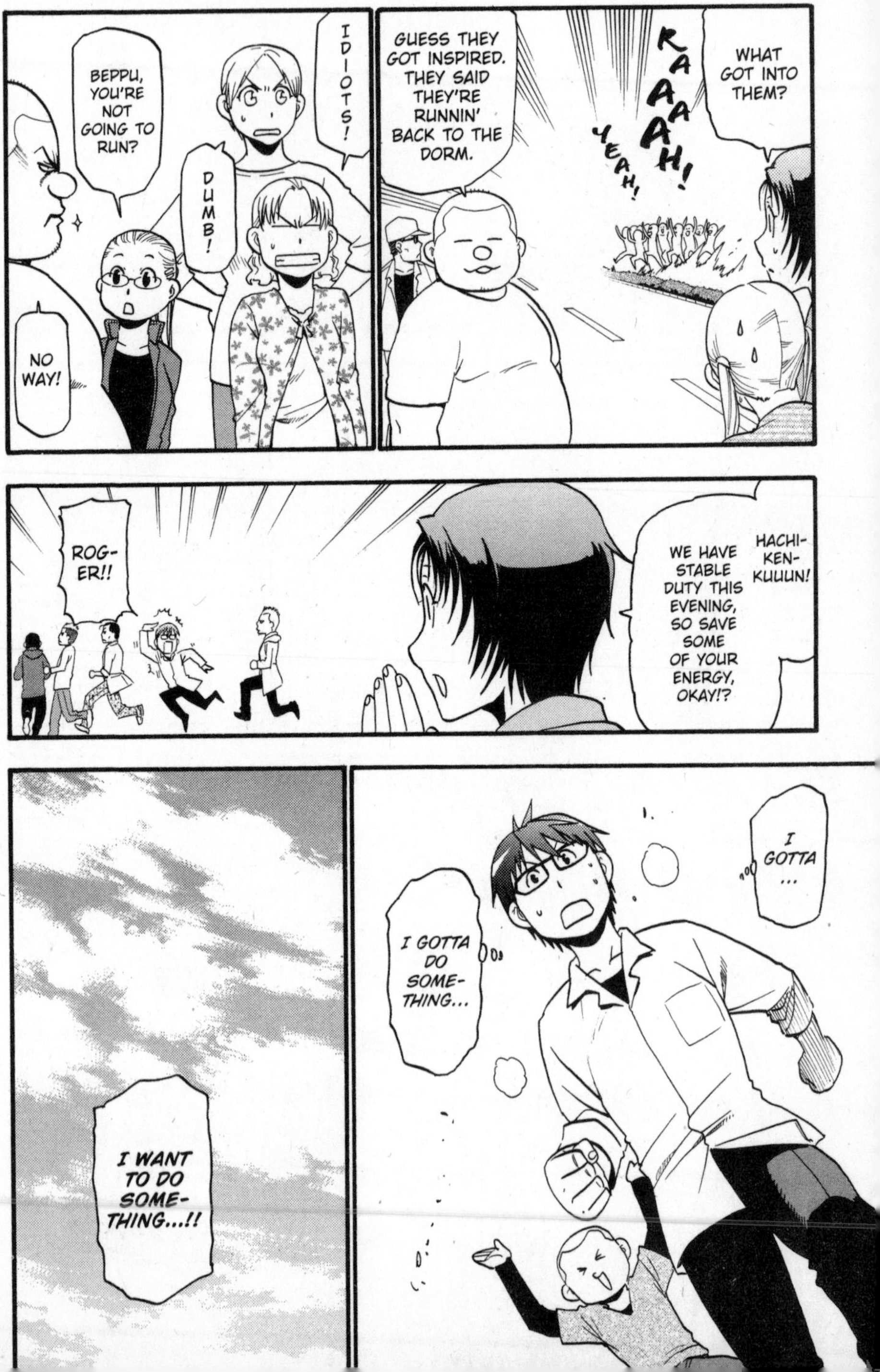
WHAT GOT INTO THEM?
RAAAAAH!
YEAH!
GUESS THEY GOT INSPIRED. THEY SAID THEY'RE RUNNIN' BACK TO THE DORM.
IDIOTS!
DUMB!
BEPPU, YOU'RE NOT GOING TO RUN?
NO WAY!
HACHI-KEN-KUUUN!
WE HAVE STABLE DUTY THIS EVENING, SO SAVE SOME OF YOUR ENERGY, OKAY!?
ROG-ER!!
I GOTTA...
I GOTTA DO SOME-THING...
I WANT TO DO SOME-THING...!!

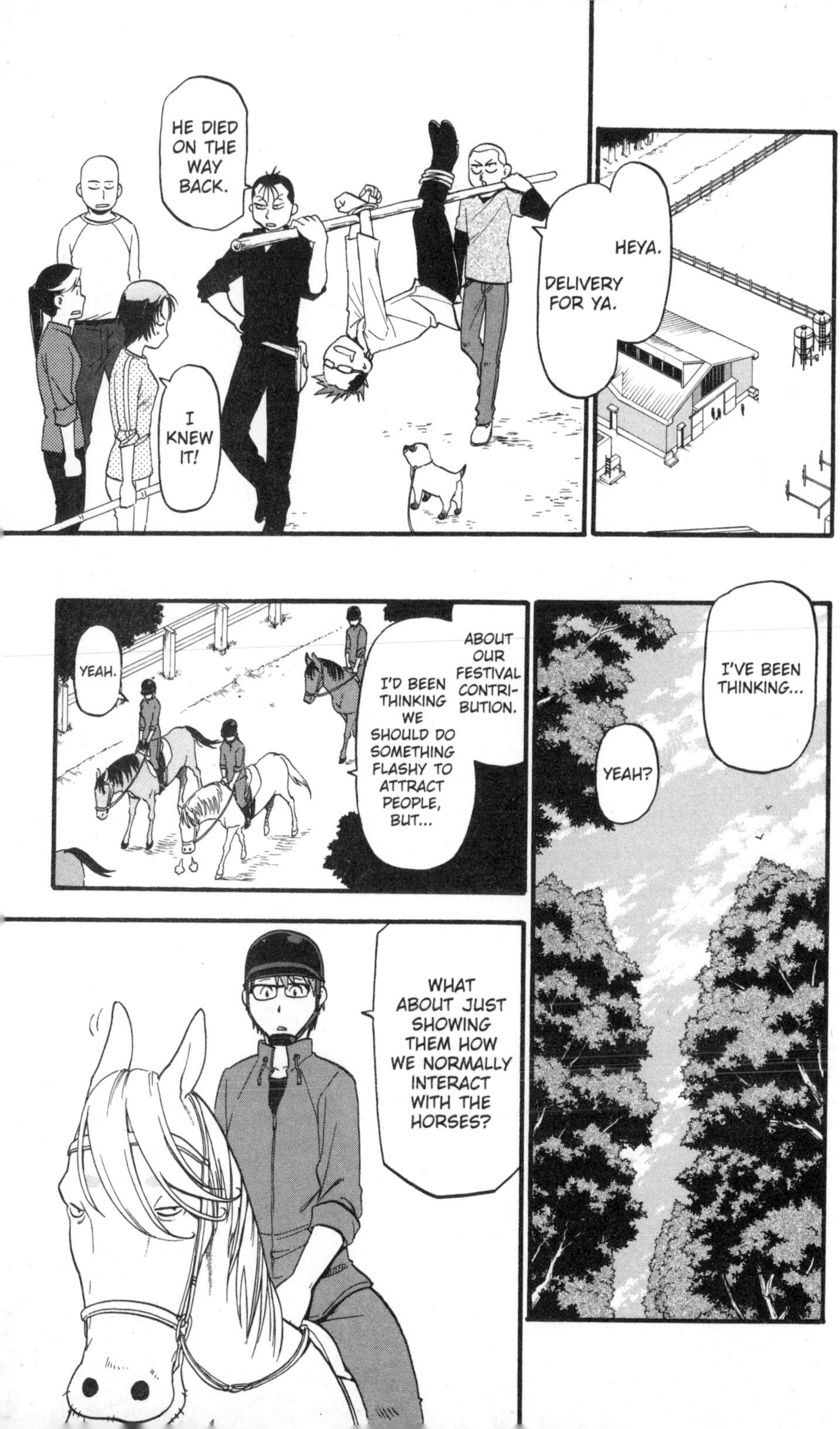
HEYA.
DELIVERY FOR YA.
HE DIED ON THE WAY BACK.
I KNEW IT!
I'VE BEEN THINKING...
YEAH?
ABOUT OUR FESTIVAL CONTRIBUTION.
I'D BEEN THINKING WE SHOULD DO SOMETHING FLASHY TO ATTRACT PEOPLE, BUT...
YEAH.
WHAT ABOUT JUST SHOWING THEM HOW WE NORMALLY INTERACT WITH THE HORSES?

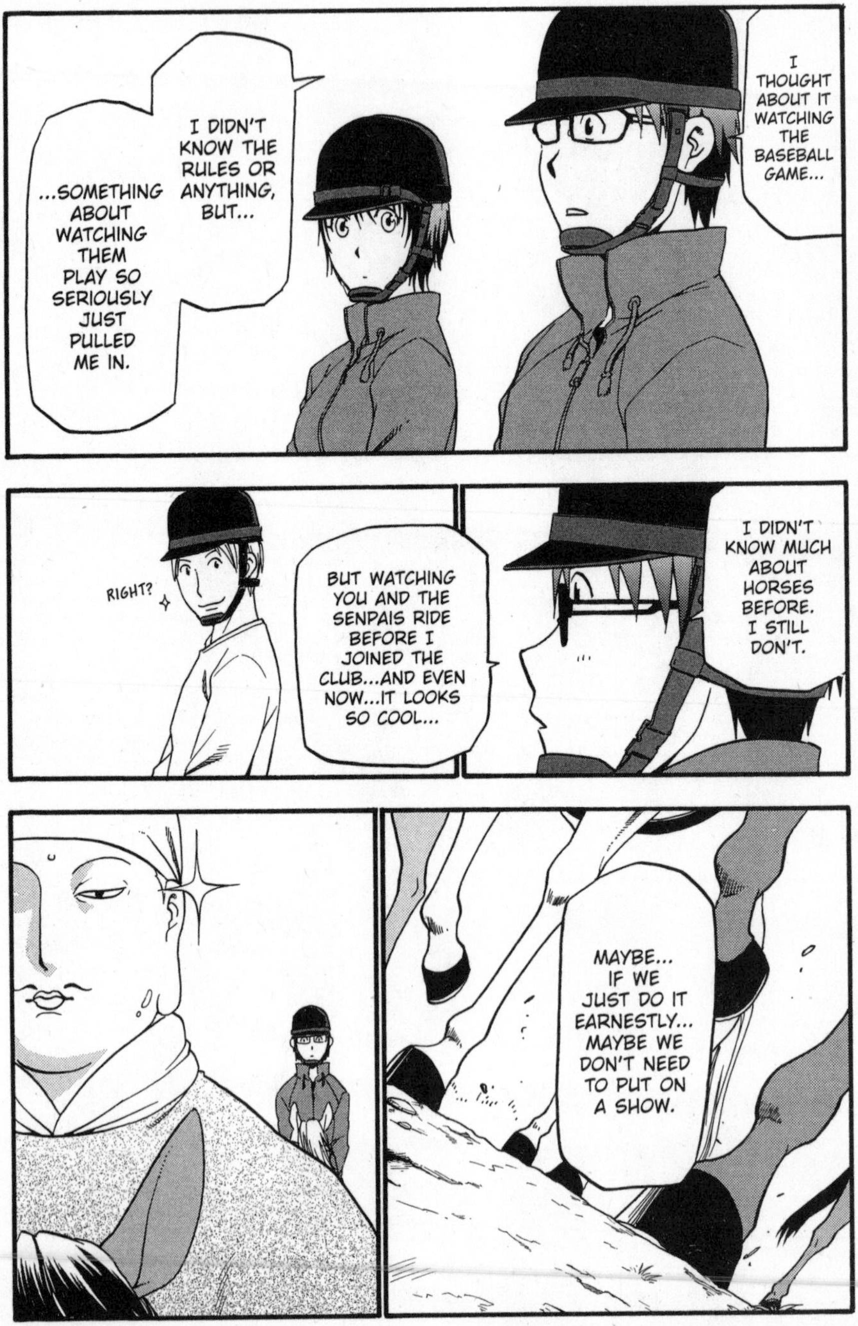
I THOUGHT ABOUT IT WATCHING THE BASEBALL GAME...
I DIDN'T KNOW THE RULES OR ANYTHING, BUT...
...SOMETHING ABOUT WATCHING THEM PLAY SO SERIOUSLY JUST PULLED ME IN.
I DIDN'T KNOW MUCH ABOUT HORSES BEFORE. I STILL DON'T.
BUT WATCHING YOU AND THE SENPAIS RIDE BEFORE I JOINED THE CLUB...AND EVEN NOW...IT LOOKS SO COOL...
RIGHT?
MAYBE... IF WE JUST DO IT EARNESTLY... MAYBE WE DON'T NEED TO PUT ON A SHOW.

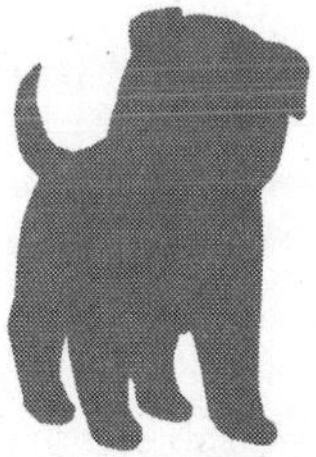

Silver Spoon

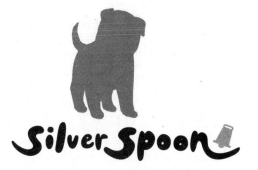

EQUESTRIAN CLUB

MANABU YODA

AGRICULTURAL SCIENCE,
YEAR 2

OBIHIRU NISHIKAWA
CENTRAL MIDDLE SCHOOL

COMMUTES TO SCHOOL
BY BIKE

Chapter 39:
Tale of Autumn ⑧

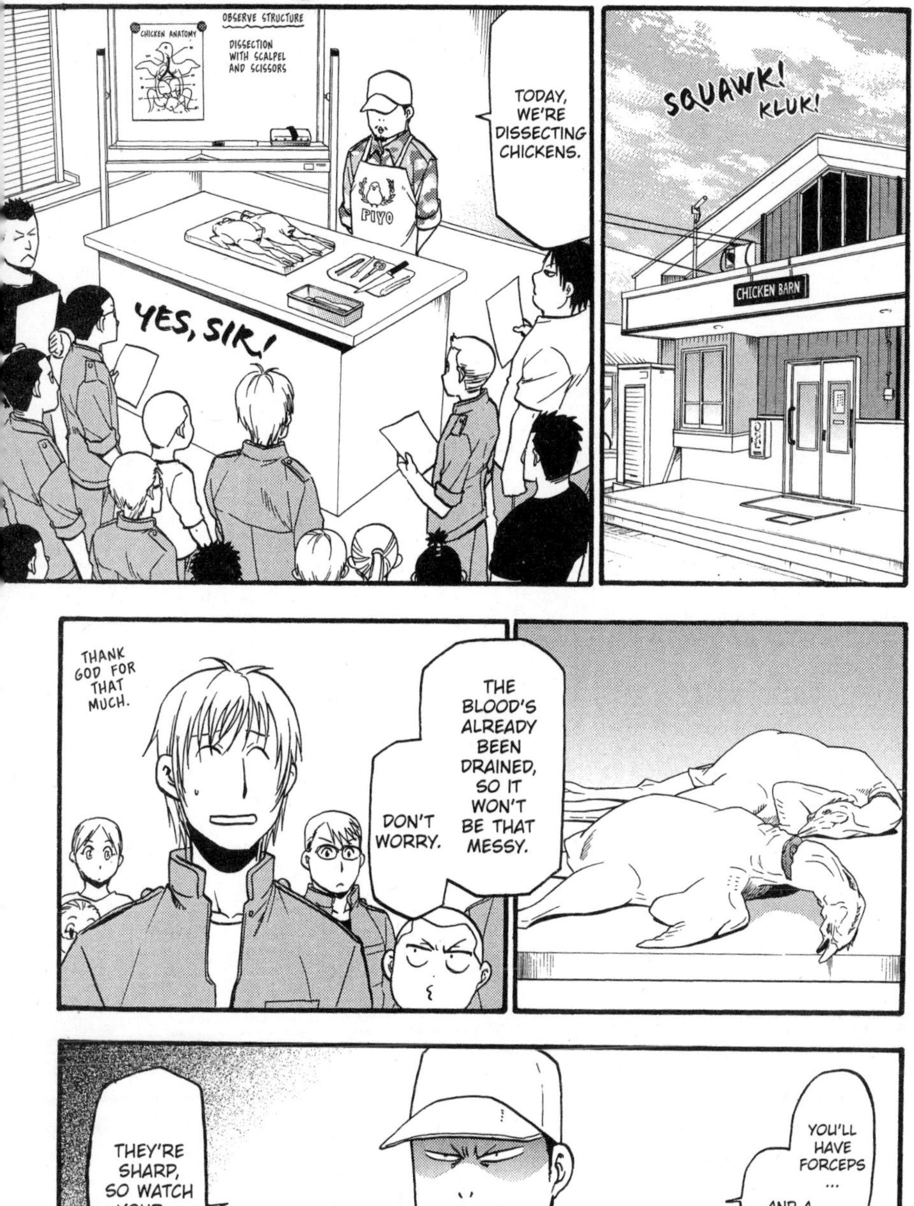
SQUAWK!
KLUK!
CHICKEN BARN
TODAY, WE'RE DISSECTING CHICKENS.
OBSERVE STRUCTURE
DISSECTION WITH SCALPEL AND SCISSORS
CHICKEN ANATOMY
PIYO
YES, SIR!
THE BLOOD'S ALREADY BEEN DRAINED, SO IT WON'T BE THAT MESSY.
DON'T WORRY.
THANK GOD FOR THAT MUCH.
YOU'LL HAVE FORCEPS...
...AND A SCALPEL.
THEY'RE SHARP, SO WATCH YOUR...

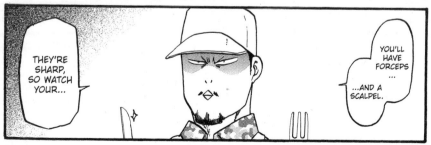

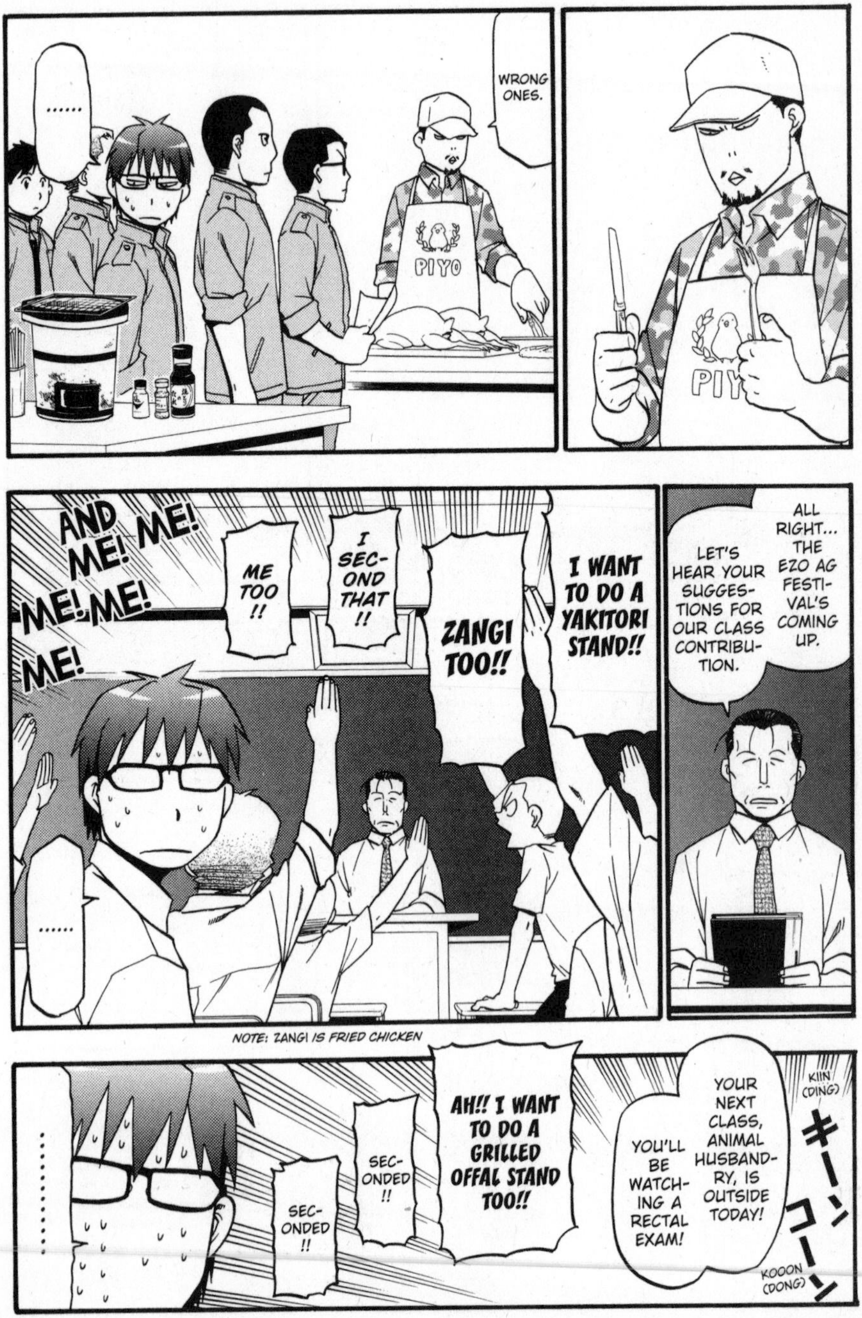
WRONG ONES.
......
ALL RIGHT... THE EZO AG FESTIVAL'S COMING UP.
LET'S HEAR YOUR SUGGESTIONS FOR OUR CLASS CONTRIBUTION.
I WANT TO DO A YAKITORI STAND!!
ZANGI TOO!!
I SECOND THAT!!
ME TOO!!
AND ME! ME! ME! ME! ME!
......
KIIN (DING)
キーン
KOOON (DONG)
コーン
YOUR NEXT CLASS, ANIMAL HUSBANDRY, IS OUTSIDE TODAY!
YOU'LL BE WATCHING A RECTAL EXAM!
AH!! I WANT TO DO A GRILLED OFFAL STAND TOO!!
SECONDED!!
SECONDED!!
....

NOTE: ZANGI IS FRIED CHICKEN

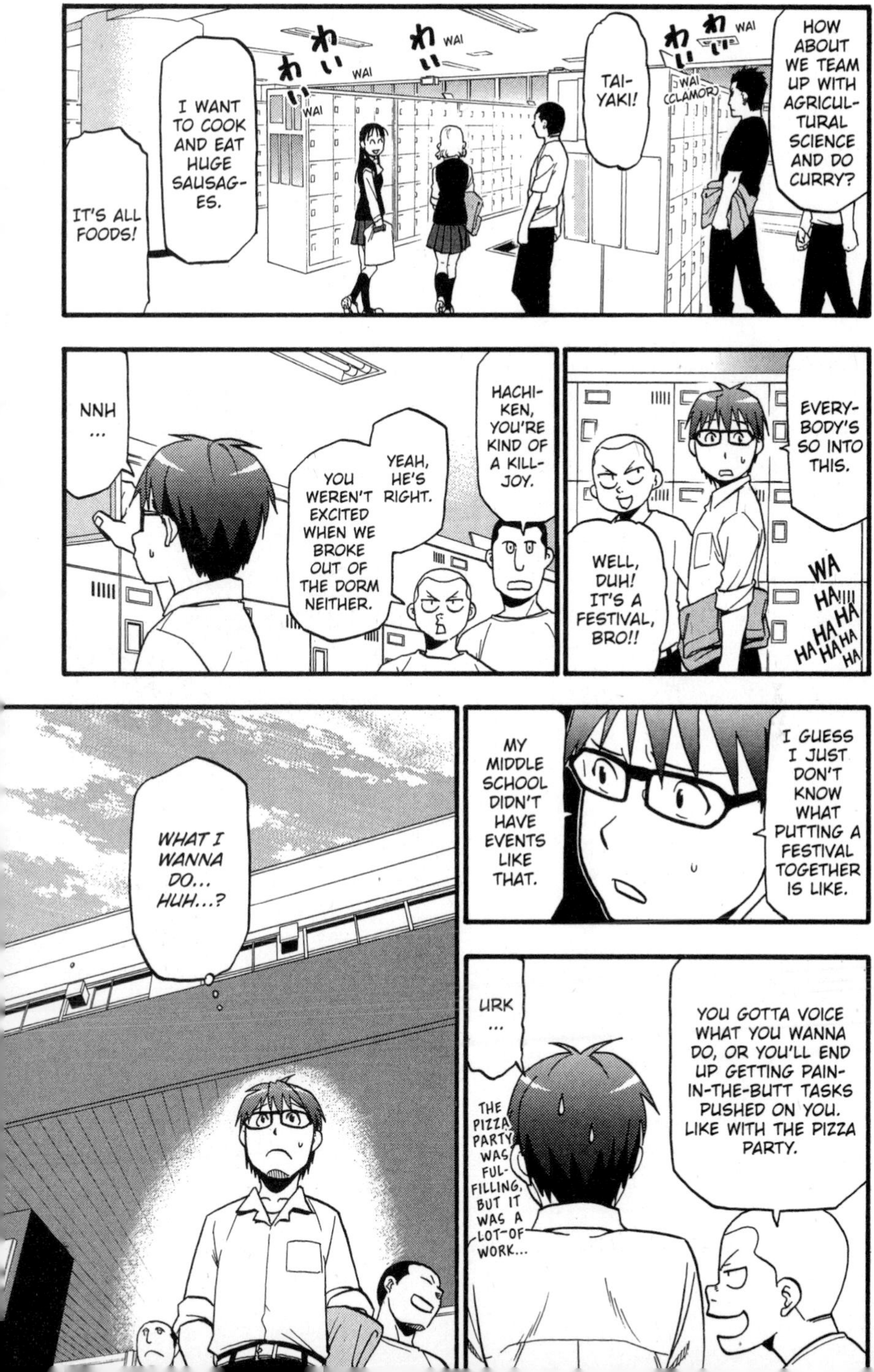
HOW ABOUT WE TEAM UP WITH AGRICULTURAL SCIENCE AND DO CURRY?
わい WAI
わい WAI (CLAMOR)
TAI-YAKI!
わい WAI
わい WAI
I WANT TO COOK AND EAT HUGE SAUSAGES.
IT'S ALL FOODS!
EVERYBODY'S SO INTO THIS.
WELL, DUH! IT'S A FESTIVAL, BRO!!
WA HA HA HA HA HA HA HA HA
HACHIKEN, YOU'RE KIND OF A KILLJOY.
YEAH, HE'S RIGHT.
YOU WEREN'T EXCITED WHEN WE BROKE OUT OF THE DORM NEITHER.
NNH...
I GUESS I JUST DON'T KNOW WHAT PUTTING A FESTIVAL TOGETHER IS LIKE.
MY MIDDLE SCHOOL DIDN'T HAVE EVENTS LIKE THAT.
YOU GOTTA VOICE WHAT YOU WANNA DO, OR YOU'LL END UP GETTING PAIN-IN-THE-BUTT TASKS PUSHED ON YOU. LIKE WITH THE PIZZA PARTY.
URK...
THE PIZZA PARTY WAS FULFILLING, BUT IT WAS A LOT OF WORK...
WHAT I WANNA DO... HUH...?

Chapter 39:
Tale of Autumn ⑧

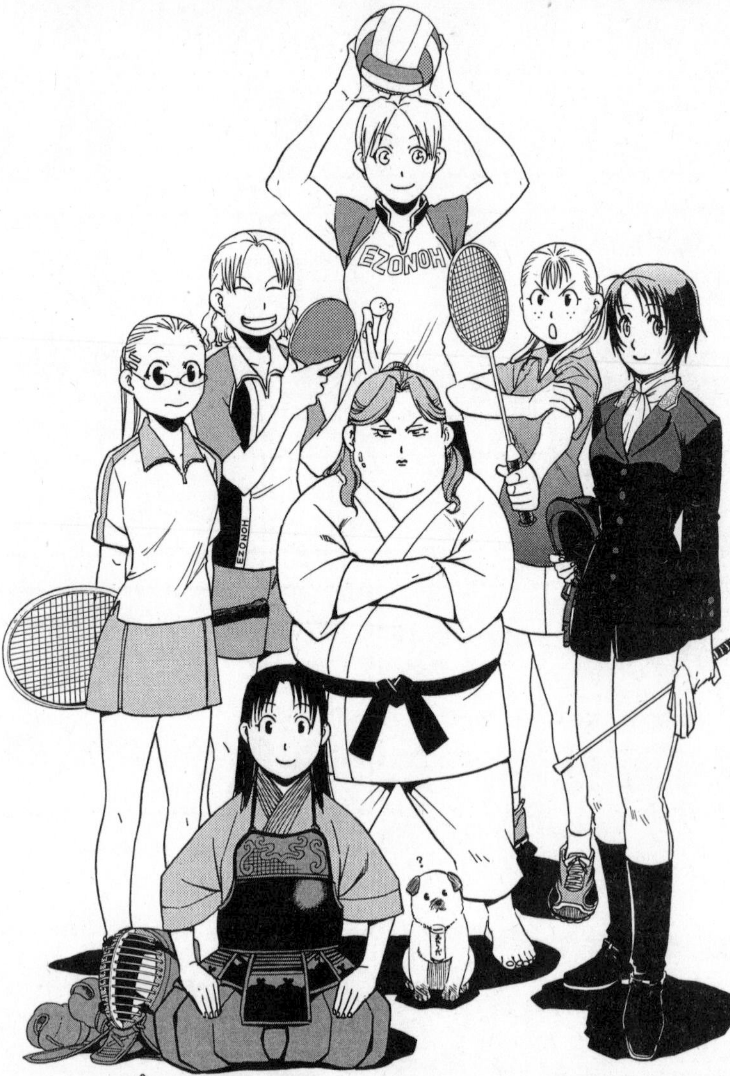
EZONOH

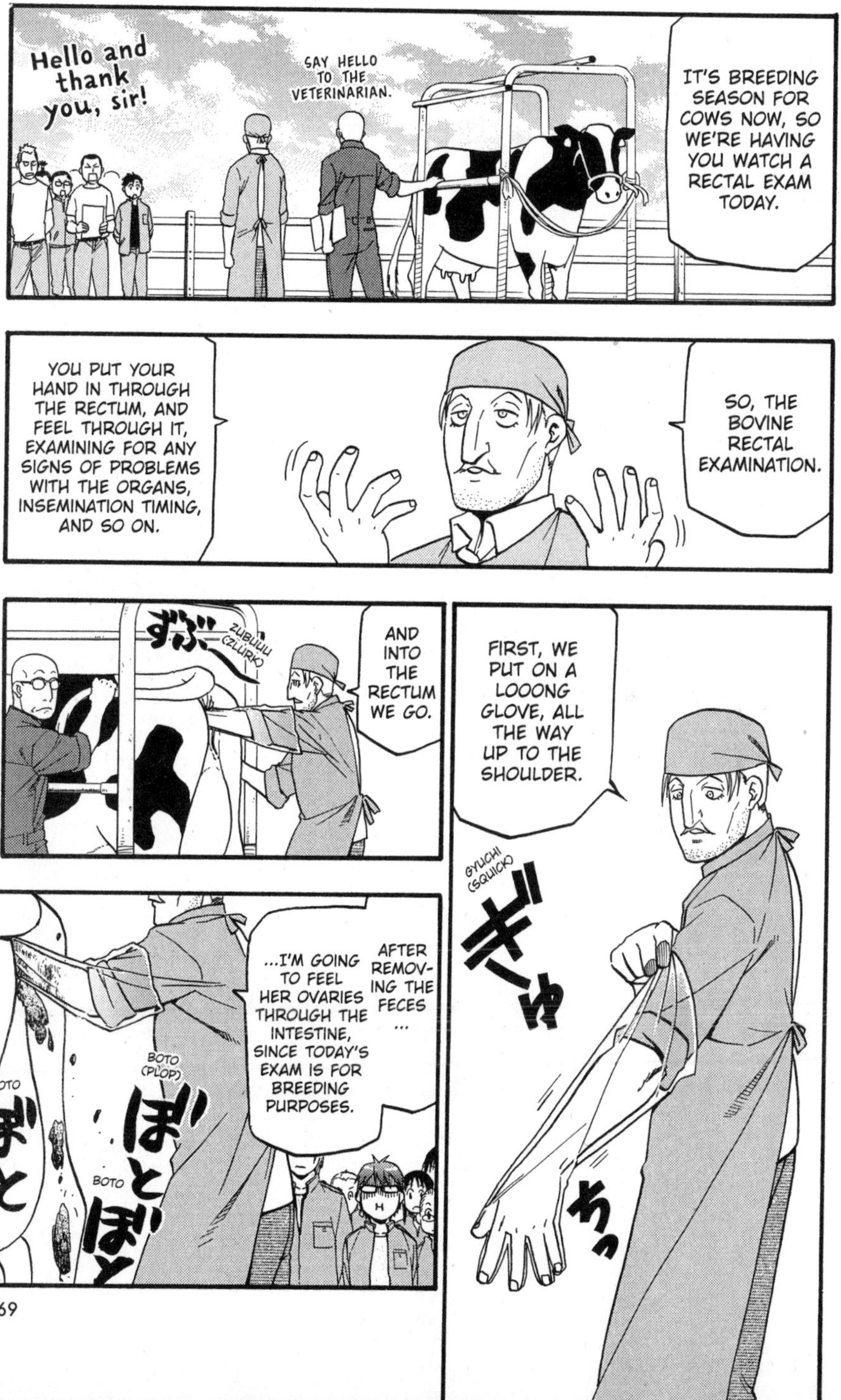

IT'S BREEDING SEASON FOR COWS NOW, SO WE'RE HAVING YOU WATCH A RECTAL EXAM TODAY.
SAY HELLO TO THE VETERINARIAN.
Hello and thank you, sir!
SO, THE BOVINE RECTAL EXAMINATION.
YOU PUT YOUR HAND IN THROUGH THE RECTUM, AND FEEL THROUGH IT, EXAMINING FOR ANY SIGNS OF PROBLEMS WITH THE ORGANS, INSEMINATION TIMING, AND SO ON.
FIRST, WE PUT ON A LOOONG GLOVE, ALL THE WAY UP TO THE SHOULDER.
GYUCHI (SQUICK)
ZUBUUU (ZLURK)
AND INTO THE RECTUM WE GO.
AFTER REMOVING THE FECES...
...I'M GOING TO FEEL HER OVARIES THROUGH THE INTESTINE, SINCE TODAY'S EXAM IS FOR BREEDING PURPOSES.
BOTO (PLOP)
BOTO
BOTO

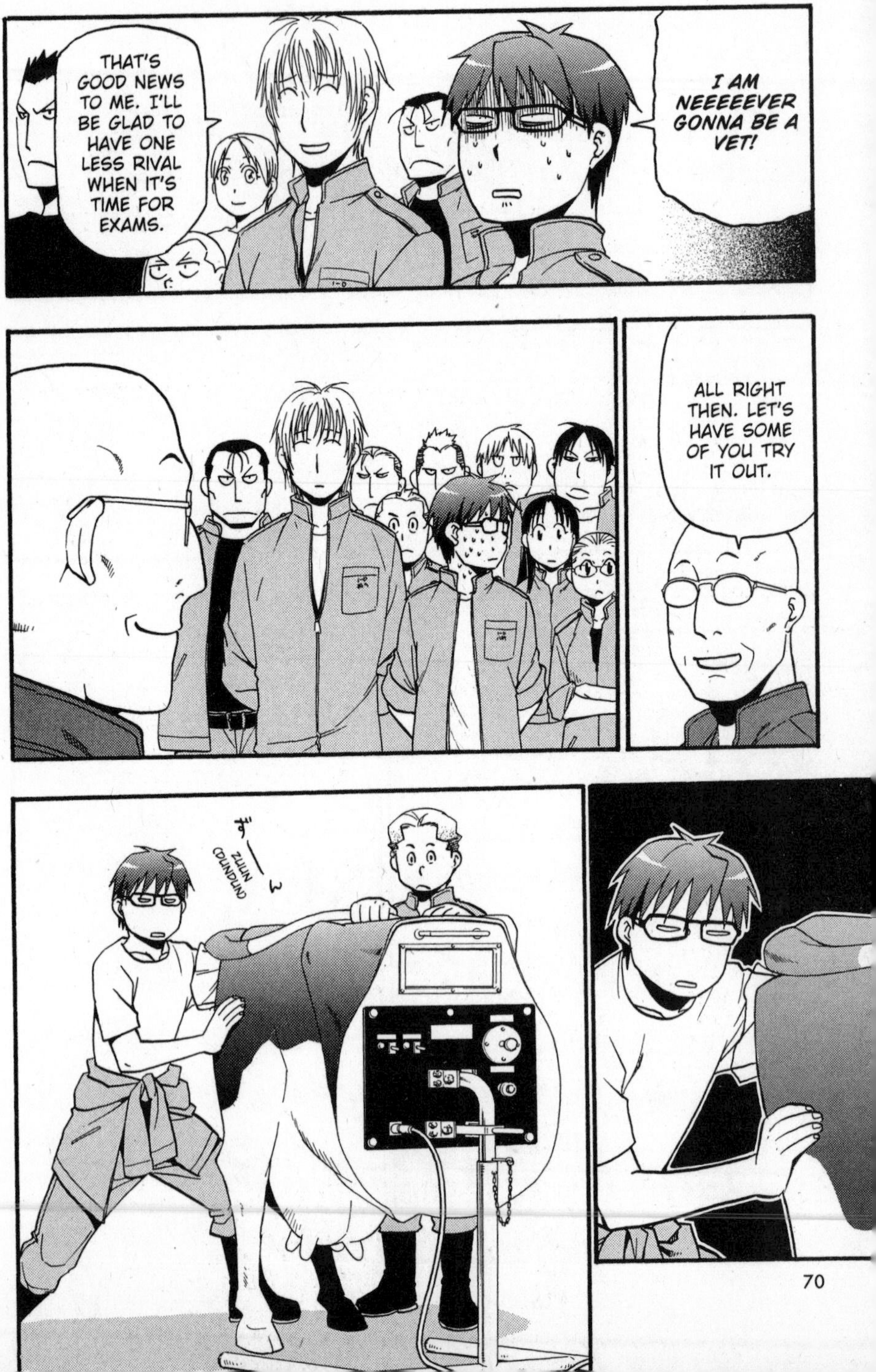
I AM NEEEEEVER GONNA BE A VET!
THAT'S GOOD NEWS TO ME. I'LL BE GLAD TO HAVE ONE LESS RIVAL WHEN IT'S TIME FOR EXAMS.
ALL RIGHT THEN. LET'S HAVE SOME OF YOU TRY IT OUT.
ずーん
ZUUN
DUNDUN

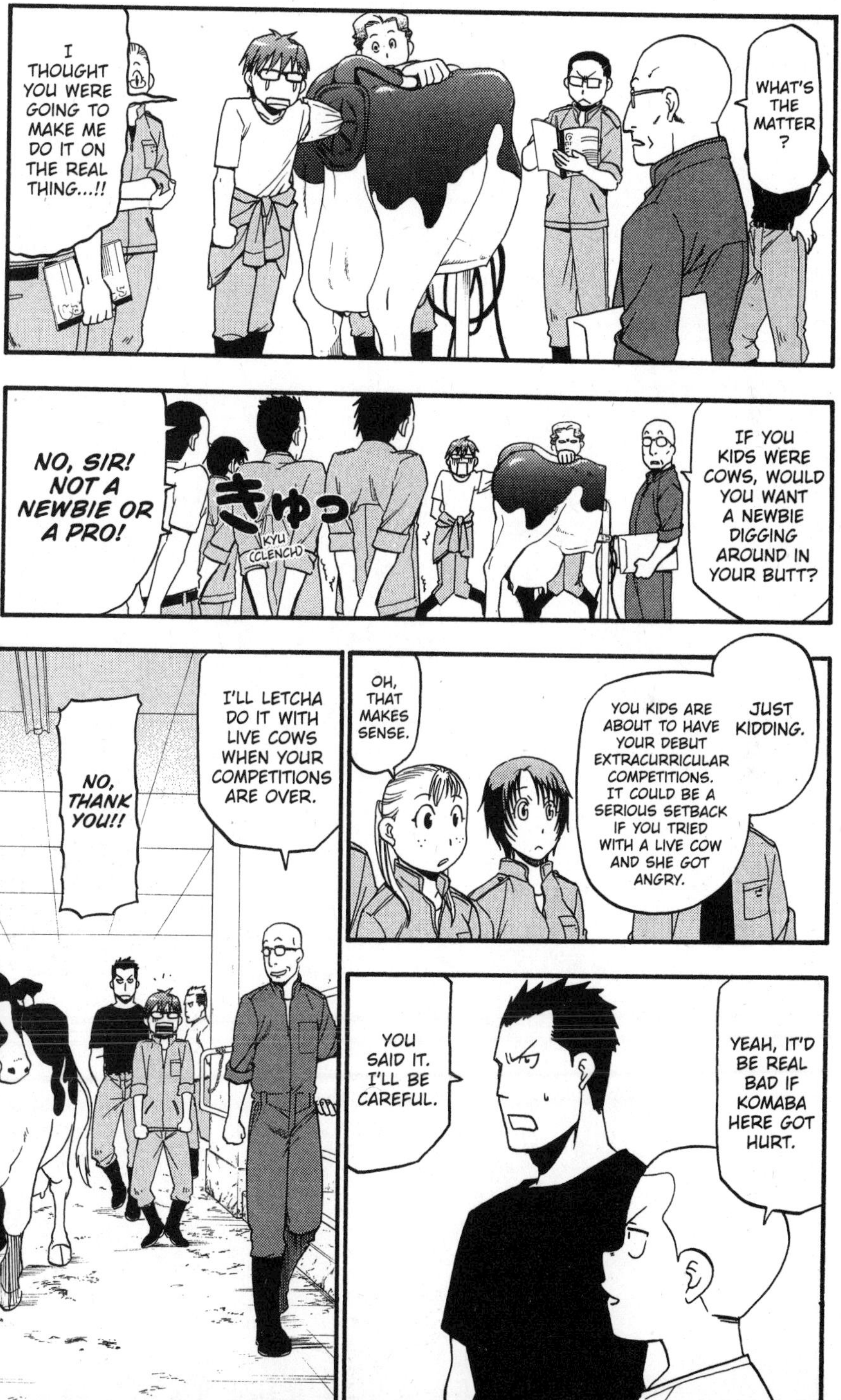
WHAT'S THE MATTER?
I THOUGHT YOU WERE GOING TO MAKE ME DO IT ON THE REAL THING...!!
IF YOU KIDS WERE COWS, WOULD YOU WANT A NEWBIE DIGGING AROUND IN YOUR BUTT?
きゅっ
KYU (CLENCH)
NO, SIR! NOT A NEWBIE OR A PRO!
JUST KIDDING.
YOU KIDS ARE ABOUT TO HAVE YOUR DEBUT EXTRACURRICULAR COMPETITIONS. IT COULD BE A SERIOUS SETBACK IF YOU TRIED WITH A LIVE COW AND SHE GOT ANGRY.
OH, THAT MAKES SENSE.
YEAH, IT'D BE REAL BAD IF KOMABA HERE GOT HURT.
YOU SAID IT. I'LL BE CAREFUL.
I'LL LETCHA DO IT WITH LIVE COWS WHEN YOUR COMPETITIONS ARE OVER.
NO, THANK YOU!!

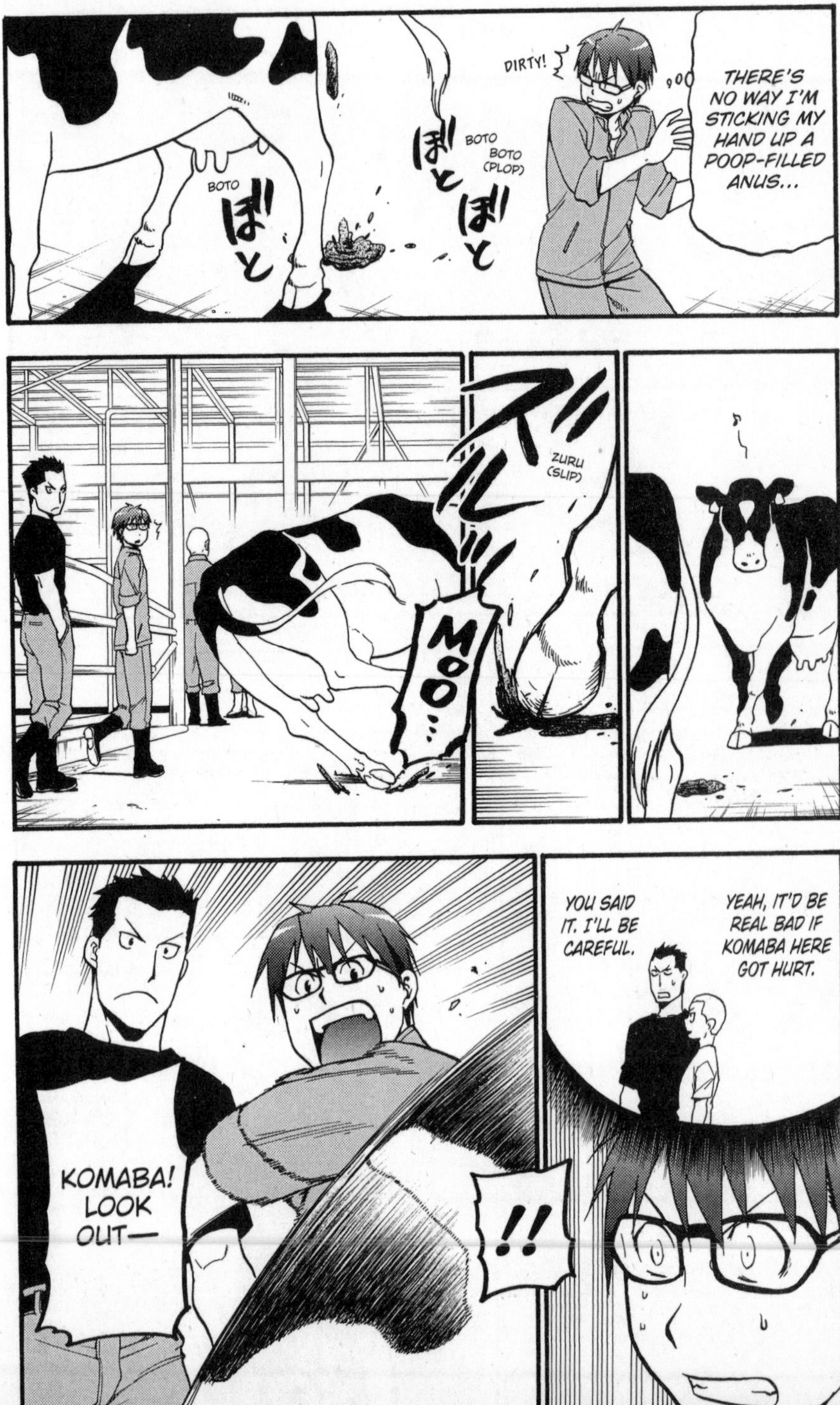
THERE'S NO WAY I'M STICKING MY HAND UP A POOP-FILLED ANUS...
DIRTY!
ぼと ぼと
BOTO BOTO (PLOP)
ぼと
BOTO
ズル
ZURU (SLIP)
MOO...
YEAH, IT'D BE REAL BAD IF KOMABA HERE GOT HURT.
YOU SAID IT. I'LL BE CAREFUL.
!!
KOMABA! LOOK OUT—

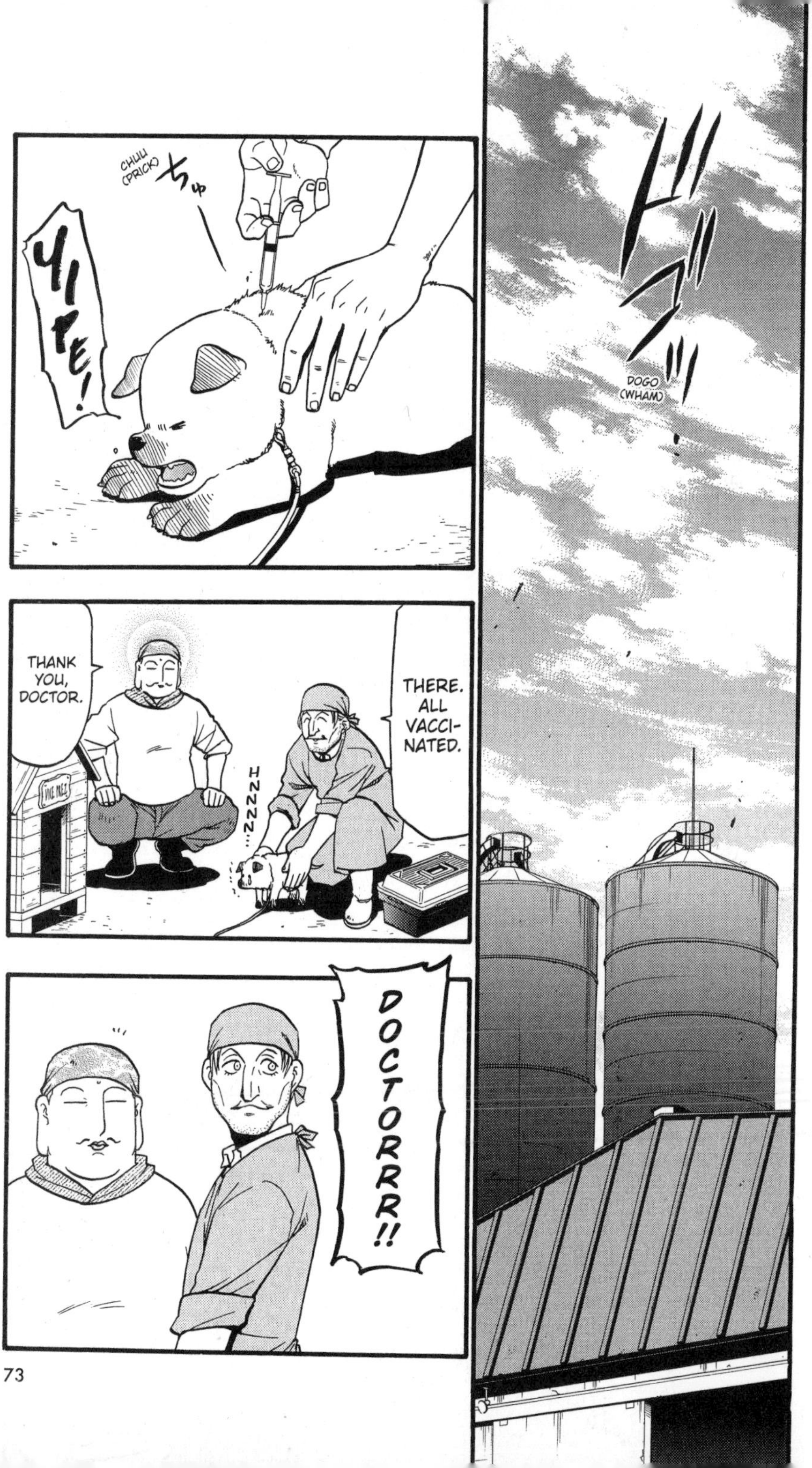
DOGO (WHAM)
CHUU (PRICK)
YIPE!
THERE. ALL VACCINATED.
HNNNN...
VICE PREZ
THANK YOU, DOCTOR.
DOCTORRR!!

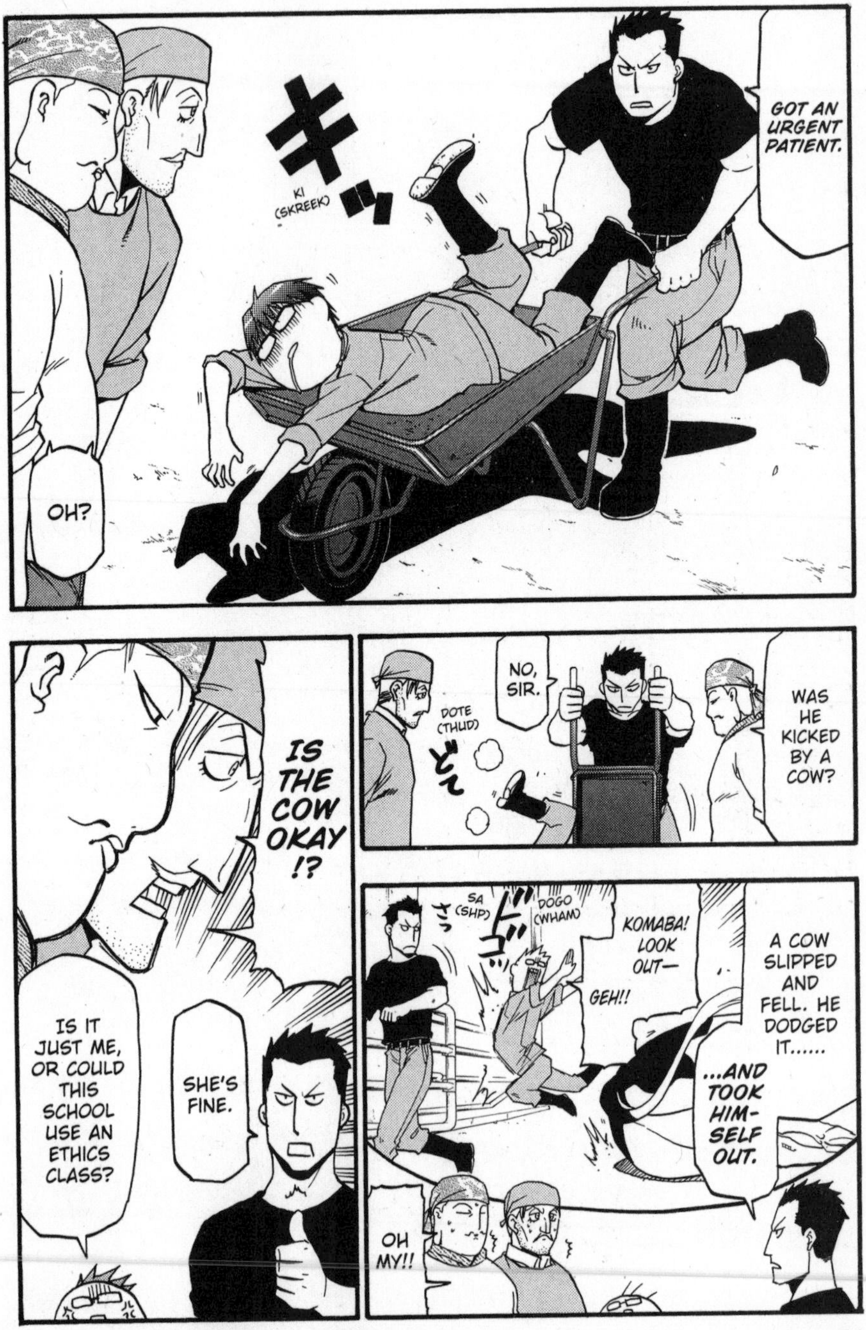
GOT AN URGENT PATIENT.
KI (SKREEK)
OH?
WAS HE KICKED BY A COW?
NO, SIR.
DOTE (THUD)
A COW SLIPPED AND FELL. HE DODGED IT......
...AND TOOK HIM-SELF OUT.
KOMABA! LOOK OUT—
GEH!!
DOGO (WHAM)
SA (SHP)
OH MY!!
IS THE COW OKAY!?
SHE'S FINE.
IS IT JUST ME, OR COULD THIS SCHOOL USE AN ETHICS CLASS?

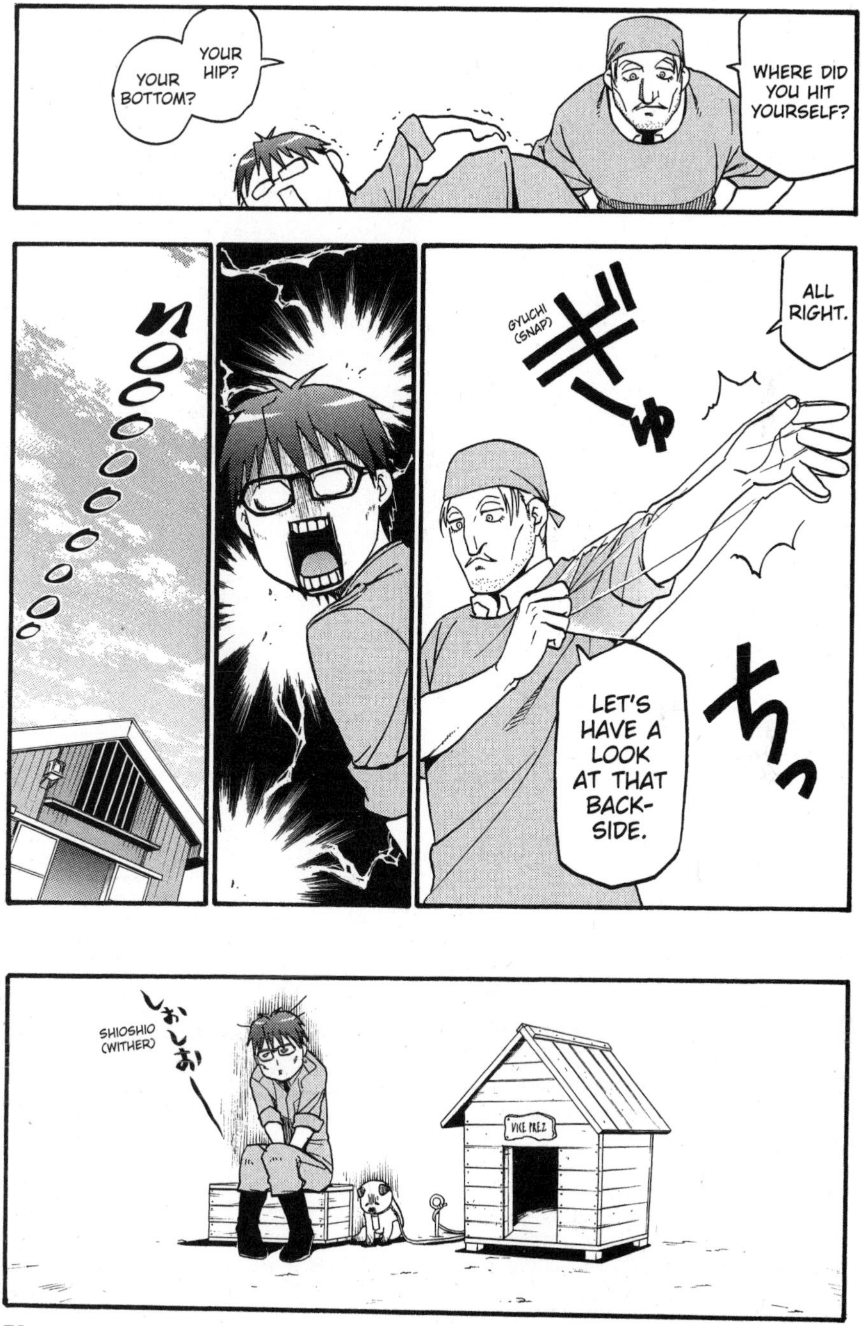
WHERE DID YOU HIT YOURSELF?
YOUR HIP? YOUR BOTTOM?
ALL RIGHT.
ぎゅ
GYUCHI (SNAP)
ちっ
LET'S HAVE A LOOK AT THAT BACK-SIDE.
しおしおー
SHIOSHIO (WITHER)
VICE PREZ

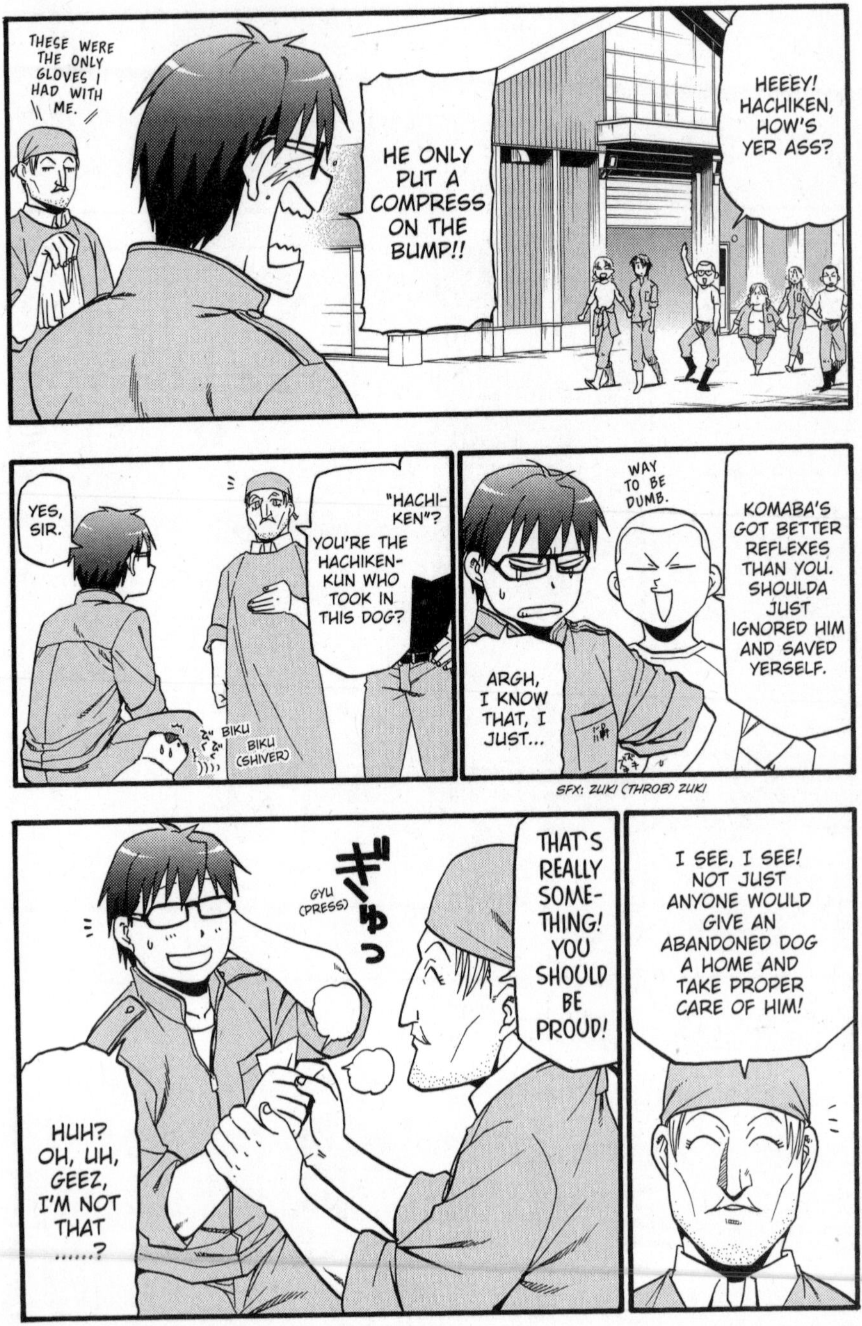
HEEEY! HACHIKEN, HOW'S YER ASS?
HE ONLY PUT A COMPRESS ON THE BUMP!!
THESE WERE THE ONLY GLOVES I HAD WITH ME.
KOMABA'S GOT BETTER REFLEXES THAN YOU. SHOULDA JUST IGNORED HIM AND SAVED YERSELF.
WAY TO BE DUMB.
ARGH, I KNOW THAT, I JUST...
SFX: ZUKI (THROB) ZUKI
"HACHI-KEN"? YOU'RE THE HACHIKEN-KUN WHO TOOK IN THIS DOG?
YES, SIR.
BIKU BIKU (SHIVER)
I SEE, I SEE! NOT JUST ANYONE WOULD GIVE AN ABANDONED DOG A HOME AND TAKE PROPER CARE OF HIM!
THAT'S REALLY SOME-THING! YOU SHOULD BE PROUD!
GYU (PRESS)
HUH? OH, UH, GEEZ, I'M NOT THAT ......?

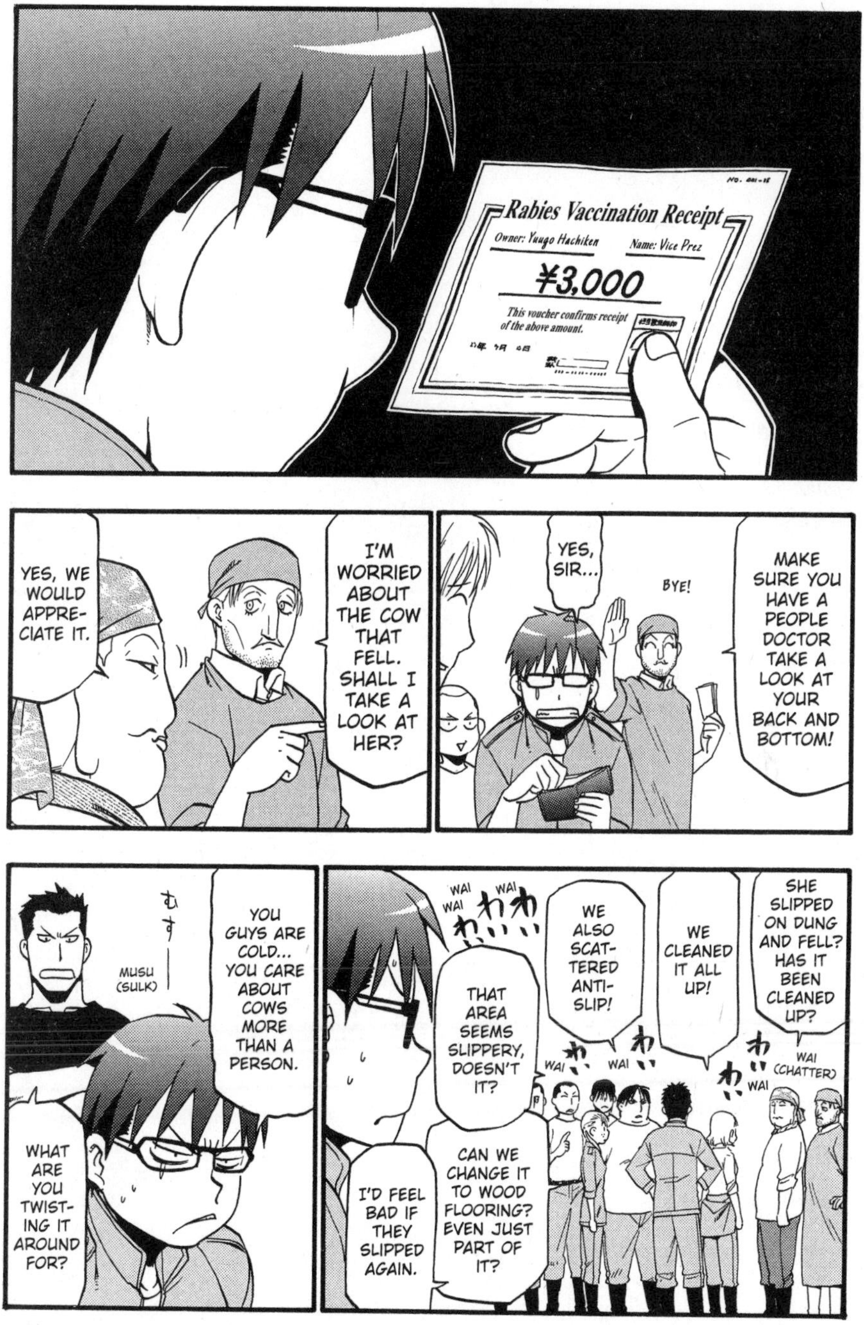

Rabies Vaccination Receipt
Owner: Yuugo Hachiken
Name: Vice Prez
¥3,000
This voucher confirms receipt of the above amount.
MAKE SURE YOU HAVE A PEOPLE DOCTOR TAKE A LOOK AT YOUR BACK AND BOTTOM!
BYE!
YES, SIR...
I'M WORRIED ABOUT THE COW THAT FELL. SHALL I TAKE A LOOK AT HER?
YES, WE WOULD APPRECIATE IT.
SHE SLIPPED ON DUNG AND FELL? HAS IT BEEN CLEANED UP?
WE CLEANED IT ALL UP!
WE ALSO SCATTERED ANTI-SLIP!
わわわ
WAI WAI
わい
WAI (CHATTER)
わい
WAI
わい
WAI
わい
WAI
THAT AREA SEEMS SLIPPERY, DOESN'T IT?
CAN WE CHANGE IT TO WOOD FLOORING? EVEN JUST PART OF IT?
I'D FEEL BAD IF THEY SLIPPED AGAIN.
YOU GUYS ARE COLD... YOU CARE ABOUT COWS MORE THAN A PERSON.
むすー
MUSU (SULK)
WHAT ARE YOU TWISTING IT AROUND FOR?

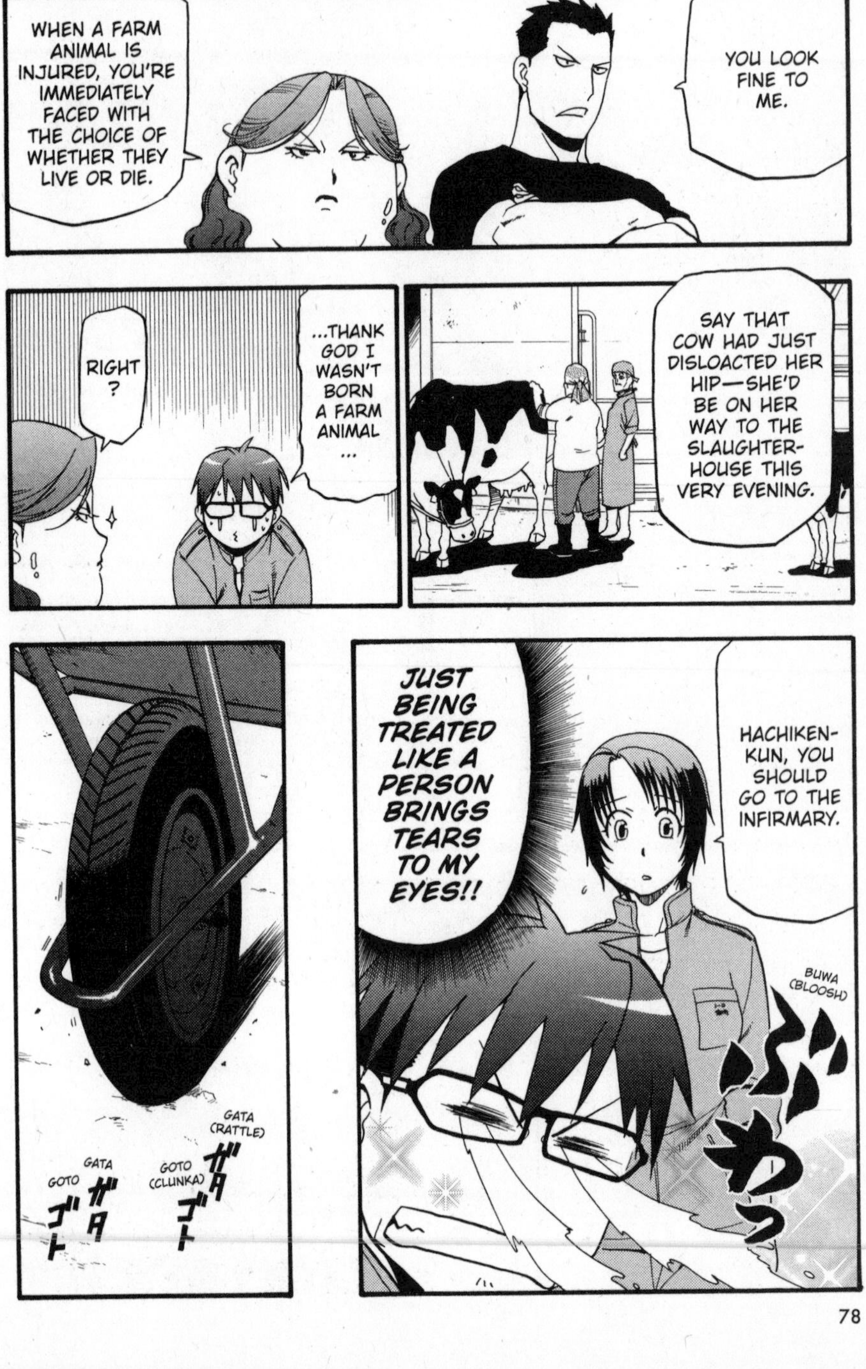
YOU LOOK FINE TO ME.
WHEN A FARM ANIMAL IS INJURED, YOU'RE IMMEDIATELY FACED WITH THE CHOICE OF WHETHER THEY LIVE OR DIE.
SAY THAT COW HAD JUST DISLOACTED HER HIP—SHE'D BE ON HER WAY TO THE SLAUGHTER-HOUSE THIS VERY EVENING.
...THANK GOD I WASN'T BORN A FARM ANIMAL ...
RIGHT ?
HACHIKEN-KUN, YOU SHOULD GO TO THE INFIRMARY.
JUST BEING TREATED LIKE A PERSON BRINGS TEARS TO MY EYES!!
BUWA (BLOOSH)
ぶわっ
GATA (RATTLE)
ガタ
GOTO (CLUNKA)
ゴト
GATA
ガタ
GOTO
ゴト

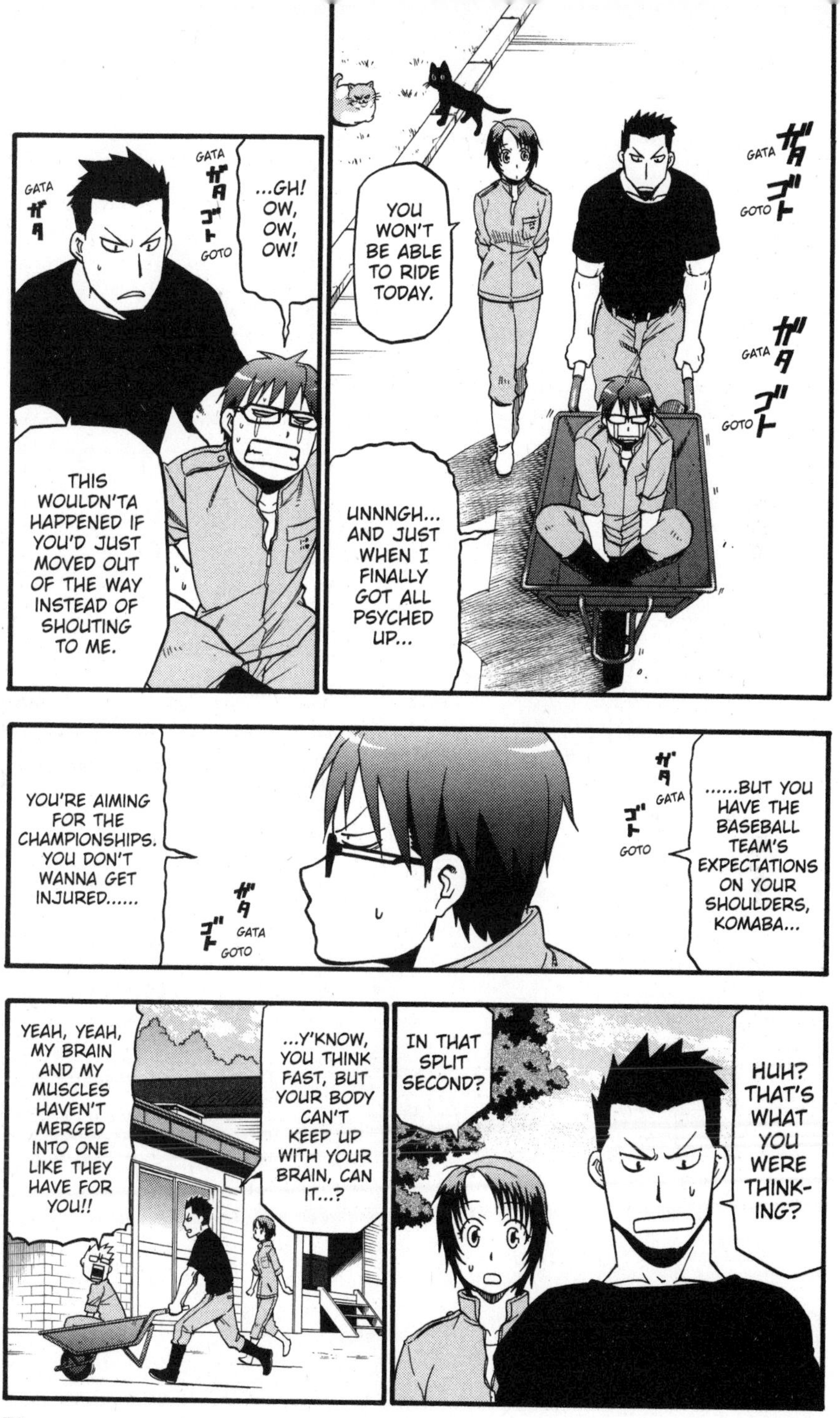
ガタ GATA
ゴト GOTO
ガタ GATA
ゴト GOTO
YOU WON'T BE ABLE TO RIDE TODAY.
UNNNGH... AND JUST WHEN I FINALLY GOT ALL PSYCHED UP...
ガタ GATA
ゴト GOTO
...GH! OW, OW, OW!
ガタ GATA
THIS WOULDN'TA HAPPENED IF YOU'D JUST MOVED OUT OF THE WAY INSTEAD OF SHOUTING TO ME.
......BUT YOU HAVE THE BASEBALL TEAM'S EXPECTATIONS ON YOUR SHOULDERS, KOMABA...
ガタ GATA
ゴト GOTO
ガタ GATA
ゴト GOTO
YOU'RE AIMING FOR THE CHAMPIONSHIPS. YOU DON'T WANNA GET INJURED......
HUH? THAT'S WHAT YOU WERE THINKING?
IN THAT SPLIT SECOND?
...Y'KNOW, YOU THINK FAST, BUT YOUR BODY CAN'T KEEP UP WITH YOUR BRAIN, CAN IT...?
YEAH, YEAH, MY BRAIN AND MY MUSCLES HAVEN'T MERGED INTO ONE LIKE THEY HAVE FOR YOU!!

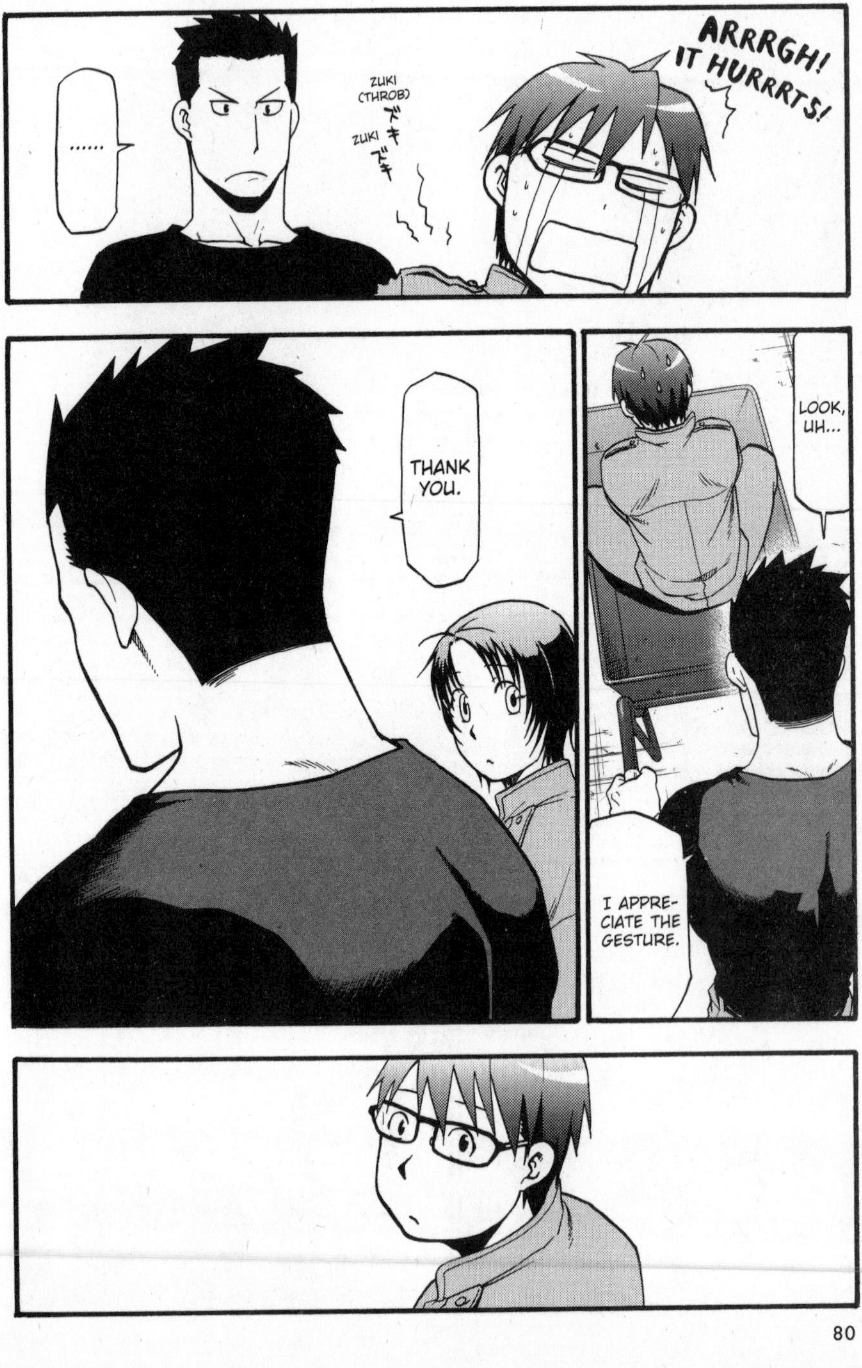
ARRRGH! IT HURRRRTS!
ZUKI (THROB)
ズキ
ZUKI
ズキ
......
LOOK, UH...
I APPRECIATE THE GESTURE.
THANK YOU.

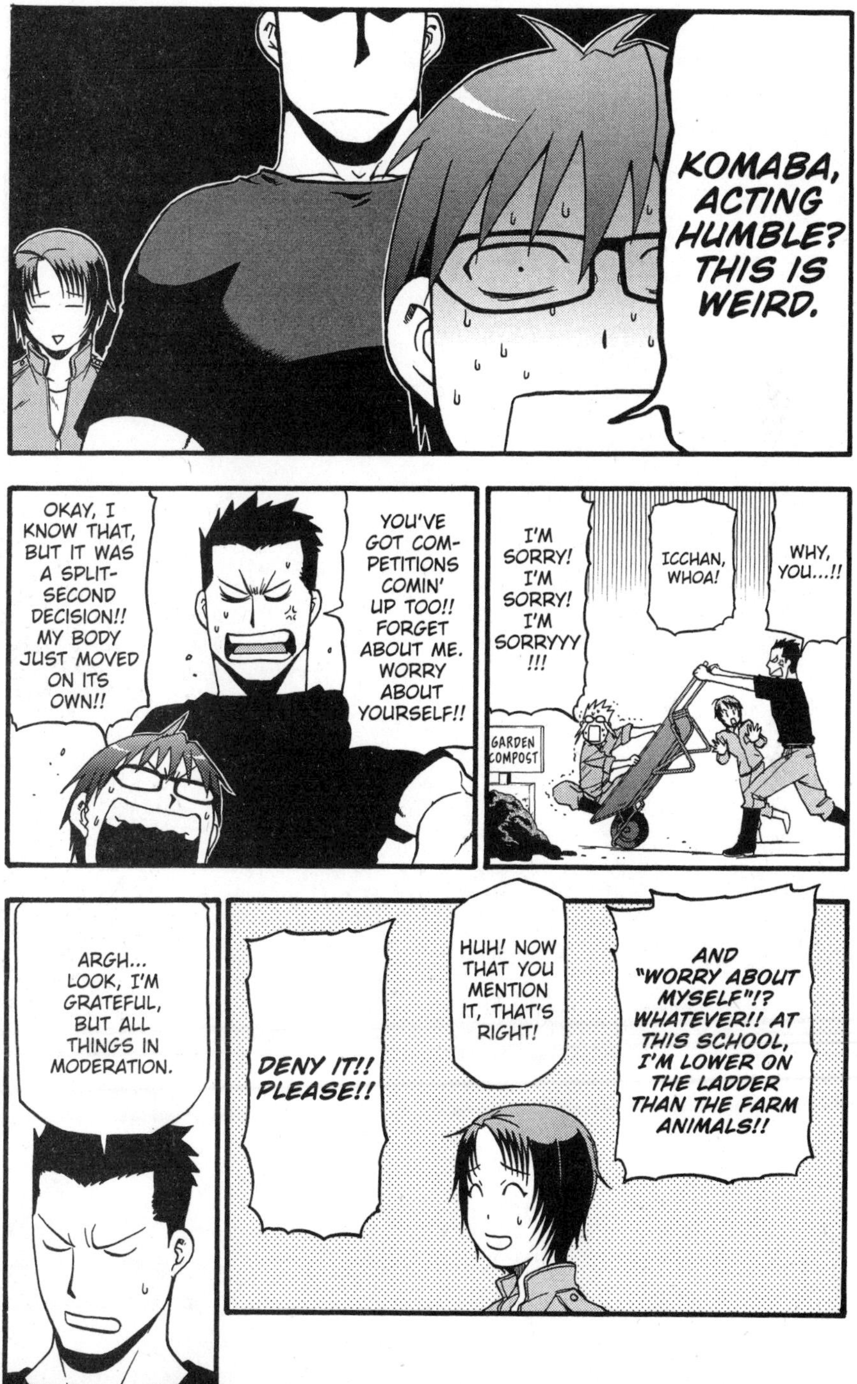
KOMABA, ACTING HUMBLE? THIS IS WEIRD.
WHY, YOU...!!
ICCHAN, WHOA!
I'M SORRY! I'M SORRY! I'M SORRYYY!!!
GARDEN COMPOST
YOU'VE GOT COM-PETITIONS COMIN' UP TOO!! FORGET ABOUT ME. WORRY ABOUT YOURSELF!!
OKAY, I KNOW THAT, BUT IT WAS A SPLIT-SECOND DECISION!! MY BODY JUST MOVED ON ITS OWN!!
AND "WORRY ABOUT MYSELF"!? WHATEVER!! AT THIS SCHOOL, I'M LOWER ON THE LADDER THAN THE FARM ANIMALS!!
HUH! NOW THAT YOU MENTION IT, THAT'S RIGHT!
DENY IT!! PLEASE!!
ARGH... LOOK, I'M GRATEFUL, BUT ALL THINGS IN MODERATION.

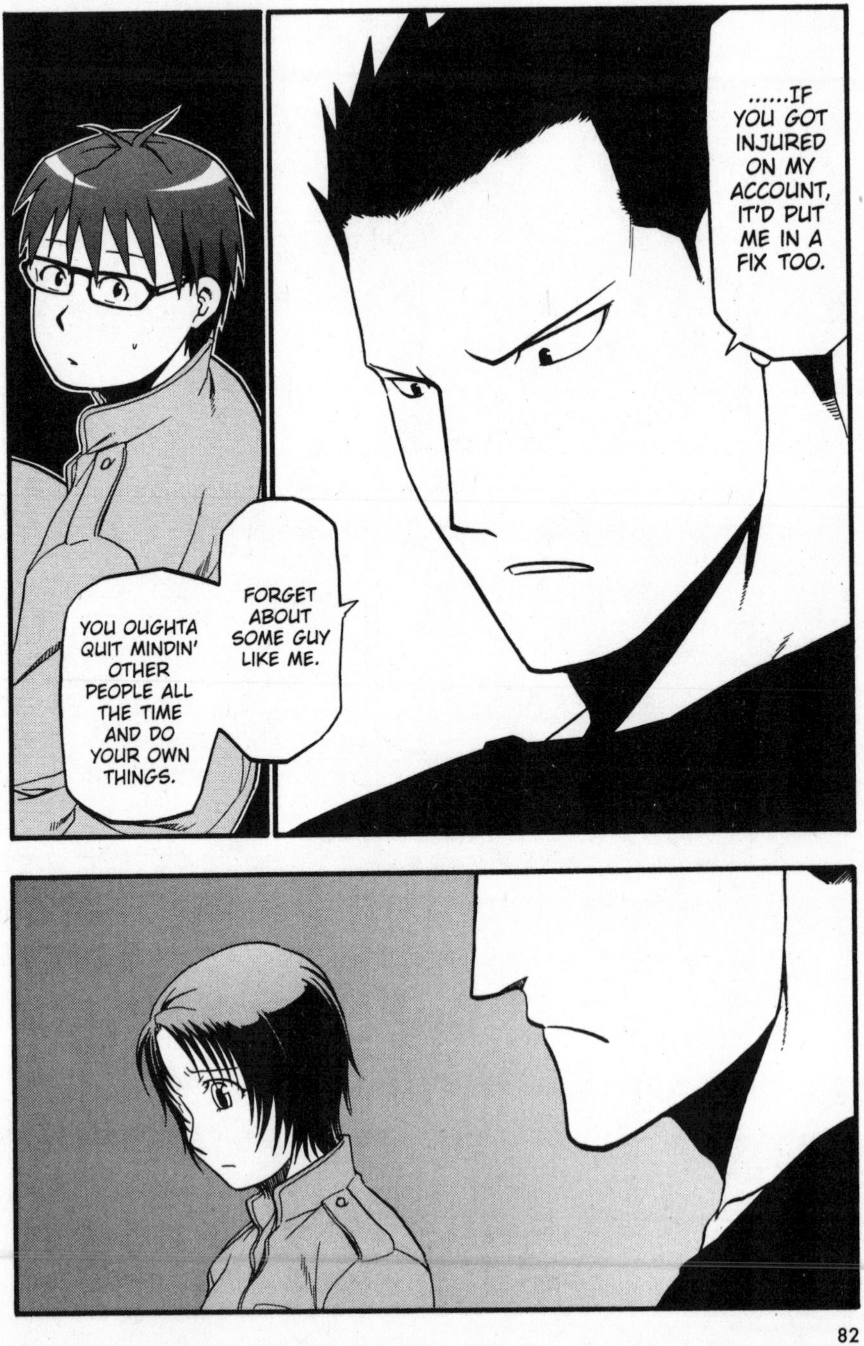
......IF YOU GOT INJURED ON MY ACCOUNT, IT'D PUT ME IN A FIX TOO.
FORGET ABOUT SOME GUY LIKE ME.
YOU OUGHTA QUIT MINDIN' OTHER PEOPLE ALL THE TIME AND DO YOUR OWN THINGS.

Silver Spoon

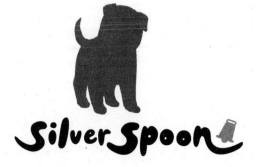

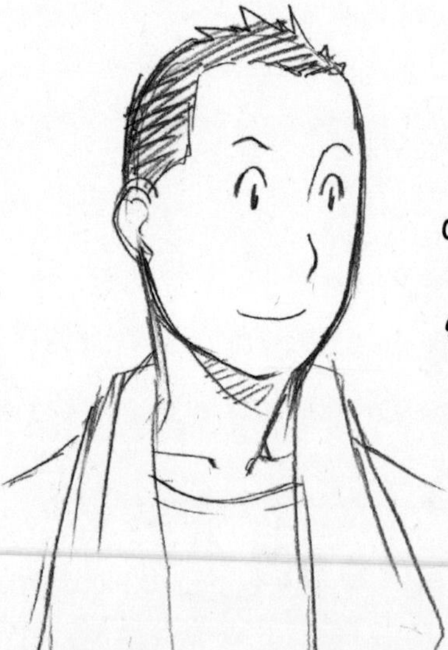

EQUESTRIAN CLUB

HIROYUKI KINO

OTOFUKE MAIN STREET MIDDLE SCHOOL

SILVICULTURE SCIENCE, YEAR 1

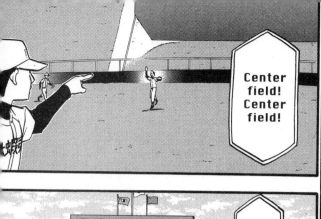

Center field! Center field!

KIN
GUINO

He's out!!

That's three outs! The game is over!!

The winner of the fall season Tokachi Preliminaries' B Block is Ooezo Agricultural High School!

Chapter 40:
Tale of Autumn ⑨

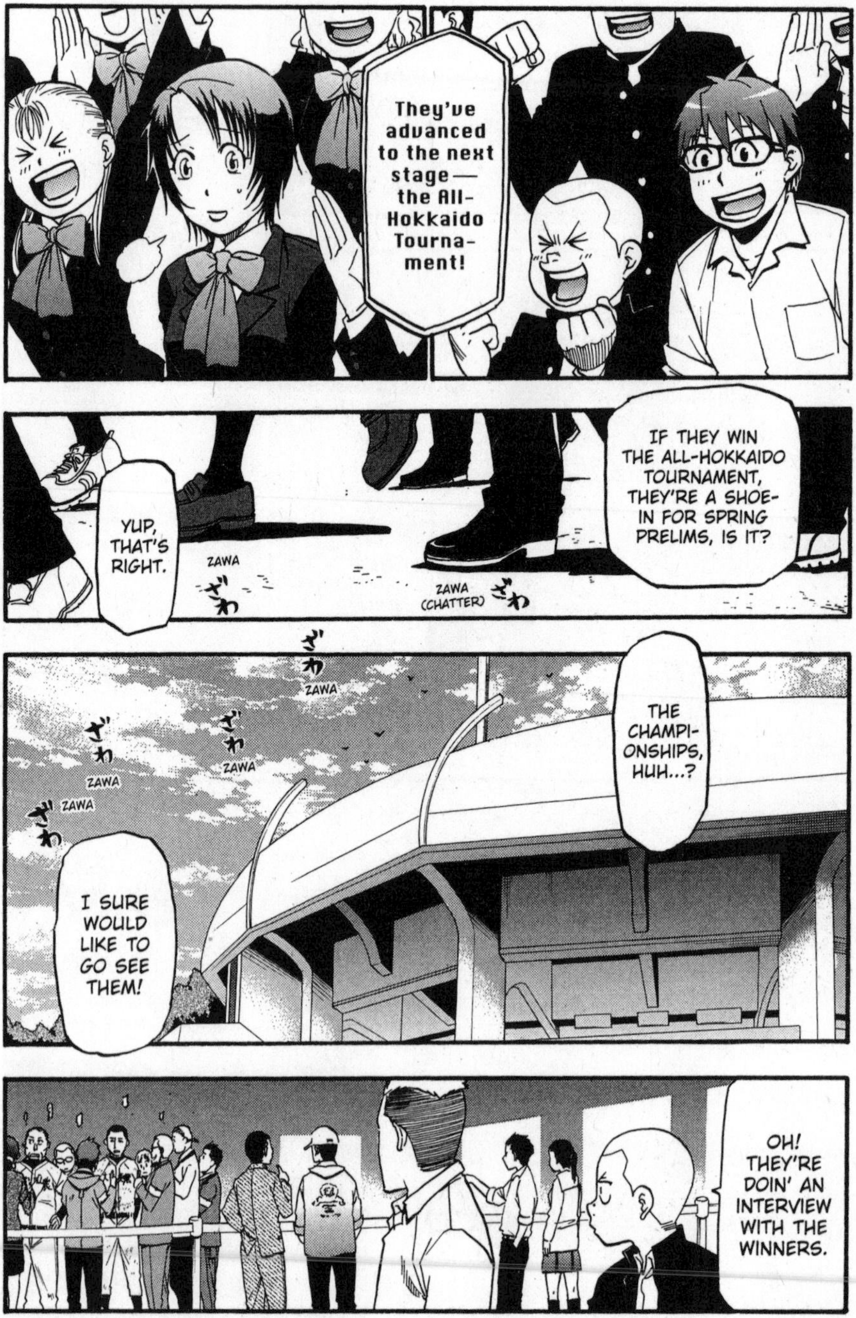
They've advanced to the next stage — the All-Hokkaido Tournament!
IF THEY WIN THE ALL-HOKKAIDO TOURNAMENT, THEY'RE A SHOE-IN FOR SPRING PRELIMS, IS IT?
YUP, THAT'S RIGHT.
ZAWA
ざわ
ZAWA (CHATTER)
ざわ
ざわ
ZAWA
THE CHAMPIONSHIPS, HUH...?
ざわ
ZAWA
ざわ
ZAWA
ZAWA
ざわ
I SURE WOULD LIKE TO GO SEE THEM!
OH! THEY'RE DOIN' AN INTERVIEW WITH THE WINNERS.

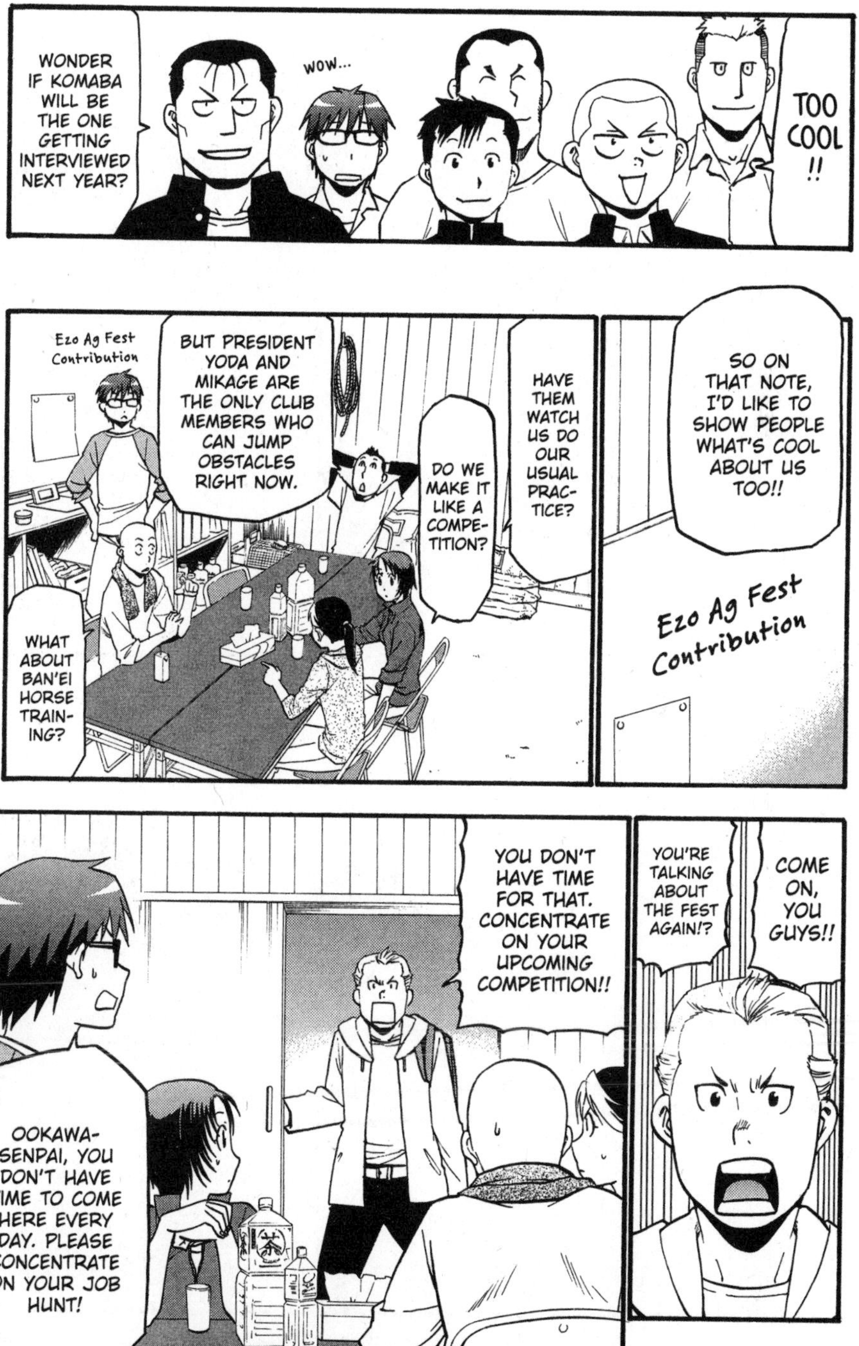
TOO COOL!!
WOW...
WONDER IF KOMABA WILL BE THE ONE GETTING INTERVIEWED NEXT YEAR?
SO ON THAT NOTE, I'D LIKE TO SHOW PEOPLE WHAT'S COOL ABOUT US TOO!!
Ezo Ag Fest Contribution
HAVE THEM WATCH US DO OUR USUAL PRACTICE?
DO WE MAKE IT LIKE A COMPETITION?
BUT PRESIDENT YODA AND MIKAGE ARE THE ONLY CLUB MEMBERS WHO CAN JUMP OBSTACLES RIGHT NOW.
Ezo Ag Fest Contribution
WHAT ABOUT BAN'EI HORSE TRAINING?
COME ON, YOU GUYS!!
YOU'RE TALKING ABOUT THE FEST AGAIN!?
YOU DON'T HAVE TIME FOR THAT. CONCENTRATE ON YOUR UPCOMING COMPETITION!!
OOKAWA-SENPAI, YOU DON'T HAVE TIME TO COME HERE EVERY DAY. PLEASE CONCENTRATE ON YOUR JOB HUNT!

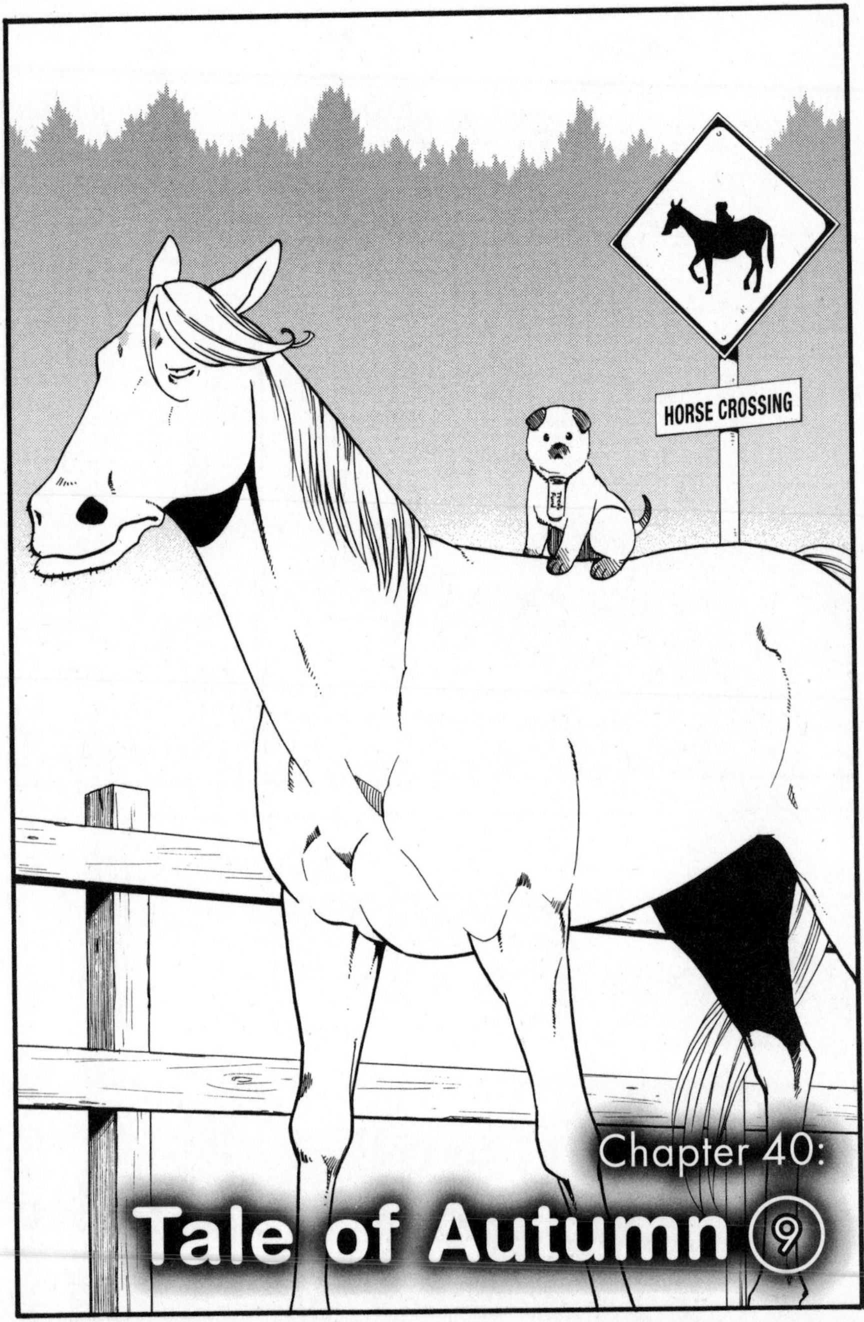
HORSE CROSSING

Chapter 40: Tale of Autumn ⑨

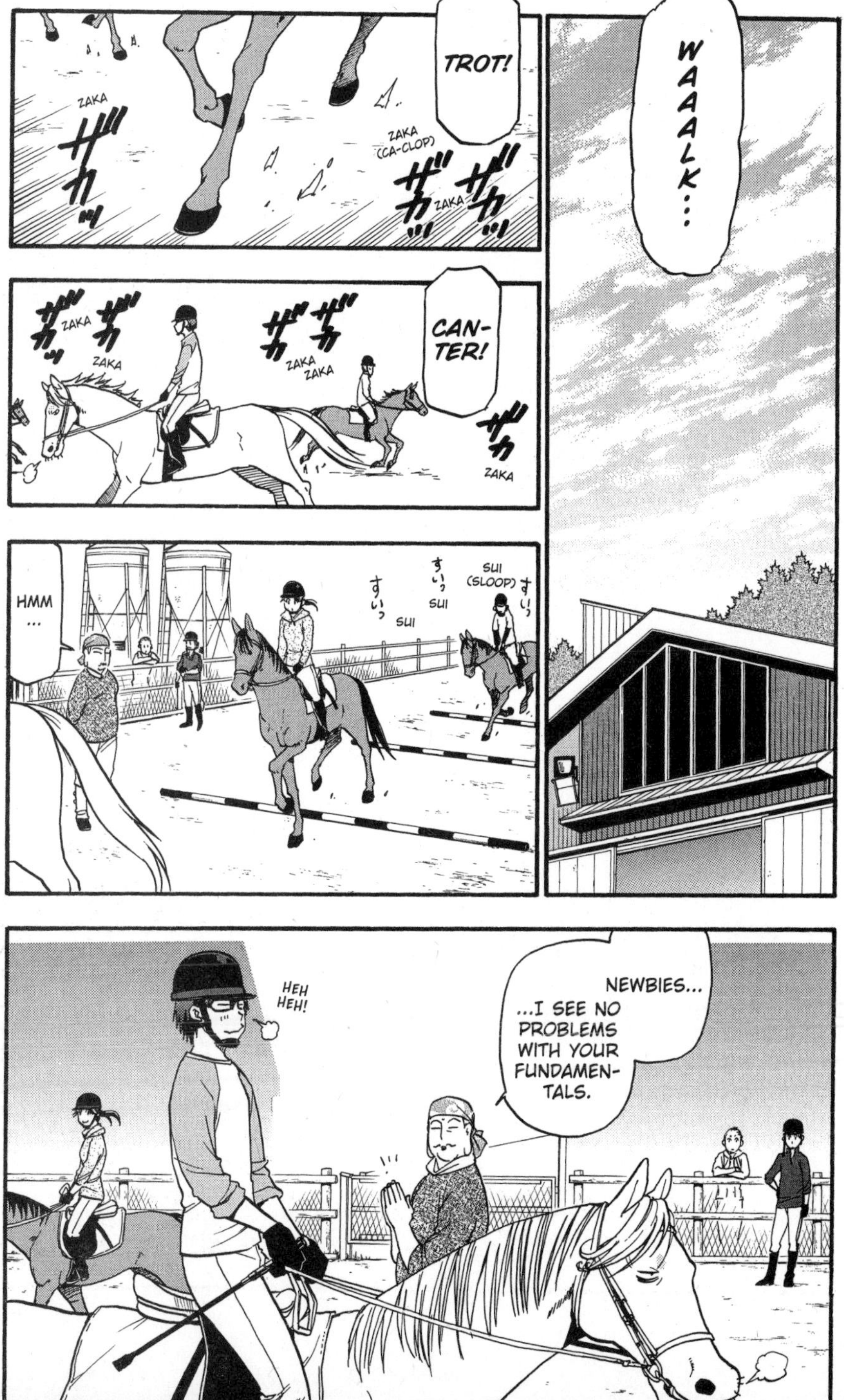
WAAAALK...
TROT!
ZAKA (CA-CLOP)
ZAKA
ZAKA
CAN-TER!
ZAKA
ZAKA ZAKA
ZAKA
ZAKA
すいっ
SUI (SLOOP)
SUI
SUI
HMM...
NEWBIES... ...I SEE NO PROBLEMS WITH YOUR FUNDAMENTALS.
HEH HEH!

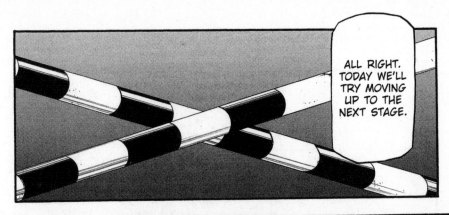

ALL RIGHT. TODAY WE'LL TRY MOVING UP TO THE NEXT STAGE.

ZAWA (MURMUR)

YOU ARE FINALLY READY FOR OBSTACLE JUMPS.

WHOA... IT'S FINALLY TIME...

CAN WE REALLY JUMP THIS...?

YES, YOU CAN.

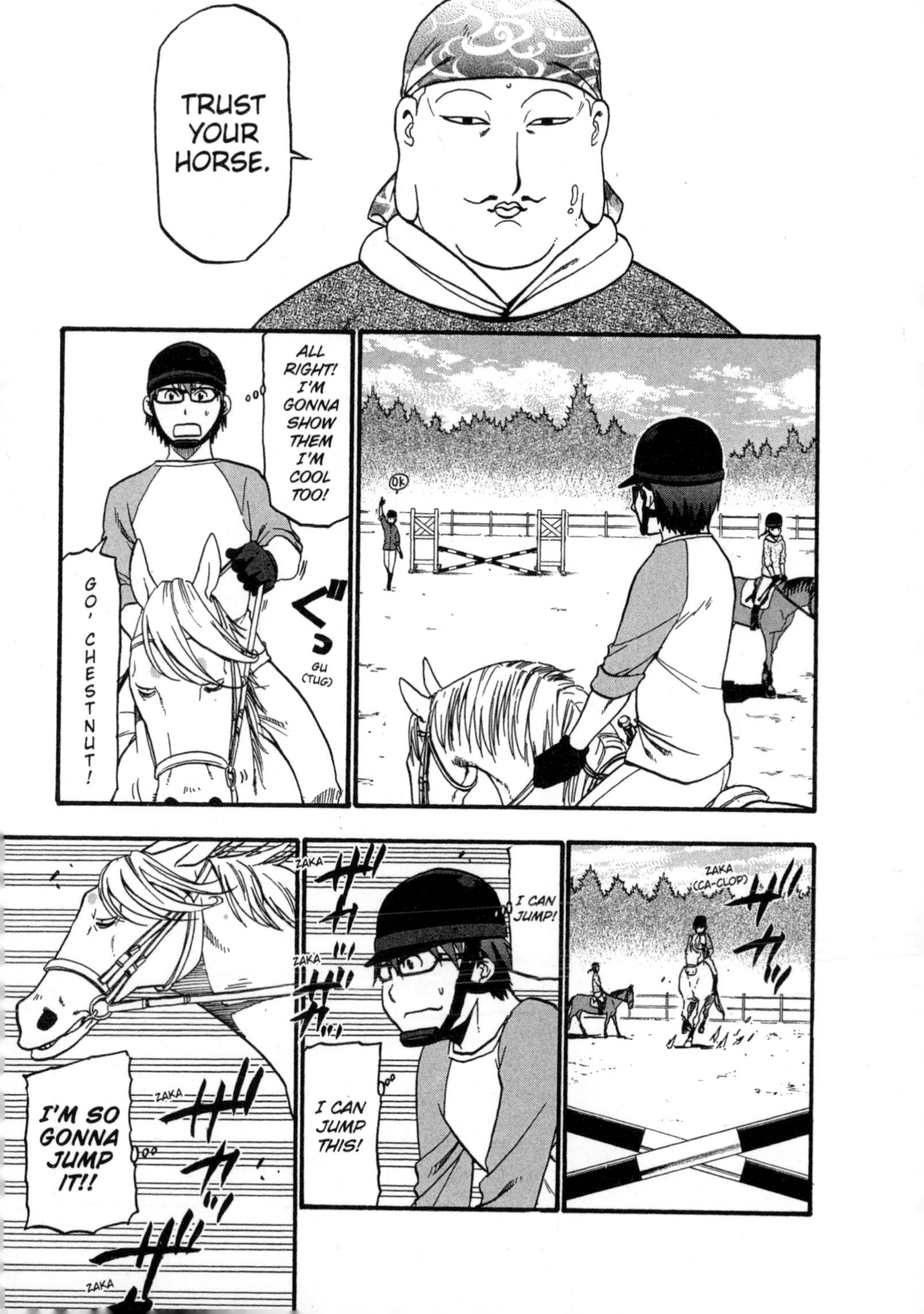
TRUST YOUR HORSE.
Ok
ALL RIGHT! I'M GONNA SHOW THEM I'M COOL TOO!
ぐっ
GU (TUG)
GO, CHESTNUT!
ザッ
ZAKA (CA-CLOP)
I CAN JUMP!
ザッ
ZAKA
ザッ
ZAKA
I CAN JUMP THIS!
I'M SO GONNA JUMP IT!!
ザッ
ZAKA
ザッ
ZAKA

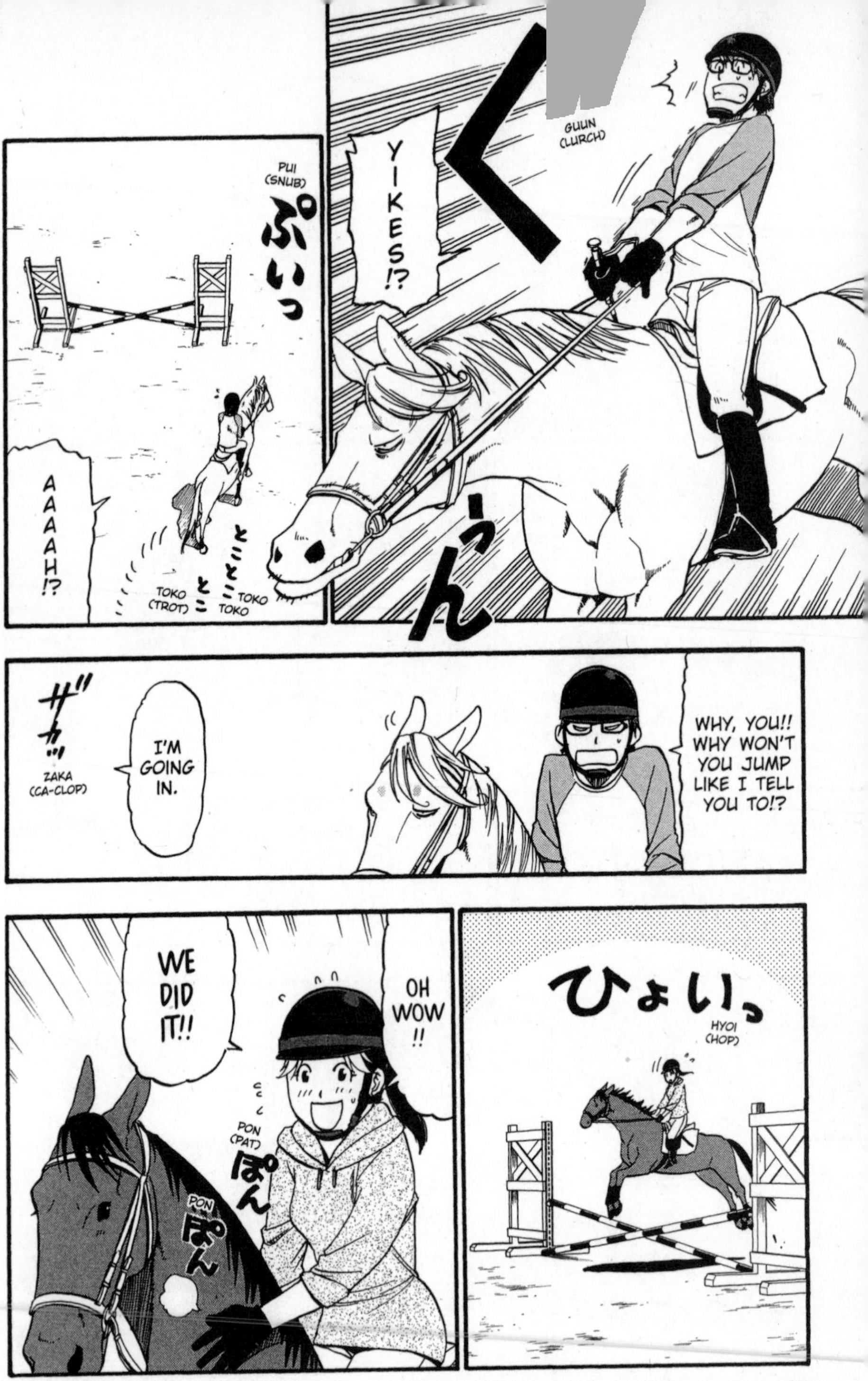
GUUN (LURCH)
YIKES!?
ぷいっ
PUI (SNUB)
AAAAH!?
とことこ
TOKO TOKO
とこ
TOKO (TROT)
WHY, YOU!! WHY WON'T YOU JUMP LIKE I TELL YOU TO!?
I'M GOING IN.
ザカッ
ZAKA (CA-CLOP)
ひょいっ
HYOI (HOP)
OH WOW!!
WE DID IT!!
ぽん
PON (PAT)
PON
ぽん

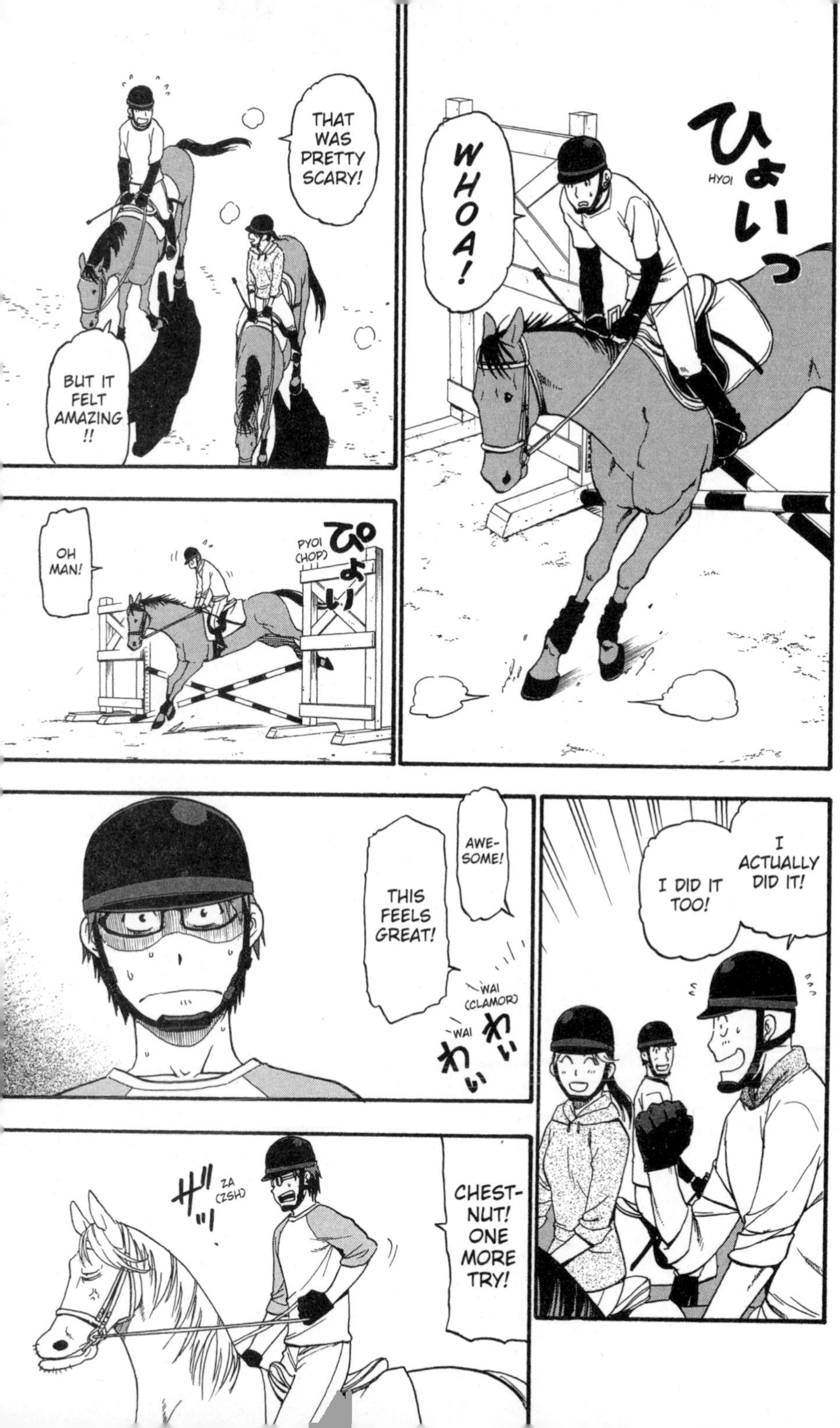
ひょいっ
HYOI
WHOA!
THAT WAS PRETTY SCARY!
BUT IT FELT AMAZING!!
PYOI (HOP)
ぴょい
OH MAN!
I ACTUALLY DID IT!
I DID IT TOO!
AWE-SOME!
THIS FEELS GREAT!
WAI (CLAMOR)
わい
WAI
わい
CHEST-NUT! ONE MORE TRY!
ZA (ZSH)
ザッ

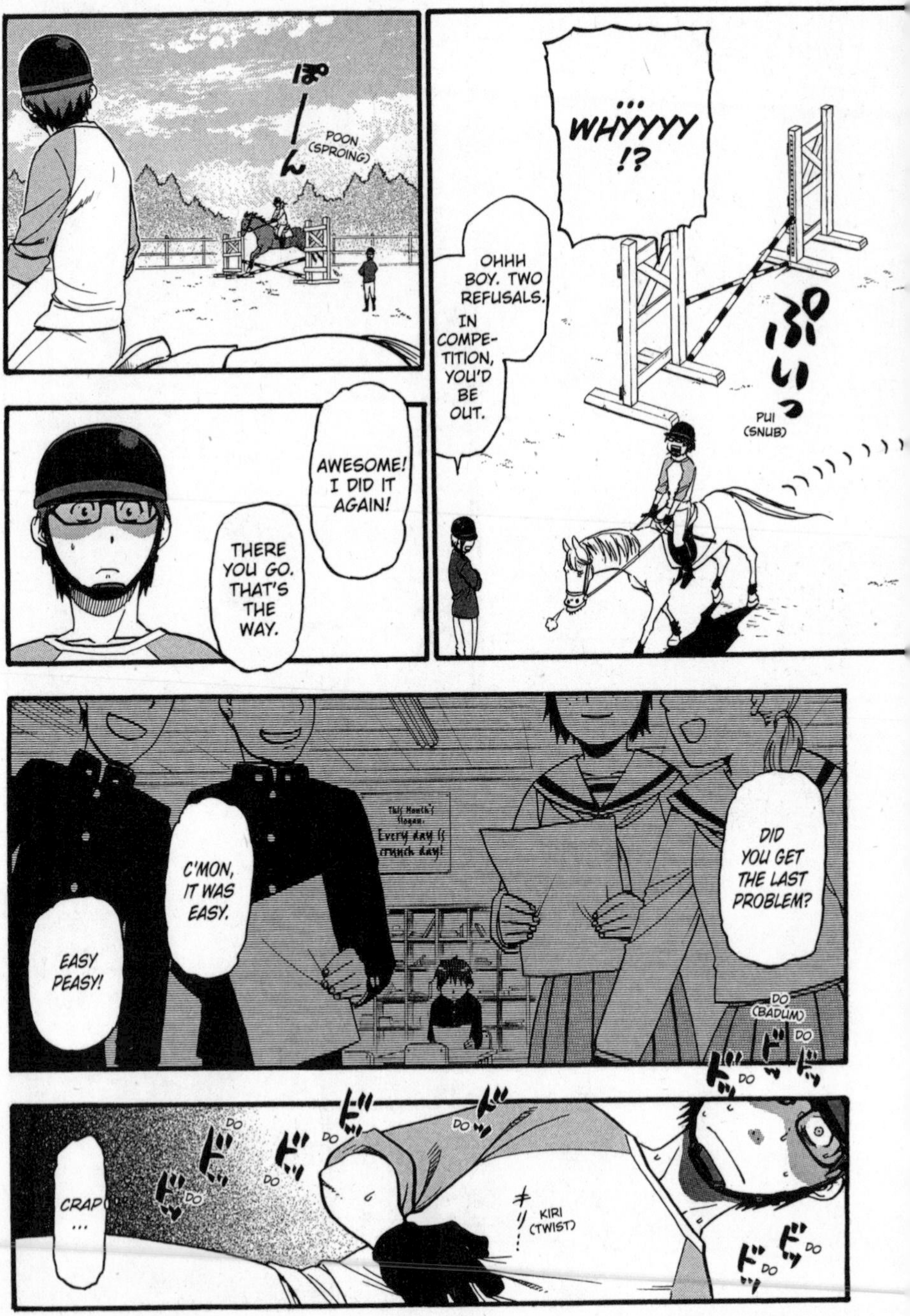

...WHYYYY!?
OHHH BOY. TWO REFUSALS.
IN COMPETITION, YOU'D BE OUT.
ぷいっ
PUI (SNUB)
ぽーん
POON (SPROING)
AWESOME! I DID IT AGAIN!
THERE YOU GO. THAT'S THE WAY.
DID YOU GET THE LAST PROBLEM?
This Month's Slogan: Every day is crunch day!
C'MON, IT WAS EASY.
EASY PEASY!
ドッ ドッ ドッ
DO (BADUM) DO DO
ドッ ドッ ドッ ドッ
DO DO DO DO
キリッ…
KIRI (TWIST)
ドッ ドッ
DO DO
CRAP...

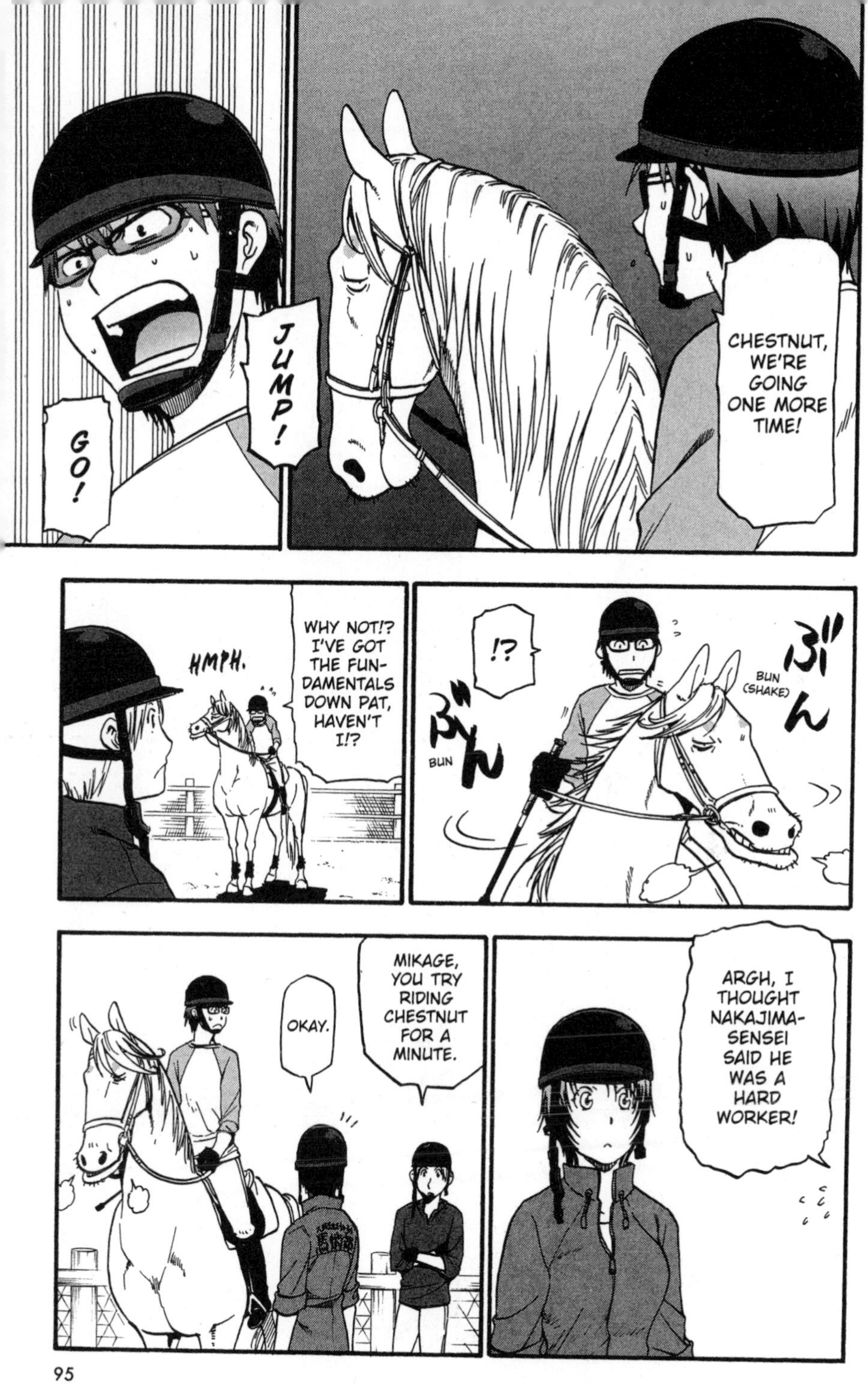
CHESTNUT, WE'RE GOING ONE MORE TIME!
JUMP!
GO!
ぶん
BUN (SHAKE)
!?
ぶん
BUN
WHY NOT!? I'VE GOT THE FUN-DAMENTALS DOWN PAT, HAVEN'T I!?
HMPH.
ARGH, I THOUGHT NAKAJIMA-SENSEI SAID HE WAS A HARD WORKER!
MIKAGE, YOU TRY RIDING CHESTNUT FOR A MINUTE.
OKAY.

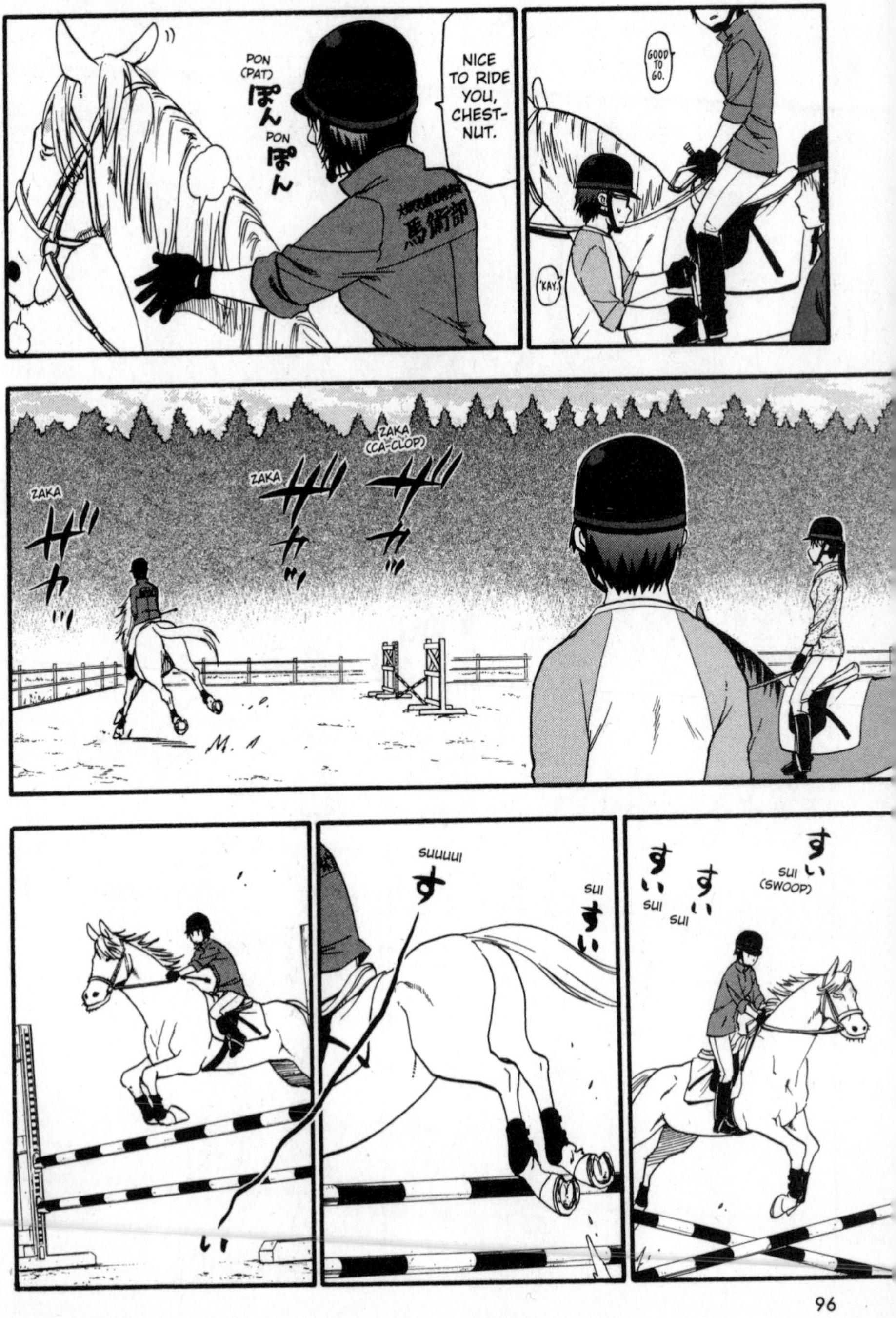
GOOD TO GO.
'KAY.
PON (PAT)
ぽん
PON
ぽん
NICE TO RIDE YOU, CHESTNUT.
ZAKA (CA-CLOP)
ザガッ
ZAKA
ザガッ
ZAKA
ザガッ
すい
SUI (SWOOP)
すい
SUI
すい
SUI
SUI
すい
SUUUUI
す
い

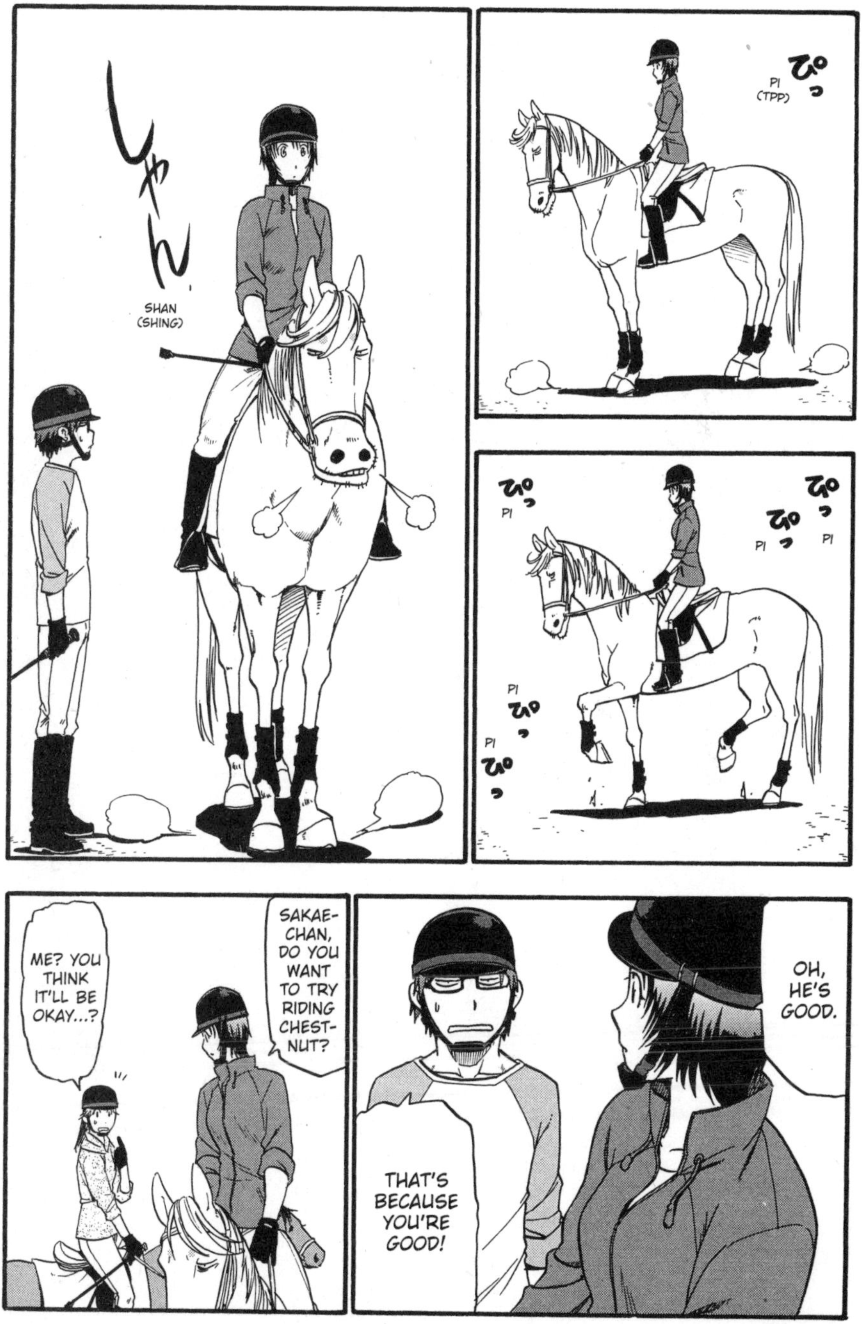
ぴっ
PI (TPP)
ぴっ
PI
ぴっ
PI
ぴっ
PI
ぴっ
PI
ぴっ
PI
しゃん
SHAN (SHING)
OH, HE'S GOOD.
THAT'S BECAUSE YOU'RE GOOD!
SAKAE-CHAN, DO YOU WANT TO TRY RIDING CHESTNUT?
ME? YOU THINK IT'LL BE OKAY...?

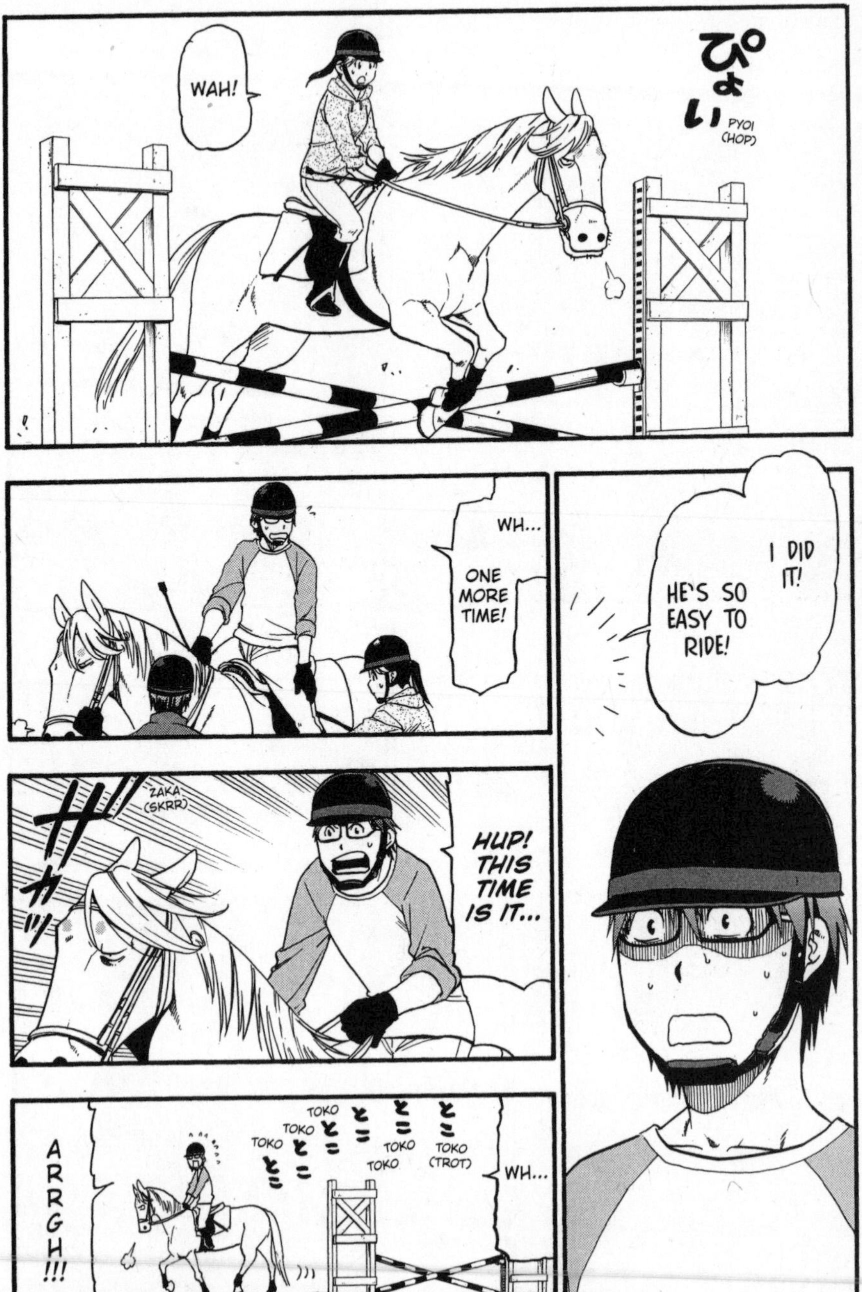
ぴょい
PYOI (HOP)
WAH!
I DID IT!
HE'S SO EASY TO RIDE!
WH...
ONE MORE TIME!
ザカッ
ZAKA (SKRR)
HUP! THIS TIME IS IT...
WH...
とこ
TOKO (TROT)
とこ
TOKO
とこ
TOKO
とこ
TOKO
とこ
TOKO
ARRGH!!!

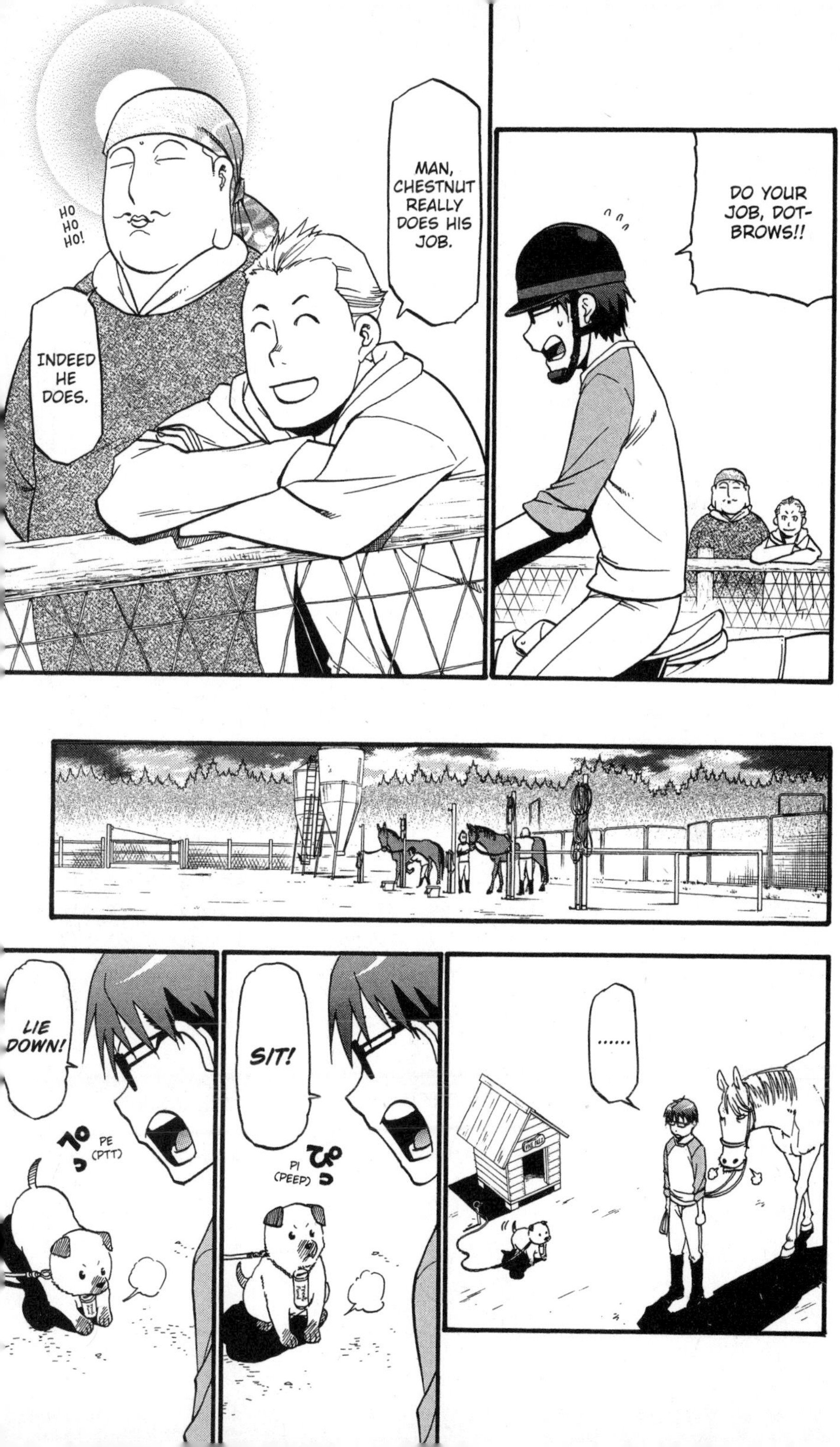
DO YOUR JOB, DOT-BROWS!!
MAN, CHESTNUT REALLY DOES HIS JOB.
HO HO HO!
INDEED HE DOES.
......
SIT!
ぴっ
PI (PEEP)
LIE DOWN!
ぺっ
PE (PTT)

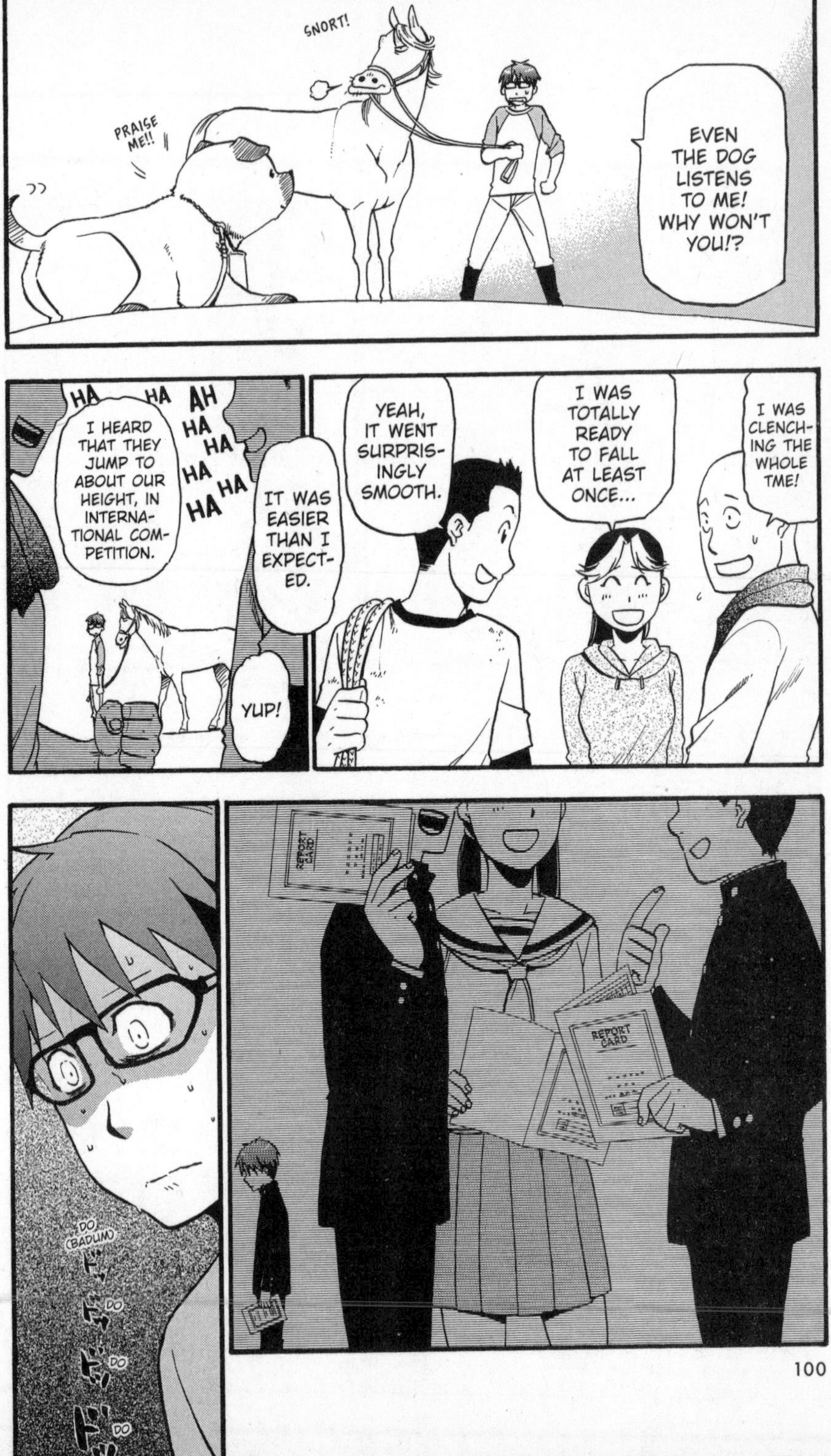
EVEN THE DOG LISTENS TO ME! WHY WON'T YOU!?
SNORT!
PRAISE ME!!
I WAS CLENCHING THE WHOLE TME!
I WAS TOTALLY READY TO FALL AT LEAST ONCE...
YEAH, IT WENT SURPRISINGLY SMOOTH.
IT WAS EASIER THAN I EXPECTED.
YUP!
I HEARD THAT THEY JUMP TO ABOUT OUR HEIGHT, IN INTERNATIONAL COMPETITION.
HA HA AH HA HA HA HA HA
REPORT CARD
REPORT CARD
DO (BADUM)
DO
DO
DO

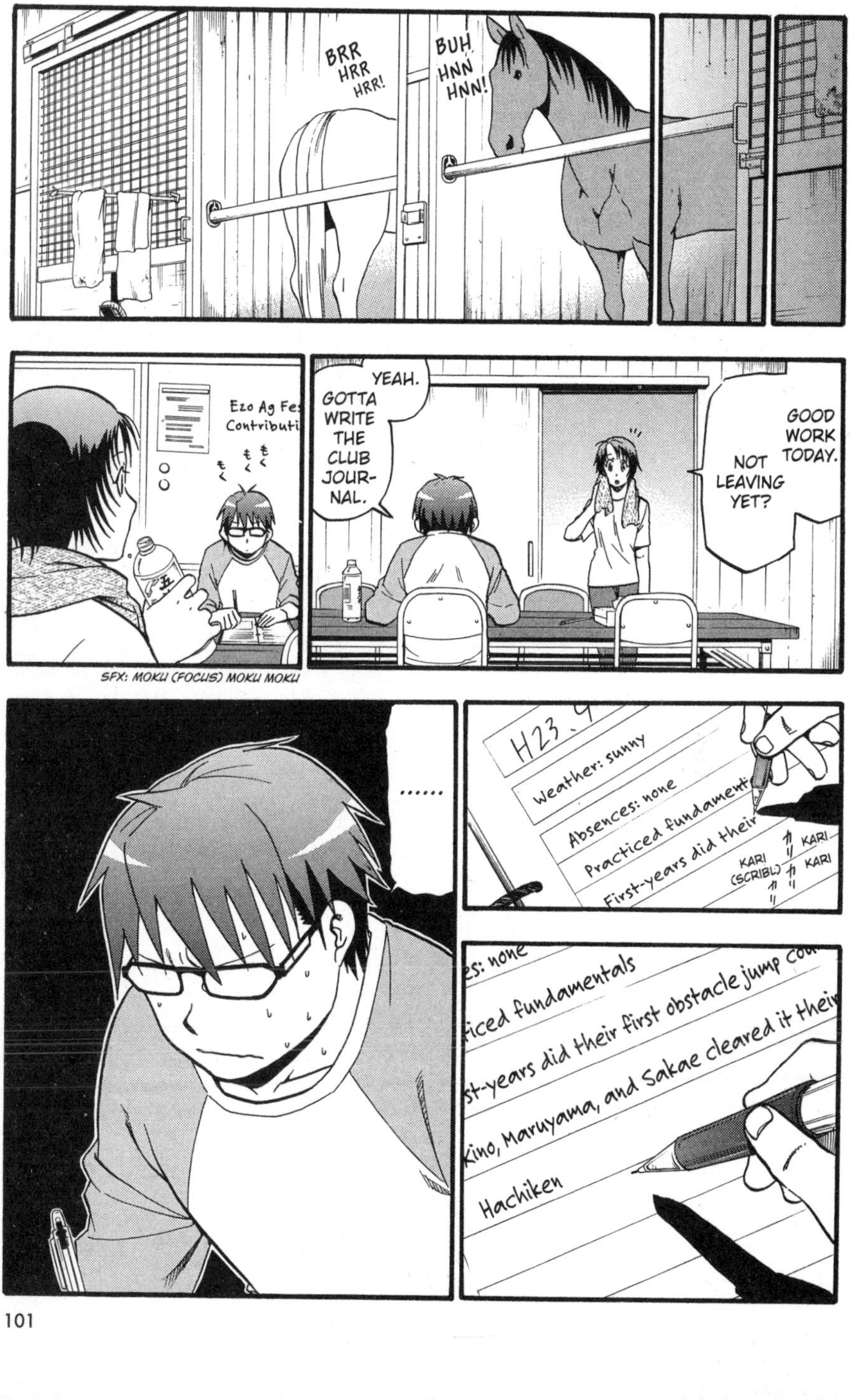
BUH HNN HNN!
BRR HRR HRR!
GOOD WORK TODAY.
NOT LEAVING YET?
YEAH. GOTTA WRITE THE CLUB JOURNAL.
Ezo Ag Fes Contributi
もくもくもく
SFX: MOKU (FOCUS) MOKU MOKU
H23. 9
Weather: sunny
Absences: none
Practiced fundament
First-years did their
カリカリカリ
KARI KARI
KARI (SCRIBL) KARI
es: none
ticed fundamentals
st-years did their first obstacle jump co
Kino, Maruyama, and Sakae cleared it their
Hachiken
......

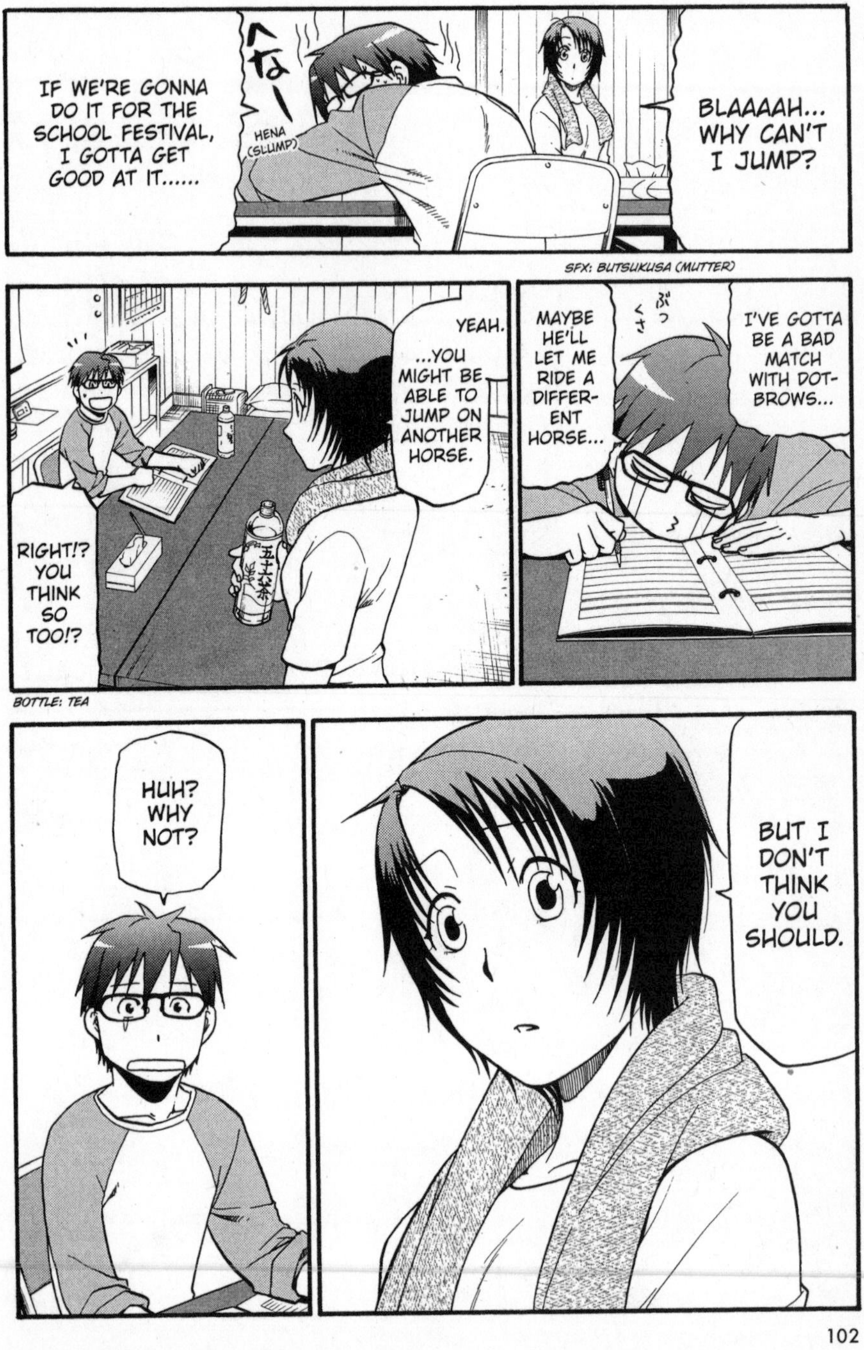
BLAAAAH... WHY CAN'T I JUMP?
へなー
HENA (SLUMP)
IF WE'RE GONNA DO IT FOR THE SCHOOL FESTIVAL, I GOTTA GET GOOD AT IT......
SFX: BUTSUKUSA (MUTTER)
I'VE GOTTA BE A BAD MATCH WITH DOT-BROWS...
ぶっくさ
MAYBE HE'LL LET ME RIDE A DIFFER-ENT HORSE...
YEAH.
...YOU MIGHT BE ABLE TO JUMP ON ANOTHER HORSE.
RIGHT!? YOU THINK SO TOO!?
五十六茶
BOTTLE: TEA
BUT I DON'T THINK YOU SHOULD.
HUH? WHY NOT?

Silver Spoon

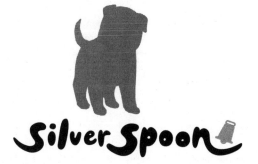

EQUESTRIAN CLUB

NOBORU
MARUYAMA

SIMOURAHORO
MIDDLE SCHOOL

FOOD SCIENCE,
YEAR 1

Chapter 41: Tale of Autumn ⑩

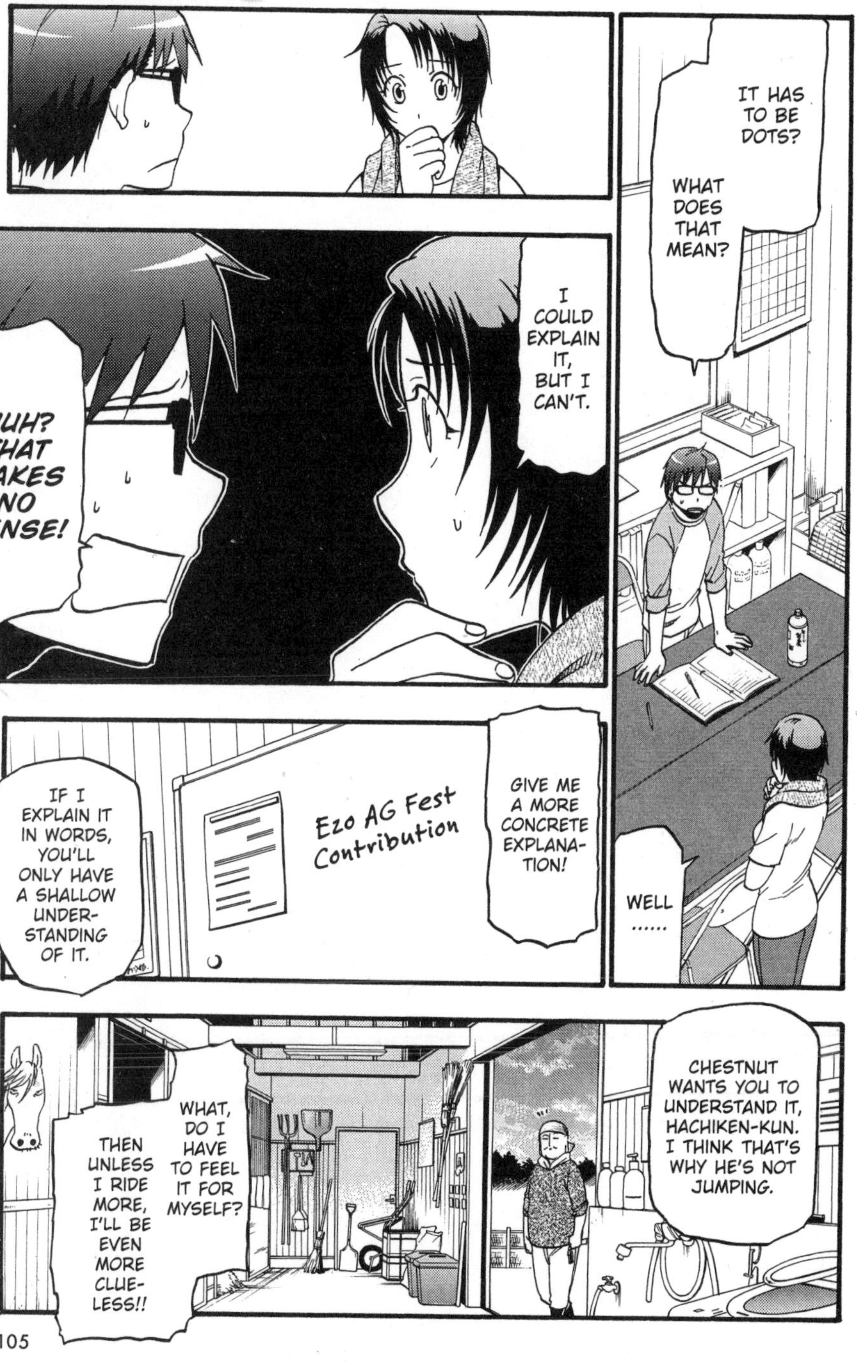

IT HAS TO BE DOTS?
WHAT DOES THAT MEAN?
WELL......
I COULD EXPLAIN IT, BUT I CAN'T.
HUH? THAT MAKES NO SENSE!
GIVE ME A MORE CONCRETE EXPLANA-TION!
Ezo AG Fest Contribution
IF I EXPLAIN IT IN WORDS, YOU'LL ONLY HAVE A SHALLOW UNDER-STANDING OF IT.
CHESTNUT WANTS YOU TO UNDERSTAND IT, HACHIKEN-KUN. I THINK THAT'S WHY HE'S NOT JUMPING.
WHAT, DO I HAVE TO FEEL IT FOR MYSELF?
THEN UNLESS I RIDE MORE, I'LL BE EVEN MORE CLUE-LESS!!

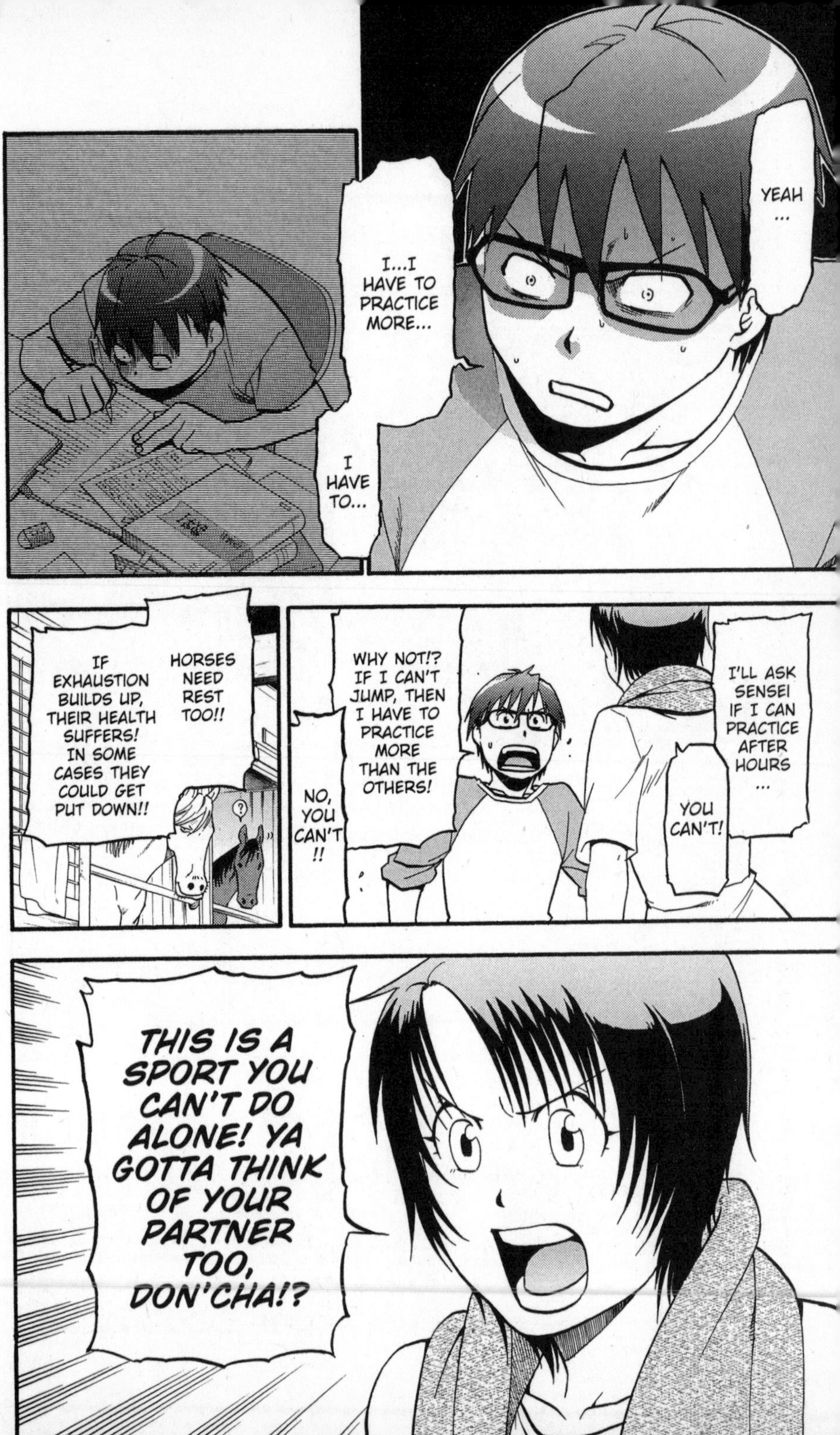
YEAH ...
I...I HAVE TO PRACTICE MORE...
I HAVE TO...
I'LL ASK SENSEI IF I CAN PRACTICE AFTER HOURS ...
YOU CAN'T!
WHY NOT!? IF I CAN'T JUMP, THEN I HAVE TO PRACTICE MORE THAN THE OTHERS!
NO, YOU CAN'T !!
HORSES NEED REST TOO!!
IF EXHAUSTION BUILDS UP, THEIR HEALTH SUFFERS! IN SOME CASES THEY COULD GET PUT DOWN!!
THIS IS A SPORT YOU CAN'T DO ALONE! YA GOTTA THINK OF YOUR PARTNER TOO, DON'CHA!?

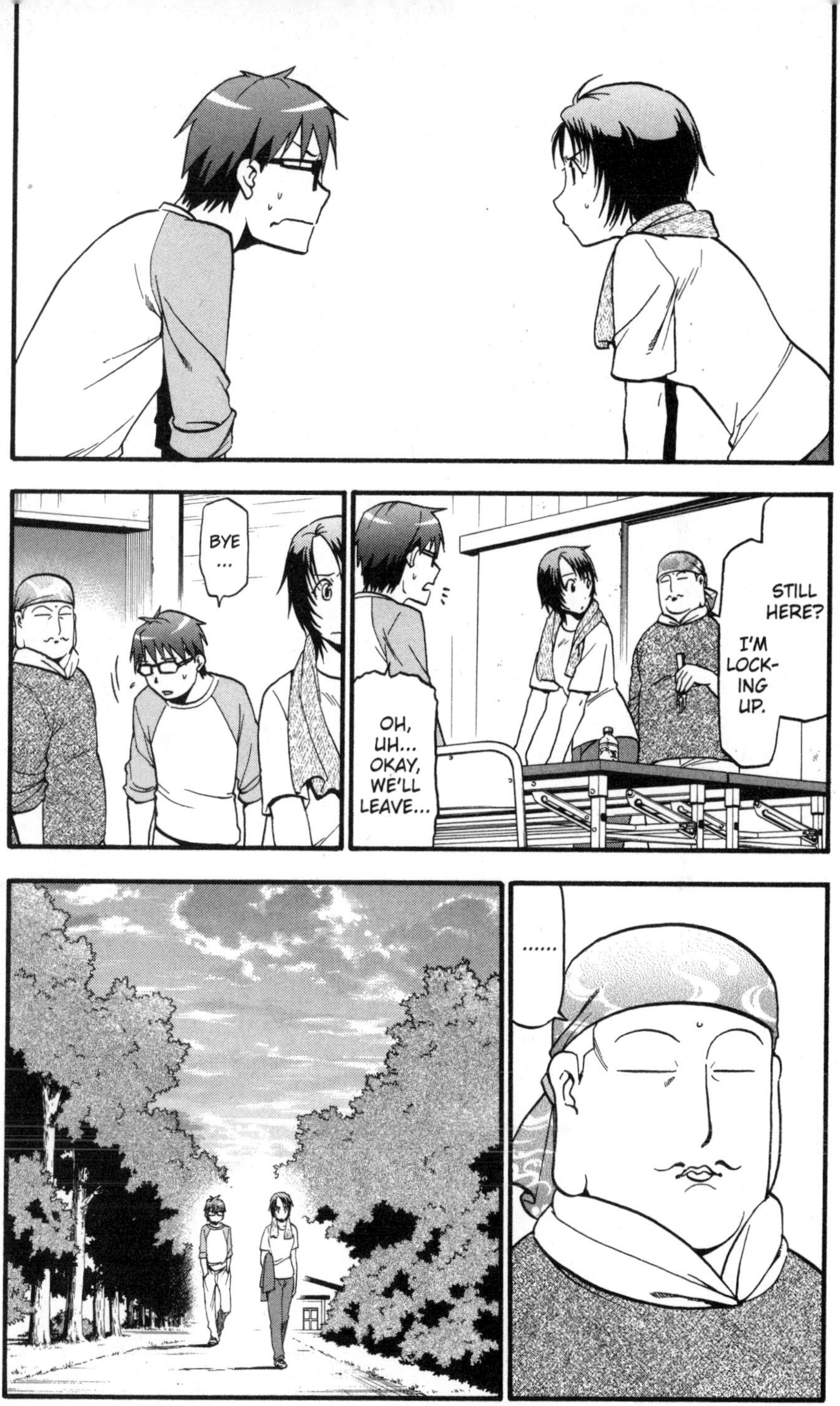
STILL HERE? I'M LOCKING UP.
OH, UH... OKAY, WE'LL LEAVE...
BYE ...
......

ARE YOU FREE NEXT SUNDAY?

HACHI-KEN-KUN.

WH-WHAT!?

CAN YOU GO SOMEWHERE WITH ME?

Chapter 41:
Tale of Autumn ⑩

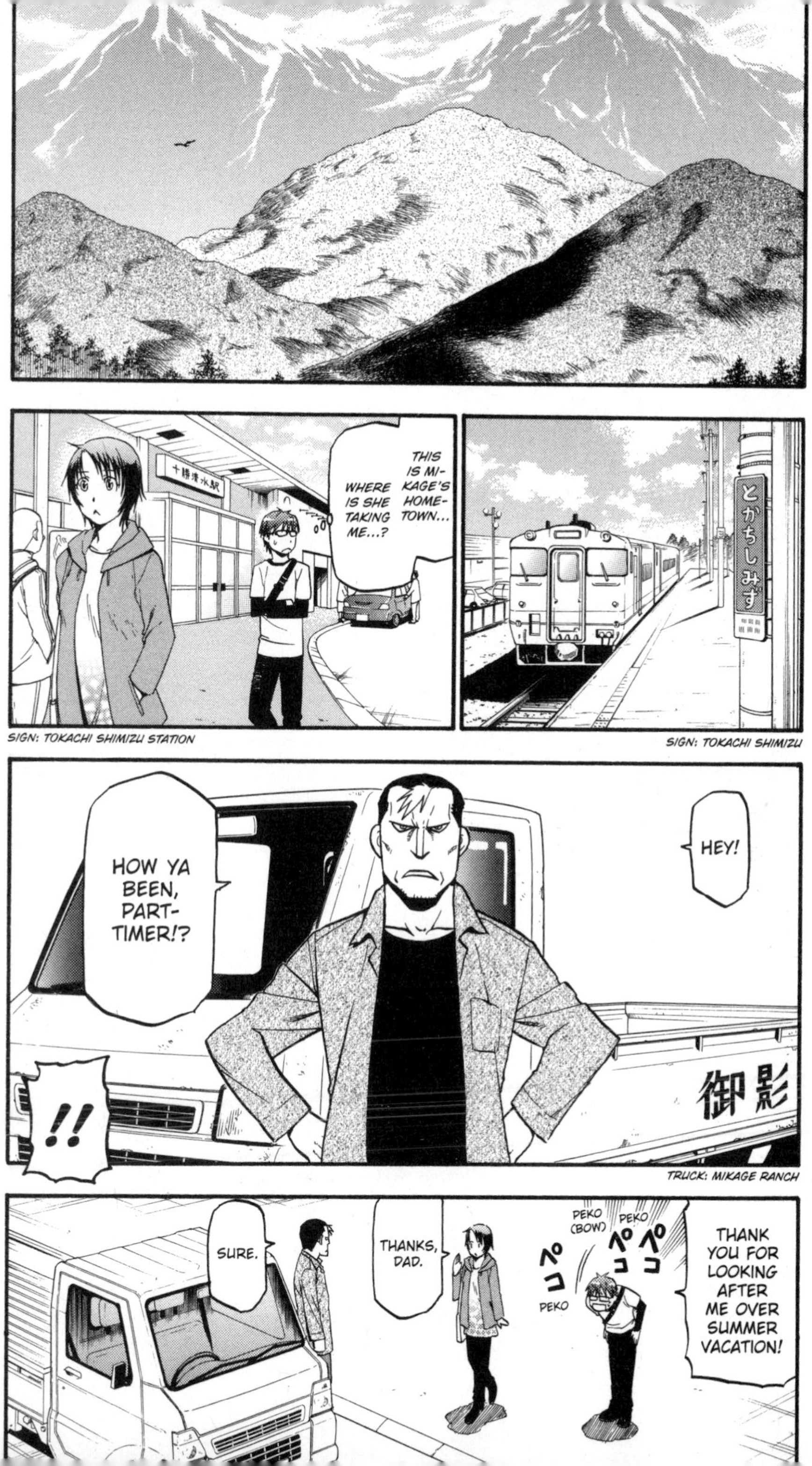
とかちしみず
SIGN: TOKACHI SHIMIZU
THIS IS MI-KAGE'S HOME-TOWN...
WHERE IS SHE TAKING ME...?
十勝清水駅
SIGN: TOKACHI SHIMIZU STATION
HEY!
HOW YA BEEN, PART-TIMER!?
!!
御影
TRUCK: MIKAGE RANCH
THANK YOU FOR LOOKING AFTER ME OVER SUMMER VACATION!
PEKO
PEKO (BOW)
PEKO
THANKS, DAD.
SURE.

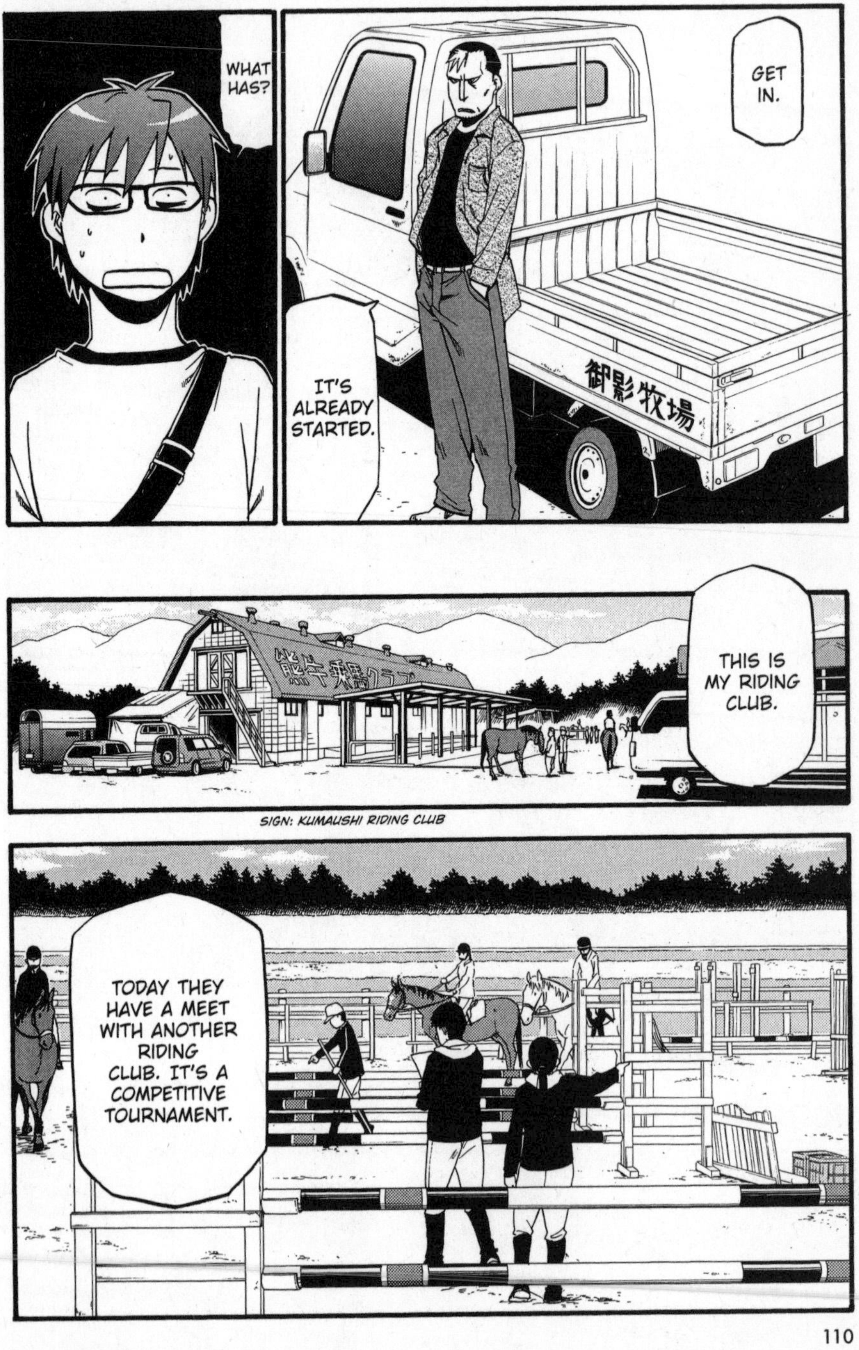
GET IN.
IT'S ALREADY STARTED.
御影牧場
WHAT HAS?
THIS IS MY RIDING CLUB.
SIGN: KUMAUSHI RIDING CLUB
TODAY THEY HAVE A MEET WITH ANOTHER RIDING CLUB. IT'S A COMPETITIVE TOURNAMENT.

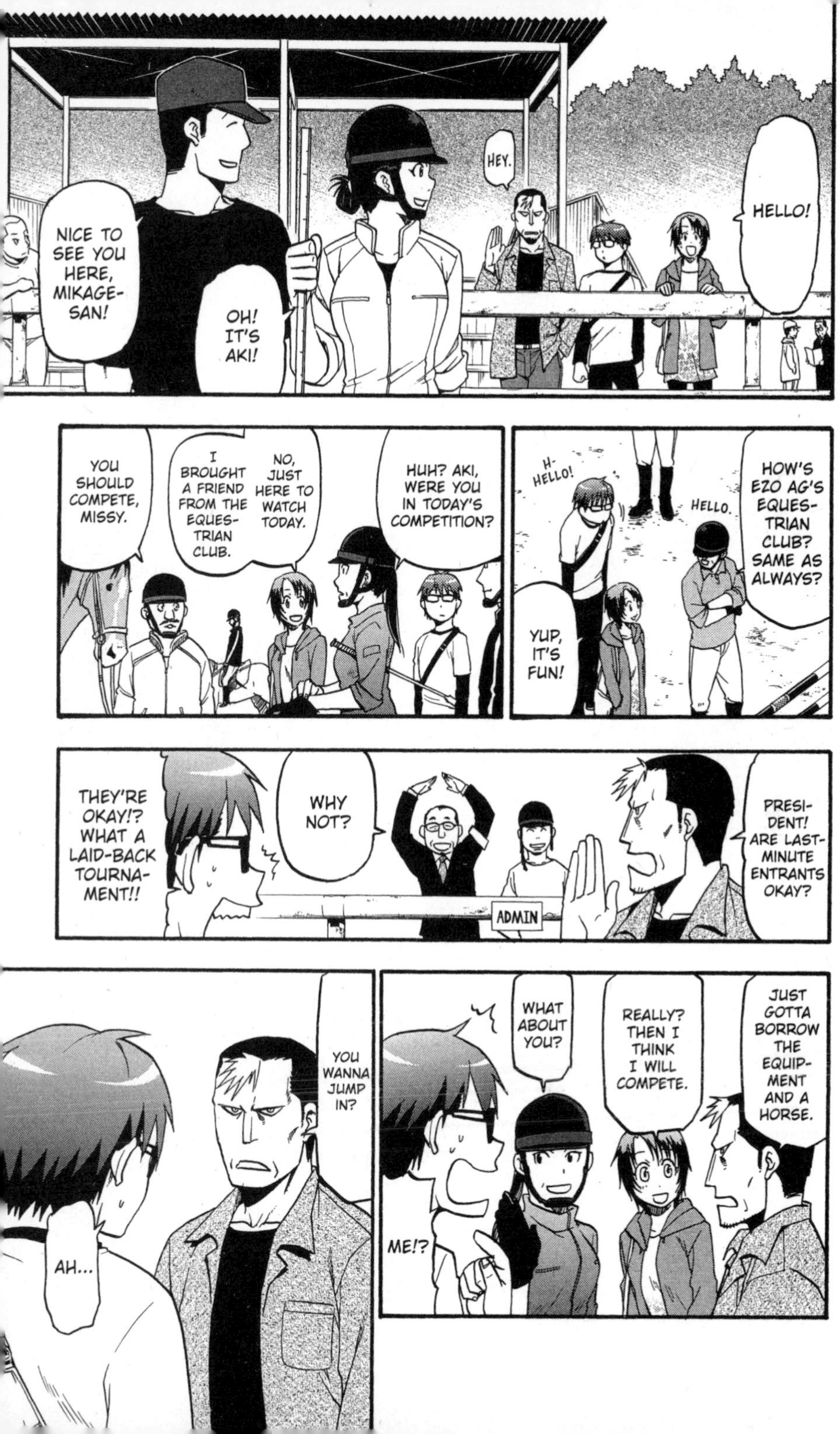
HELLO!
HEY.
OH! IT'S AKI!
NICE TO SEE YOU HERE, MIKAGE-SAN!
HOW'S EZO AG'S EQUES-TRIAN CLUB? SAME AS ALWAYS?
HELLO.
H-HELLO!
YUP, IT'S FUN!
HUH? AKI, WERE YOU IN TODAY'S COMPETITION?
NO, JUST HERE TO WATCH TODAY.
I BROUGHT A FRIEND FROM THE EQUES-TRIAN CLUB.
YOU SHOULD COMPETE, MISSY.
PRESI-DENT! ARE LAST-MINUTE ENTRANTS OKAY?
ADMIN
WHY NOT?
THEY'RE OKAY!? WHAT A LAID-BACK TOURNA-MENT!!
JUST GOTTA BORROW THE EQUIP-MENT AND A HORSE.
REALLY? THEN I THINK I WILL COMPETE.
WHAT ABOUT YOU?
ME!?
YOU WANNA JUMP IN?
AH...

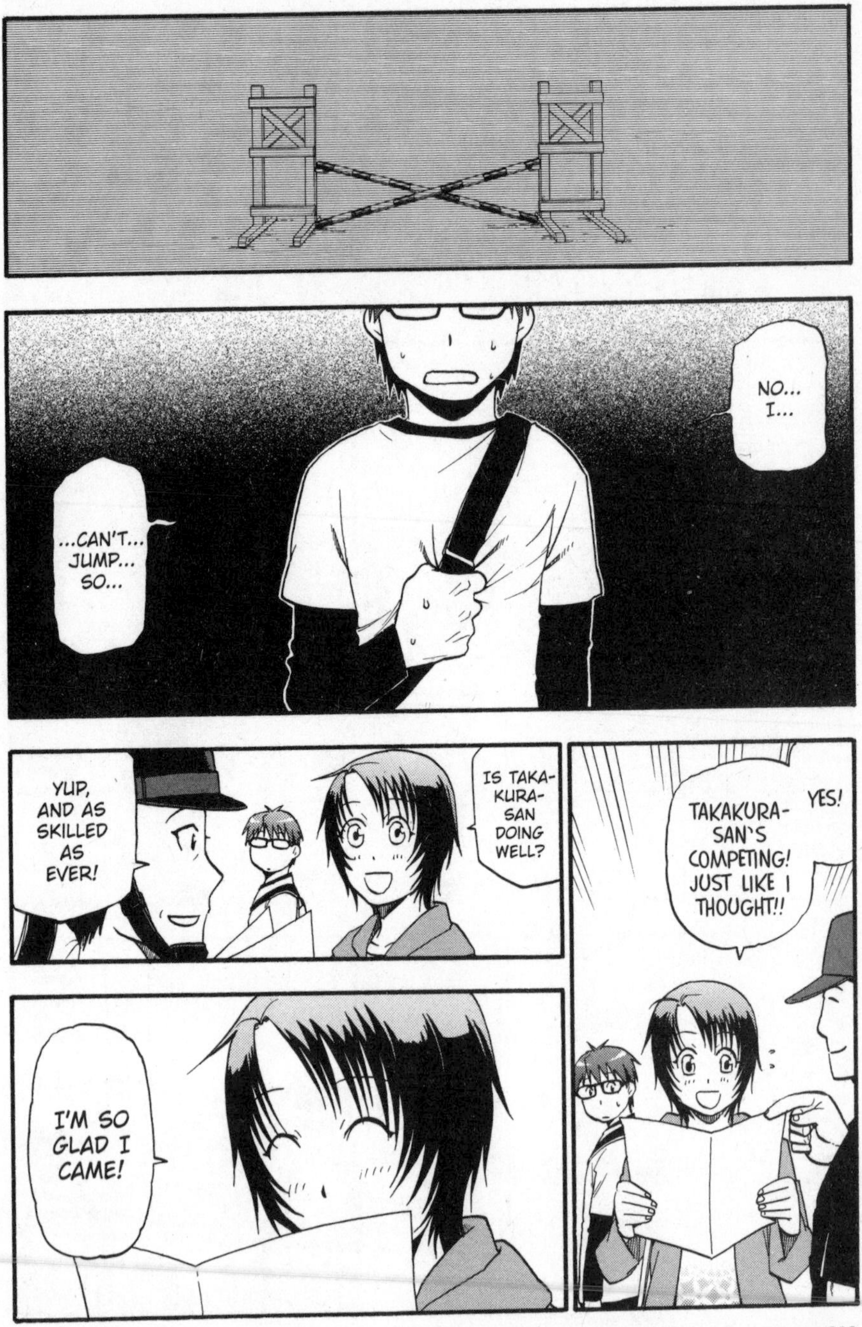
NO... I...
...CAN'T... JUMP... SO...
YES!
TAKAKURA-SAN'S COMPETING! JUST LIKE I THOUGHT!!
IS TAKA-KURA-SAN DOING WELL?
YUP, AND AS SKILLED AS EVER!
I'M SO GLAD I CAME!

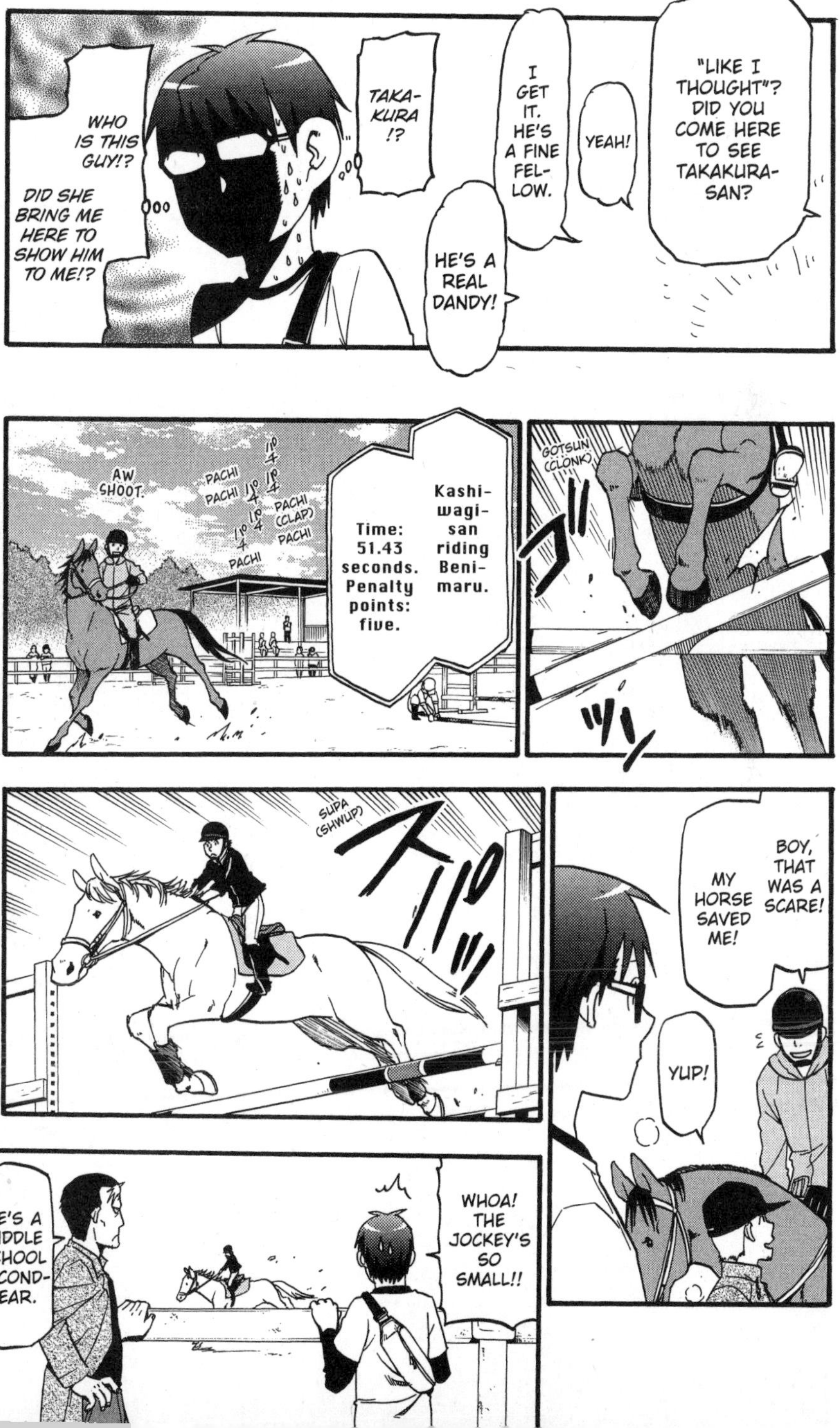
"LIKE I THOUGHT"? DID YOU COME HERE TO SEE TAKAKURA-SAN?
YEAH!
I GET IT. HE'S A FINE FEL-LOW.
HE'S A REAL DANDY!
TAKA-KURA!?
WHO IS THIS GUY!?
DID SHE BRING ME HERE TO SHOW HIM TO ME!?
GOTSUN (CLONK)
Kashi-wagi-san riding Beni-maru.
Time: 51.43 seconds. Penalty points: five.
PACHI PACHI PACHI (CLAP) PACHI PACHI
AW SHOOT.
BOY, THAT WAS A SCARE!
MY HORSE SAVED ME!
YUP!
SUPA (SHWUP)
WHOA! THE JOCKEY'S SO SMALL!!
HE'S A MIDDLE SCHOOL SECOND-YEAR.

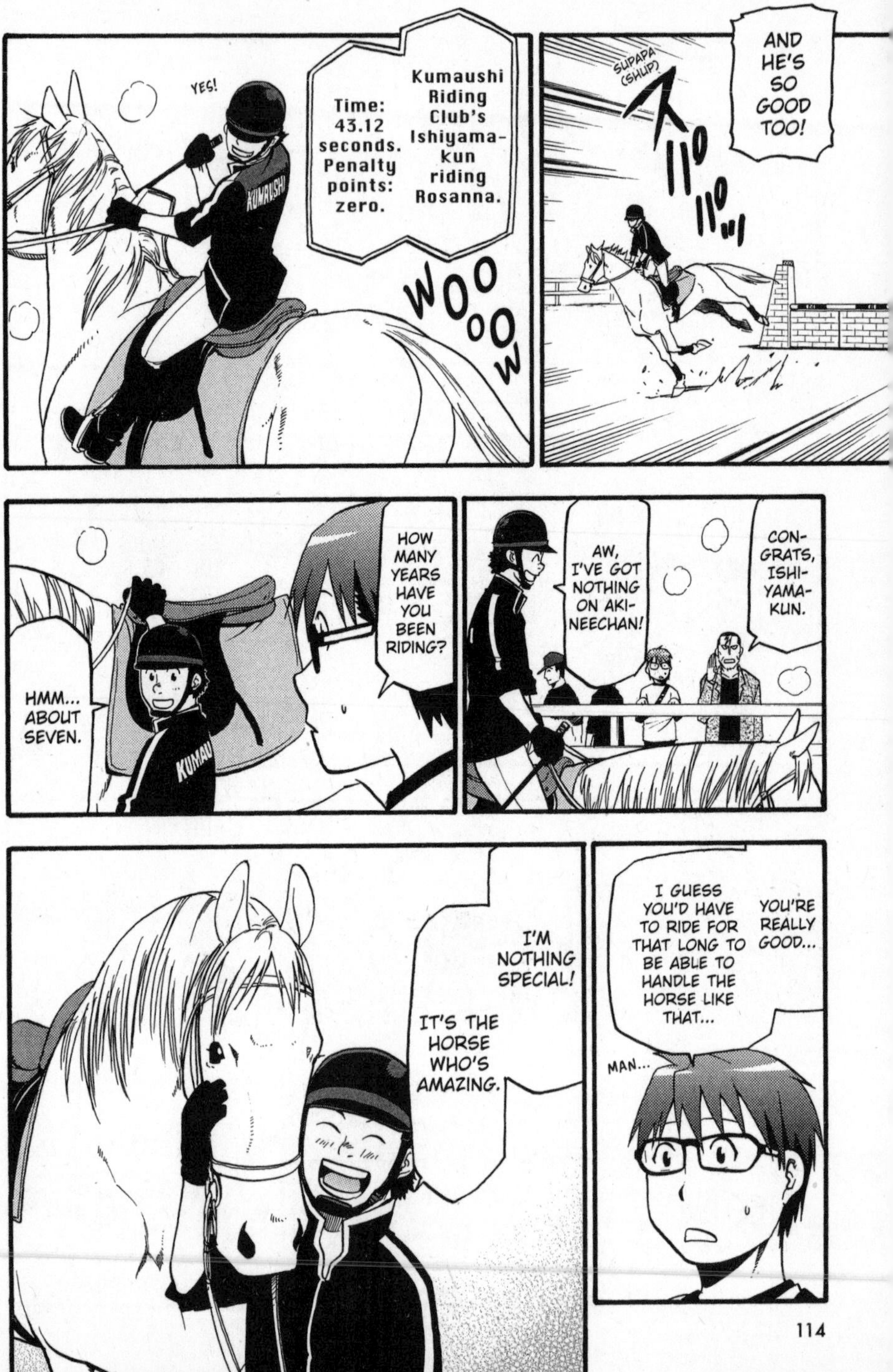
AND HE'S SO GOOD TOO!
SUPAPA (SHUP)
Kumaushi Riding Club's Ishiyama-kun riding Rosanna.
Time: 43.12 seconds. Penalty points: zero.
YES!
WOOOOW
CON-GRATS, ISHI-YAMA-KUN.
AW, I'VE GOT NOTHING ON AKI-NEECHAN!
HOW MANY YEARS HAVE YOU BEEN RIDING?
HMM... ABOUT SEVEN.
YOU'RE REALLY GOOD...
I GUESS YOU'D HAVE TO RIDE FOR THAT LONG TO BE ABLE TO HANDLE THE HORSE LIKE THAT...
MAN...
I'M NOTHING SPECIAL!
IT'S THE HORSE WHO'S AMAZING.

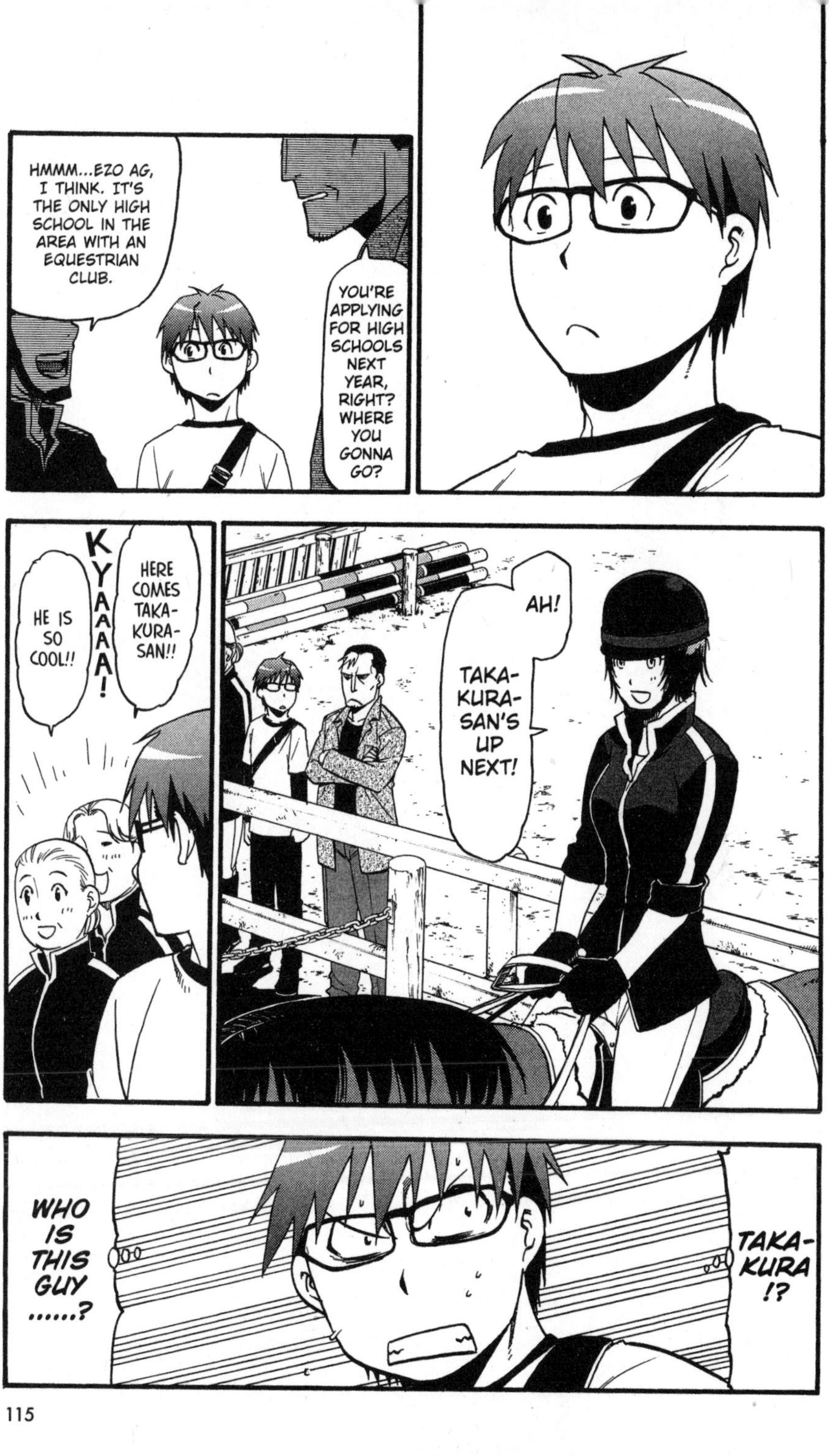
YOU'RE APPLYING FOR HIGH SCHOOLS NEXT YEAR, RIGHT? WHERE YOU GONNA GO?
HMMM...EZO AG, I THINK. IT'S THE ONLY HIGH SCHOOL IN THE AREA WITH AN EQUESTRIAN CLUB.
AH!
TAKA-KURA-SAN'S UP NEXT!
HERE COMES TAKA-KURA-SAN!!
KYAAAA!
HE IS SO COOL!!
TAKA-KURA!?
WHO IS THIS GUY......?

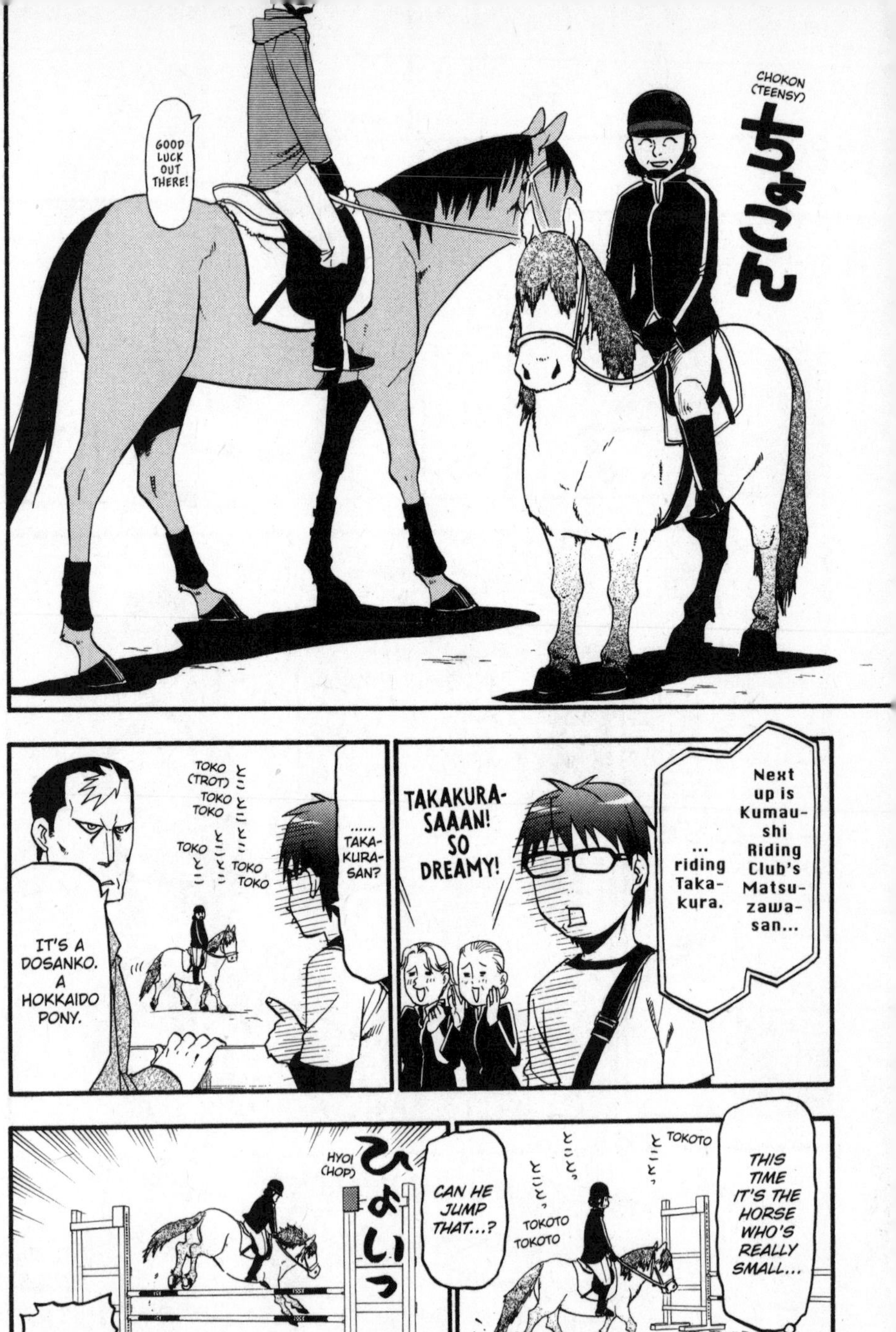
CHOKON (TEENSY)
ちょこん
GOOD LUCK OUT THERE!
Next up is Kumaushi Riding Club's Matsuzawa-san...
... riding Takakura.
TAKAKURA-SAAAN! SO DREAMY!
...... TAKAKURA-SAN?
TOKO (TROT) TOKO TOKO
TOKO
TOKO TOKO
とことこ
とことこ
とこ
IT'S A DOSANKO. A HOKKAIDO PONY.
THIS TIME IT'S THE HORSE WHO'S REALLY SMALL...
TOKOTO
とことっ
TOKOTO TOKOTO
とことっ
とことっ
CAN HE JUMP THAT...?
HYOI (HOP)
ひょいっ
!!?

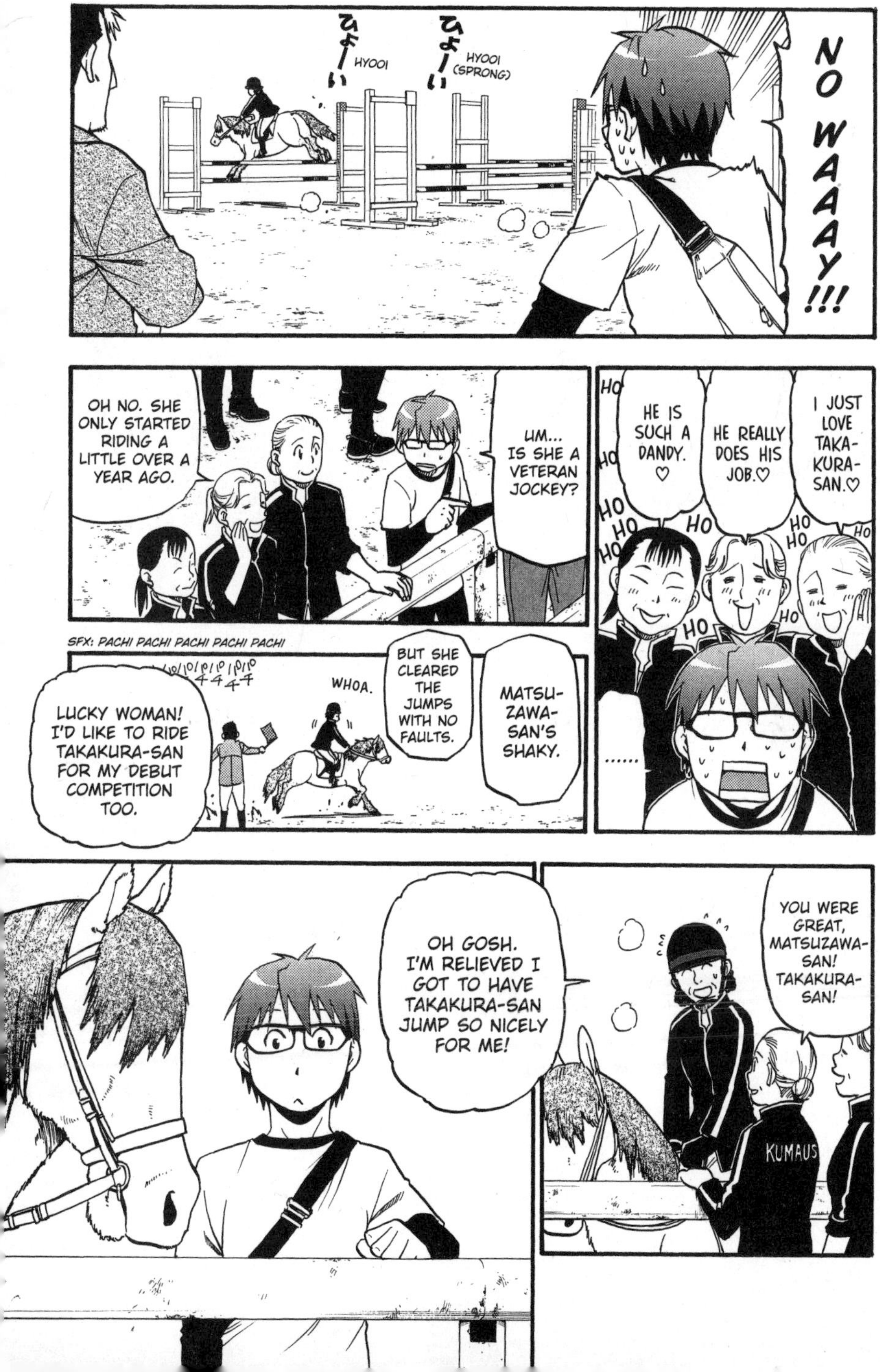
NO WAAAAY!!!
ひよーい
HYOOI (SPRONG)
ひよーい
HYOOI
UM... IS SHE A VETERAN JOCKEY?
OH NO. SHE ONLY STARTED RIDING A LITTLE OVER A YEAR AGO.
SFX: PACHI PACHI PACHI PACHI PACHI
MATSU-ZAWA-SAN'S SHAKY.
BUT SHE CLEARED THE JUMPS WITH NO FAULTS.
WHOA.
LUCKY WOMAN! I'D LIKE TO RIDE TAKAKURA-SAN FOR MY DEBUT COMPETITION TOO.
I JUST LOVE TAKA-KURA-SAN.♡
HE REALLY DOES HIS JOB.♡
HE IS SUCH A DANDY.♡
HO HO HO HO HO HO HO HO HO HO HO HO
......
YOU WERE GREAT, MATSUZAWA-SAN! TAKAKURA-SAN!
KUMAUS
OH GOSH. I'M RELIEVED I GOT TO HAVE TAKAKURA-SAN JUMP SO NICELY FOR ME!

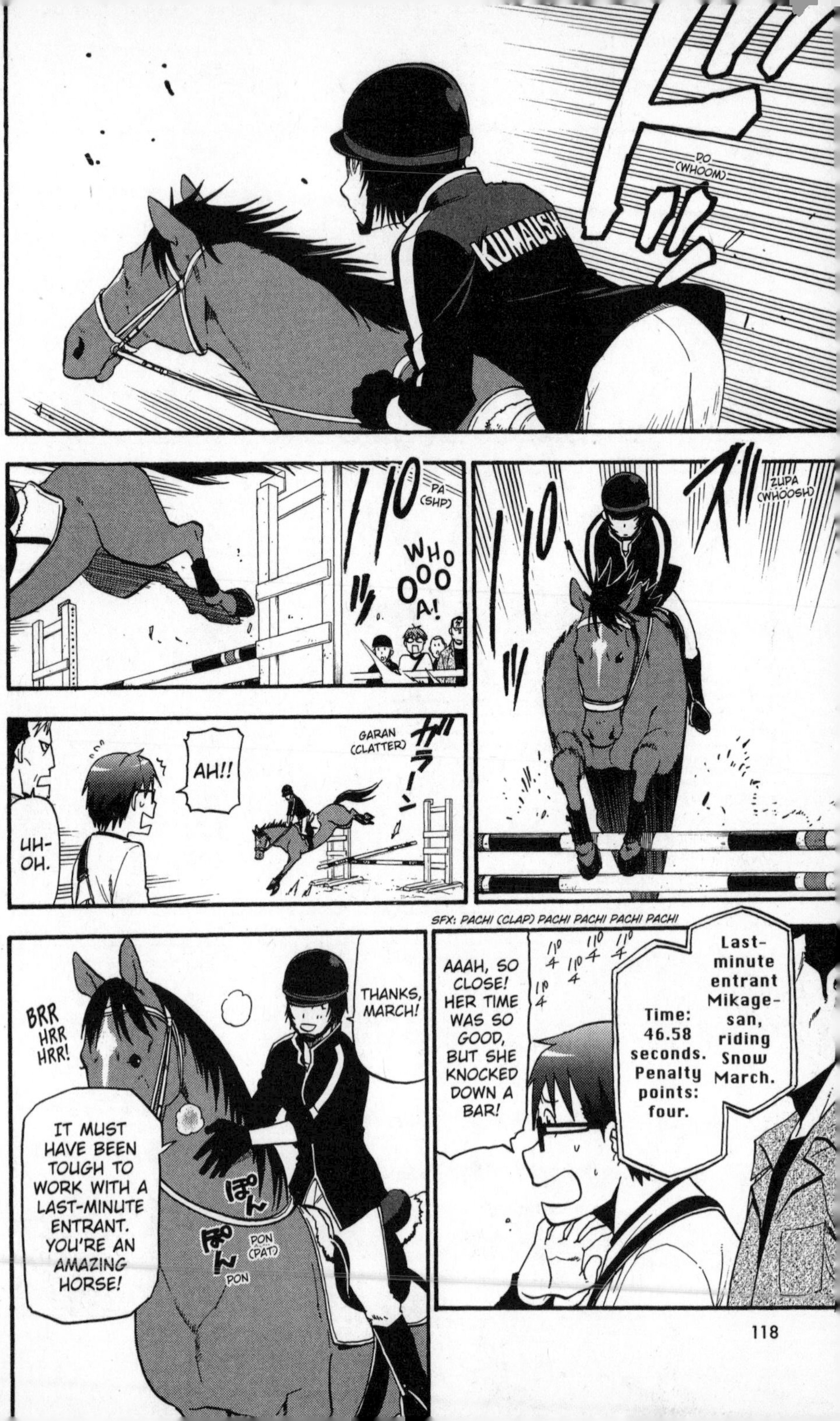
DO
(WHOOM)
KUMAUSH
ZUPA
(WHOOSH)
PA
(SHP)
WHOOOOA!
GARAN
(CLATTER)
AH!!
UH-OH.
SFX: PACHI (CLAP) PACHI PACHI PACHI PACHI
Last-minute entrant Mikage-san, riding Snow March.
Time: 46.58 seconds. Penalty points: four.
AAAH, SO CLOSE! HER TIME WAS SO GOOD, BUT SHE KNOCKED DOWN A BAR!
THANKS, MARCH!
BRR HRR HRR!
IT MUST HAVE BEEN TOUGH TO WORK WITH A LAST-MINUTE ENTRANT. YOU'RE AN AMAZING HORSE!
PON
(PAT)
PON

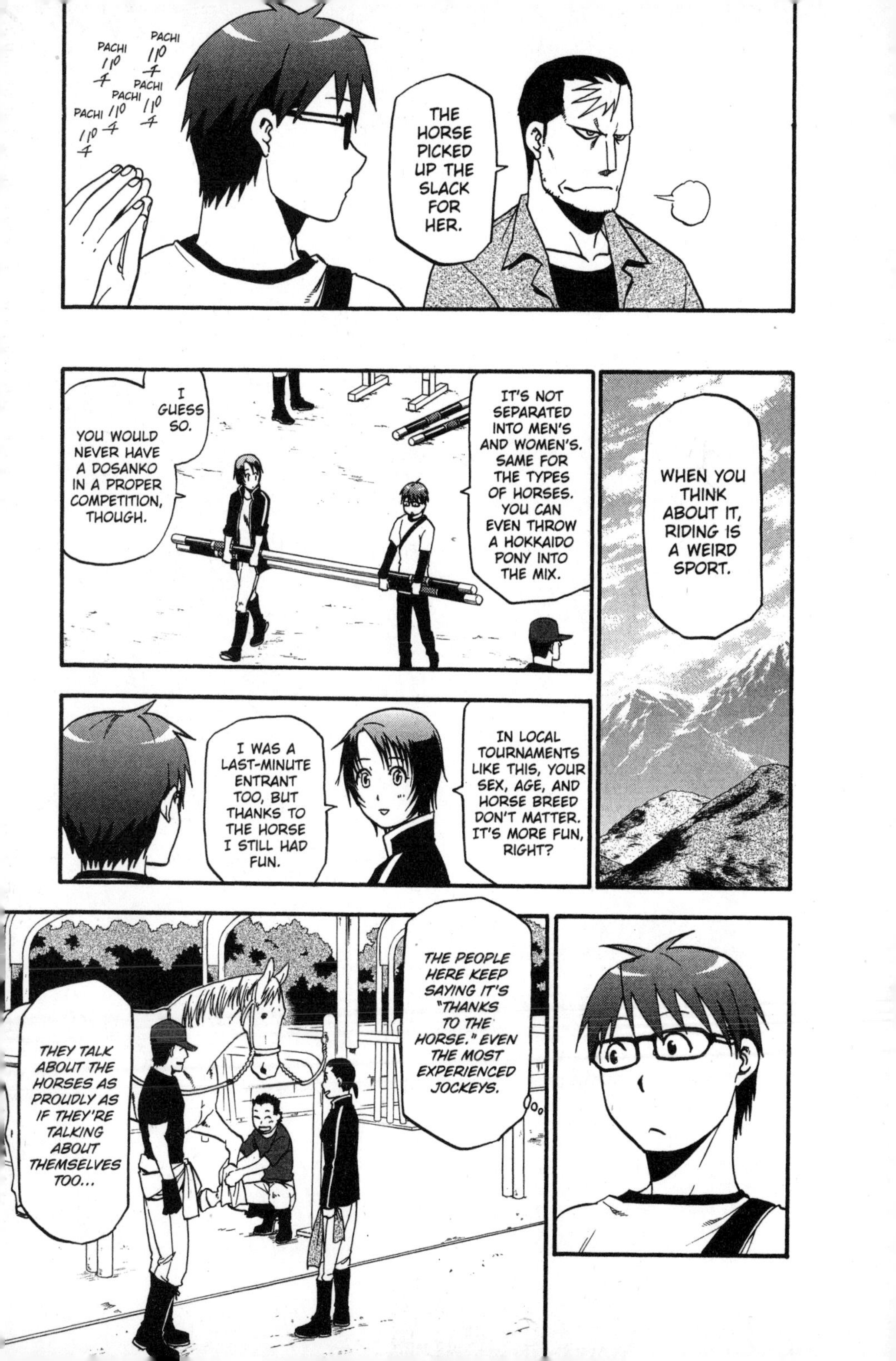
PACHI PACHI PACHI PACHI
THE HORSE PICKED UP THE SLACK FOR HER.
WHEN YOU THINK ABOUT IT, RIDING IS A WEIRD SPORT.
IT'S NOT SEPARATED INTO MEN'S AND WOMEN'S. SAME FOR THE TYPES OF HORSES. YOU CAN EVEN THROW A HOKKAIDO PONY INTO THE MIX.
I GUESS SO.
YOU WOULD NEVER HAVE A DOSANKO IN A PROPER COMPETITION, THOUGH.
IN LOCAL TOURNAMENTS LIKE THIS, YOUR SEX, AGE, AND HORSE BREED DON'T MATTER. IT'S MORE FUN, RIGHT?
I WAS A LAST-MINUTE ENTRANT TOO, BUT THANKS TO THE HORSE I STILL HAD FUN.
THE PEOPLE HERE KEEP SAYING IT'S "THANKS TO THE HORSE." EVEN THE MOST EXPERIENCED JOCKEYS.
THEY TALK ABOUT THE HORSES AS PROUDLY AS IF THEY'RE TALKING ABOUT THEMSELVES TOO...

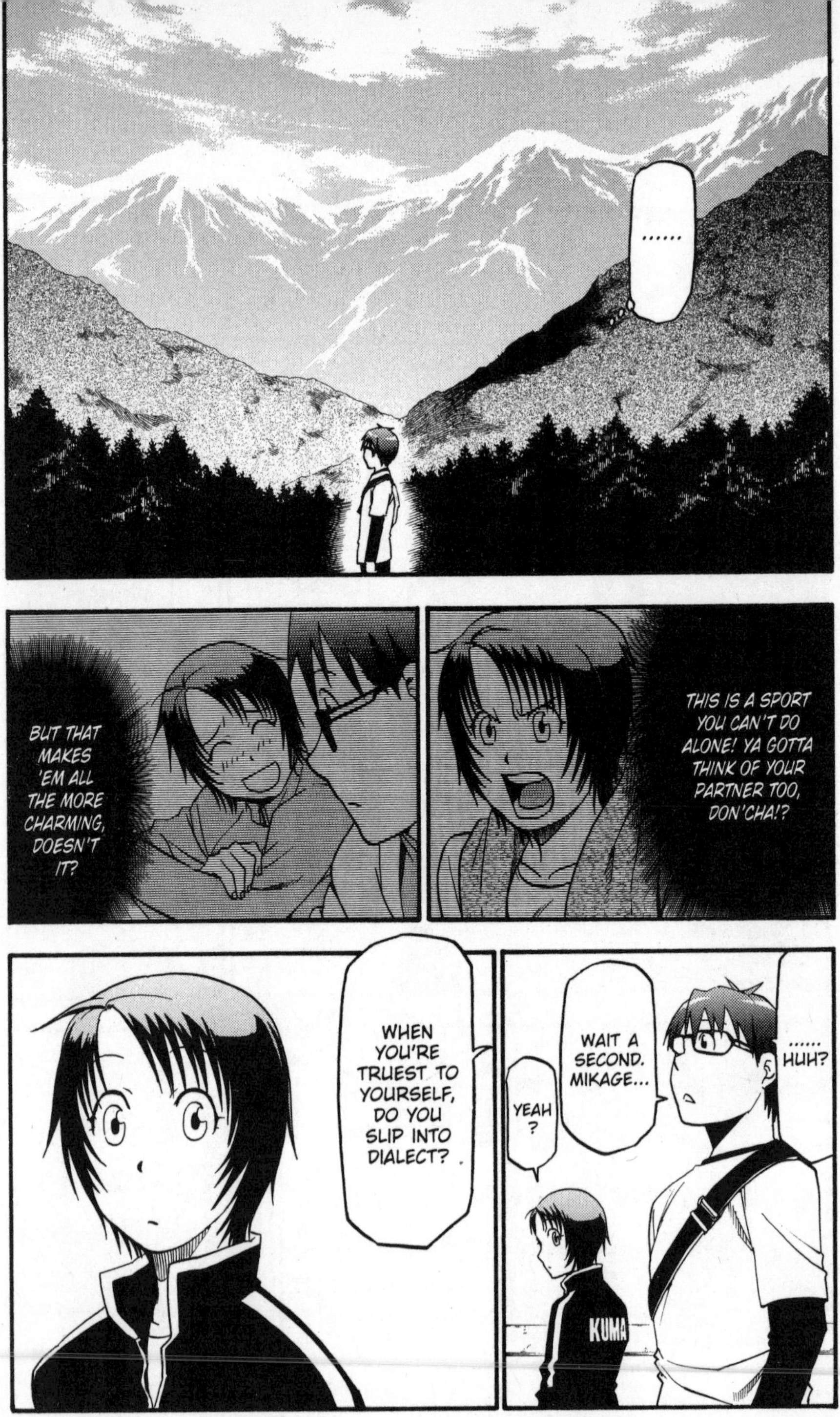
......
THIS IS A SPORT YOU CAN'T DO ALONE! YA GOTTA THINK OF YOUR PARTNER TOO, DON'CHA!?
BUT THAT MAKES 'EM ALL THE MORE CHARMING, DOESN'T IT?
......HUH?
WAIT A SECOND. MIKAGE...
YEAH?
KUMA
WHEN YOU'RE TRUEST TO YOURSELF, DO YOU SLIP INTO DIALECT?

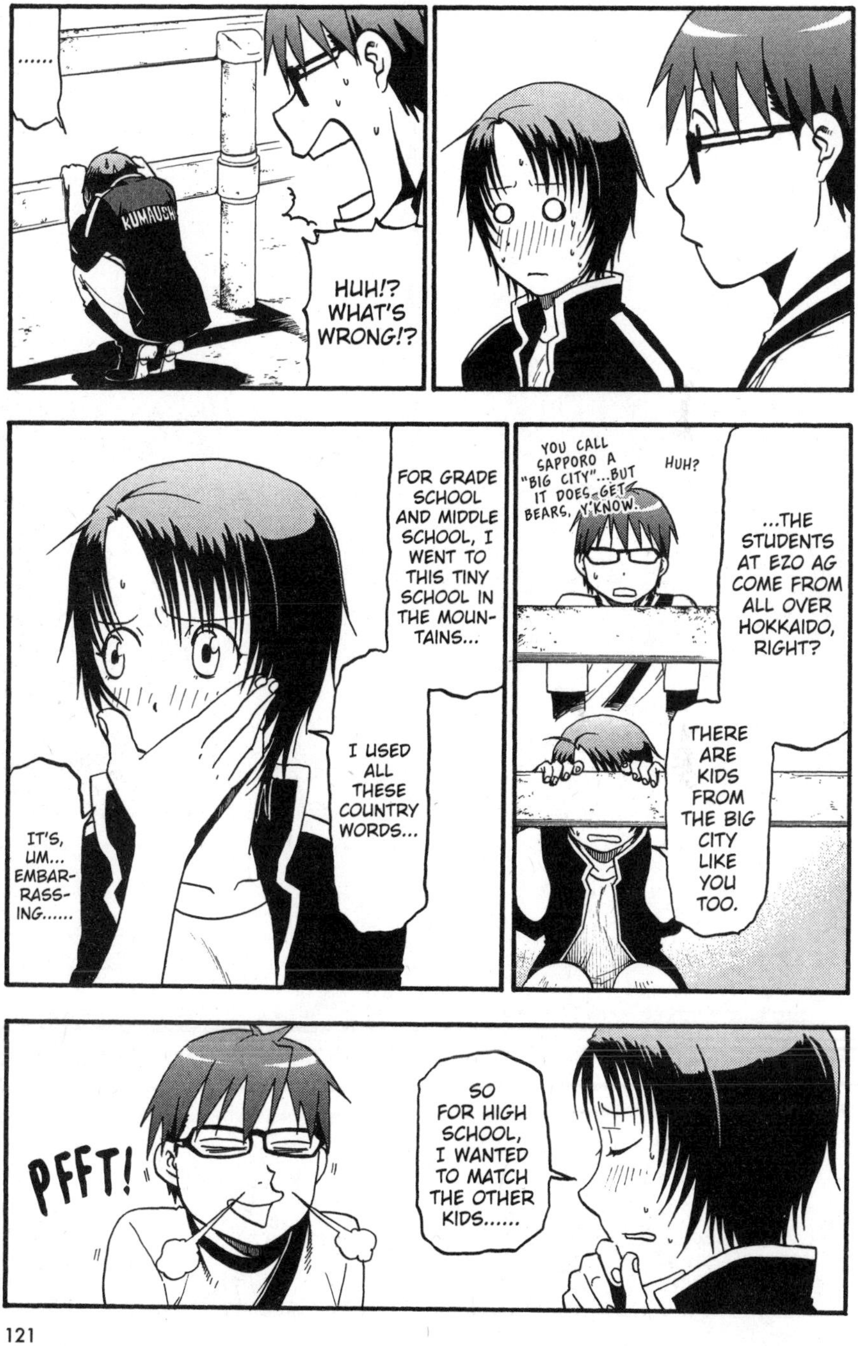
......
HUH!? WHAT'S WRONG!?
KUMAUCHI
...THE STUDENTS AT EZO AG COME FROM ALL OVER HOKKAIDO, RIGHT?
THERE ARE KIDS FROM THE BIG CITY LIKE YOU TOO.
HUH?
YOU CALL SAPPORO A "BIG CITY"...BUT IT DOES GET BEARS, Y'KNOW.
FOR GRADE SCHOOL AND MIDDLE SCHOOL, I WENT TO THIS TINY SCHOOL IN THE MOUN-TAINS...
I USED ALL THESE COUNTRY WORDS...
IT'S, UM... EMBAR-RASS-ING......
SO FOR HIGH SCHOOL, I WANTED TO MATCH THE OTHER KIDS......
PFFT!

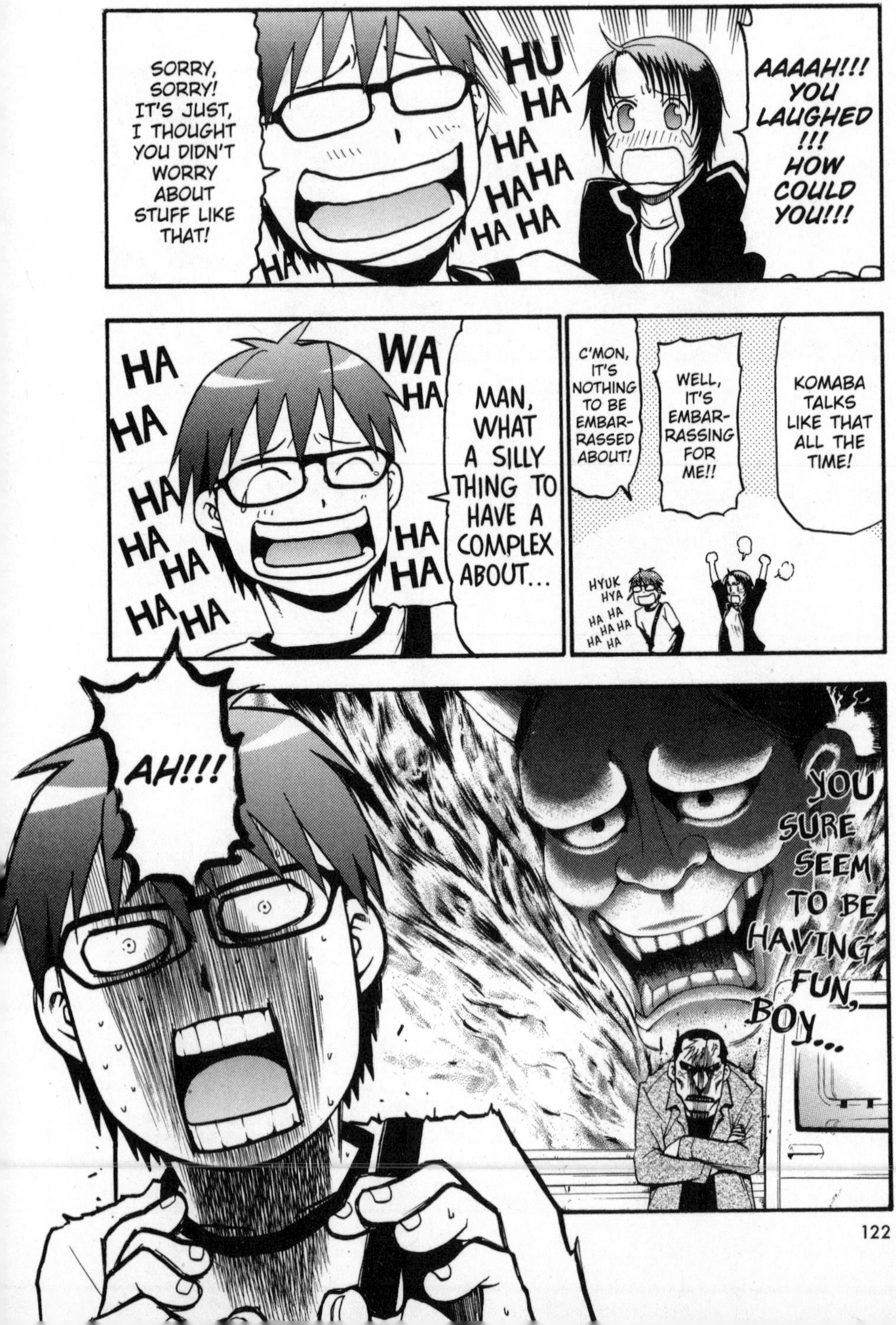
AAAAH!!! YOU LAUGHED!!! HOW COULD YOU!!!
HU HA HA HA HA HA HA HA
SORRY, SORRY! IT'S JUST, I THOUGHT YOU DIDN'T WORRY ABOUT STUFF LIKE THAT!
KOMABA TALKS LIKE THAT ALL THE TIME!
WELL, IT'S EMBARRASSING FOR ME!!
C'MON, IT'S NOTHING TO BE EMBARRASSED ABOUT!
HYUK HYA HA HA HA HA HA HA HA
WA HA
MAN, WHAT A SILLY THING TO HAVE A COMPLEX ABOUT...
HA HA
HA HA HA HA HA HA HA HA
YOU SURE SEEM TO BE HAVING FUN, BOY...
AH!!!

Silver Spoon

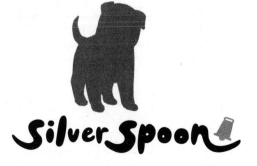

EQUESTRIAN CLUB

MANAMI SAKAE

MAKUBETSU EAST
MIDDLE SCHOOL

AGRICULTURAL
SCIENCE, YEAR 1

Chapter 42:

Tale of Autumn ⑪

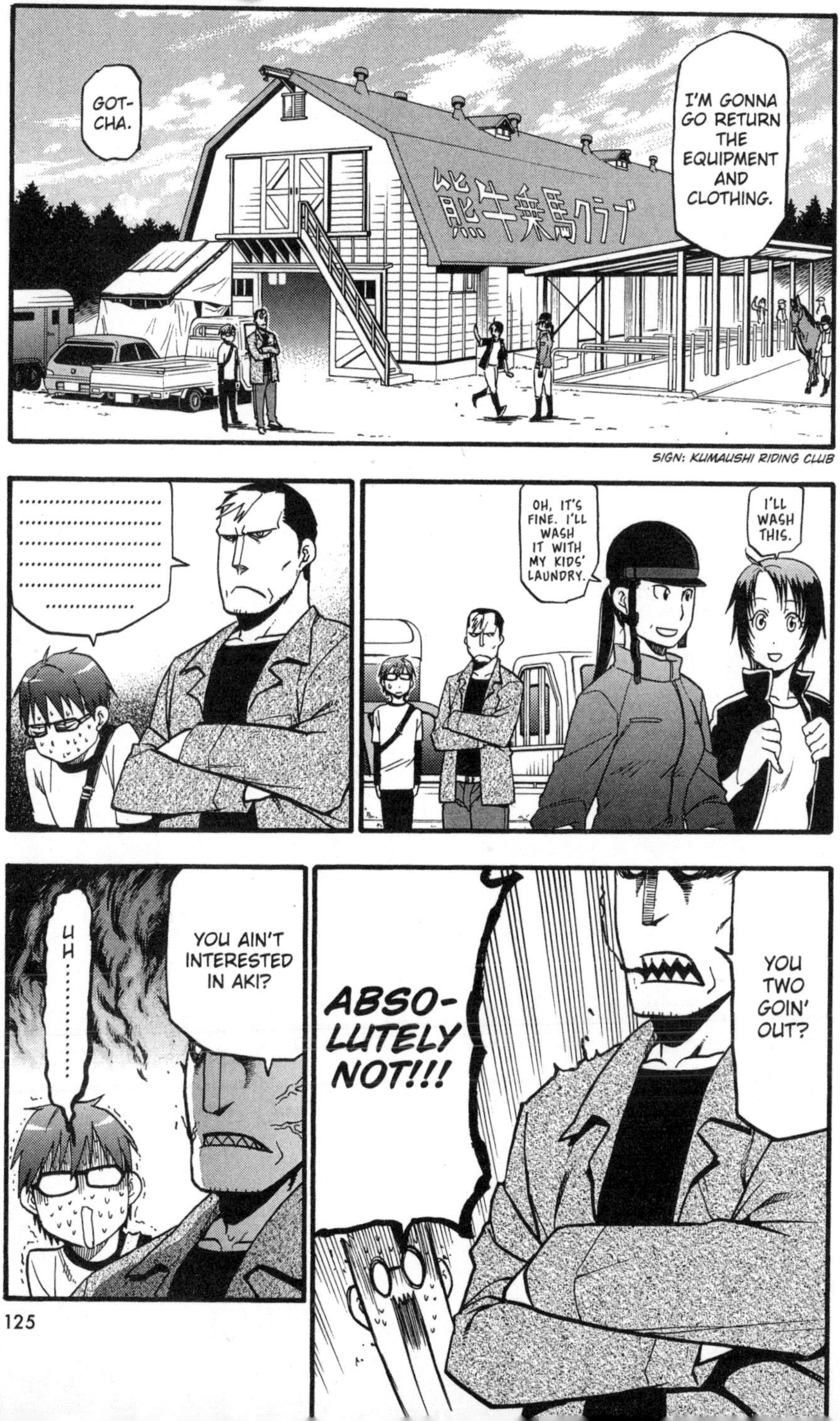
I'M GONNA GO RETURN THE EQUIPMENT AND CLOTHING.
熊牛乗馬クラブ
GOT-CHA.
SIGN: KUMAUSHI RIDING CLUB
I'LL WASH THIS.
OH, IT'S FINE. I'LL WASH IT WITH MY KIDS' LAUNDRY.
....
YOU TWO GOIN' OUT?
ABSO-LUTELY NOT!!!
YOU AIN'T INTERESTED IN AKI?
UH.........

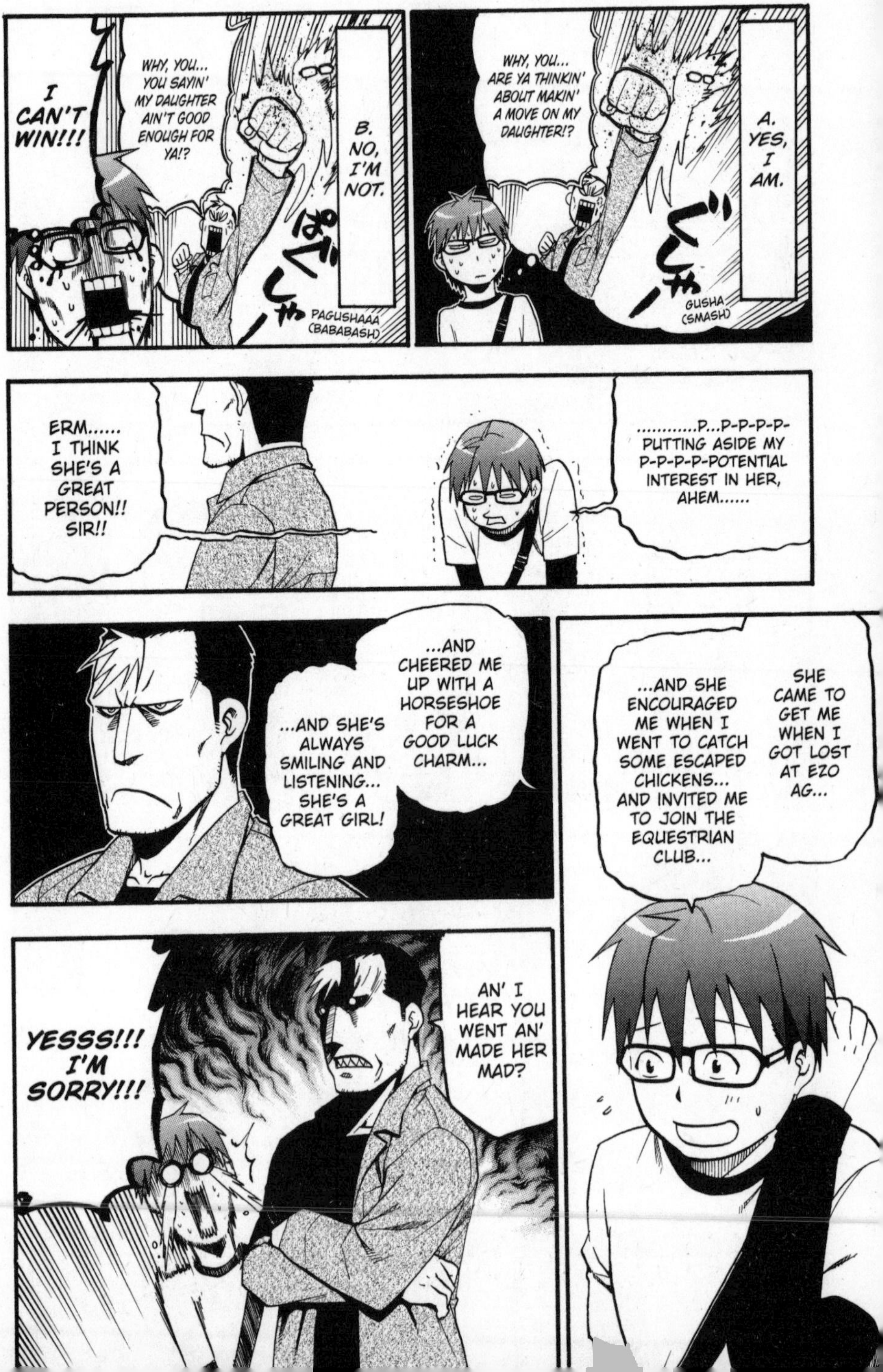
A. YES, I AM.
WHY, YOU... ARE YA THINKIN' ABOUT MAKIN' A MOVE ON MY DAUGHTER!?
GUSHA (SMASH)
B. NO, I'M NOT.
WHY, YOU... YOU SAYIN' MY DAUGHTER AIN'T GOOD ENOUGH FOR YA!?
I CAN'T WIN!!!
PAGUSHAAA (BABABASH)
............P...P-P-P-P- PUTTING ASIDE MY P-P-P-P-POTENTIAL INTEREST IN HER, AHEM......
ERM...... I THINK SHE'S A GREAT PERSON!! SIR!!
SHE CAME TO GET ME WHEN I GOT LOST AT EZO AG...
...AND SHE ENCOURAGED ME WHEN I WENT TO CATCH SOME ESCAPED CHICKENS... AND INVITED ME TO JOIN THE EQUESTRIAN CLUB...
...AND CHEERED ME UP WITH A HORSESHOE FOR A GOOD LUCK CHARM...
...AND SHE'S ALWAYS SMILING AND LISTENING... SHE'S A GREAT GIRL!
AN' I HEAR YOU WENT AN' MADE HER MAD?
YESSS!!! I'M SORRY!!!

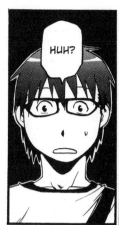

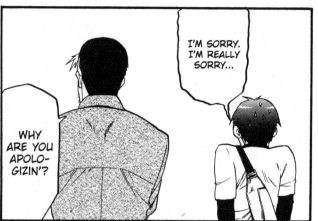

I'M SORRY. I'M REALLY SORRY...
WHY ARE YOU APOLO-GIZIN'?
HUH?
DAD! ARE YOU PICKING ON HACHIKEN-KUN AGAIN?
I'M READY NOW.
I AIN'T PICKIN' ON HIM.
I WAS JUST WONDERIN' WHETHER YOU TWO MADE UP OR NOT.
AH.
RIGHT... I FORGOT. WE HAD THAT FIGHT......
STRAIGHT FROM ONE AWKWARD SITUATION TO ANOTHER ...
GATA (RATTLE) ガタ
GOTO (RUMBLE) ゴト
ガタ GATA
GOTO ゴト
GATA ガタ
GOTO

Chapter 42:

Tale of Autumn ⑪

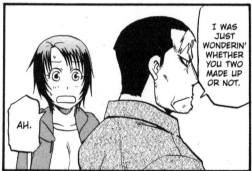

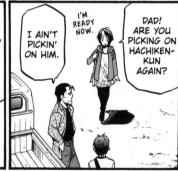

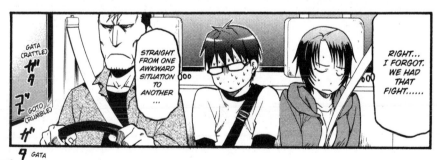

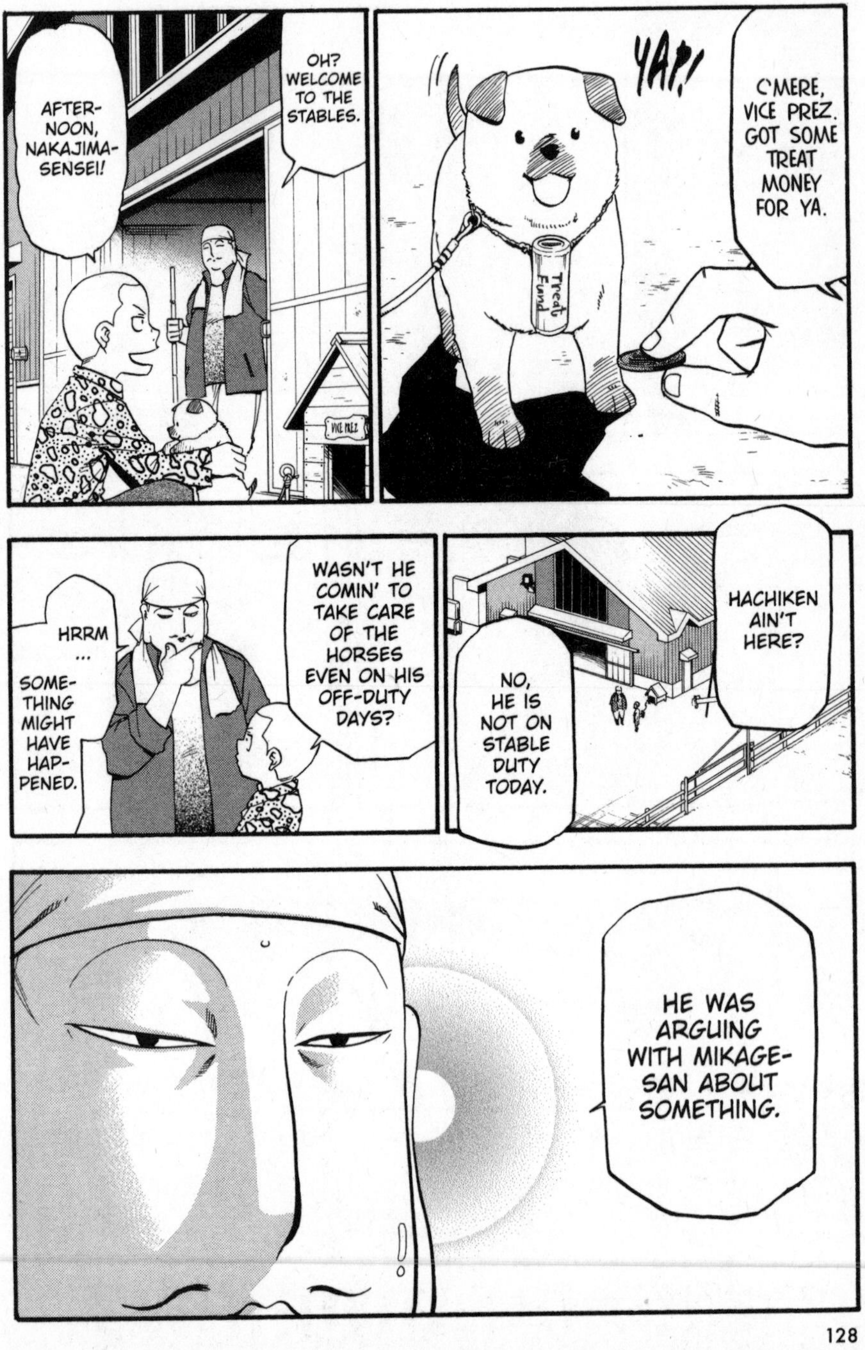
C'MERE, VICE PREZ. GOT SOME TREAT MONEY FOR YA.
YAP!
Treat Fund
OH? WELCOME TO THE STABLES.
AFTERNOON, NAKAJIMA-SENSEI!
VICE PREZ
HACHIKEN AIN'T HERE?
NO, HE IS NOT ON STABLE DUTY TODAY.
WASN'T HE COMIN' TO TAKE CARE OF THE HORSES EVEN ON HIS OFF-DUTY DAYS?
HRRM ...
SOMETHING MIGHT HAVE HAPPENED.
HE WAS ARGUING WITH MIKAGE-SAN ABOUT SOMETHING.

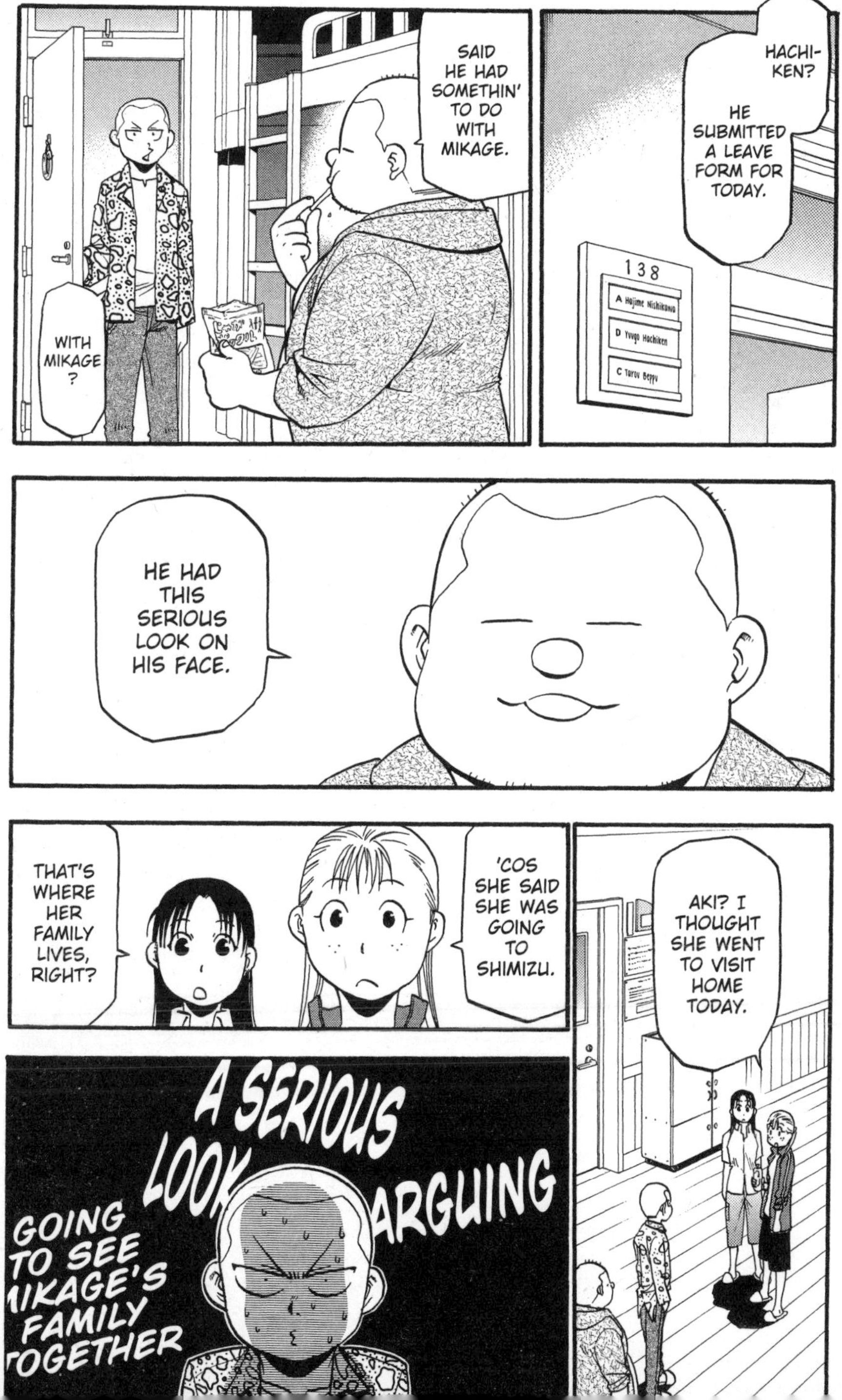
HACHI-KEN?
HE SUBMITTED A LEAVE FORM FOR TODAY.
138
A Hajime Nishikawa
D Yuugo Hachiken
C Tarou Beppu
SAID HE HAD SOMETHIN' TO DO WITH MIKAGE.
WITH MIKAGE?
HE HAD THIS SERIOUS LOOK ON HIS FACE.
AKI? I THOUGHT SHE WENT TO VISIT HOME TODAY.
'COS SHE SAID SHE WAS GOING TO SHIMIZU.
THAT'S WHERE HER FAMILY LIVES, RIGHT?
A SERIOUS LOOK
ARGUING
GOING TO SEE IKAGE'S FAMILY TOGETHER

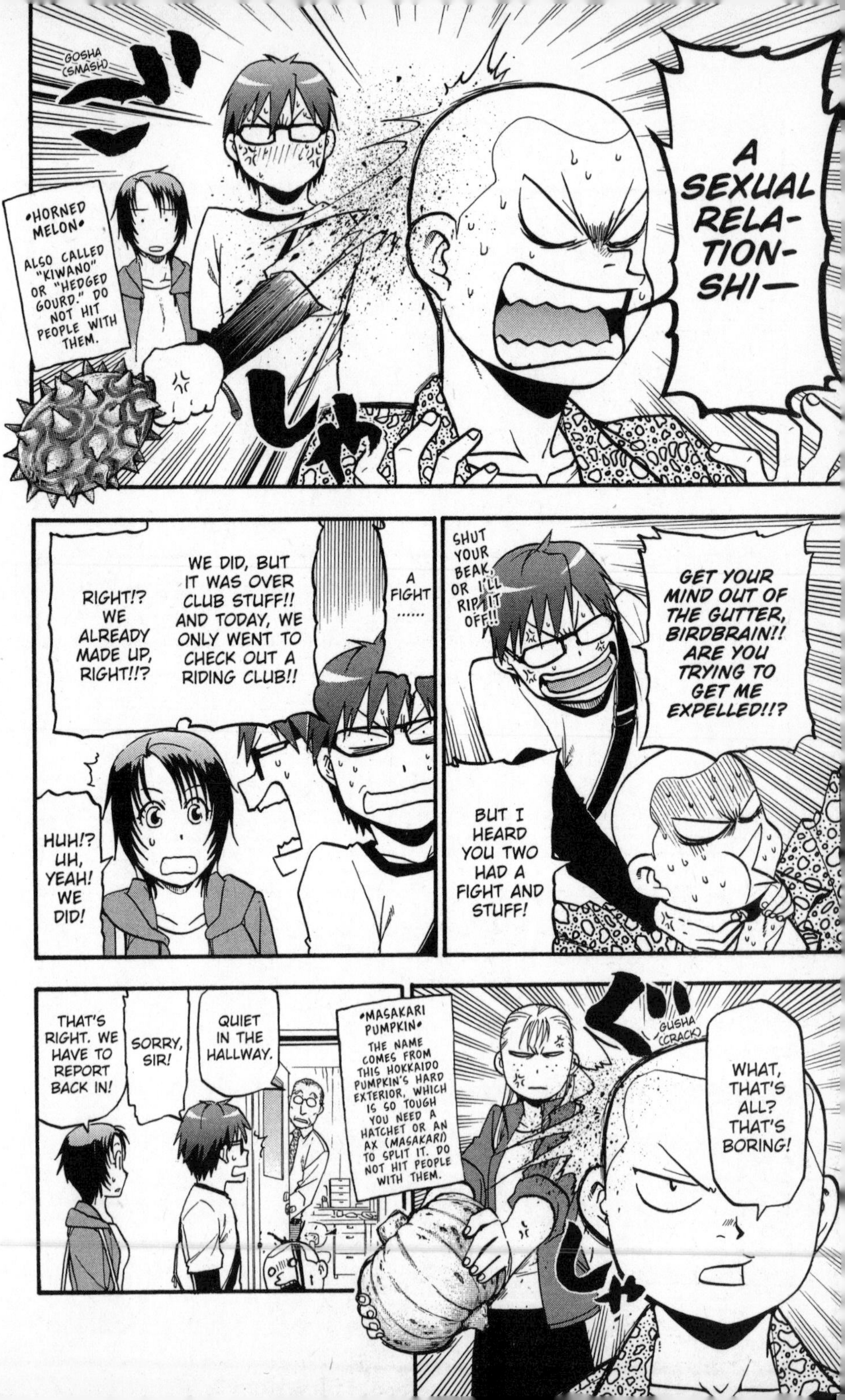
A SEXUAL RELA-TION-SHI—
GOSHA (SMASH)
•HORNED MELON• ALSO CALLED "KIWANO" OR "HEDGED GOURD." DO NOT HIT PEOPLE WITH THEM.
GET YOUR MIND OUT OF THE GUTTER, BIRDBRAIN!! ARE YOU TRYING TO GET ME EXPELLED!!?
SHUT YOUR BEAK, OR I'LL RIP IT OFF!!
BUT I HEARD YOU TWO HAD A FIGHT AND STUFF!
A FIGHT......
WE DID, BUT IT WAS OVER CLUB STUFF!! AND TODAY, WE ONLY WENT TO CHECK OUT A RIDING CLUB!!
RIGHT!? WE ALREADY MADE UP, RIGHT!!?
HUH!? UH, YEAH! WE DID!
GUSHA (CRACK)
WHAT, THAT'S ALL? THAT'S BORING!
•MASAKARI PUMPKIN• THE NAME COMES FROM THIS HOKKAIDO PUMPKIN'S HARD EXTERIOR, WHICH IS SO TOUGH YOU NEED A HATCHET OR AN AX (MASAKARI) TO SPLIT IT. DO NOT HIT PEOPLE WITH THEM.
QUIET IN THE HALLWAY.
SORRY, SIR!
THAT'S RIGHT. WE HAVE TO REPORT BACK IN!

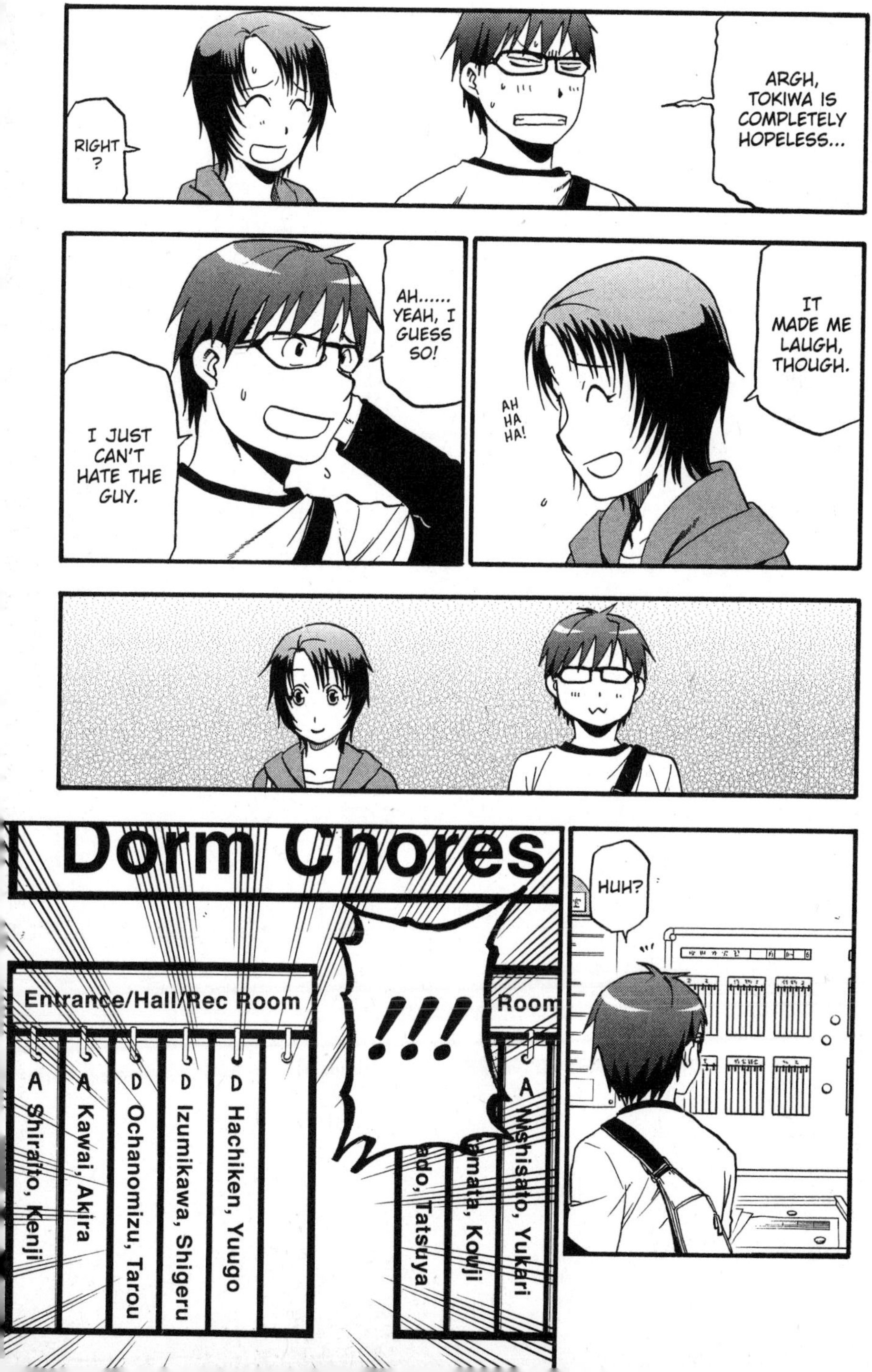
ARGH, TOKIWA IS COMPLETELY HOPELESS...
RIGHT?
IT MADE ME LAUGH, THOUGH.
AH HA HA!
AH...... YEAH, I GUESS SO!
I JUST CAN'T HATE THE GUY.
HUH?
Dorm Chores
!!!
Entrance/Hall/Rec Room
A Shiraito, Kenji
A Kawai, Akira
D Ochanomizu, Tarou
D Izumikawa, Shigeru
D Hachiken, Yuugo
Room

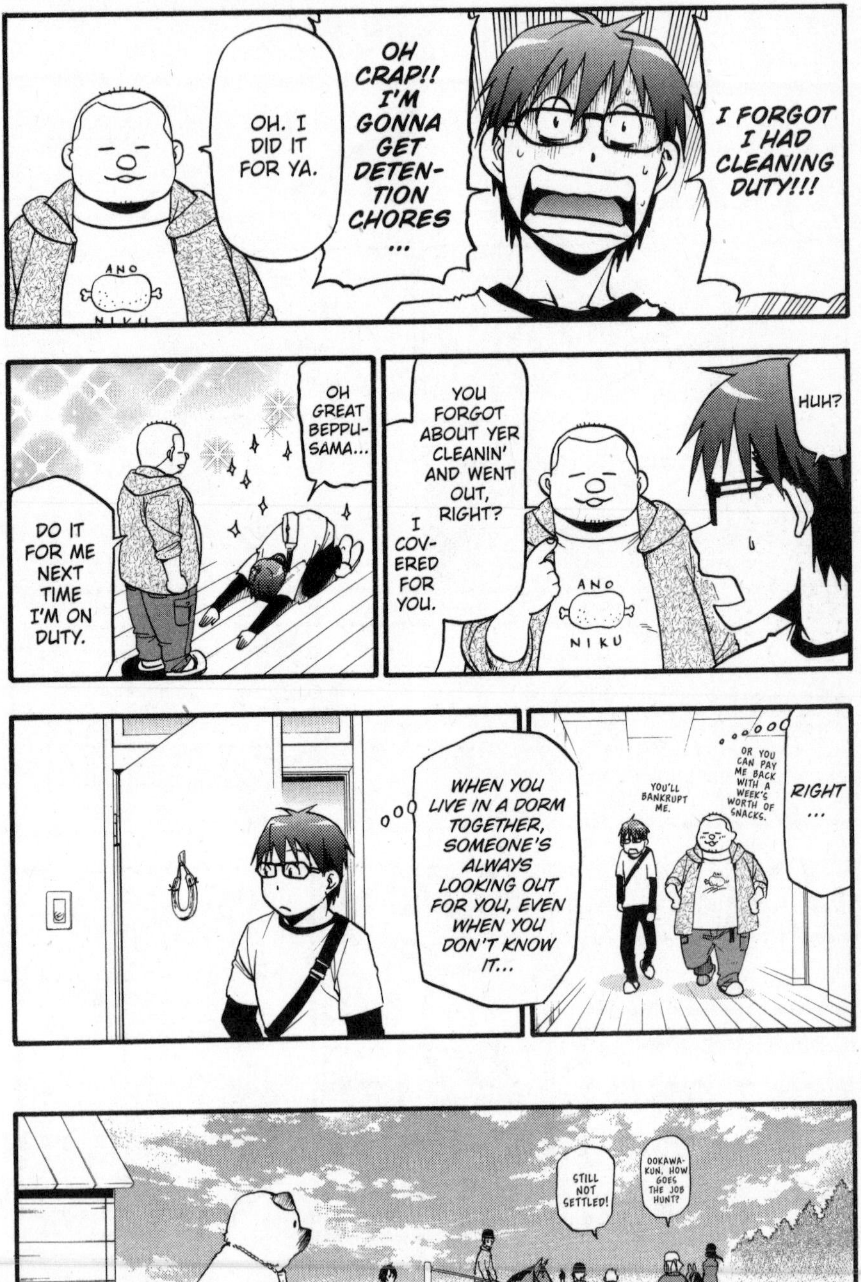
I FORGOT I HAD CLEANING DUTY!!!
OH CRAP!! I'M GONNA GET DETEN-TION CHORES ...
OH. I DID IT FOR YA.
ANO NIKU
HUH?
YOU FORGOT ABOUT YER CLEANIN' AND WENT OUT, RIGHT?
I COV-ERED FOR YOU.
OH GREAT BEPPU-SAMA...
DO IT FOR ME NEXT TIME I'M ON DUTY.
RIGHT ...
OR YOU CAN PAY ME BACK WITH A WEEK'S WORTH OF SNACKS.
YOU'LL BANKRUPT ME.
WHEN YOU LIVE IN A DORM TOGETHER, SOMEONE'S ALWAYS LOOKING OUT FOR YOU, EVEN WHEN YOU DON'T KNOW IT...
OOKAWA-KUN, HOW GOES THE JOB HUNT?
STILL NOT SETTLED!

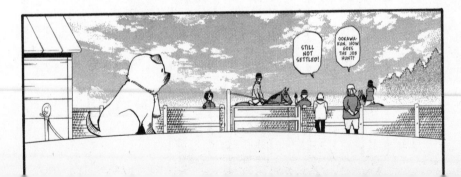

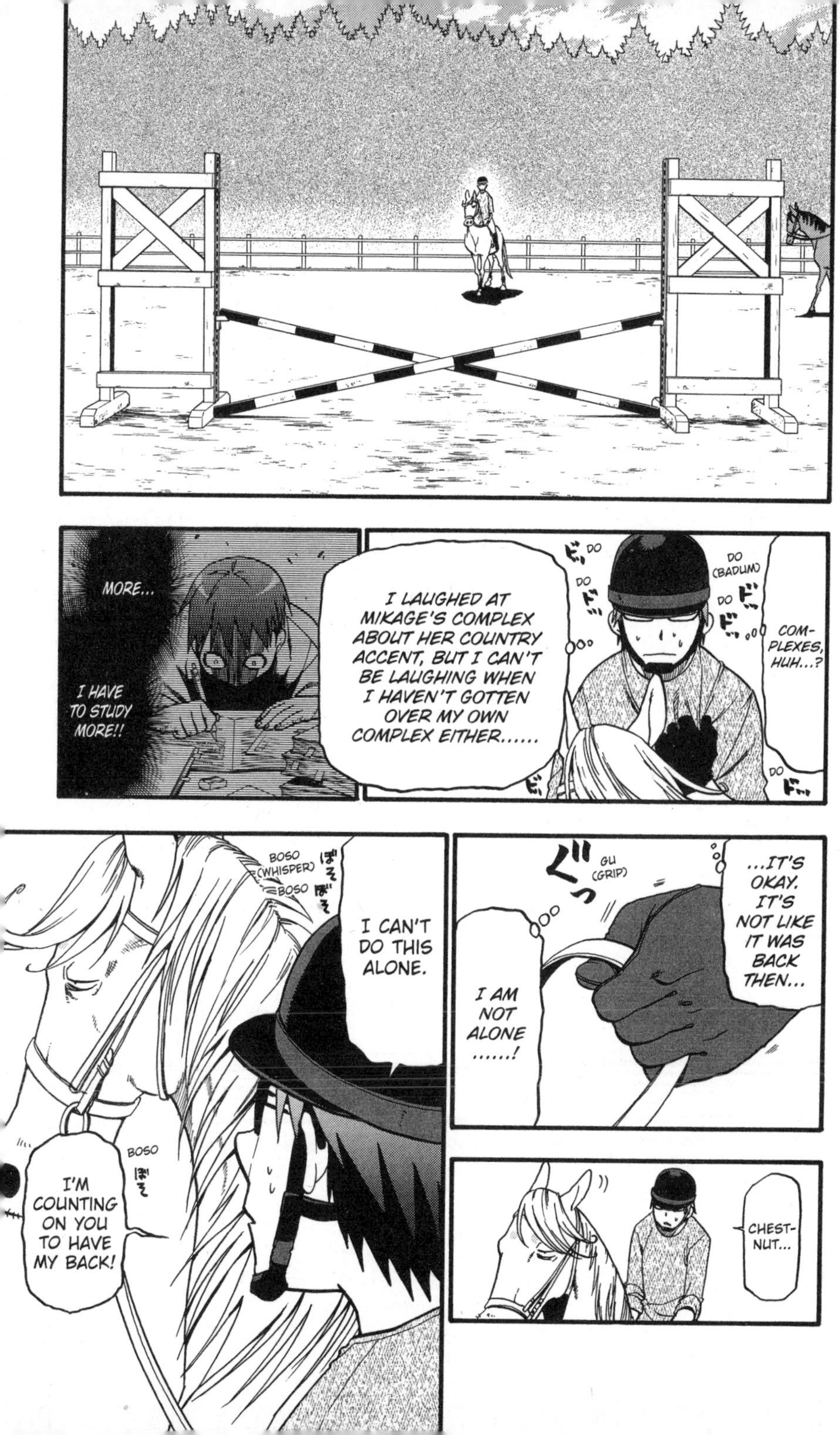

DO (BADUM)
DO
COMPLEXES, HUH...?
DO
DO
DO
I LAUGHED AT MIKAGE'S COMPLEX ABOUT HER COUNTRY ACCENT, BUT I CAN'T BE LAUGHING WHEN I HAVEN'T GOTTEN OVER MY OWN COMPLEX EITHER......
MORE...
I HAVE TO STUDY MORE!!
...IT'S OKAY. IT'S NOT LIKE IT WAS BACK THEN...
GU (GRIP)
I AM NOT ALONE ......!
CHEST-NUT...
BOSO (WHISPER)
BOSO
I CAN'T DO THIS ALONE.
BOSO
I'M COUNTING ON YOU TO HAVE MY BACK!

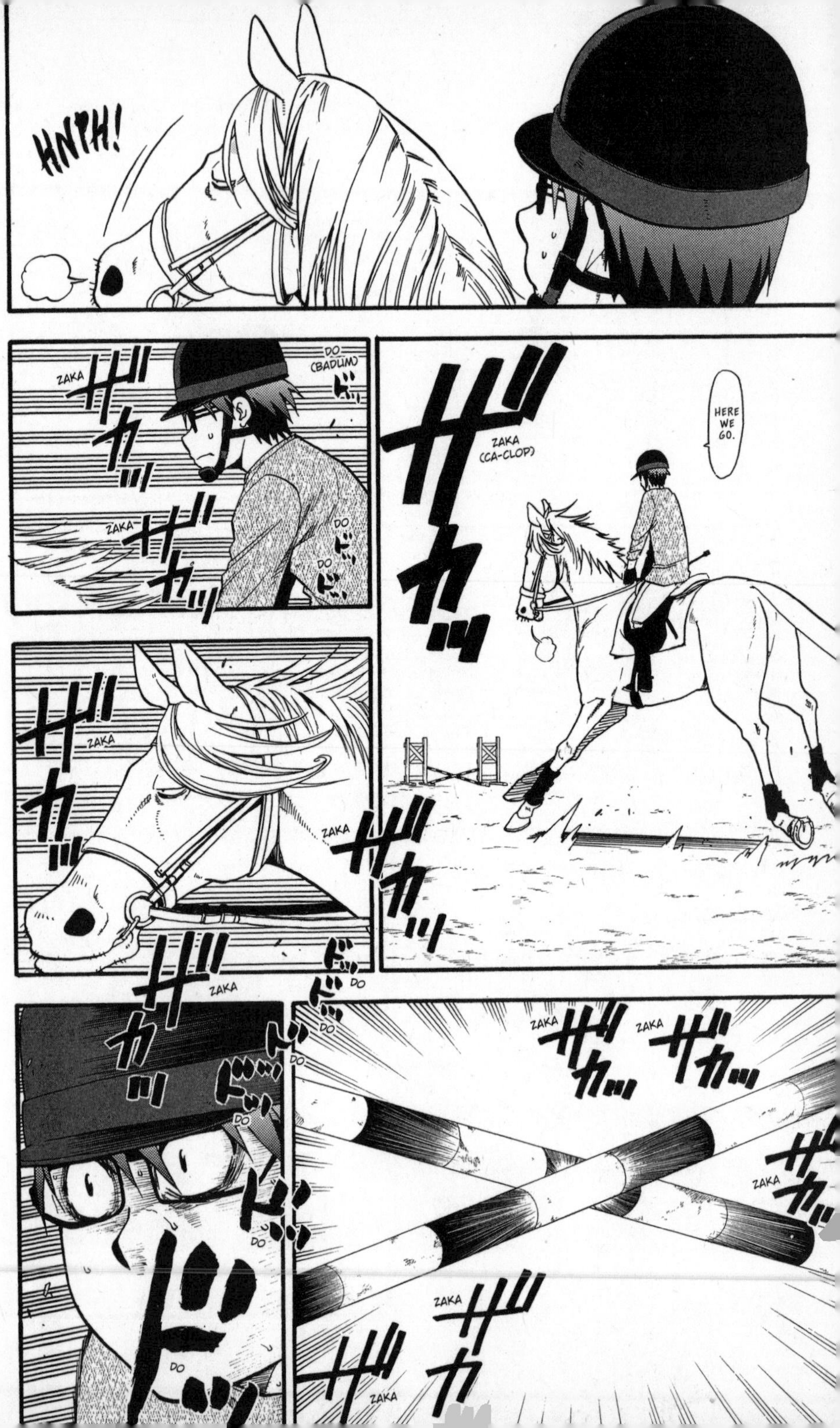
HNPH!
ZAKA (CA-CLOP)
HERE WE GO.
ZAKA
DO (BADUM)
ZAKA
DO
DO
ZAKA
ZAKA
ZAKA
ZAKA
ZAKA
ZAKA
ZAKA
ZAKA
ZAKA
DO
DO
DO
DO
DO
DO

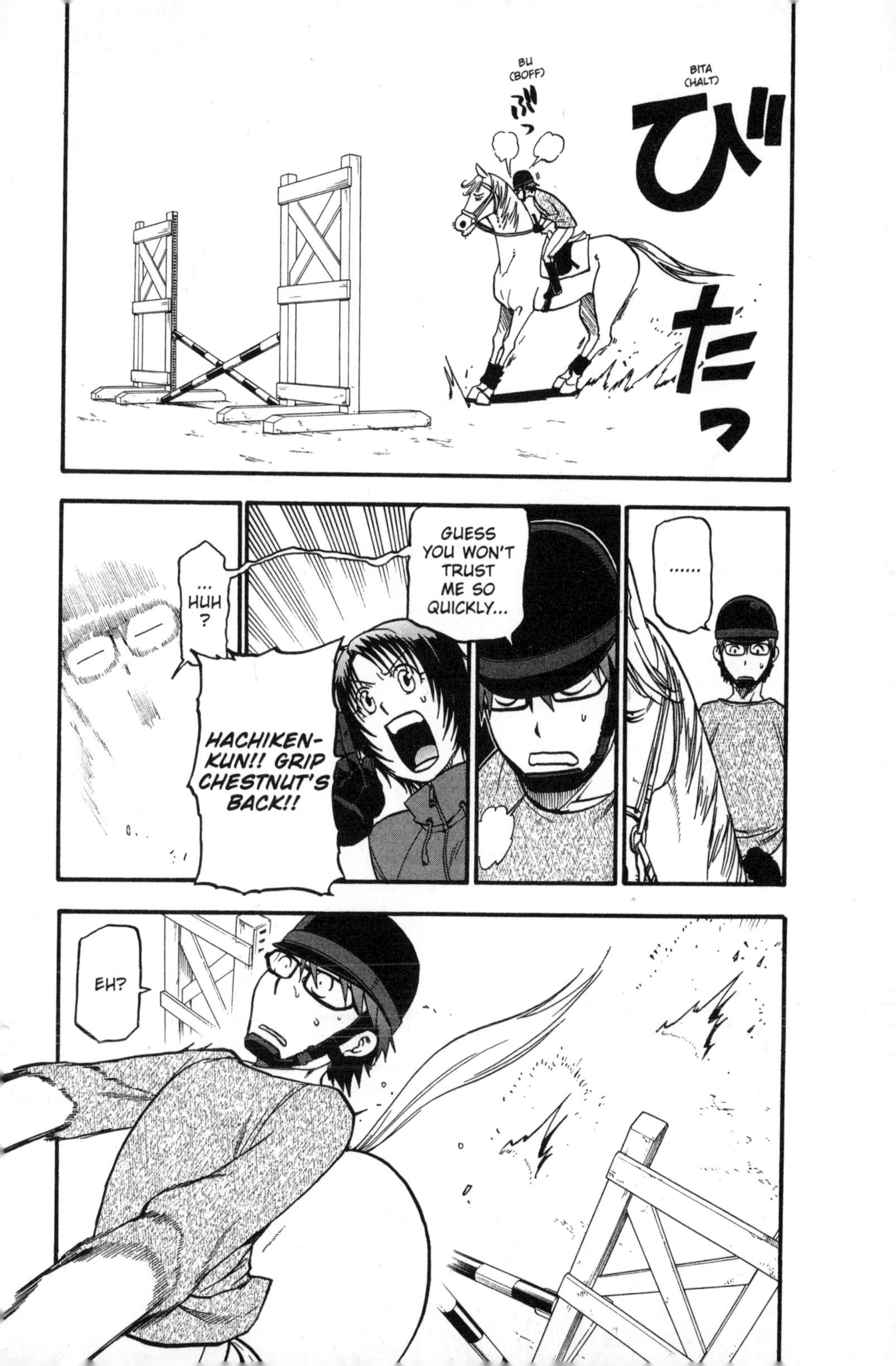
BITA
(HALT)
びたっ
BU
(BOFF)
ぶっ
......
GUESS YOU WON'T TRUST ME SO QUICKLY...
HACHIKEN-KUN!! GRIP CHESTNUT'S BACK!!
... HUH ?
EH?

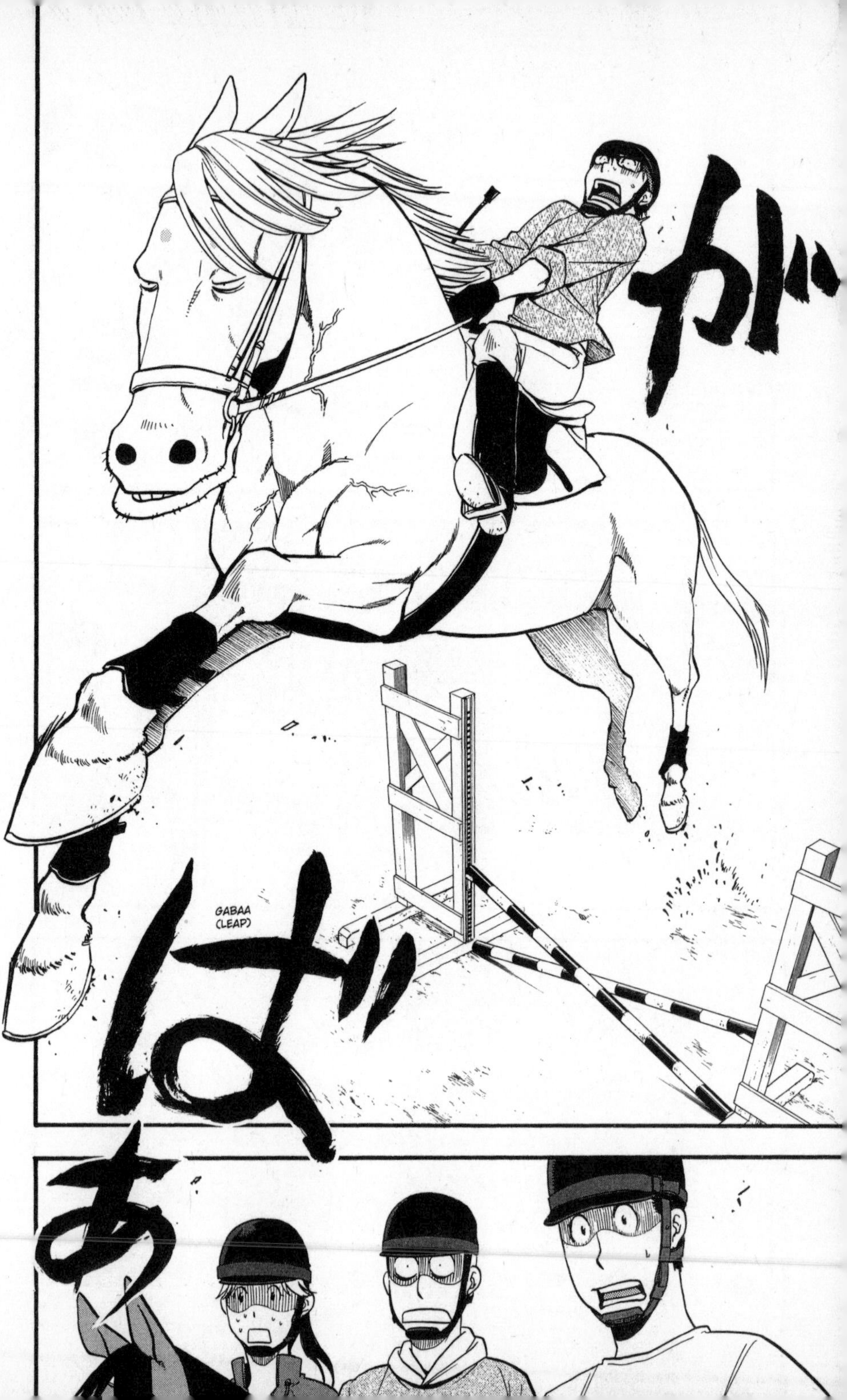
ガ
GABAA
(LEAP)
ばあ

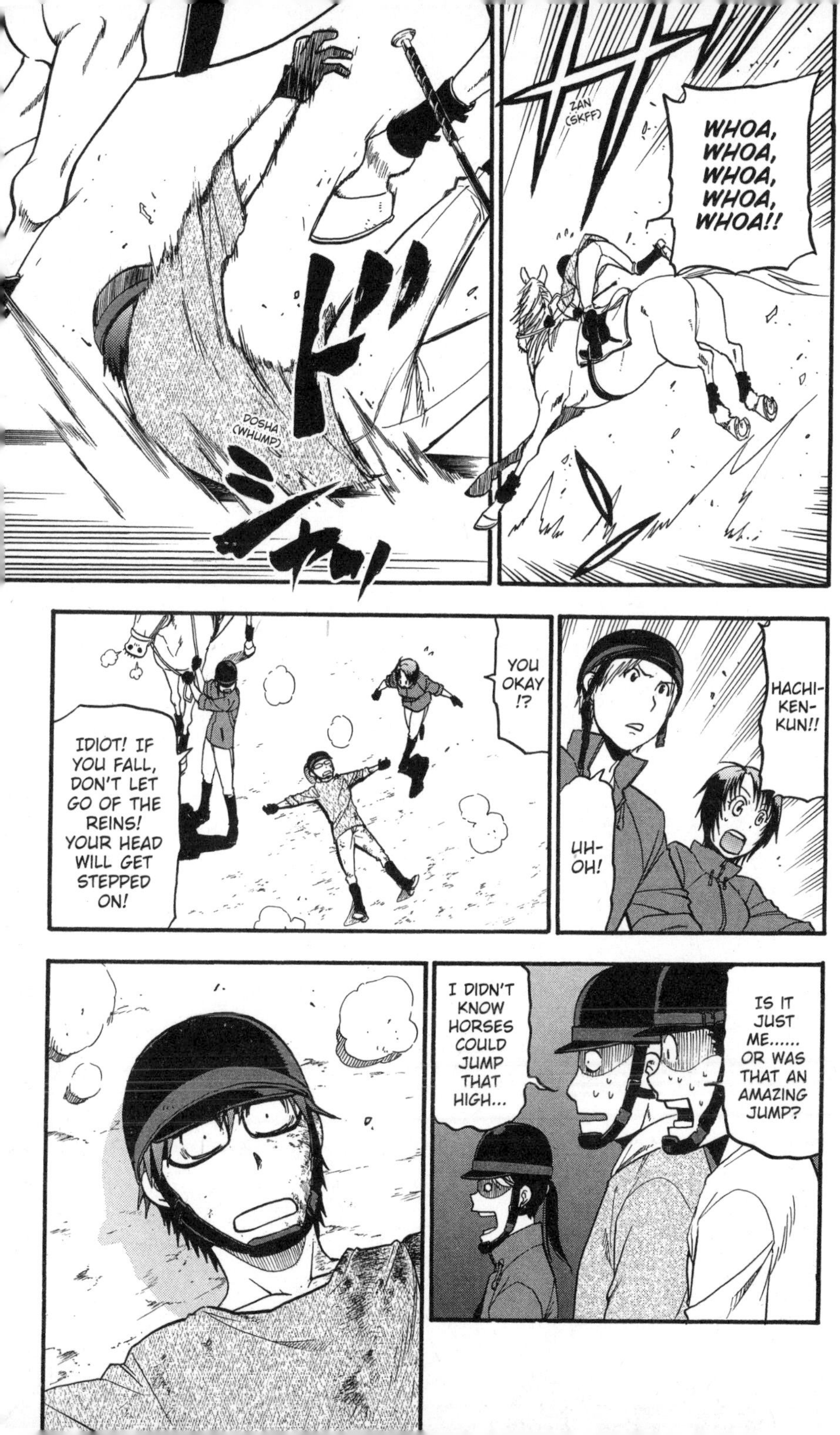
ZAN (SKFF)
WHOA, WHOA, WHOA, WHOA, WHOA!!
DOSHA (WHUMP)
HACHI-KEN-KUN!!
UH-OH!
YOU OKAY!?
IDIOT! IF YOU FALL, DON'T LET GO OF THE REINS! YOUR HEAD WILL GET STEPPED ON!
IS IT JUST ME...... OR WAS THAT AN AMAZING JUMP?
I DIDN'T KNOW HORSES COULD JUMP THAT HIGH...

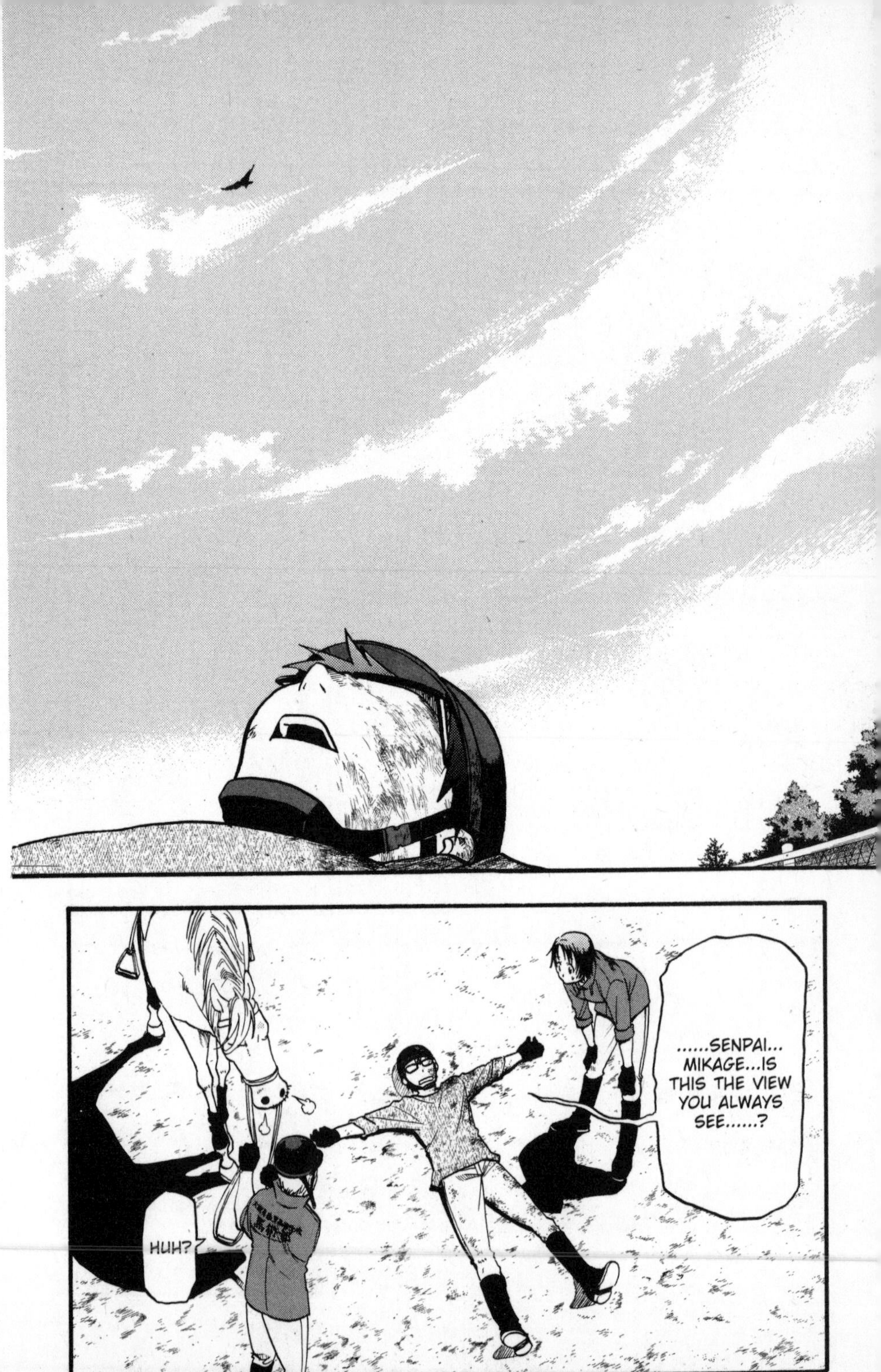
......SENPAI... MIKAGE...IS THIS THE VIEW YOU ALWAYS SEE......?
HUH?

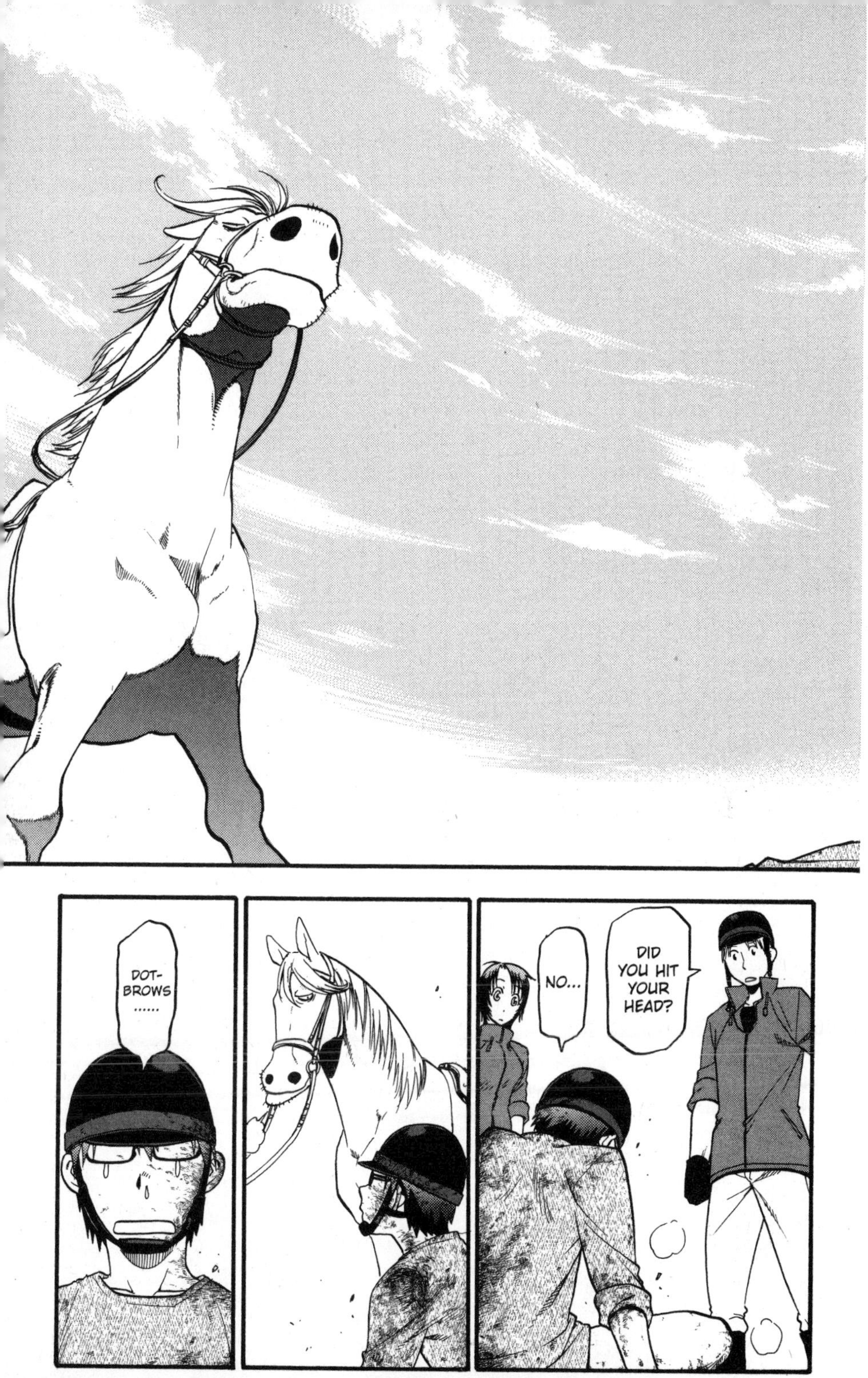
DID YOU HIT YOUR HEAD?
NO...
DOT-BROWS ......

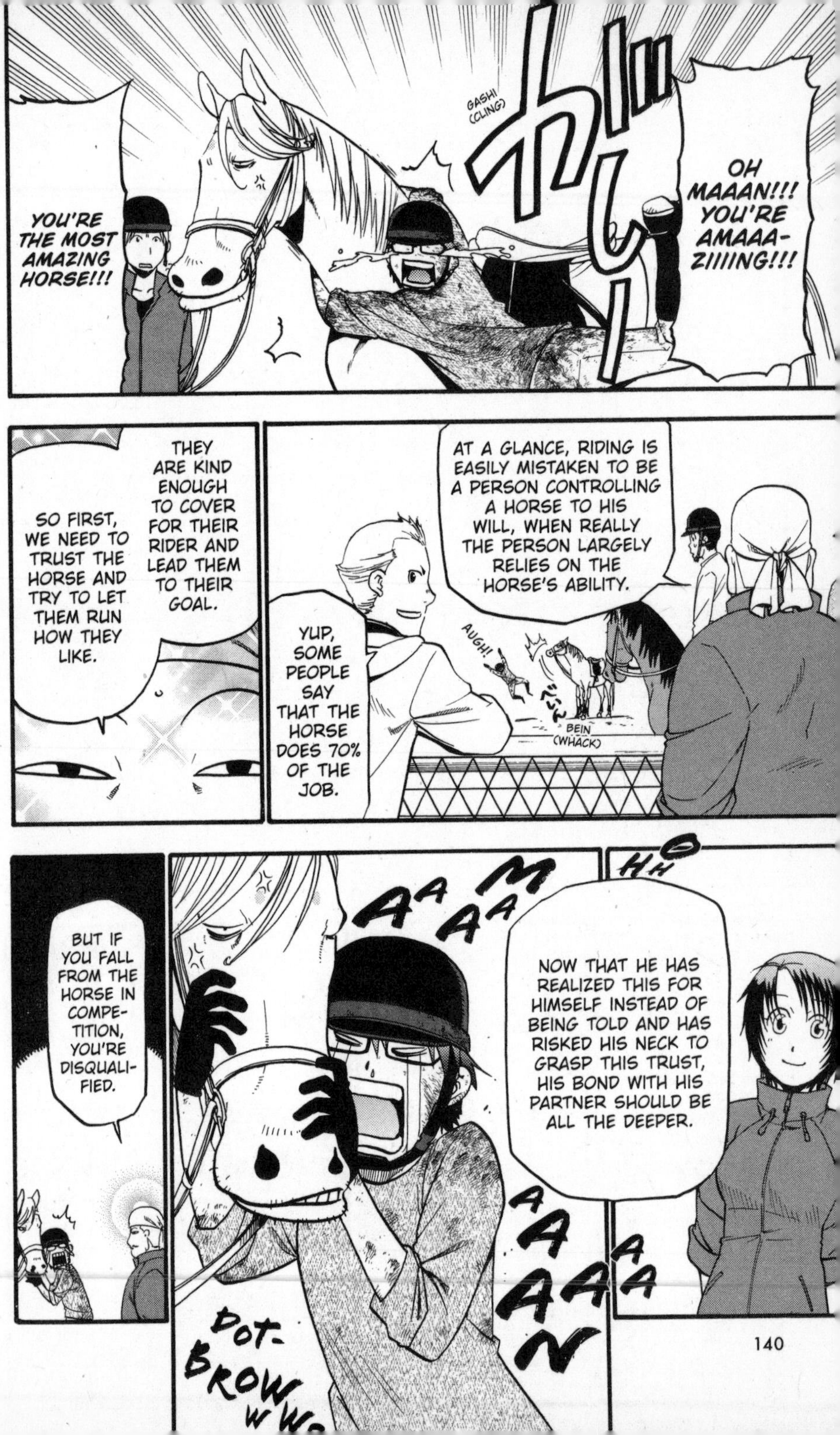
OH MAAAN!!! YOU'RE AMAAA-ZIIIING!!!
GASHI (CLING)
YOU'RE THE MOST AMAZING HORSE!!!
AT A GLANCE, RIDING IS EASILY MISTAKEN TO BE A PERSON CONTROLLING A HORSE TO HIS WILL, WHEN REALLY THE PERSON LARGELY RELIES ON THE HORSE'S ABILITY.
AUGH!
BEIN (WHACK)
YUP, SOME PEOPLE SAY THAT THE HORSE DOES 70% OF THE JOB.
THEY ARE KIND ENOUGH TO COVER FOR THEIR RIDER AND LEAD THEM TO THEIR GOAL.
SO FIRST, WE NEED TO TRUST THE HORSE AND TRY TO LET THEM RUN HOW THEY LIKE.
NOW THAT HE HAS REALIZED THIS FOR HIMSELF INSTEAD OF BEING TOLD AND HAS RISKED HIS NECK TO GRASP THIS TRUST, HIS BOND WITH HIS PARTNER SHOULD BE ALL THE DEEPER.
MAAAAAAAAAAAAAN
DOT-BROWWW
BUT IF YOU FALL FROM THE HORSE IN COMPE-TITION, YOU'RE DISQUALI-FIED.

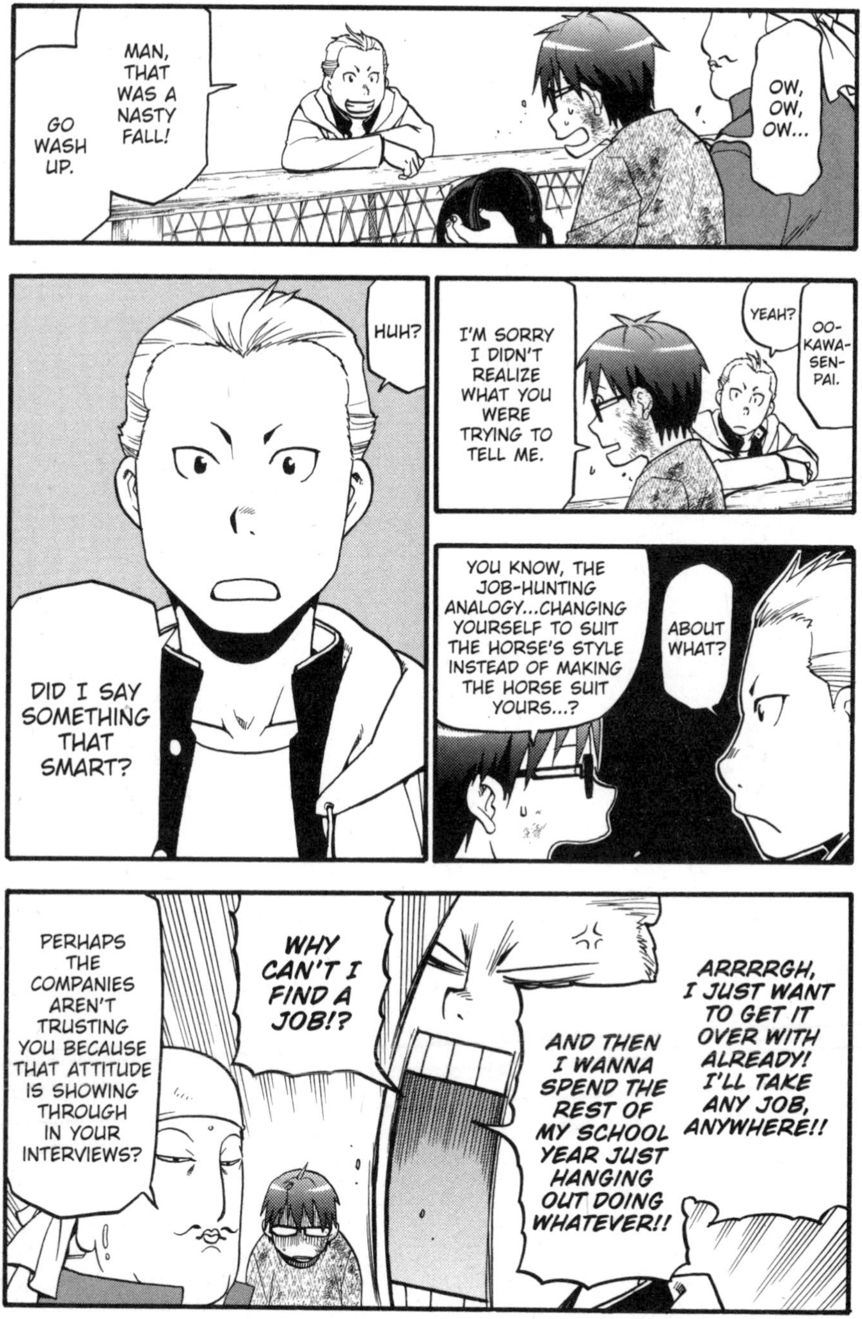
OW, OW, OW...
MAN, THAT WAS A NASTY FALL!
GO WASH UP.
OO-KAWA-SENPAI.
YEAH?
I'M SORRY I DIDN'T REALIZE WHAT YOU WERE TRYING TO TELL ME.
ABOUT WHAT?
YOU KNOW, THE JOB-HUNTING ANALOGY...CHANGING YOURSELF TO SUIT THE HORSE'S STYLE INSTEAD OF MAKING THE HORSE SUIT YOURS...?
HUH?
DID I SAY SOMETHING THAT SMART?
ARRRRGH, I JUST WANT TO GET IT OVER WITH ALREADY! I'LL TAKE ANY JOB, ANYWHERE!!
AND THEN I WANNA SPEND THE REST OF MY SCHOOL YEAR JUST HANGING OUT DOING WHATEVER!!
WHY CAN'T I FIND A JOB!?
PERHAPS THE COMPANIES AREN'T TRUSTING YOU BECAUSE THAT ATTITUDE IS SHOWING THROUGH IN YOUR INTERVIEWS?

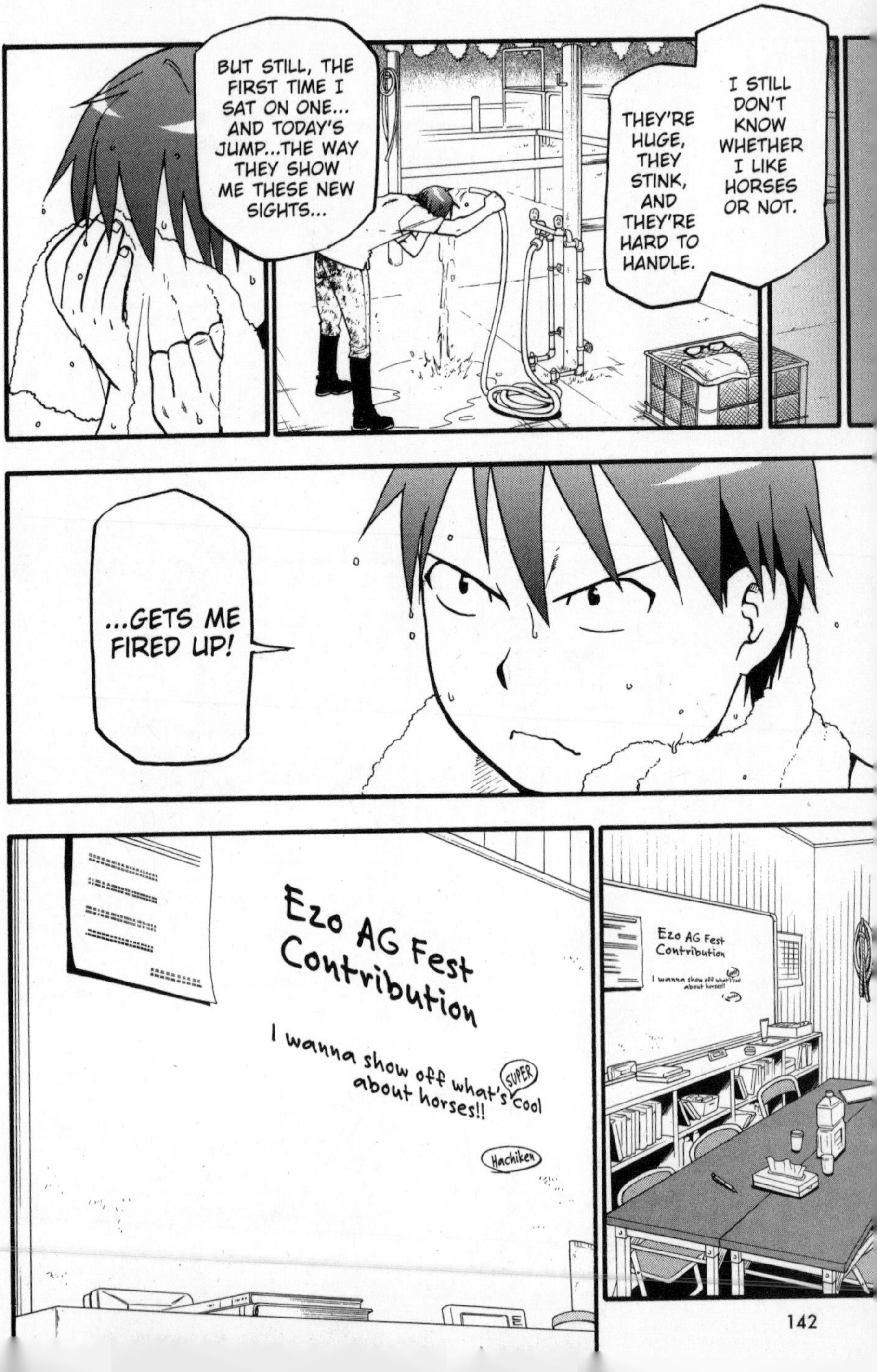
I STILL DON'T KNOW WHETHER I LIKE HORSES OR NOT.
THEY'RE HUGE, THEY STINK, AND THEY'RE HARD TO HANDLE.
BUT STILL, THE FIRST TIME I SAT ON ONE... AND TODAY'S JUMP...THE WAY THEY SHOW ME THESE NEW SIGHTS...
...GETS ME FIRED UP!
Ezo AG Fest Contribution
Ezo AG Fest Contribution
I wanna show off what's SUPER cool about horses!!
Hachiken

Silver Spoon

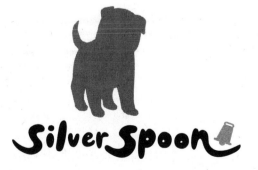

EQUESTRIAN CLUB

YOSHIYUKI NAKAJIMA

YOU MIGHT THINK THE CHARACTERS FOR HIS NAME READ "MIYUKI," BUT NO. IT'S "YOSHIYUKI."

TEACHES FOOD CHEMISTRY

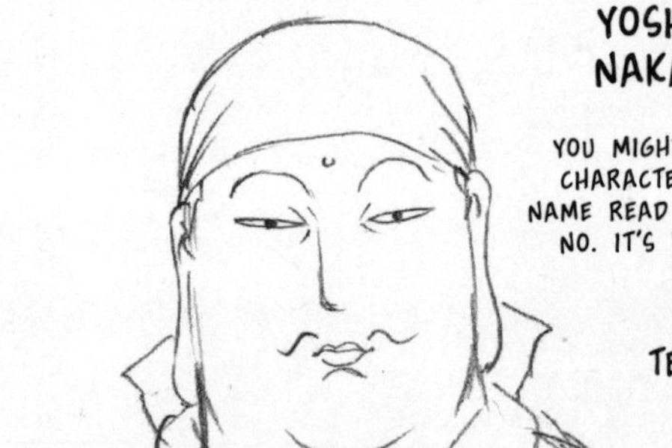

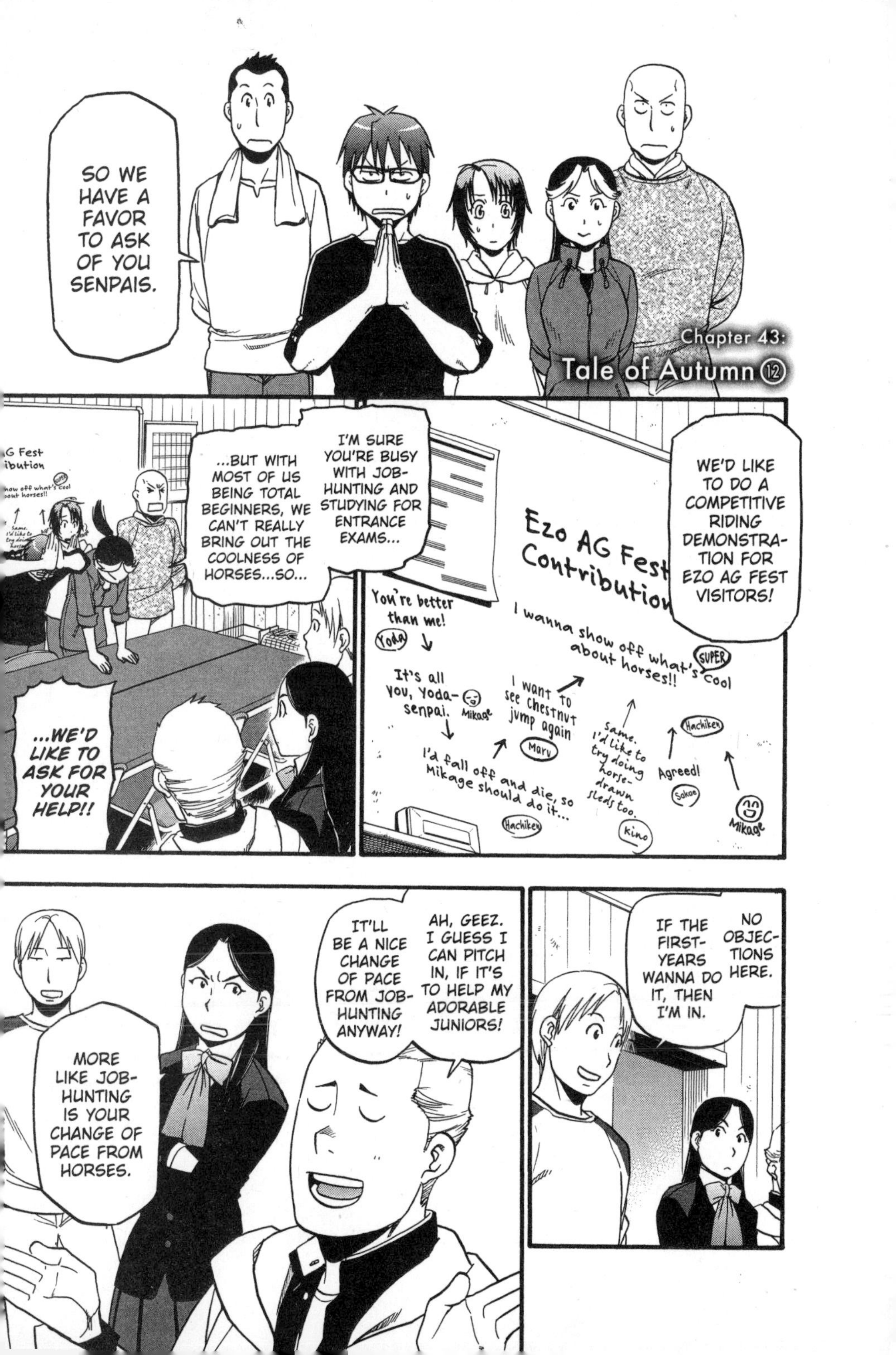
SO WE HAVE A FAVOR TO ASK OF YOU SENPAIS.
Chapter 43:
Tale of Autumn ⑫
WE'D LIKE TO DO A COMPETITIVE RIDING DEMONSTRATION FOR EZO AG FEST VISITORS!
Ezo AG Fest Contribution
I wanna show off what's cool about horses!! SUPER
Mikage
Agreed! Sakae
Hachiken
Same. I'd like to try doing horse-drawn sleds too. Kino
I want to see Chestnut jump again Maru
I'd fall off and die, so Mikage should do it... Hachiken
It's all you, Yoda-senpai. Mikage
You're better than me! Yoda
I'M SURE YOU'RE BUSY WITH JOB-HUNTING AND STUDYING FOR ENTRANCE EXAMS...
...BUT WITH MOST OF US BEING TOTAL BEGINNERS, WE CAN'T REALLY BRING OUT THE COOLNESS OF HORSES...SO...
...WE'D LIKE TO ASK FOR YOUR HELP!!
NO OBJECTIONS HERE.
IF THE FIRST-YEARS WANNA DO IT, THEN I'M IN.
AH, GEEZ. I GUESS I CAN PITCH IN, IF IT'S TO HELP MY ADORABLE JUNIORS!
IT'LL BE A NICE CHANGE OF PACE FROM JOB-HUNTING ANYWAY!
MORE LIKE JOB-HUNTING IS YOUR CHANGE OF PACE FROM HORSES.

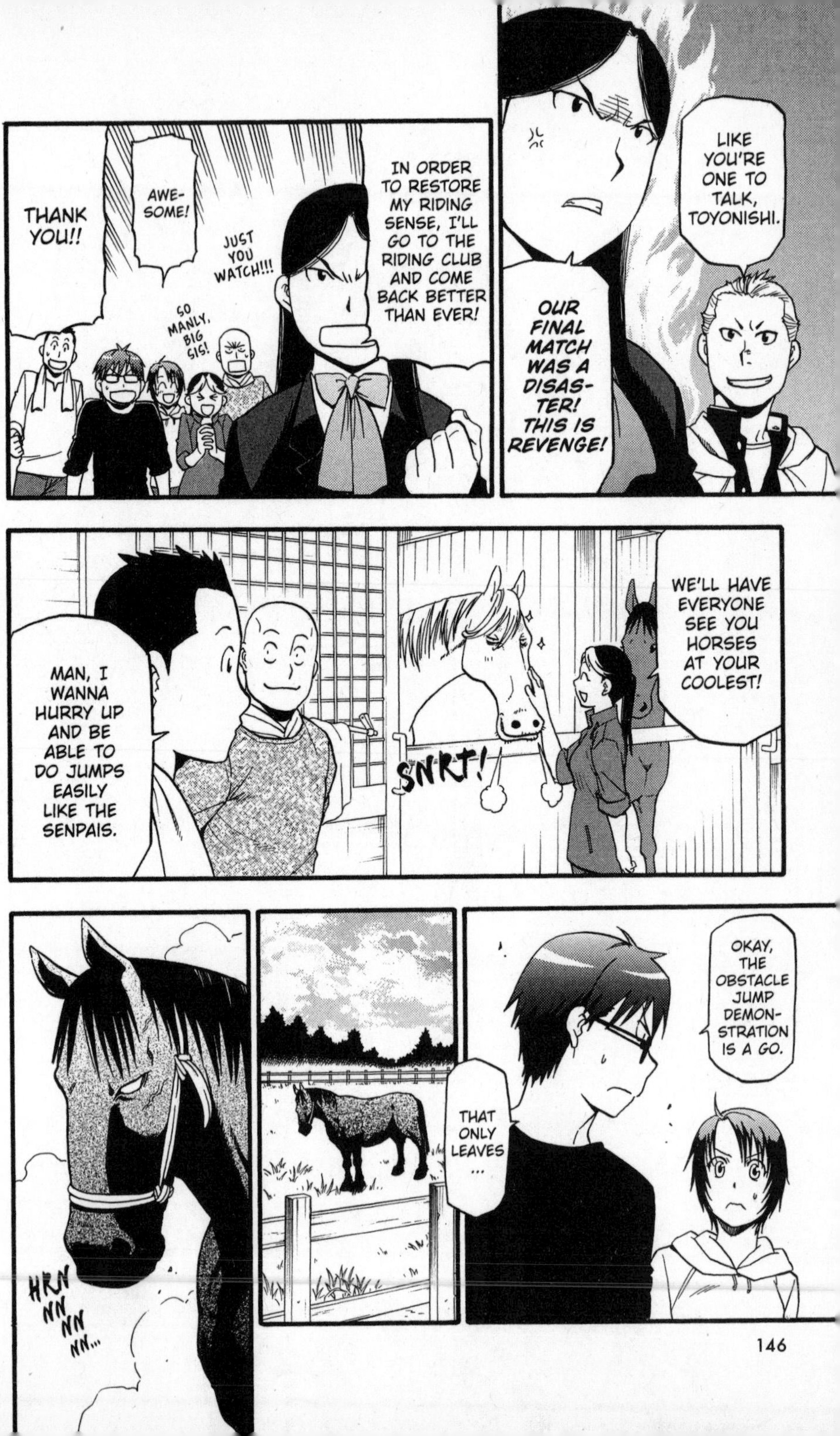
LIKE YOU'RE ONE TO TALK, TOYONISHI.
OUR FINAL MATCH WAS A DISASTER! THIS IS REVENGE!
IN ORDER TO RESTORE MY RIDING SENSE, I'LL GO TO THE RIDING CLUB AND COME BACK BETTER THAN EVER!
JUST YOU WATCH!!!
AWE-SOME!
SO MANLY, BIG SIS!
THANK YOU!!
WE'LL HAVE EVERYONE SEE YOU HORSES AT YOUR COOLEST!
SNRT!
MAN, I WANNA HURRY UP AND BE ABLE TO DO JUMPS EASILY LIKE THE SENPAIS.
OKAY, THE OBSTACLE JUMP DEMON-STRATION IS A GO.
THAT ONLY LEAVES ...
HRNNNNNNNN...

Chapter 43:

Tale of Autumn ⑫

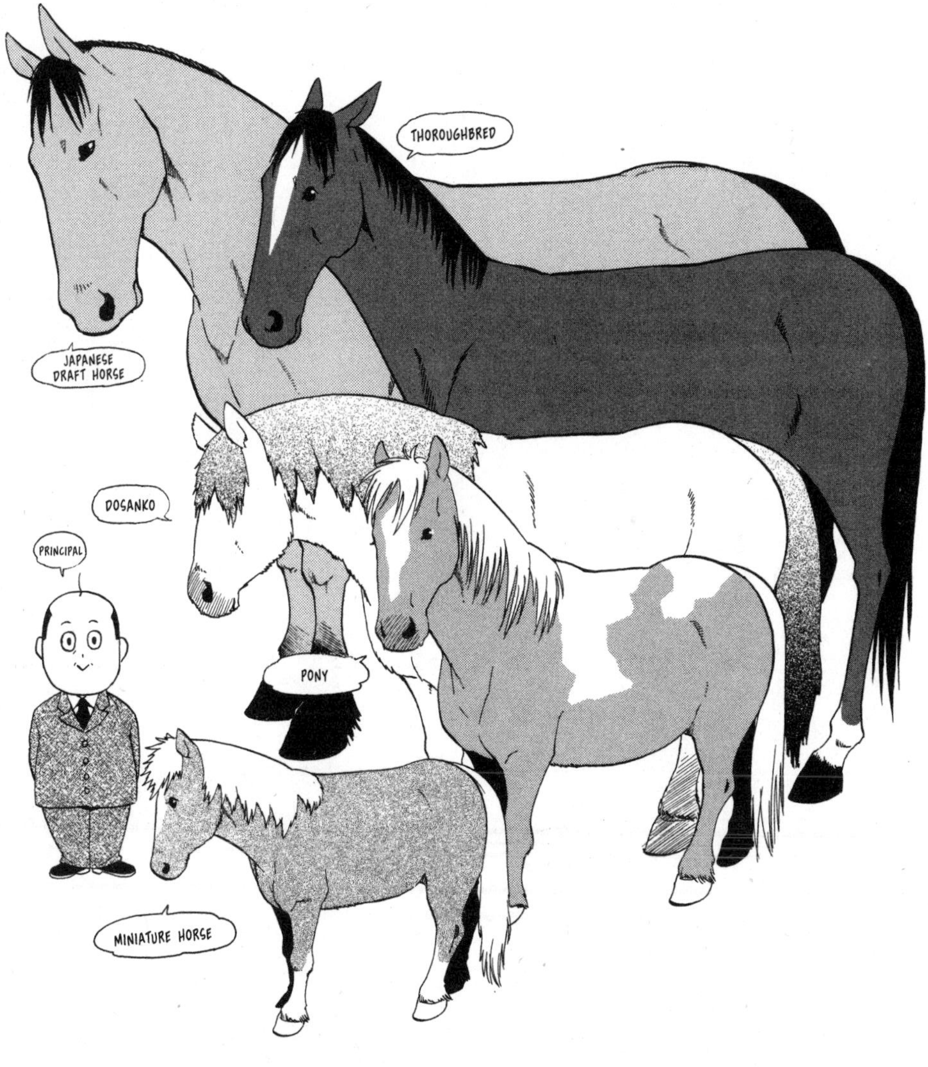
THOROUGHBRED
JAPANESE DRAFT HORSE
DOSANKO
PRINCIPAL
PONY
MINIATURE HORSE

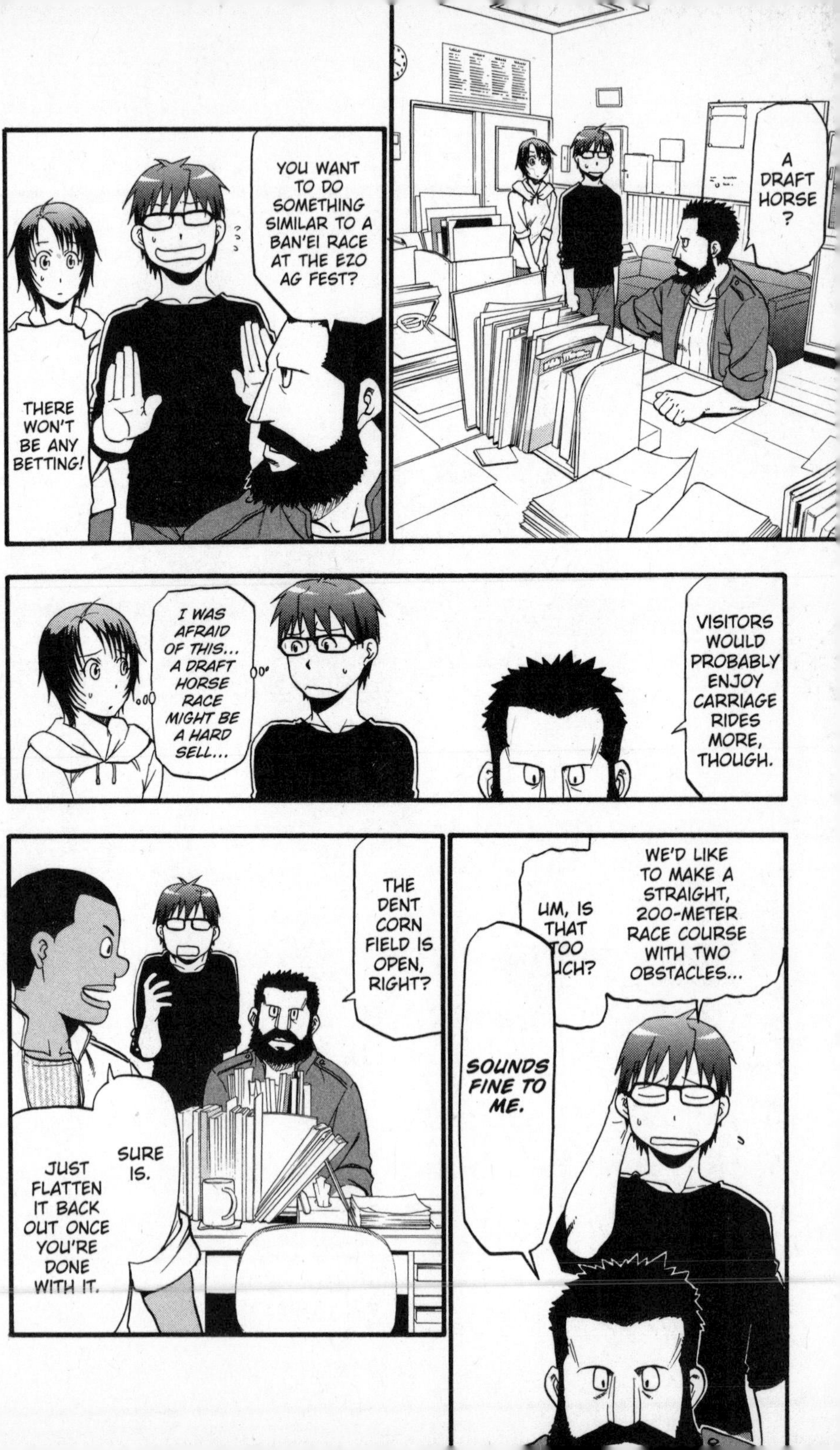
A DRAFT HORSE?
YOU WANT TO DO SOMETHING SIMILAR TO A BAN'EI RACE AT THE EZO AG FEST?
THERE WON'T BE ANY BETTING!
VISITORS WOULD PROBABLY ENJOY CARRIAGE RIDES MORE, THOUGH.
I WAS AFRAID OF THIS... A DRAFT HORSE RACE MIGHT BE A HARD SELL...
WE'D LIKE TO MAKE A STRAIGHT, 200-METER RACE COURSE WITH TWO OBSTACLES...
UM, IS THAT
SOUNDS FINE TO ME.
THE DENT CORN FIELD IS OPEN, RIGHT?
SURE IS.
JUST FLATTEN IT BACK OUT ONCE YOU'RE DONE WITH IT.

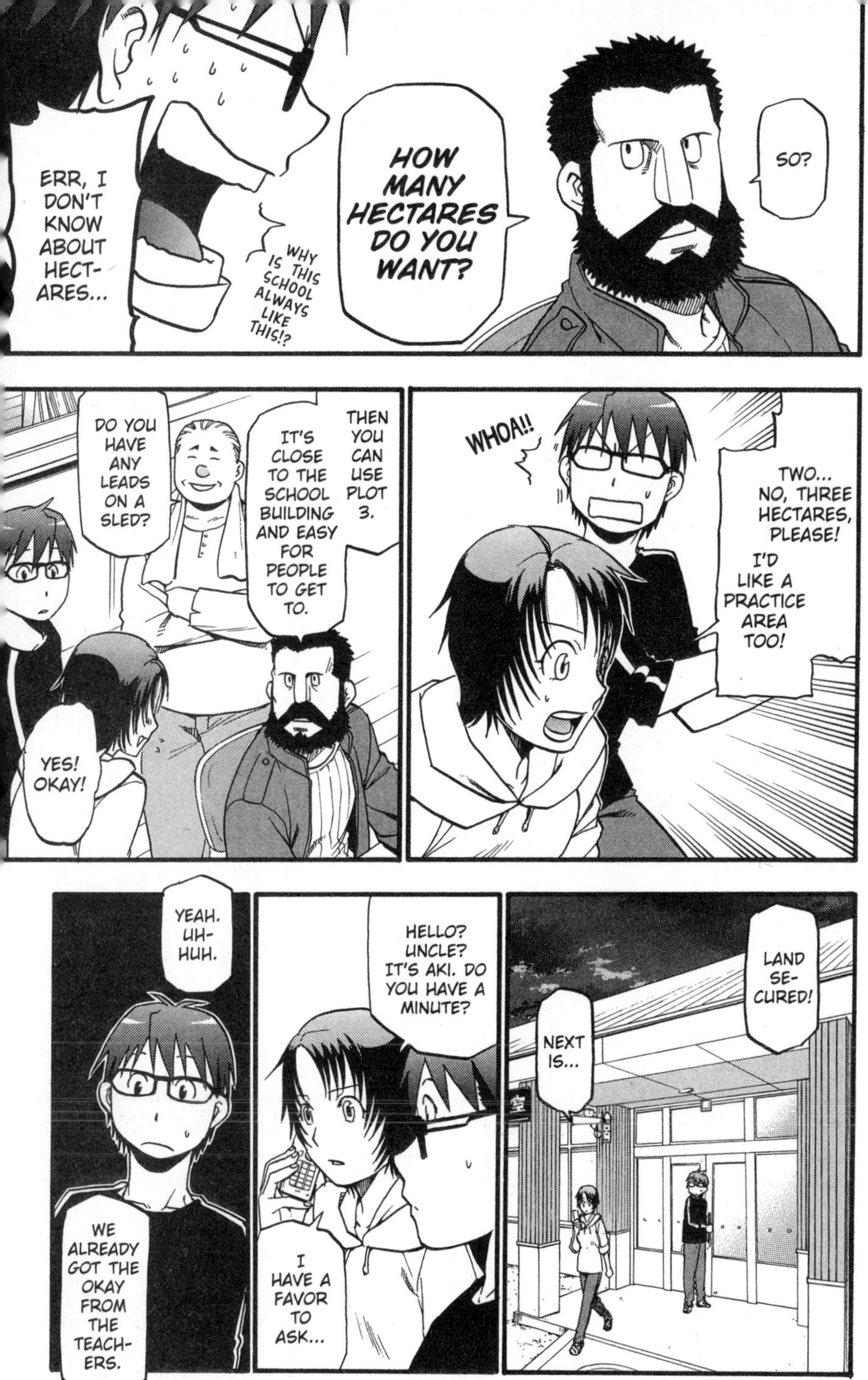
SO?
HOW MANY HECTARES DO YOU WANT?
WHY IS THIS SCHOOL ALWAYS LIKE THIS!?
ERR, I DON'T KNOW ABOUT HECT-ARES...
TWO... NO, THREE HECTARES, PLEASE!
I'D LIKE A PRACTICE AREA TOO!
WHOA!!
THEN YOU CAN USE PLOT 3.
IT'S CLOSE TO THE SCHOOL BUILDING AND EASY FOR PEOPLE TO GET TO.
DO YOU HAVE ANY LEADS ON A SLED?
YES! OKAY!
LAND SE-CURED!
NEXT IS...
HELLO? UNCLE? IT'S AKI. DO YOU HAVE A MINUTE?
I HAVE A FAVOR TO ASK...
YEAH. UH-HUH.
WE ALREADY GOT THE OKAY FROM THE TEACH-ERS.

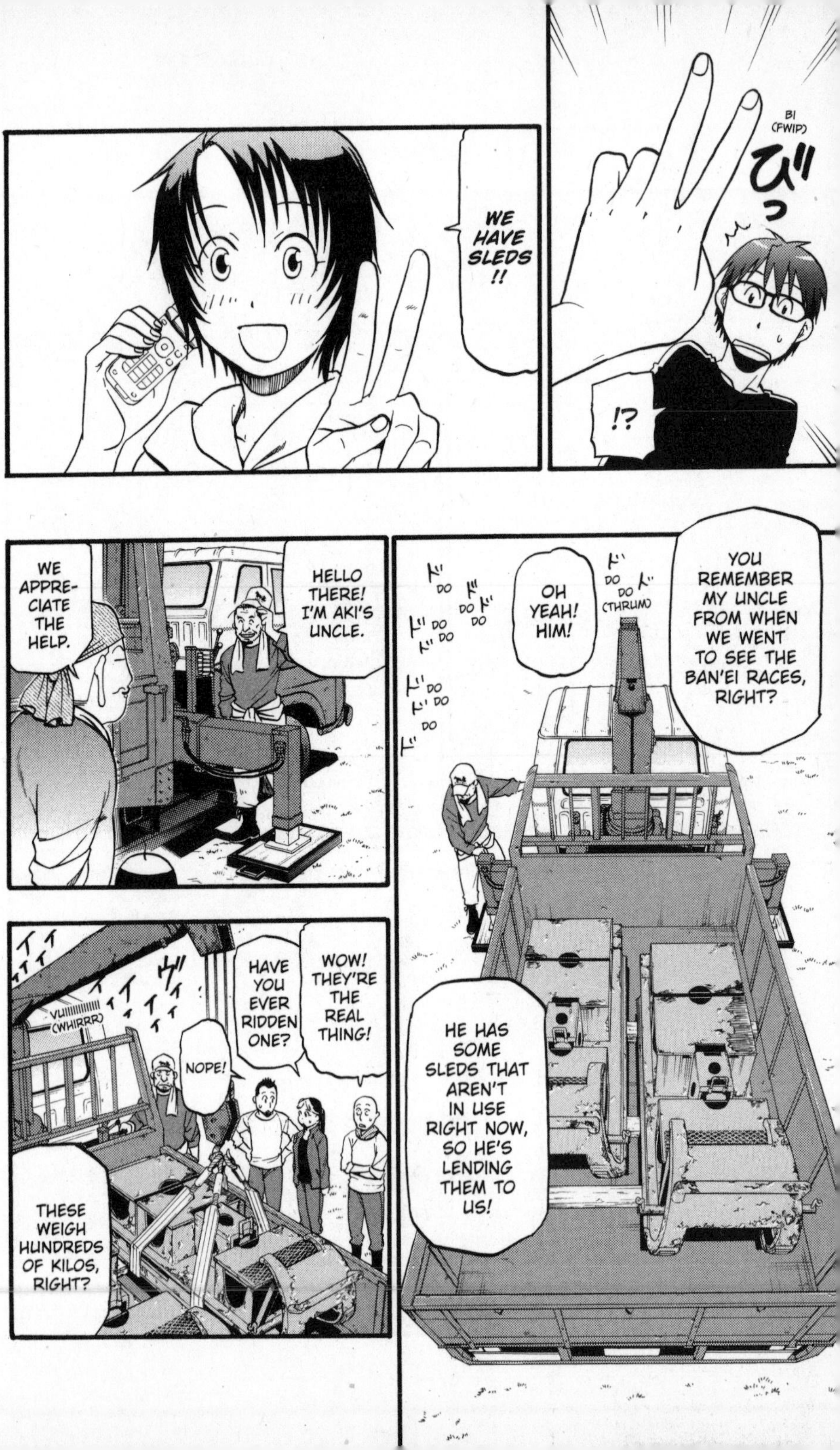

BI (FWIP)
びっ
!?
WE HAVE SLEDS!!
YOU REMEMBER MY UNCLE FROM WHEN WE WENT TO SEE THE BAN'EI RACES, RIGHT?
ド DO ド DO (THRUM)
OH YEAH! HIM!
ド DO ド DO ド DO ド DO ド DO ド DO ド DO ド DO ド
HE HAS SOME SLEDS THAT AREN'T IN USE RIGHT NOW, SO HE'S LENDING THEM TO US!
HELLO THERE! I'M AKI'S UNCLE.
WE APPRECIATE THE HELP.
WOW! THEY'RE THE REAL THING!
HAVE YOU EVER RIDDEN ONE?
NOPE!
VUIIIIIIIII (WHIRRR)
THESE WEIGH HUNDREDS OF KILOS, RIGHT?

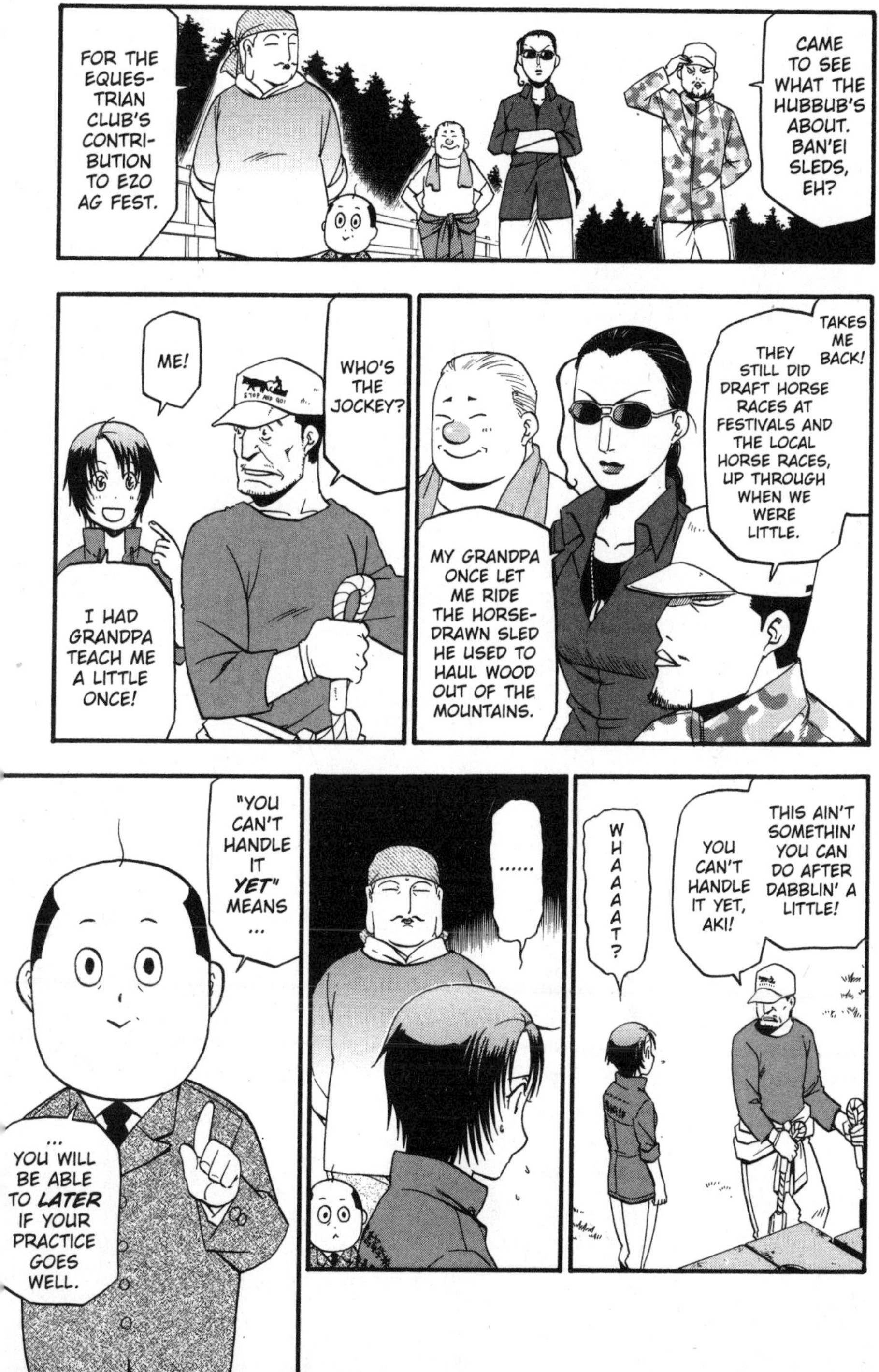
CAME TO SEE WHAT THE HUBBUB'S ABOUT. BAN'EI SLEDS, EH?
FOR THE EQUES-TRIAN CLUB'S CONTRI-BUTION TO EZO AG FEST.
TAKES ME BACK!
THEY STILL DID DRAFT HORSE RACES AT FESTIVALS AND THE LOCAL HORSE RACES, UP THROUGH WHEN WE WERE LITTLE.
MY GRANDPA ONCE LET ME RIDE THE HORSE-DRAWN SLED HE USED TO HAUL WOOD OUT OF THE MOUNTAINS.
WHO'S THE JOCKEY?
ME!
I HAD GRANDPA TEACH ME A LITTLE ONCE!
THIS AIN'T SOMETHIN' YOU CAN DO AFTER DABBLIN' A LITTLE!
YOU CAN'T HANDLE IT YET, AKI!
WHAAAAAT?
......
"YOU CAN'T HANDLE IT *YET*" MEANS ...
... YOU WILL BE ABLE TO *LATER* IF YOUR PRACTICE GOES WELL.

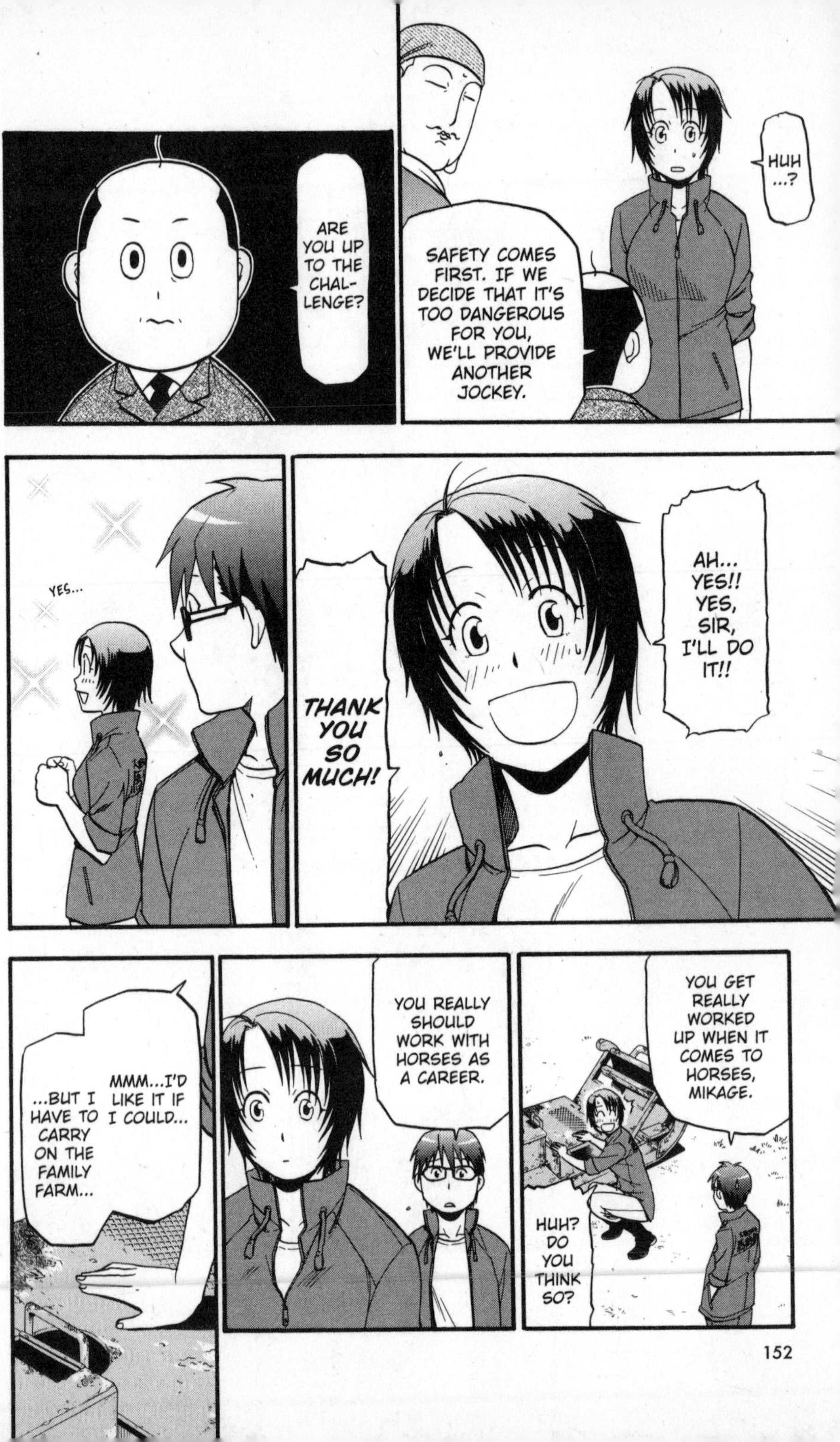
HUH ...?
SAFETY COMES FIRST. IF WE DECIDE THAT IT'S TOO DANGEROUS FOR YOU, WE'LL PROVIDE ANOTHER JOCKEY.
ARE YOU UP TO THE CHAL-LENGE?
AH... YES!! YES, SIR, I'LL DO IT!!
THANK YOU SO MUCH!
YES...
YOU GET REALLY WORKED UP WHEN IT COMES TO HORSES, MIKAGE.
HUH? DO YOU THINK SO?
YOU REALLY SHOULD WORK WITH HORSES AS A CAREER.
MMM...I'D LIKE IT IF I COULD...
...BUT I HAVE TO CARRY ON THE FAMILY FARM...

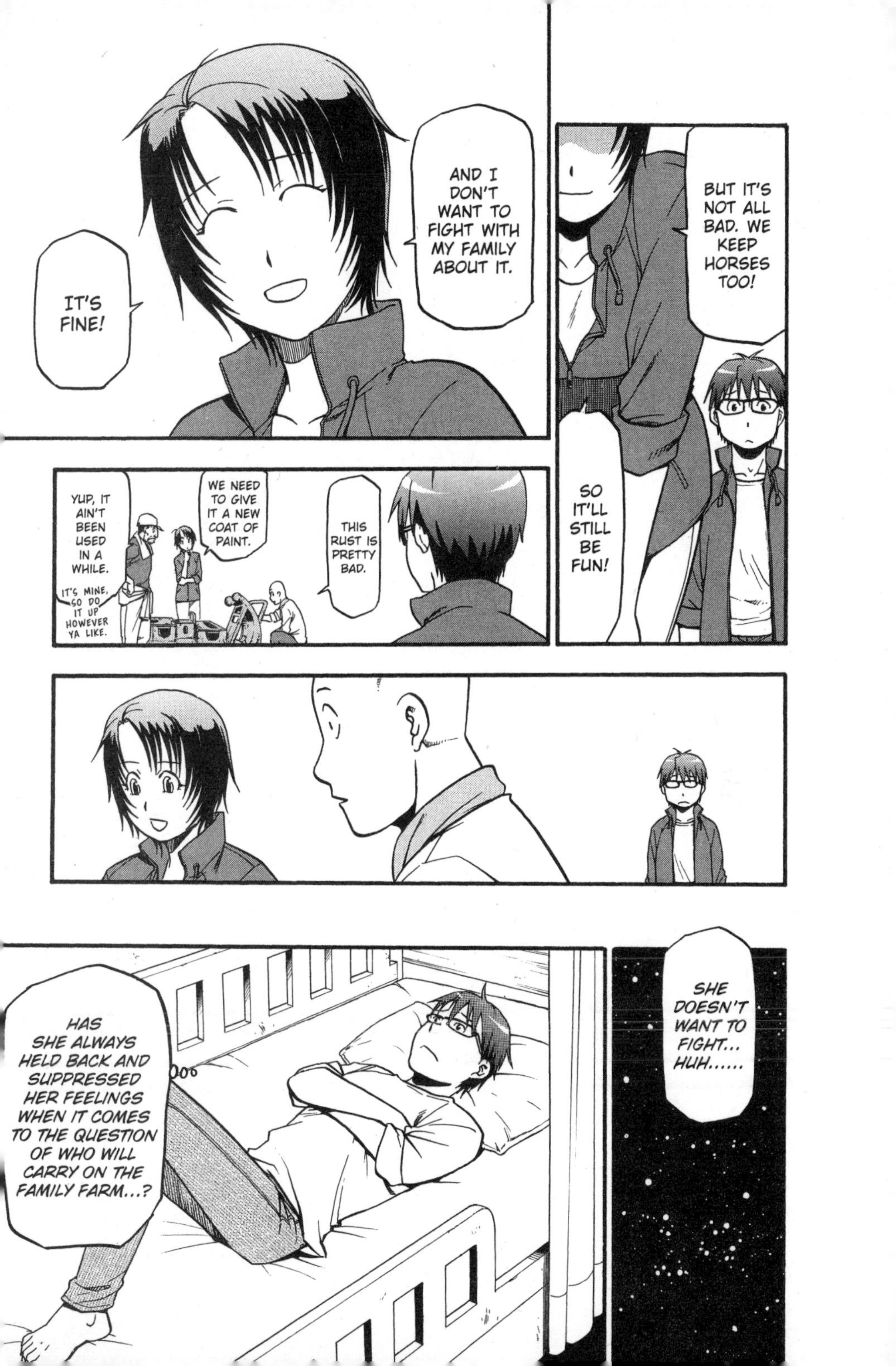

AND I DON'T WANT TO FIGHT WITH MY FAMILY ABOUT IT.
IT'S FINE!
BUT IT'S NOT ALL BAD. WE KEEP HORSES TOO!
SO IT'LL STILL BE FUN!
THIS RUST IS PRETTY BAD.
WE NEED TO GIVE IT A NEW COAT OF PAINT.
YUP, IT AIN'T BEEN USED IN A WHILE.
IT'S MINE, SO DO IT UP HOWEVER YA LIKE.
SHE DOESN'T WANT TO FIGHT... HUH......
HAS SHE ALWAYS HELD BACK AND SUPPRESSED HER FEELINGS WHEN IT COMES TO THE QUESTION OF WHO WILL CARRY ON THE FAMILY FARM...?

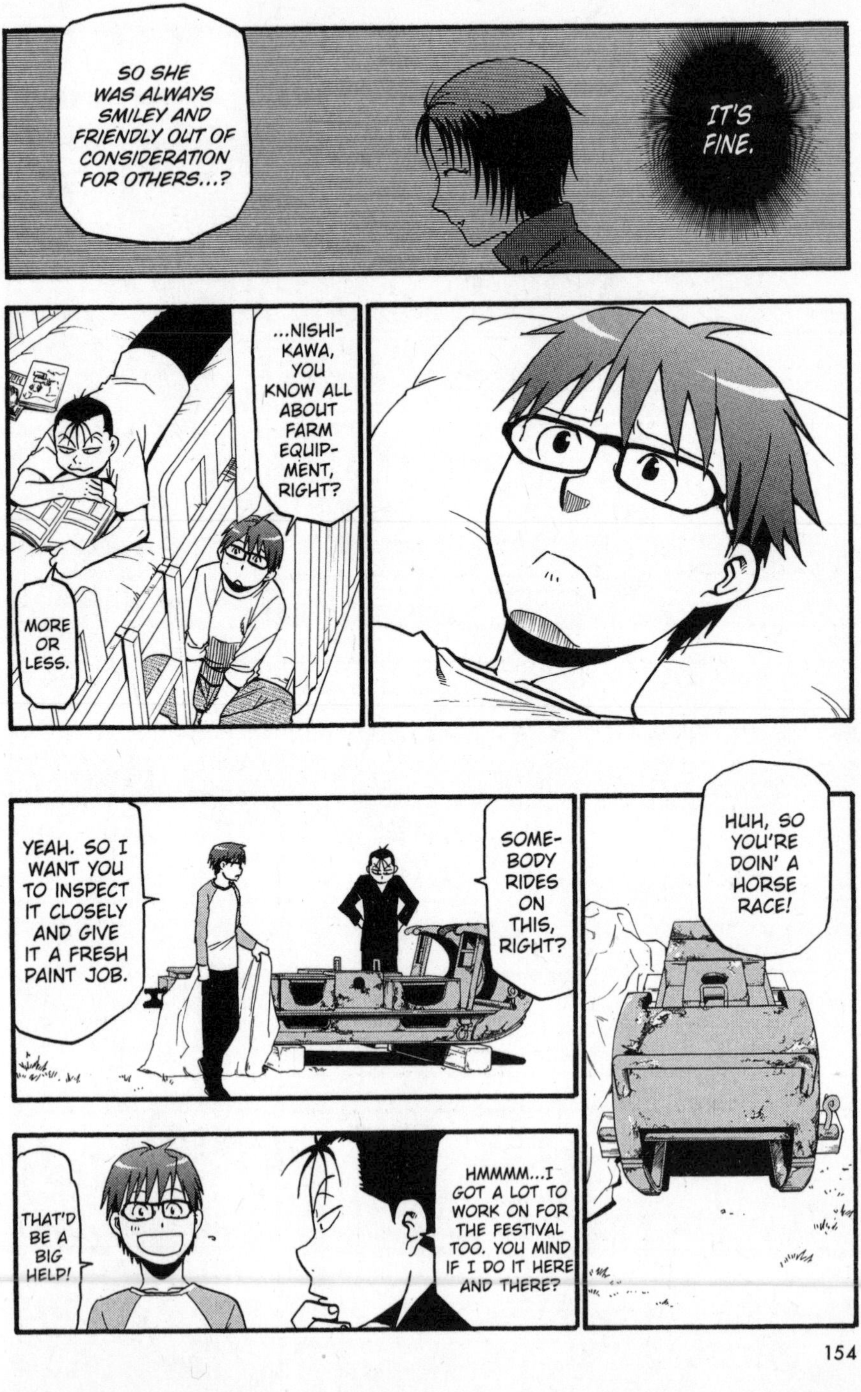
IT'S FINE.
SO SHE WAS ALWAYS SMILEY AND FRIENDLY OUT OF CONSIDERATION FOR OTHERS...?
...NISHIKAWA, YOU KNOW ALL ABOUT FARM EQUIPMENT, RIGHT?
MORE OR LESS.
HUH, SO YOU'RE DOIN' A HORSE RACE!
SOMEBODY RIDES ON THIS, RIGHT?
YEAH. SO I WANT YOU TO INSPECT IT CLOSELY AND GIVE IT A FRESH PAINT JOB.
HMMMM...I GOT A LOT TO WORK ON FOR THE FESTIVAL TOO. YOU MIND IF I DO IT HERE AND THERE?
THAT'D BE A BIG HELP!

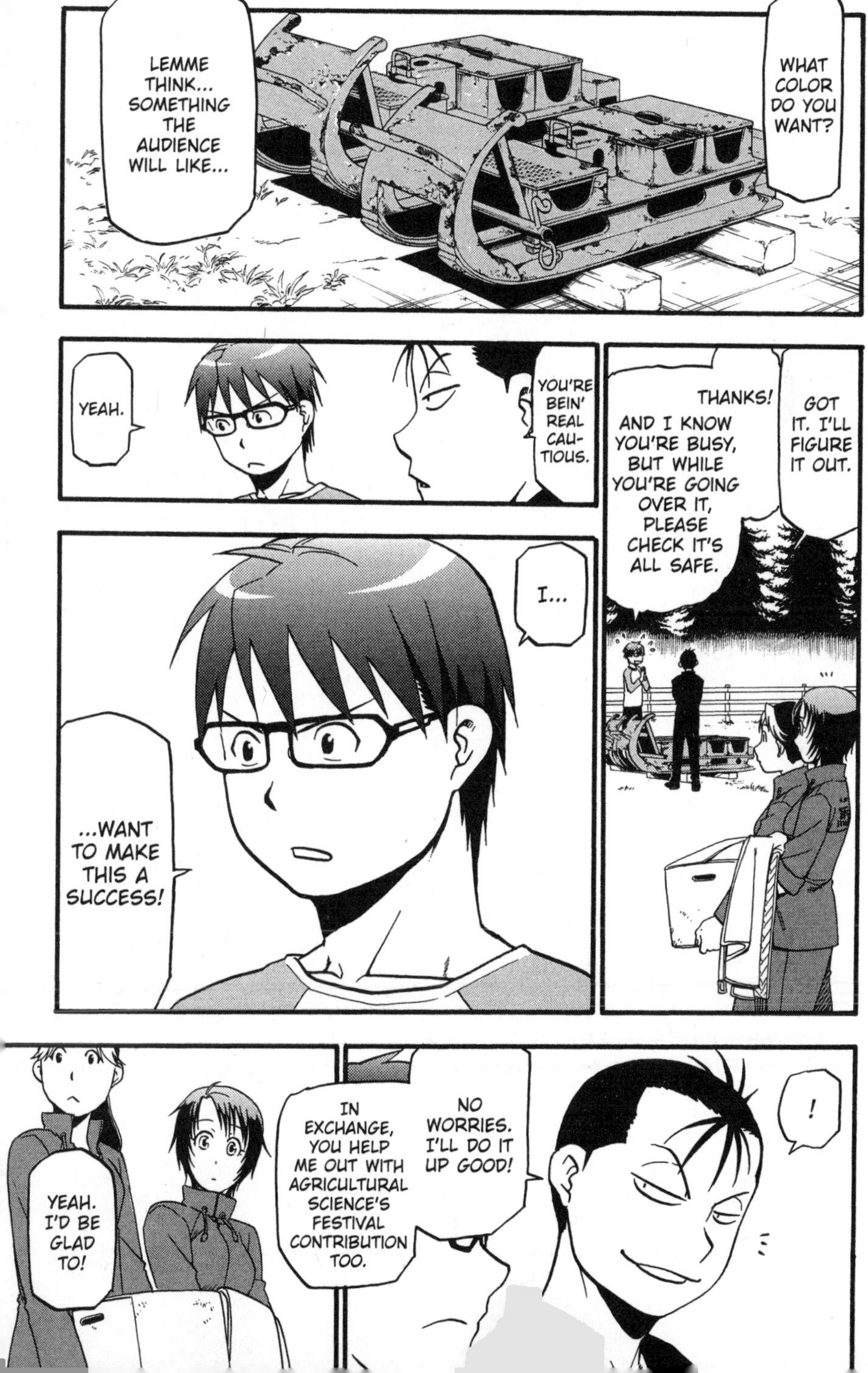
WHAT COLOR DO YOU WANT?
LEMME THINK... SOMETHING THE AUDIENCE WILL LIKE...
GOT IT. I'LL FIGURE IT OUT.
THANKS! AND I KNOW YOU'RE BUSY, BUT WHILE YOU'RE GOING OVER IT, PLEASE CHECK IT'S ALL SAFE.
YOU'RE BEIN' REAL CAU-TIOUS.
YEAH.
I...
...WANT TO MAKE THIS A SUCCESS!
!
NO WORRIES. I'LL DO IT UP GOOD!
IN EXCHANGE, YOU HELP ME OUT WITH AGRICULTURAL SCIENCE'S FESTIVAL CONTRIBUTION TOO.
YEAH. I'D BE GLAD TO!

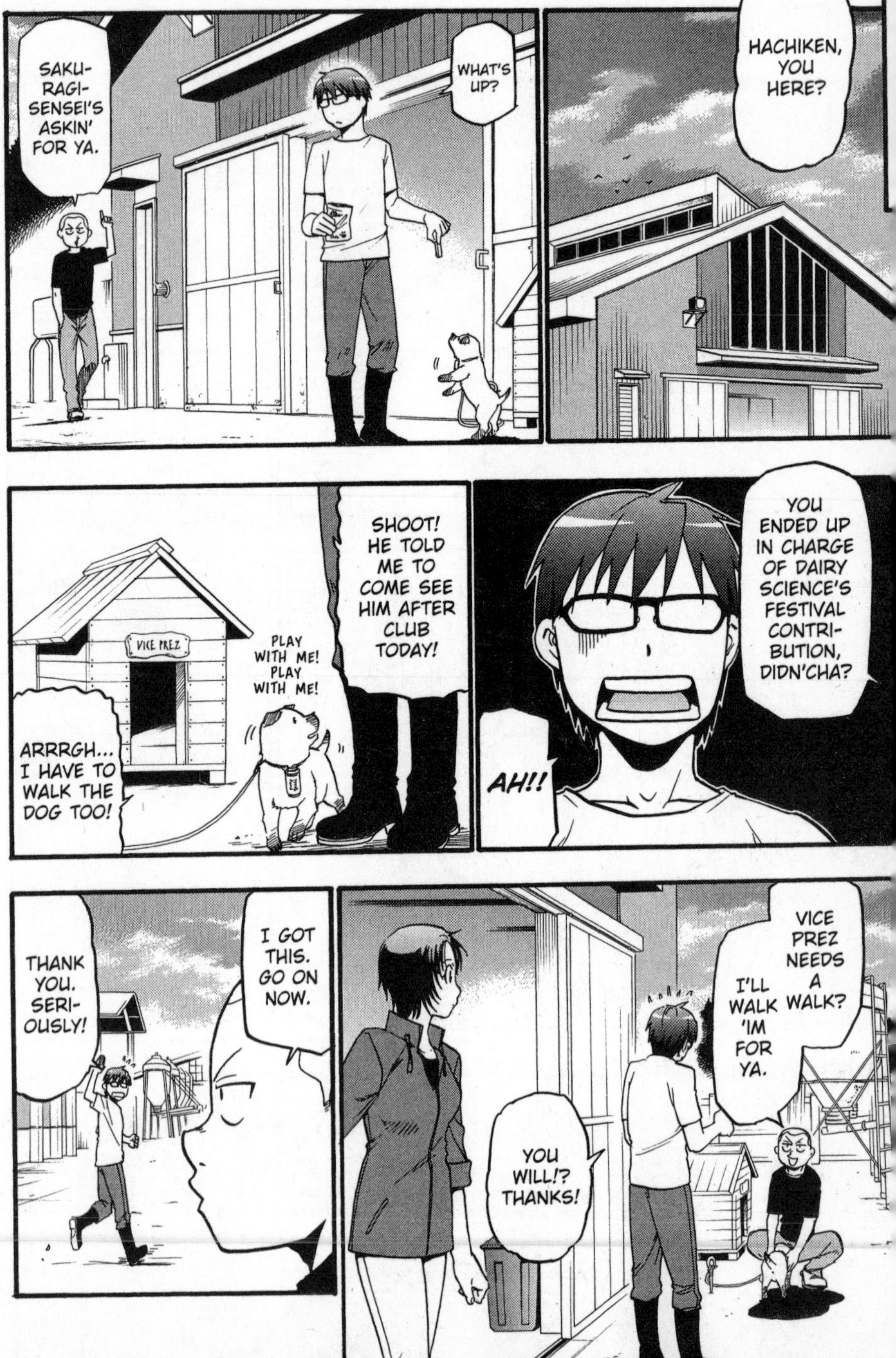
HACHIKEN, YOU HERE?
WHAT'S UP?
SAKURAGI-SENSEI'S ASKIN' FOR YA.
YOU ENDED UP IN CHARGE OF DAIRY SCIENCE'S FESTIVAL CONTRIBUTION, DIDN'CHA?
AH!!
SHOOT! HE TOLD ME TO COME SEE HIM AFTER CLUB TODAY!
PLAY WITH ME! PLAY WITH ME!
VICE PREZ
ARRRGH... I HAVE TO WALK THE DOG TOO!
VICE PREZ NEEDS A WALK?
I'LL WALK 'IM FOR YA.
YOU WILL!? THANKS!
I GOT THIS. GO ON NOW.
THANK YOU. SERIOUSLY!

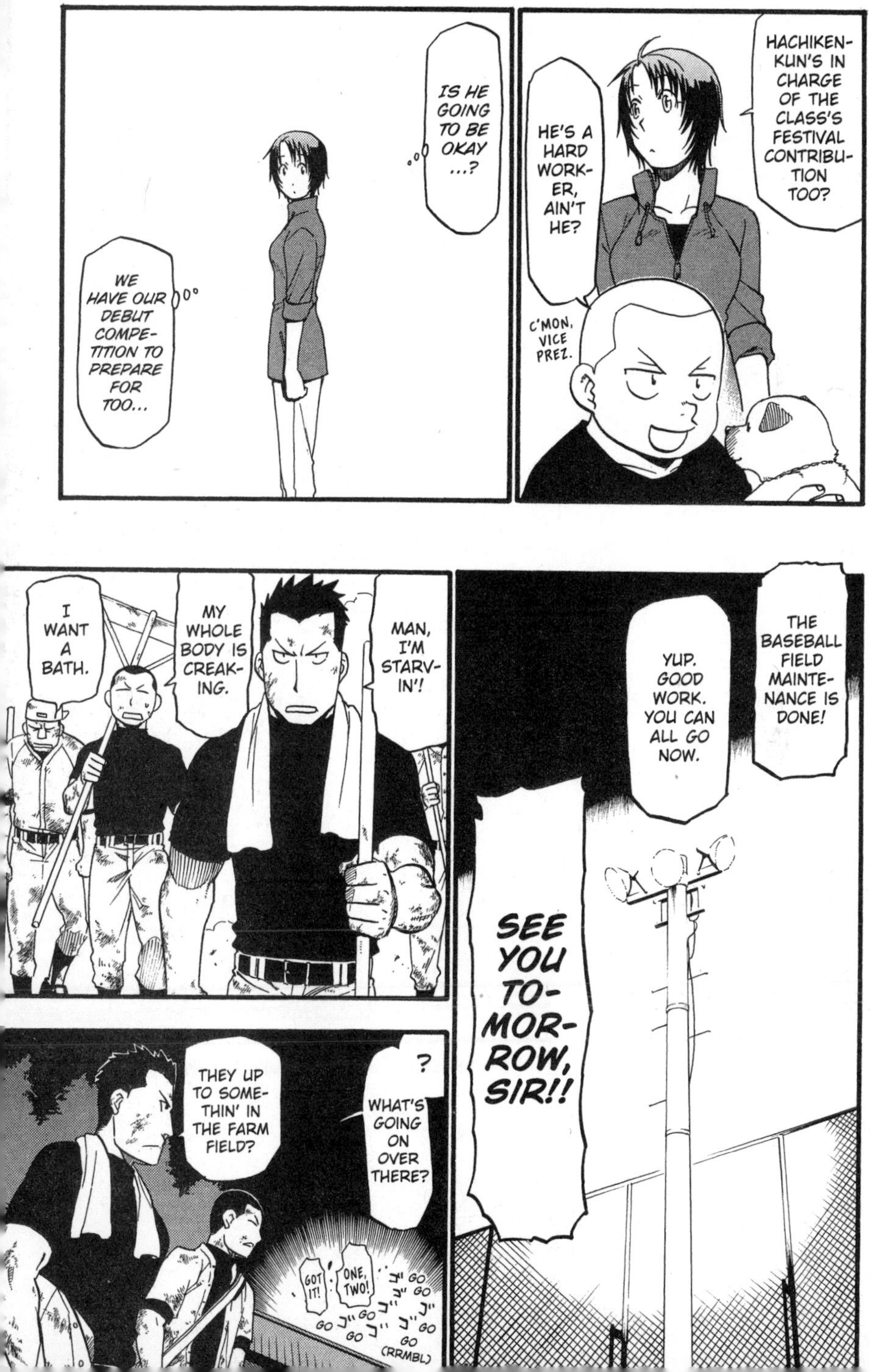
HACHIKEN-KUN'S IN CHARGE OF THE CLASS'S FESTIVAL CONTRIBUTION TOO?
HE'S A HARD WORKER, AIN'T HE?
C'MON, VICE PREZ.
IS HE GOING TO BE OKAY ...?
WE HAVE OUR DEBUT COMPETITION TO PREPARE FOR TOO...
THE BASEBALL FIELD MAINTENANCE IS DONE!
YUP. GOOD WORK. YOU CAN ALL GO NOW.
SEE YOU TOMORROW, SIR!!
MAN, I'M STARVIN'!
MY WHOLE BODY IS CREAKING.
I WANT A BATH.
?
WHAT'S GOING ON OVER THERE?
THEY UP TO SOMETHIN' IN THE FARM FIELD?
ONE, TWO!
GOT IT!
GO GO GO GO GO GO GO GO
(RRMBL)

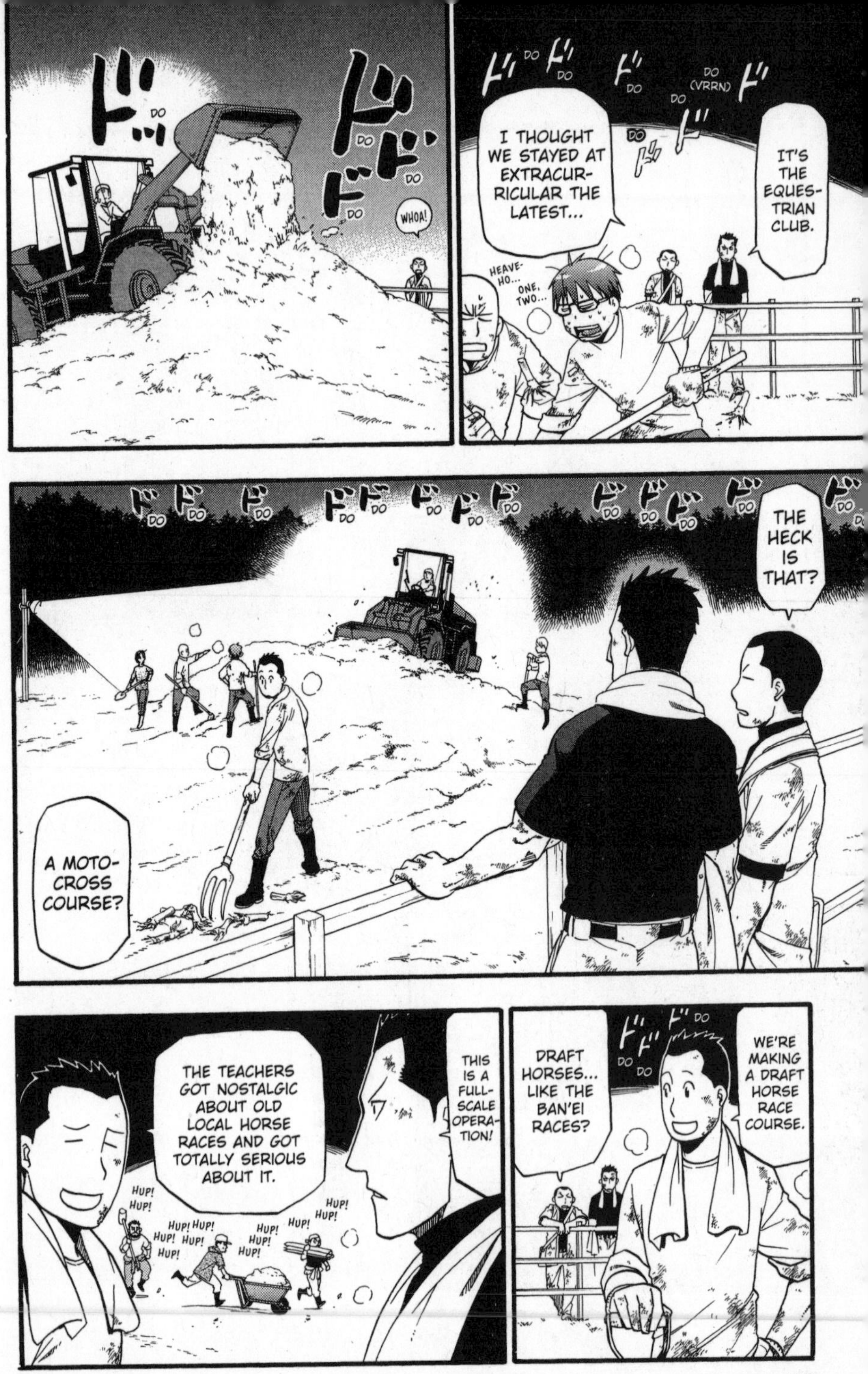
DO DO DO DO DO (VRRN) DO DO
IT'S THE EQUES-TRIAN CLUB.
I THOUGHT WE STAYED AT EXTRACUR-RICULAR THE LATEST...
HEAVE-HO... ONE, TWO...
DO
DO DO DO
WHOA!
THE HECK IS THAT?
DO DO DO DO DO DO DO DO DO DO DO DO DO
A MOTO-CROSS COURSE?
WE'RE MAKING A DRAFT HORSE RACE COURSE.
DO DO DO
DRAFT HORSES... LIKE THE BAN'EI RACES?
THIS IS A FULL-SCALE OPERA-TION!
THE TEACHERS GOT NOSTALGIC ABOUT OLD LOCAL HORSE RACES AND GOT TOTALLY SERIOUS ABOUT IT.
HUP! HUP! HUP! HUP! HUP! HUP! HUP! HUP! HUP! HUP! HUP! HUP!

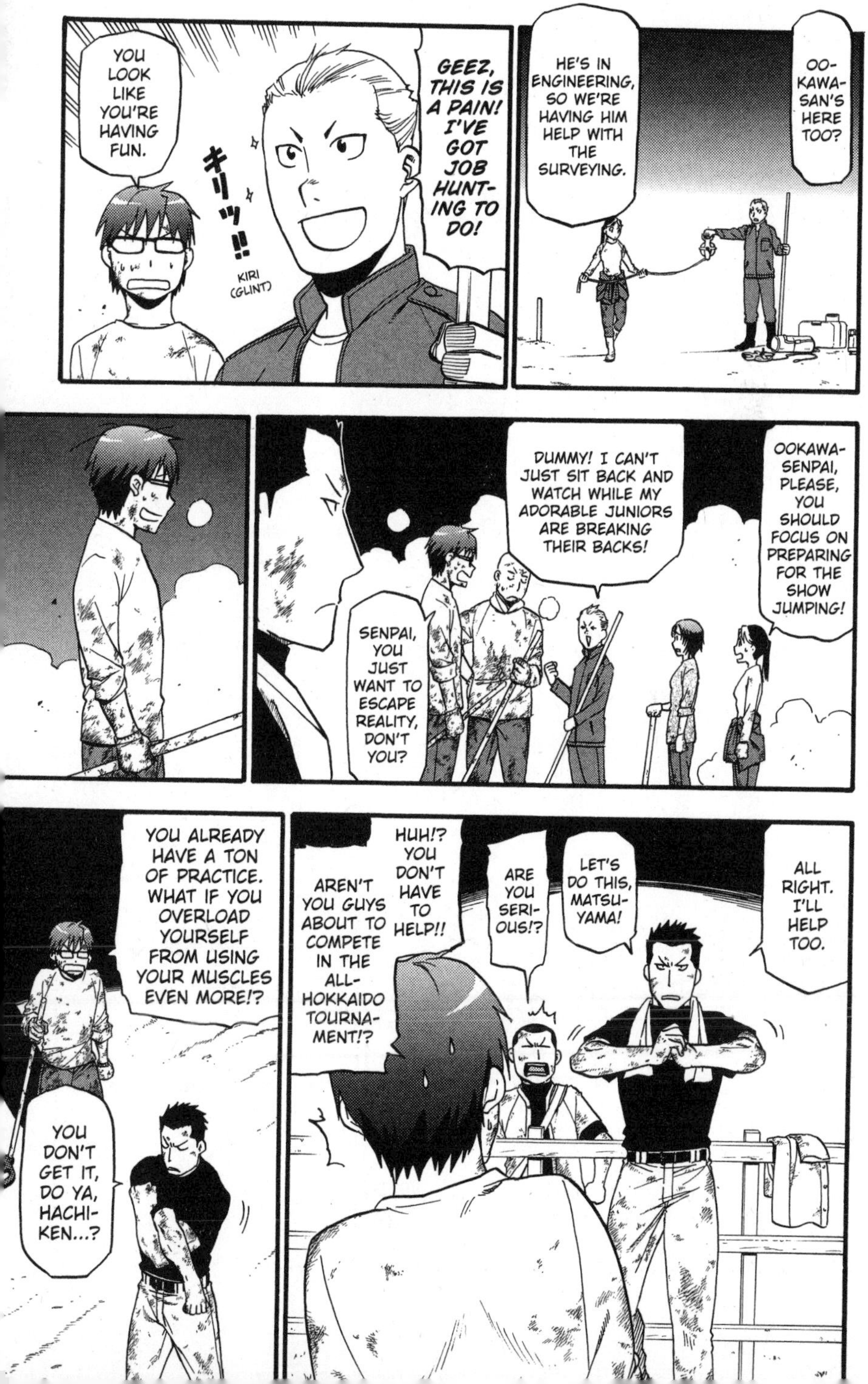
OO-KAWA-SAN'S HERE TOO?
HE'S IN ENGINEERING, SO WE'RE HAVING HIM HELP WITH THE SURVEYING.
GEEZ, THIS IS A PAIN! I'VE GOT JOB HUNTING TO DO!
キリッ!!
KIRI (GLINT)
YOU LOOK LIKE YOU'RE HAVING FUN.
OOKAWA-SENPAI, PLEASE, YOU SHOULD FOCUS ON PREPARING FOR THE SHOW JUMPING!
DUMMY! I CAN'T JUST SIT BACK AND WATCH WHILE MY ADORABLE JUNIORS ARE BREAKING THEIR BACKS!
SENPAI, YOU JUST WANT TO ESCAPE REALITY, DON'T YOU?
ALL RIGHT. I'LL HELP TOO.
LET'S DO THIS, MATSUYAMA!
ARE YOU SERIOUS!?
HUH!? YOU DON'T HAVE TO HELP!!
AREN'T YOU GUYS ABOUT TO COMPETE IN THE ALL-HOKKAIDO TOURNAMENT!?
YOU ALREADY HAVE A TON OF PRACTICE. WHAT IF YOU OVERLOAD YOURSELF FROM USING YOUR MUSCLES EVEN MORE!?
YOU DON'T GET IT, DO YA, HACHIKEN...?

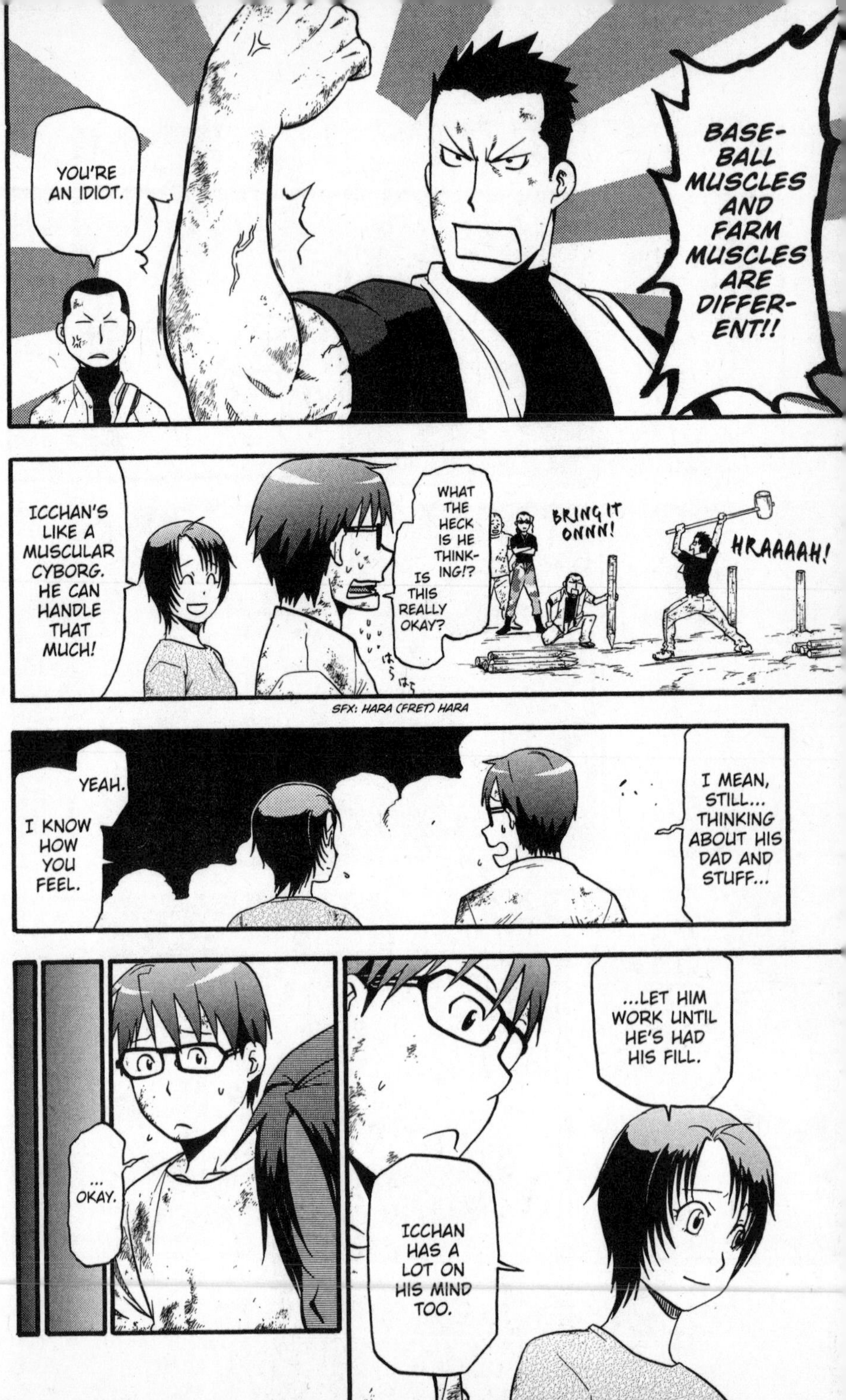
BASE-BALL MUSCLES AND FARM MUSCLES ARE DIFFER-ENT!!
YOU'RE AN IDIOT.
HRAAAAH!
BRING IT ONNN!
WHAT THE HECK IS HE THINKING!?
IS THIS REALLY OKAY?
ICCHAN'S LIKE A MUSCULAR CYBORG. HE CAN HANDLE THAT MUCH!
SFX: HARA (FRET) HARA
I MEAN, STILL... THINKING ABOUT HIS DAD AND STUFF...
YEAH.
I KNOW HOW YOU FEEL.
...LET HIM WORK UNTIL HE'S HAD HIS FILL.
ICCHAN HAS A LOT ON HIS MIND TOO.
...OKAY.

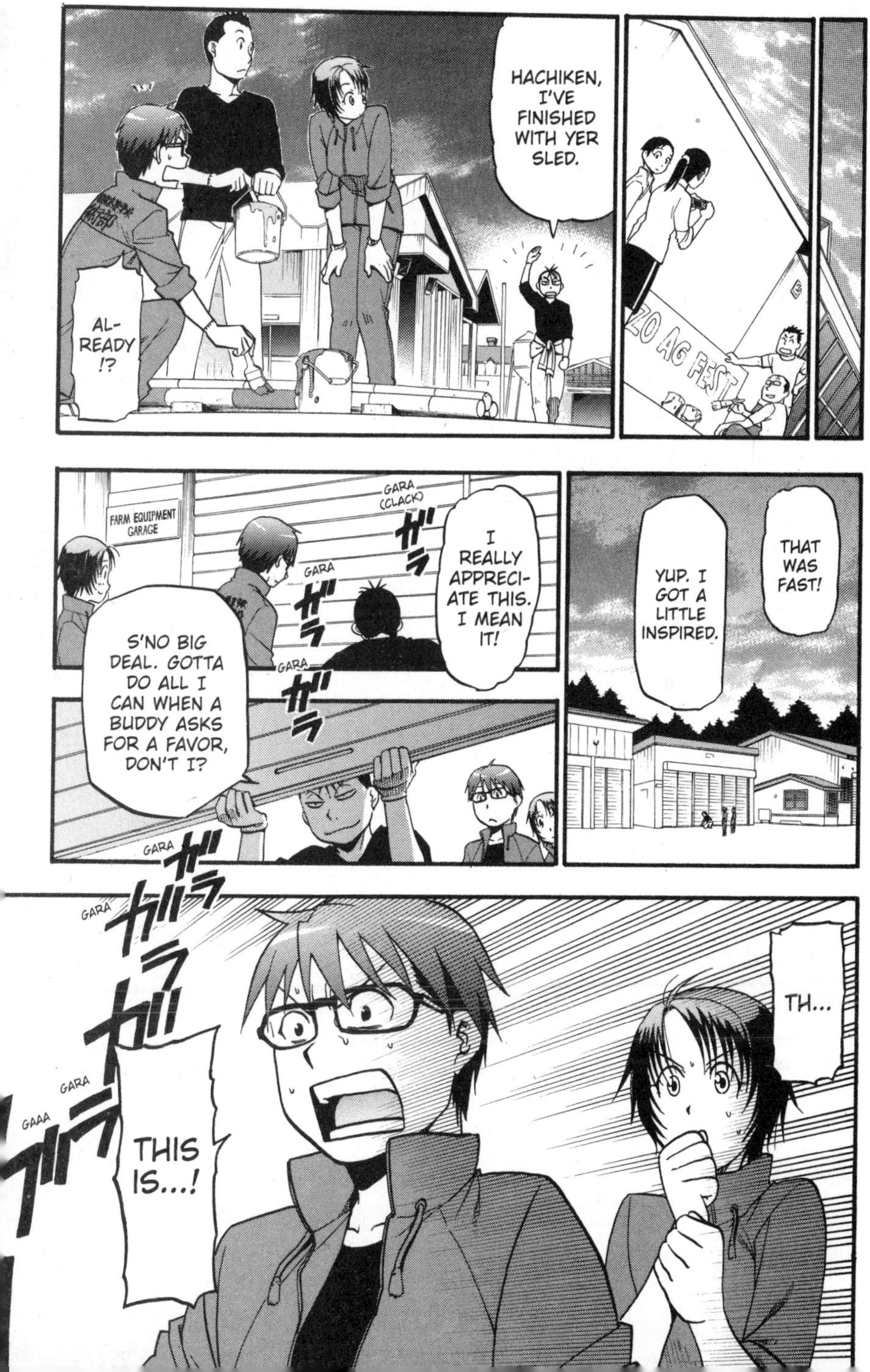
ZO AG FEST
HACHIKEN, I'VE FINISHED WITH YER SLED.
AL-READY!?
THAT WAS FAST!
YUP. I GOT A LITTLE INSPIRED.
FARM EQUIPMENT GARAGE
GARA (CLACK)
ガラ
I REALLY APPRECIATE THIS. I MEAN IT!
GARA
ガラ
GARA
ガラ
S'NO BIG DEAL. GOTTA DO ALL I CAN WHEN A BUDDY ASKS FOR A FAVOR, DON'T I?
GARA
ガラ
TH...
GARA
GARA
GAAA
THIS IS...!

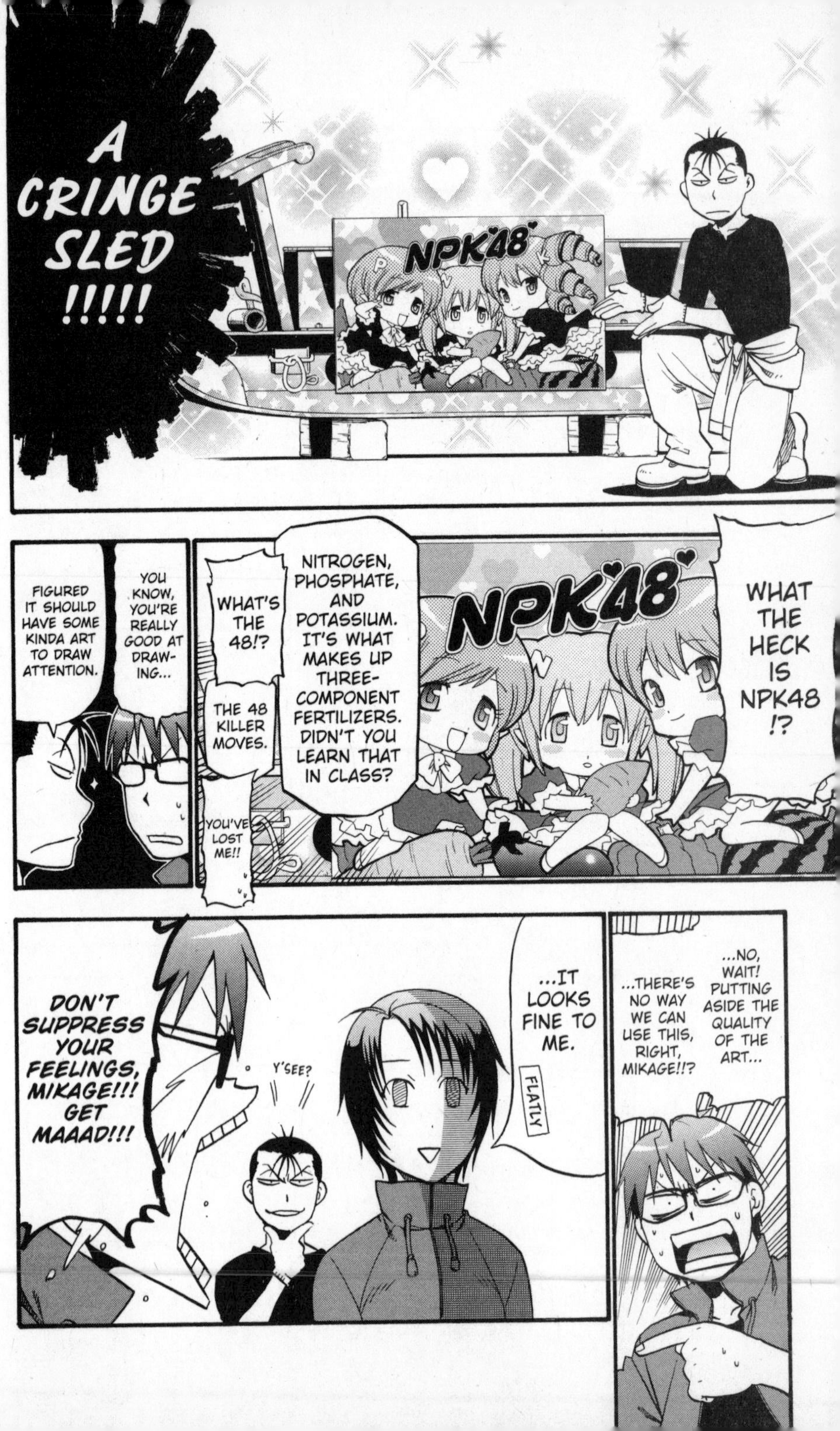
A CRINGE SLED !!!!!
NPK48
WHAT THE HECK IS NPK48 !?
NPK48
NITROGEN, PHOSPHATE, AND POTASSIUM. IT'S WHAT MAKES UP THREE-COMPONENT FERTILIZERS. DIDN'T YOU LEARN THAT IN CLASS?
WHAT'S THE 48!?
THE 48 KILLER MOVES.
YOU'VE LOST ME!!
YOU KNOW, YOU'RE REALLY GOOD AT DRAWING...
FIGURED IT SHOULD HAVE SOME KINDA ART TO DRAW ATTENTION.
...NO, WAIT! PUTTING ASIDE THE QUALITY OF THE ART...
...THERE'S NO WAY WE CAN USE THIS, RIGHT, MIKAGE!!?
...IT LOOKS FINE TO ME.
FLATLY
Y'SEE?
DON'T SUPPRESS YOUR FEELINGS, MIKAGE!!! GET MAAAD!!!

Silver Spoon

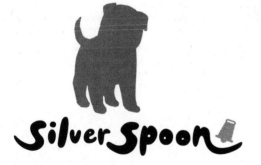

THE PRINCIPAL

HE HAS HIS OWN HORSE IN THE CARE OF THE EQUESTRIAN CLUB.

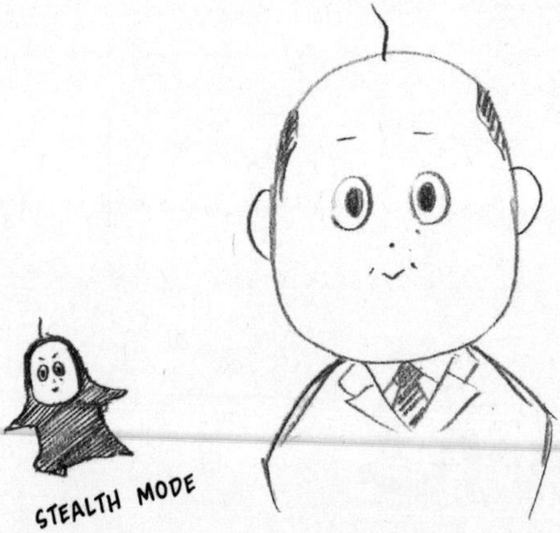
STEALTH MODE

Chapter 44: Tale of Autumn ⑬

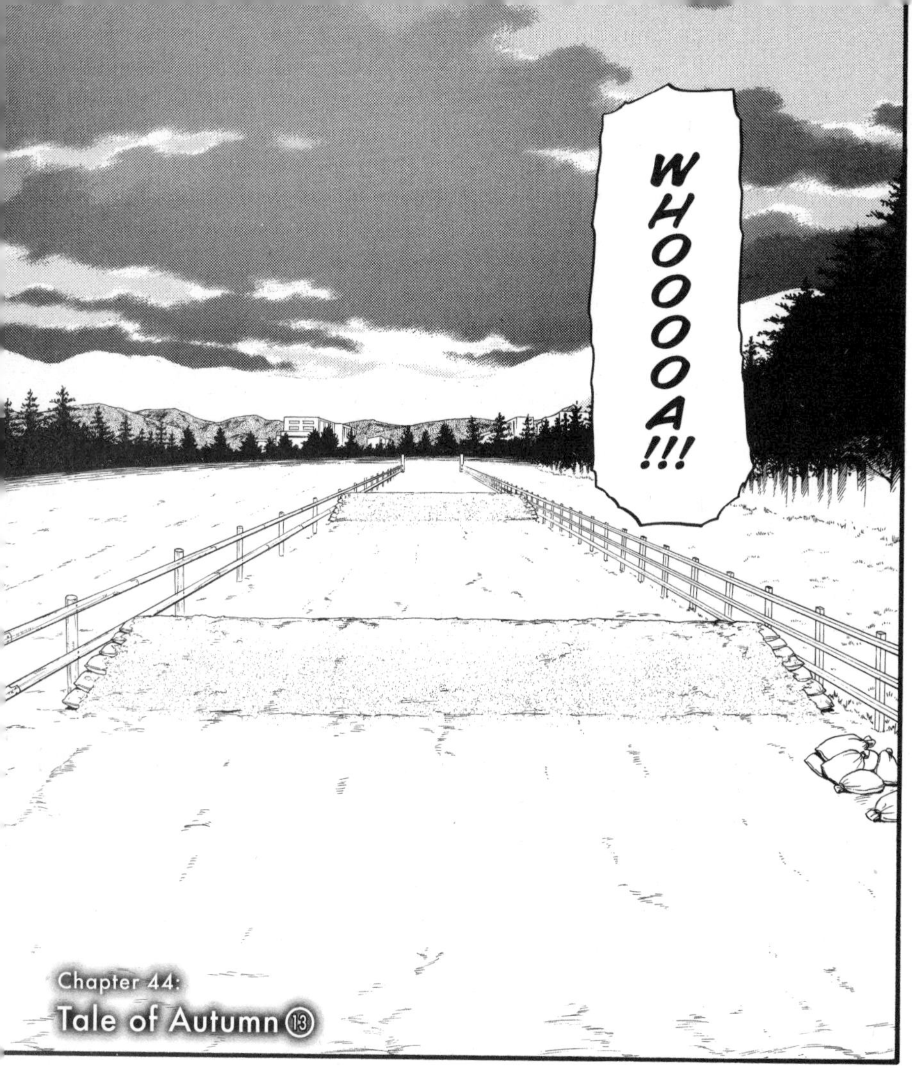
WHOOOOOA!!!

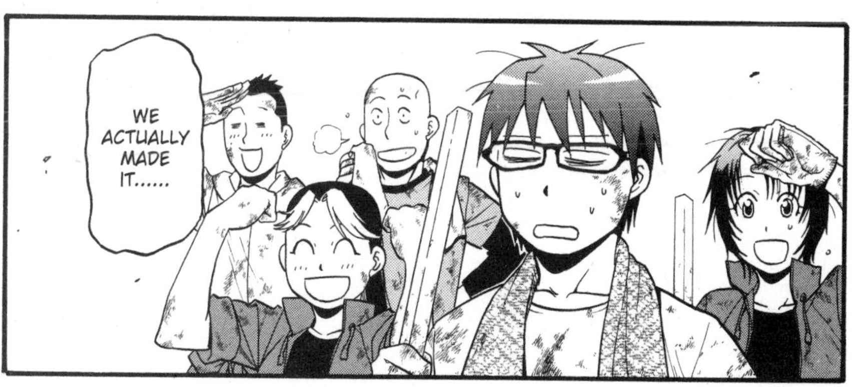
WE ACTUALLY MADE IT......

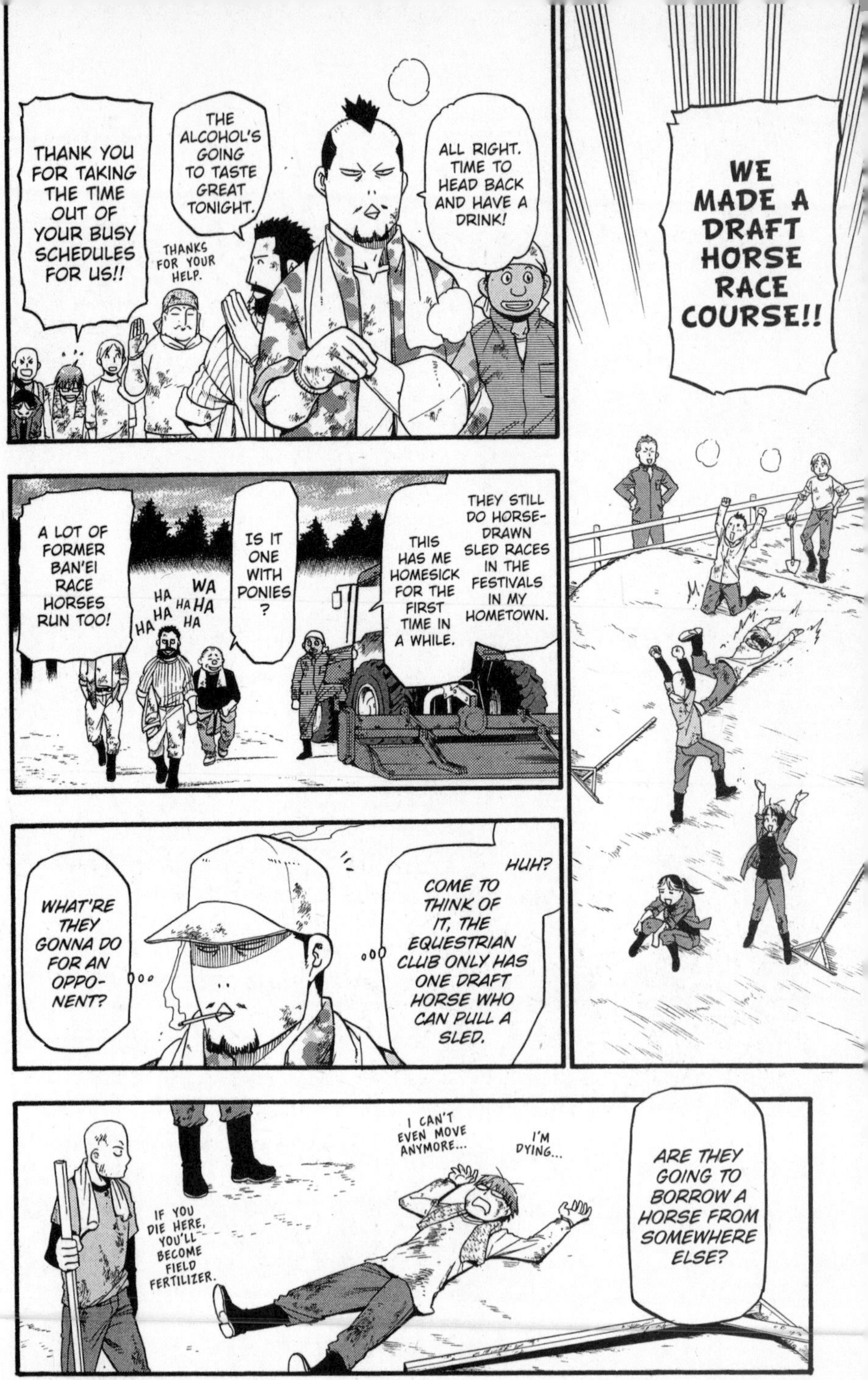
WE MADE A DRAFT HORSE RACE COURSE!!
ALL RIGHT. TIME TO HEAD BACK AND HAVE A DRINK!
THE ALCOHOL'S GOING TO TASTE GREAT TONIGHT.
THANKS FOR YOUR HELP.
THANK YOU FOR TAKING THE TIME OUT OF YOUR BUSY SCHEDULES FOR US!!
THEY STILL DO HORSE-DRAWN SLED RACES IN THE FESTIVALS IN MY HOMETOWN.
THIS HAS ME HOMESICK FOR THE FIRST TIME IN A WHILE.
IS IT ONE WITH PONIES?
WA HA HA HA HA HA HA HA
A LOT OF FORMER BAN'EI RACE HORSES RUN TOO!
HUH? COME TO THINK OF IT, THE EQUESTRIAN CLUB ONLY HAS ONE DRAFT HORSE WHO CAN PULL A SLED.
WHAT'RE THEY GONNA DO FOR AN OPPONENT?
ARE THEY GOING TO BORROW A HORSE FROM SOMEWHERE ELSE?
I'M DYING...
I CAN'T EVEN MOVE ANYMORE...
IF YOU DIE HERE, YOU'LL BECOME FIELD FERTILIZER.

Chapter 44: Tale of Autumn ⑬

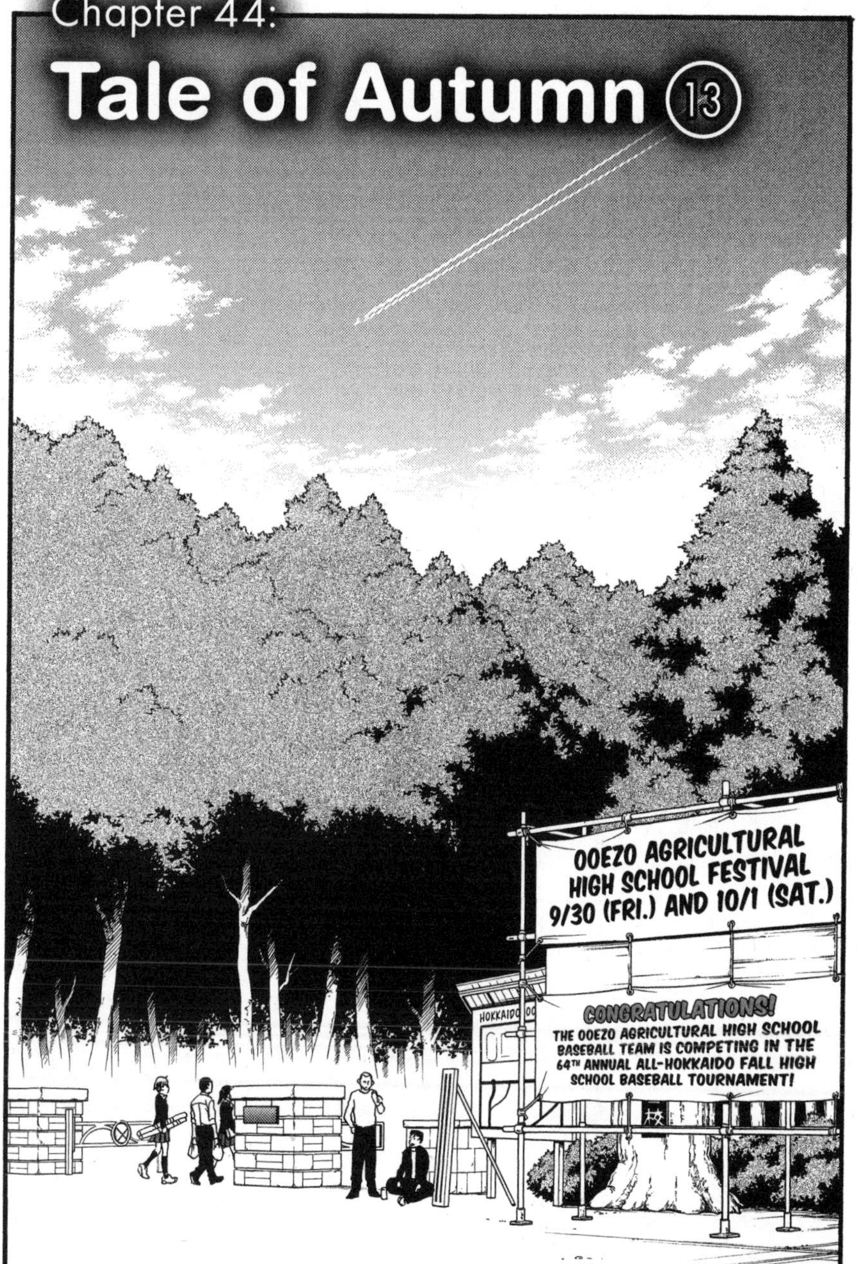
OOEZO AGRICULTURAL HIGH SCHOOL FESTIVAL 9/30 (FRI.) AND 10/1 (SAT.)
CONGRATULATIONS!
THE OOEZO AGRICULTURAL HIGH SCHOOL BASEBALL TEAM IS COMPETING IN THE 64TH ANNUAL ALL-HOKKAIDO FALL HIGH SCHOOL BASEBALL TOURNAMENT!

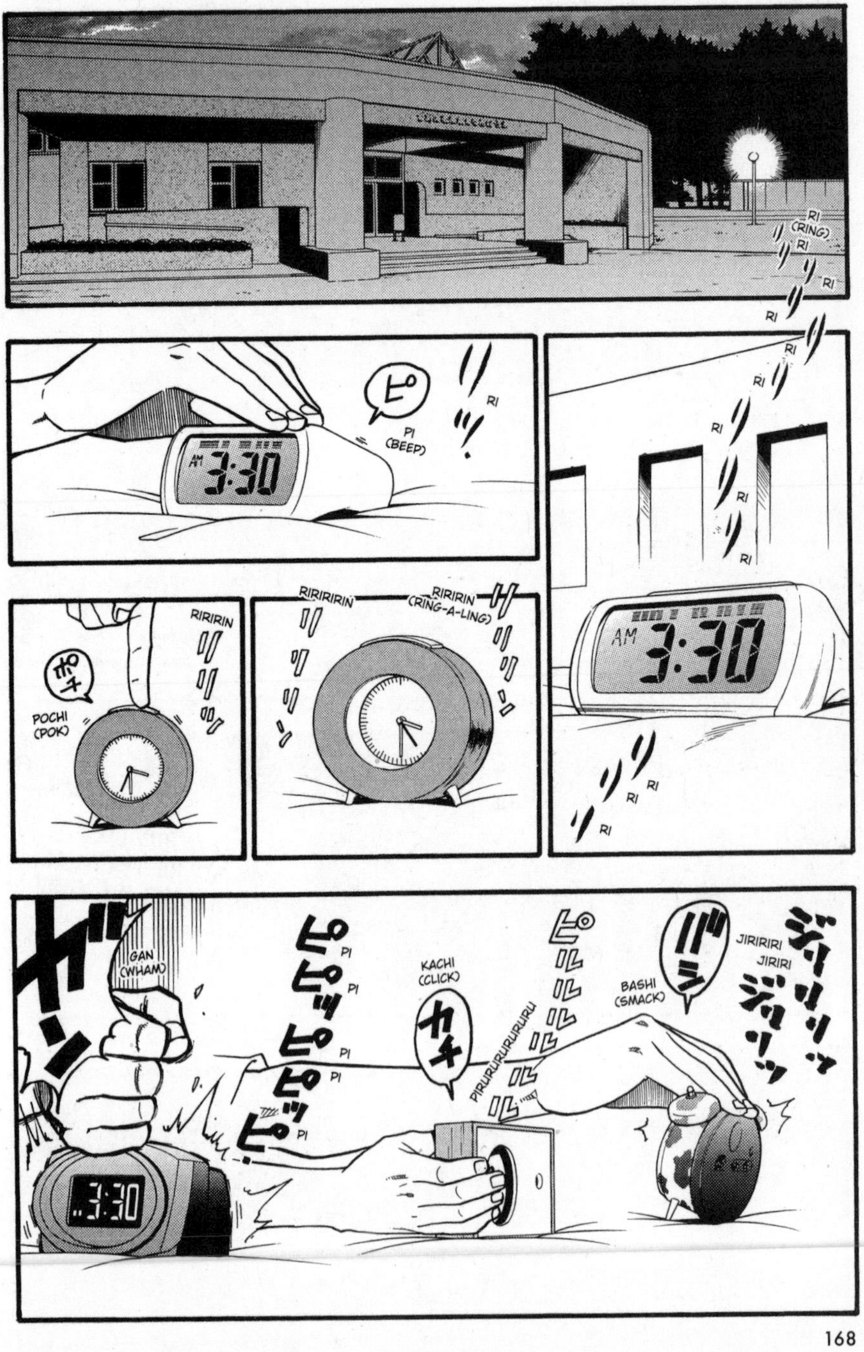

RI (RING) RI
RI
RI
RI
RI
RI
RI
RI
RI
RI
RI
ピ
PI (BEEP)
RI
RIRIRIN (RING-A-LING)
RIRIRIRIN
ポチ
POCHI (POK)
RIRIRIN
JIRIRIRI JIRIRI
バシ
BASHI (SMACK)
PIRURURURURU
カチ
KACHI (CLICK)
PI PI PI PI PI
GAN (WHAM)

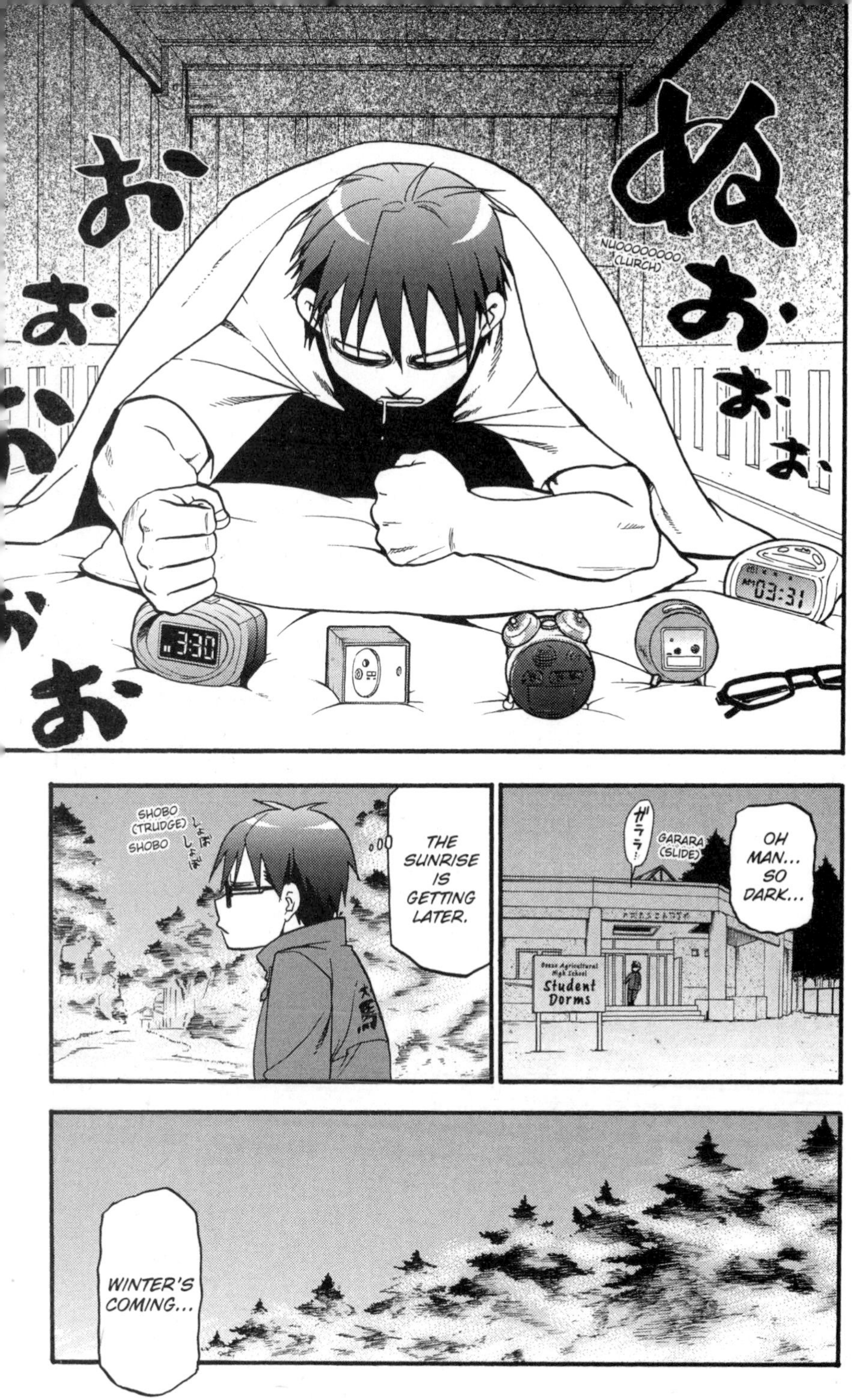
NUOOOOOOOO (LURCH)
AM 03:31
GARARA (SLIDE)
ガララ…
OH MAN... SO DARK...
Student Dorms
SHOBO (TRUDGE) SHOBO
しょぼしょぼ
THE SUNRISE IS GETTING LATER.
WINTER'S COMING...

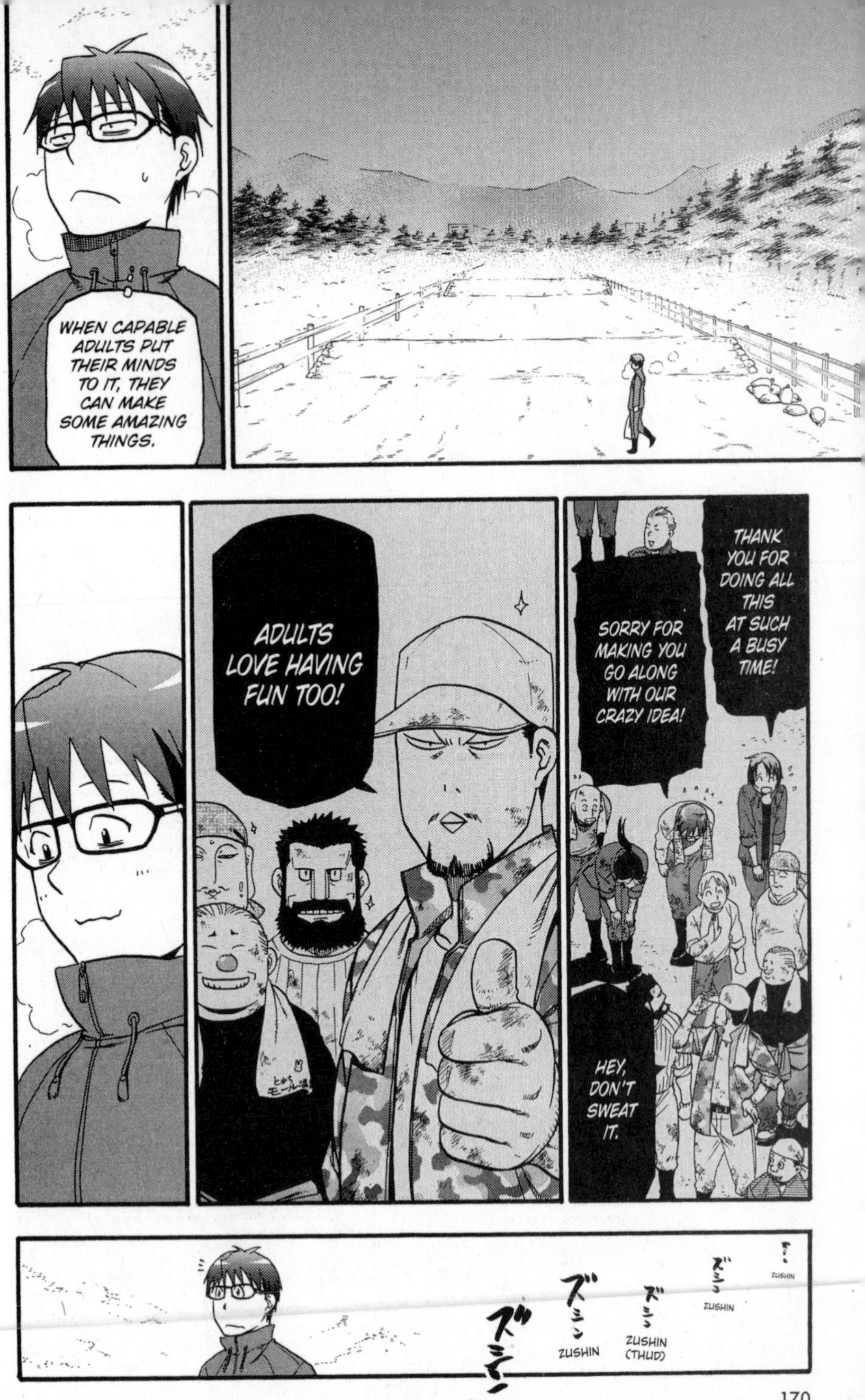
WHEN CAPABLE ADULTS PUT THEIR MINDS TO IT, THEY CAN MAKE SOME AMAZING THINGS.
THANK YOU FOR DOING ALL THIS AT SUCH A BUSY TIME!
SORRY FOR MAKING YOU GO ALONG WITH OUR CRAZY IDEA!
HEY, DON'T SWEAT IT.
ADULTS LOVE HAVING FUN TOO!
ZUSHIN
ZUSHIN
ZUSHIN (THUD)
ZUSHIN
ZUSHIN

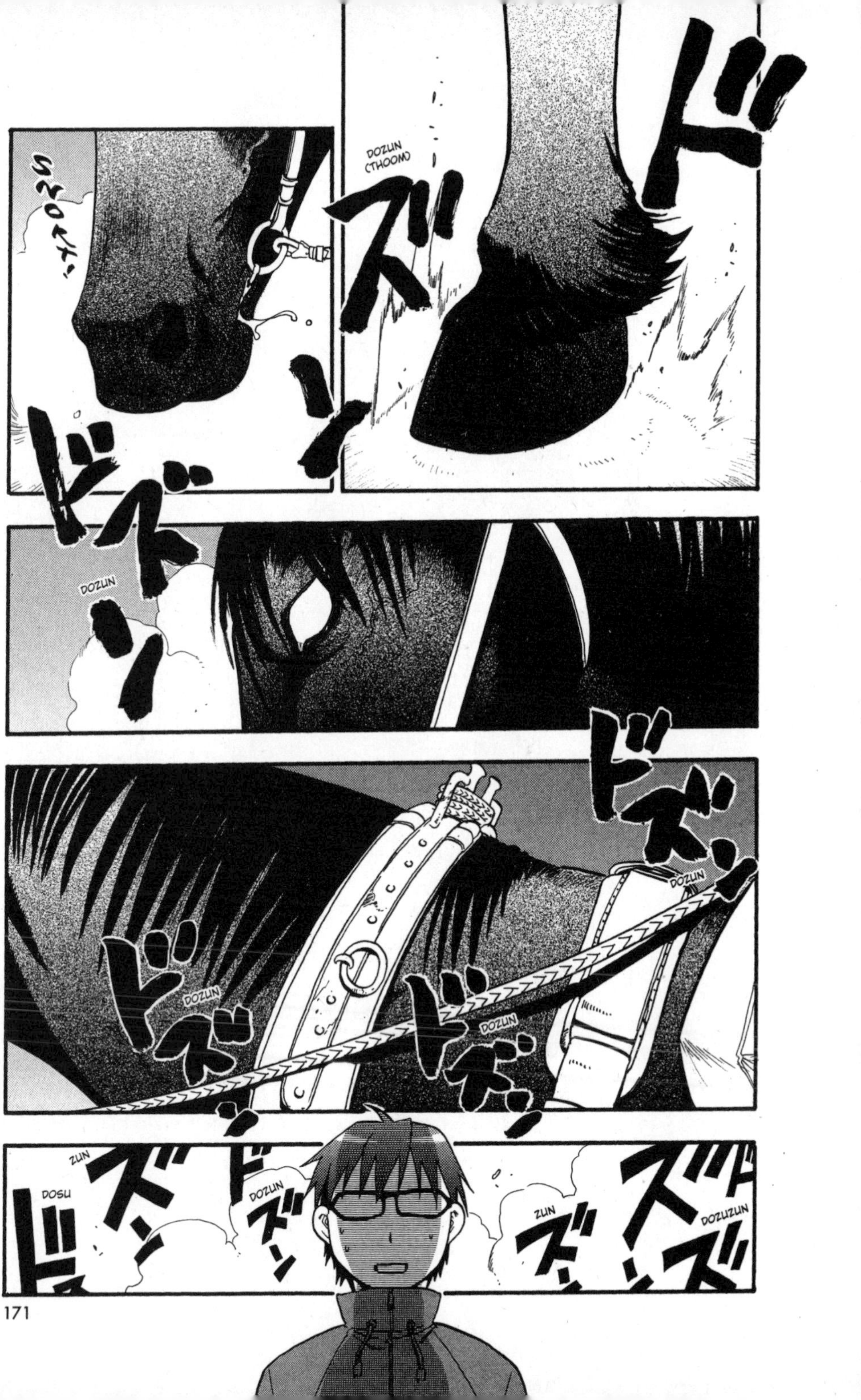
DOZUN (THOOM)
SNORT!
DOZUN
DOZUN
DOZUN
DOZUN
DOZUZUN
ZUN
DOZUN
ZUN
DOSU

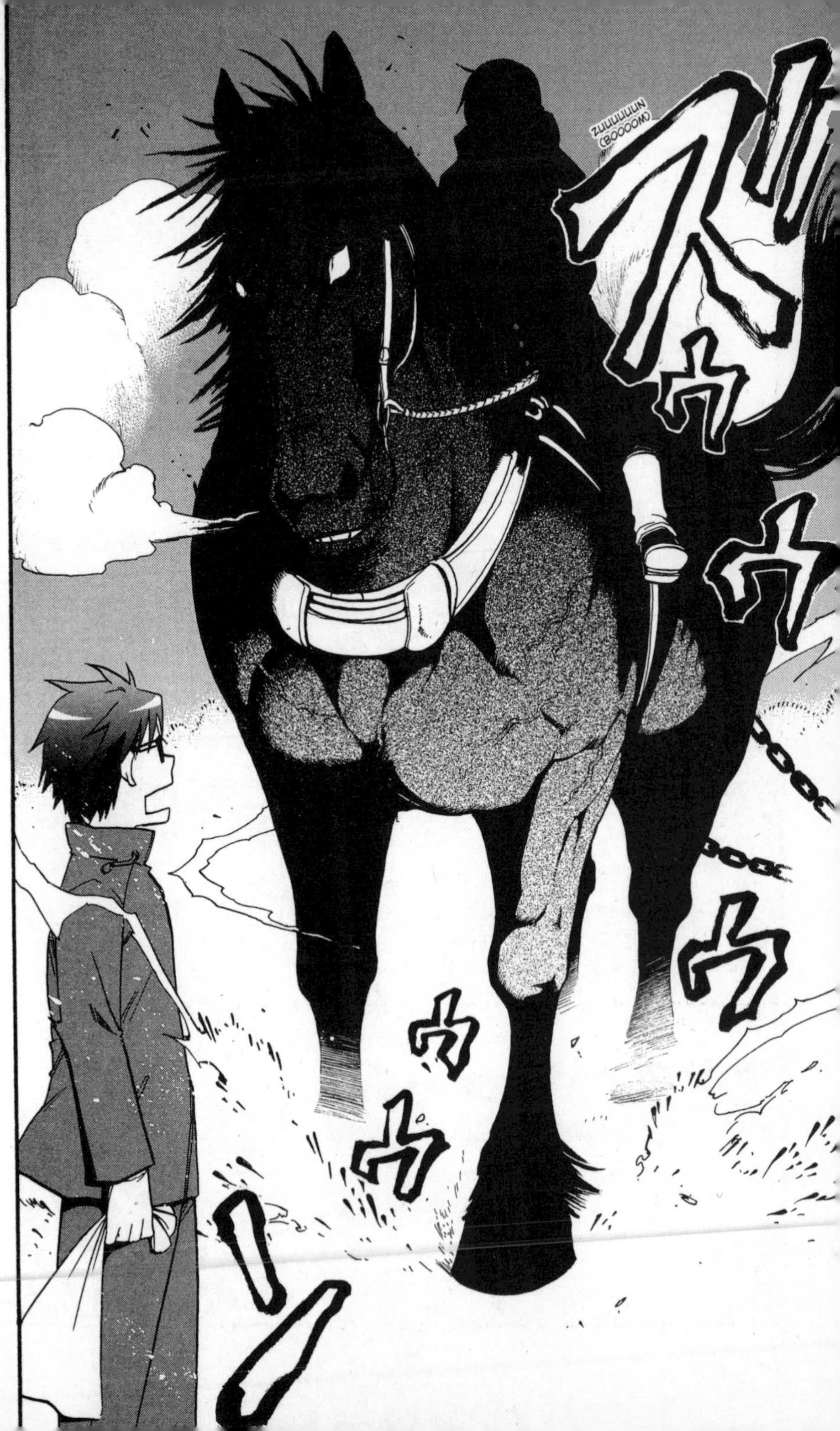
ズウウウウウン
ZUUUUUUN (BOOOOM)

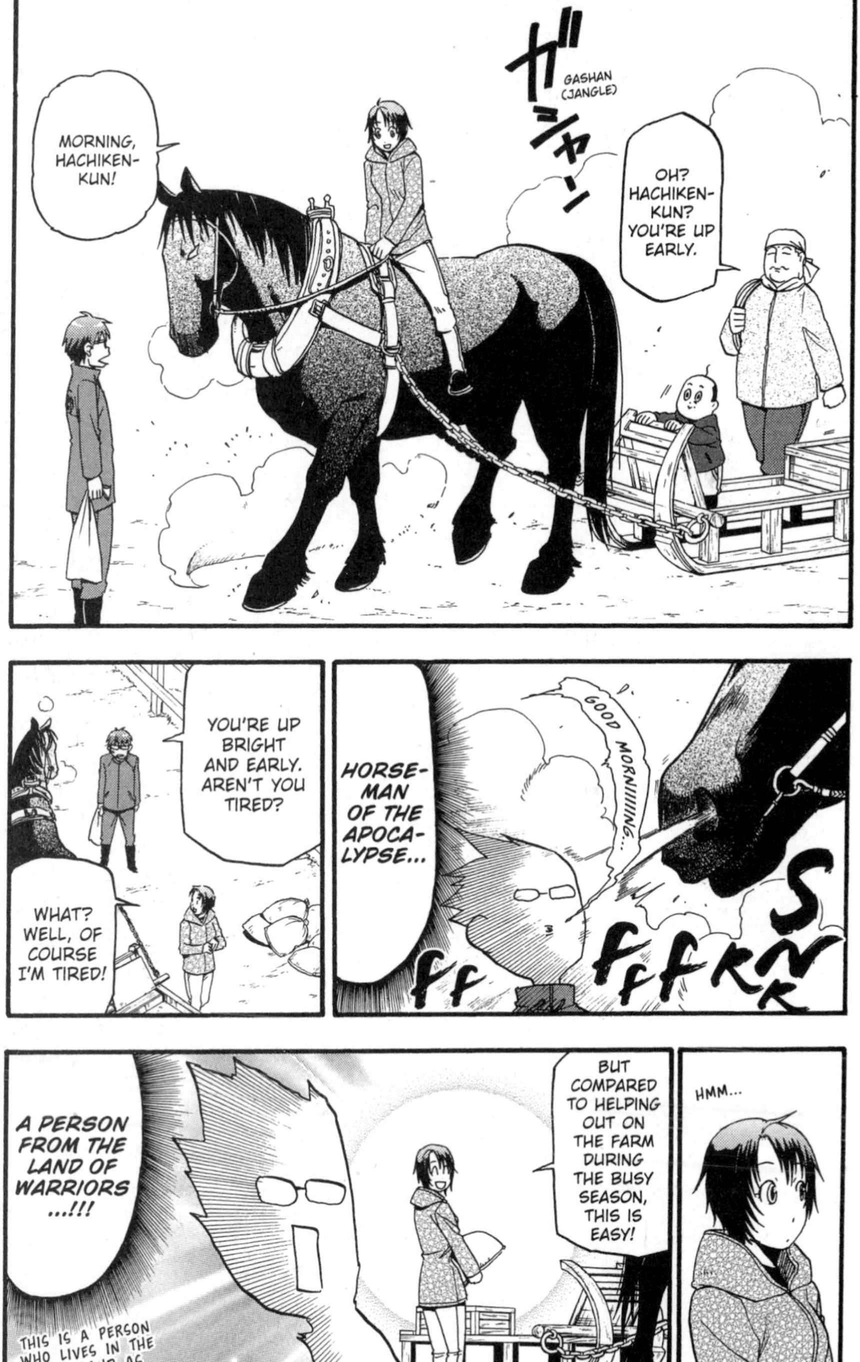

ガシャン
GASHAN (JANGLE)
OH? HACHIKEN-KUN? YOU'RE UP EARLY.
MORNING, HACHIKEN-KUN!
GOOD MORNIIIIING...
HORSE-MAN OF THE APOCA-LYPSE...
YOU'RE UP BRIGHT AND EARLY. AREN'T YOU TIRED?
WHAT? WELL, OF COURSE I'M TIRED!
HMM...
BUT COMPARED TO HELPING OUT ON THE FARM DURING THE BUSY SEASON, THIS IS EASY!
A PERSON FROM THE LAND OF WARRIORS ...!!!
THIS IS A PERSON WHO LIVES IN THE SAME LAND AS KOMABAAAA!

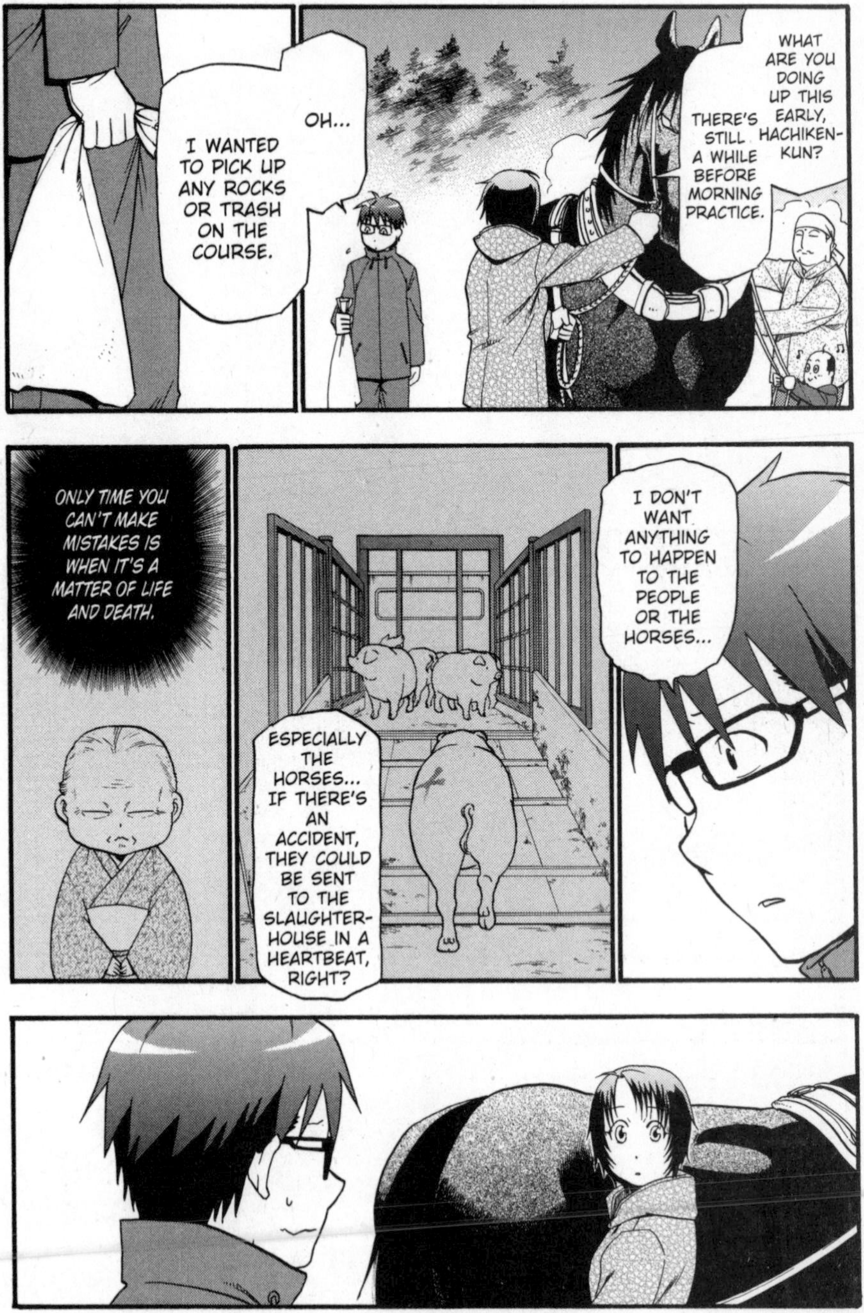
WHAT ARE YOU DOING UP THIS EARLY, HACHIKEN-KUN?
THERE'S STILL A WHILE BEFORE MORNING PRACTICE.
OH...
I WANTED TO PICK UP ANY ROCKS OR TRASH ON THE COURSE.
I DON'T WANT ANYTHING TO HAPPEN TO THE PEOPLE OR THE HORSES...
ESPECIALLY THE HORSES... IF THERE'S AN ACCIDENT, THEY COULD BE SENT TO THE SLAUGHTER-HOUSE IN A HEARTBEAT, RIGHT?
ONLY TIME YOU CAN'T MAKE MISTAKES IS WHEN IT'S A MATTER OF LIFE AND DEATH.

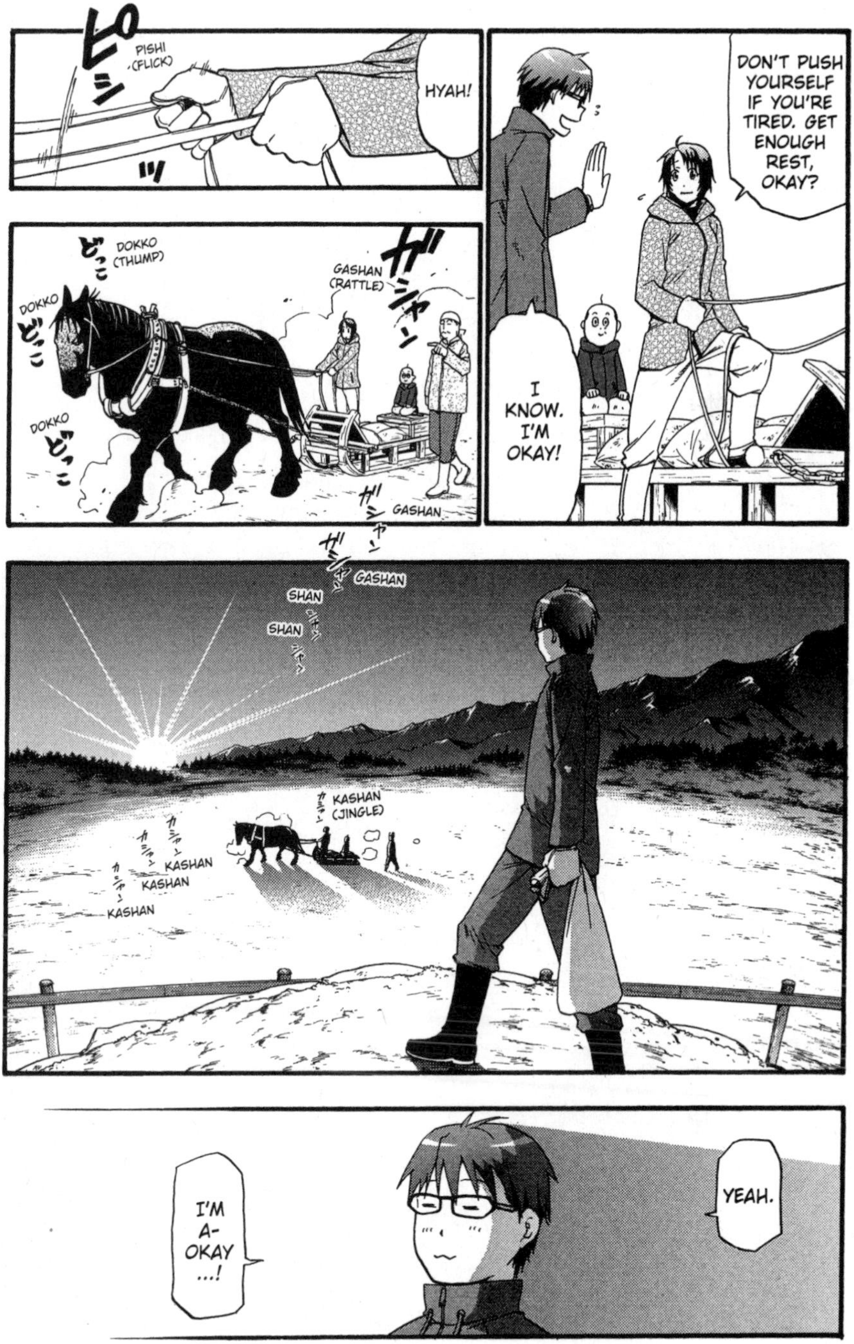
DON'T PUSH YOURSELF IF YOU'RE TIRED. GET ENOUGH REST, OKAY?
I KNOW. I'M OKAY!
ピシッ
PISHI (FLICK)
HYAH!
どっこ
DOKKO (THUMP)
どっこ
DOKKO
どっこ
DOKKO
ガシャン
GASHAN (RATTLE)
ガシャン
GASHAN
ガシャン
GASHAN
シャン
SHAN
シャン
SHAN
カシャ
KASHAN (JINGLE)
カシャ
KASHAN
カシャ
KASHAN
カシャ
KASHAN
YEAH.
I'M A-OKAY ...!

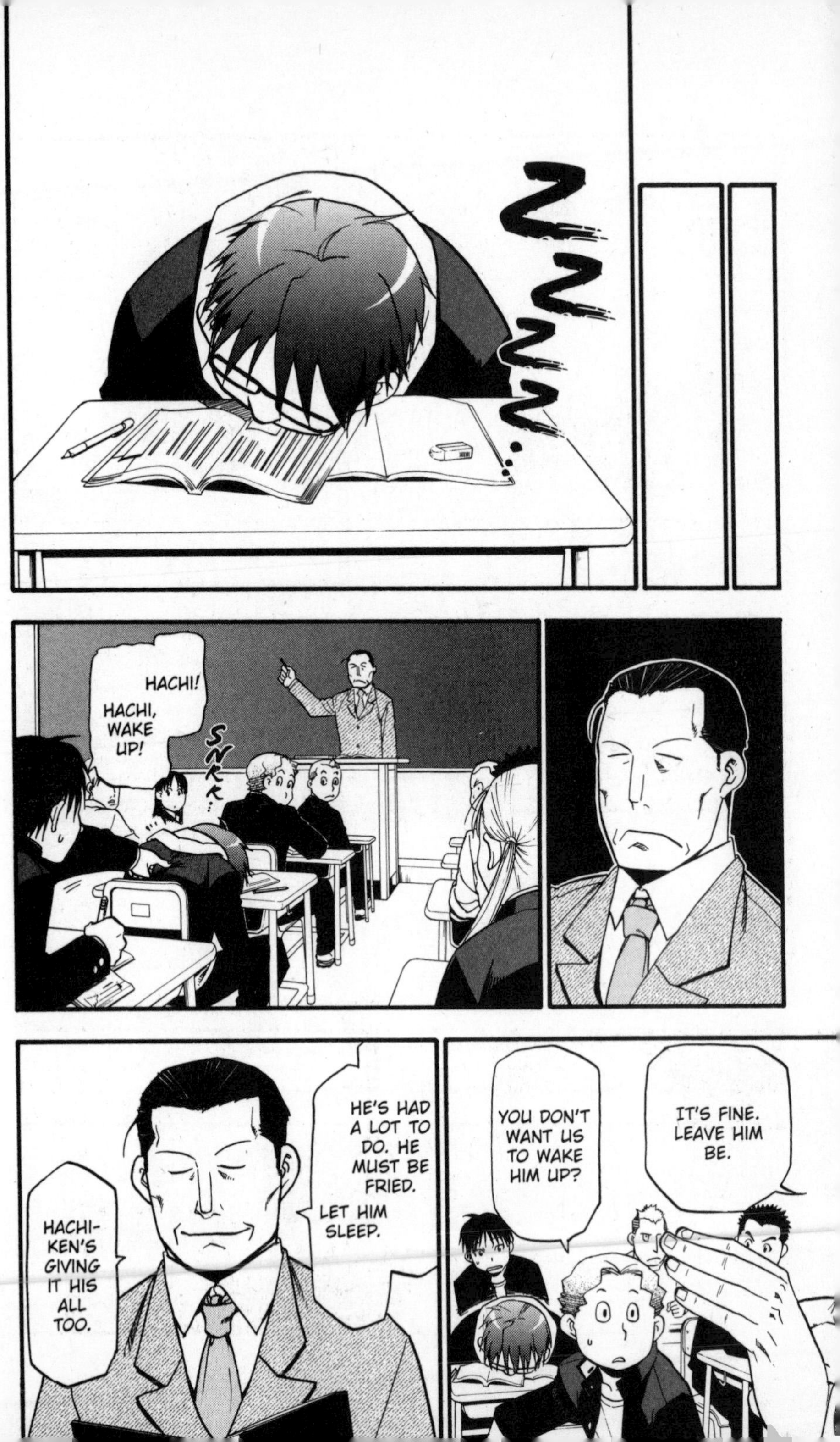
ZZZZ
HACHI! HACHI, WAKE UP!
SNKK...
IT'S FINE. LEAVE HIM BE.
YOU DON'T WANT US TO WAKE HIM UP?
HE'S HAD A LOT TO DO. HE MUST BE FRIED.
LET HIM SLEEP.
HACHI-KEN'S GIVING IT HIS ALL TOO.

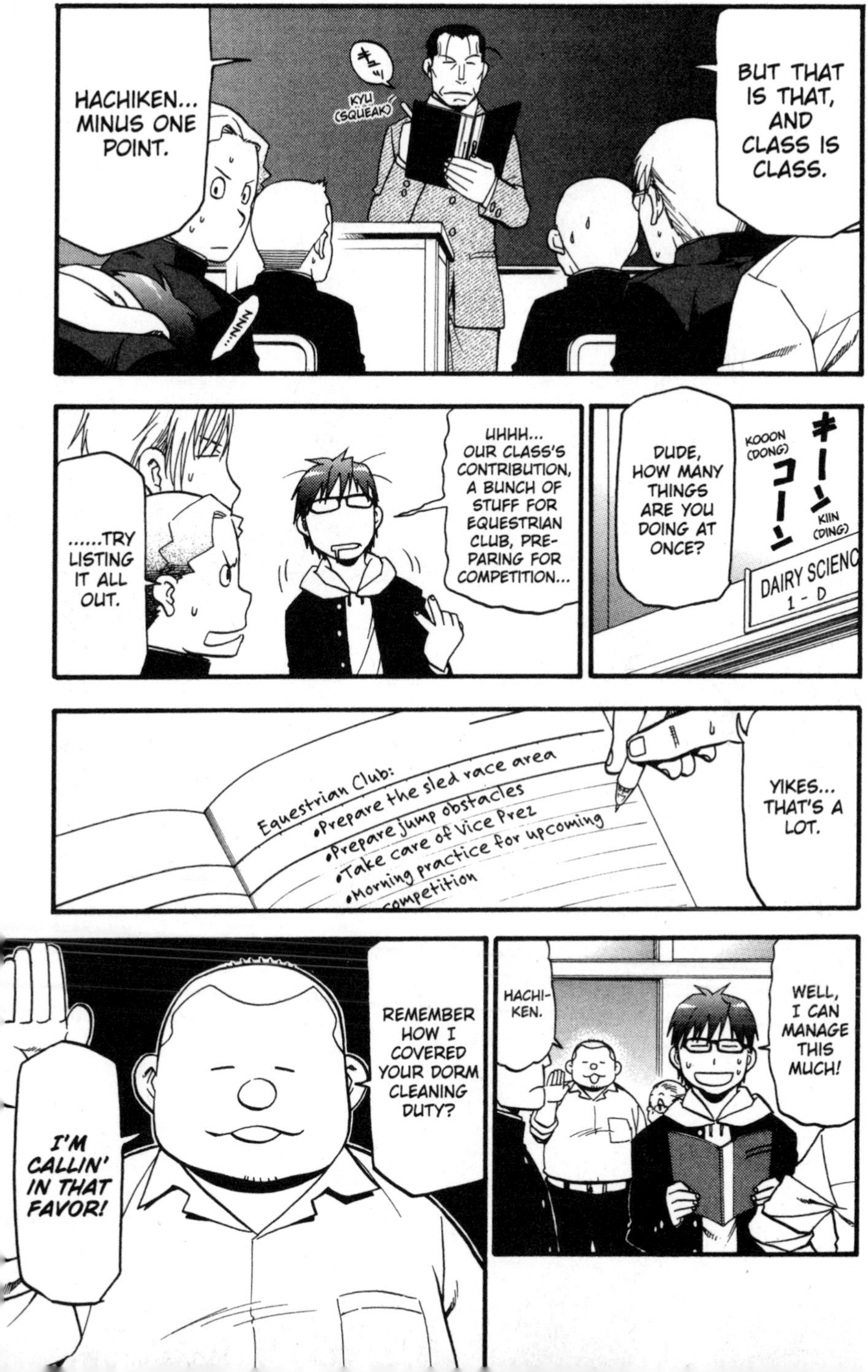
BUT THAT IS THAT, AND CLASS IS CLASS.
KYU (SQUEAK)
HACHIKEN... MINUS ONE POINT.
NNN...
KIIN (DING)
KOOON (DONG)
DUDE, HOW MANY THINGS ARE YOU DOING AT ONCE?
DAIRY SCIENC
1 - D
UHHH... OUR CLASS'S CONTRIBUTION, A BUNCH OF STUFF FOR EQUESTRIAN CLUB, PRE-PARING FOR COMPETITION...
......TRY LISTING IT ALL OUT.
YIKES... THAT'S A LOT.
Equestrian Club:
•Prepare the sled race area
•Prepare jump obstacles
•Take care of Vice Prez
•Morning practice for upcoming competition
WELL, I CAN MANAGE THIS MUCH!
HACHI-KEN.
REMEMBER HOW I COVERED YOUR DORM CLEANING DUTY?
I'M CALLIN' IN THAT FAVOR!

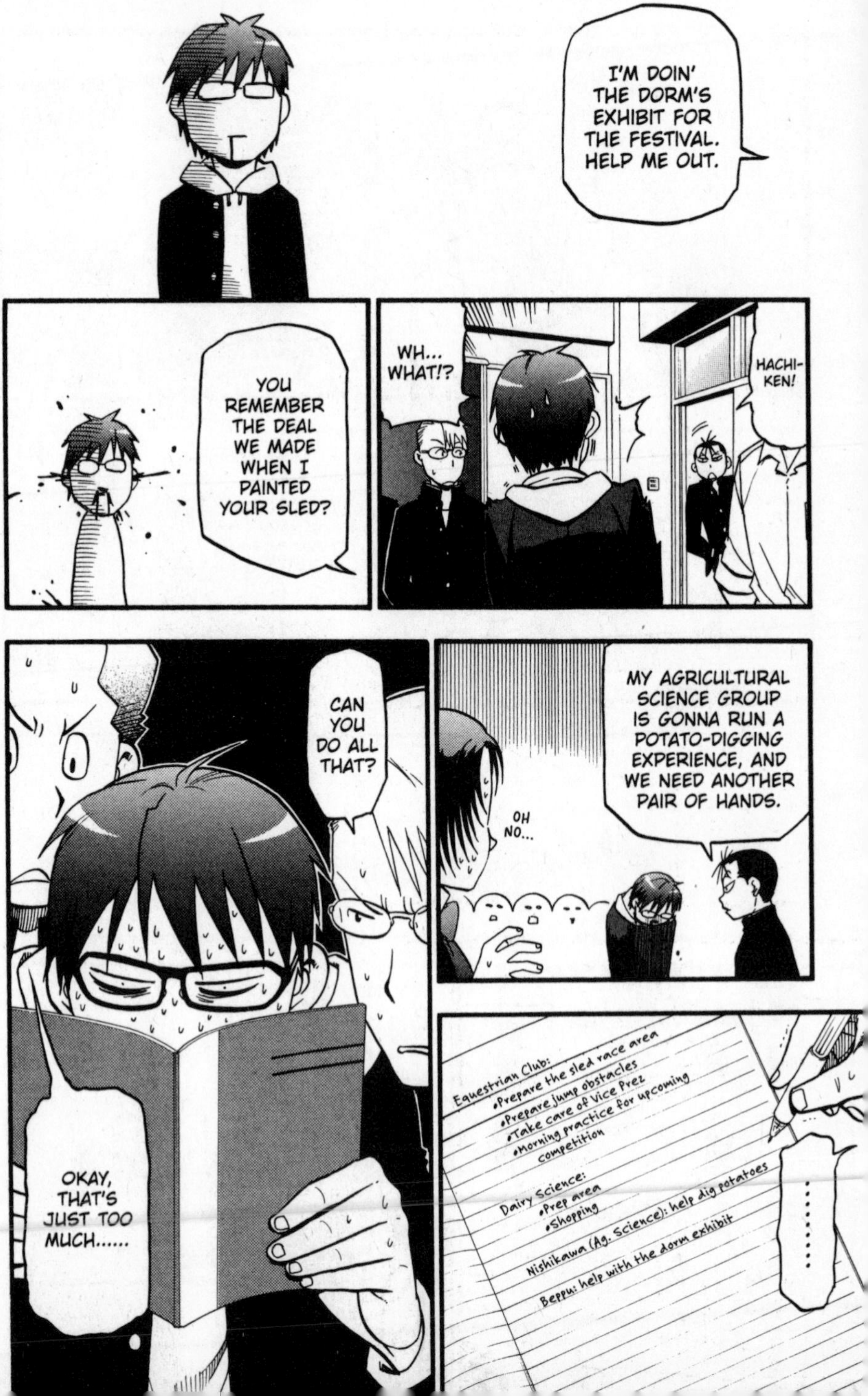
I'M DOIN' THE DORM'S EXHIBIT FOR THE FESTIVAL. HELP ME OUT.
HACHI-KEN!
WH... WHAT!?
YOU REMEMBER THE DEAL WE MADE WHEN I PAINTED YOUR SLED?
MY AGRICULTURAL SCIENCE GROUP IS GONNA RUN A POTATO-DIGGING EXPERIENCE, AND WE NEED ANOTHER PAIR OF HANDS.
OH NO...
Equestrian Club:
•Prepare the sled race area
•Prepare jump obstacles
•Take care of Vice Prez
•Morning practice for upcoming competition
Dairy Science:
•Prep area
•Shopping
Nishikawa (Ag. Science): help dig potatoes
Beppu: help with the dorm exhibit
......
CAN YOU DO ALL THAT?
OKAY, THAT'S JUST TOO MUCH......

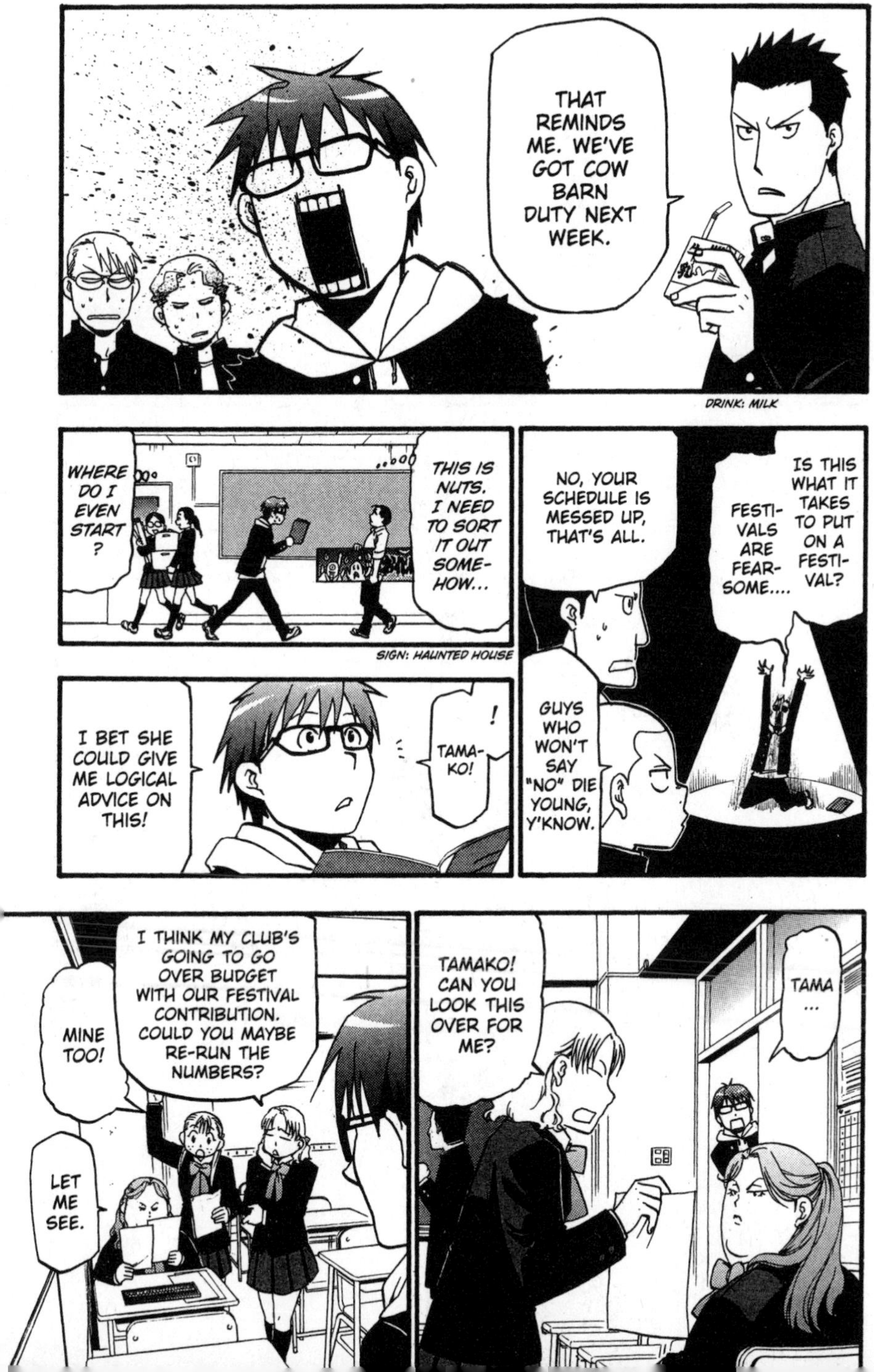
THAT REMINDS ME. WE'VE GOT COW BARN DUTY NEXT WEEK.
DRINK: MILK
IS THIS WHAT IT TAKES TO PUT ON A FESTIVAL?
FESTIVALS ARE FEARSOME....
NO, YOUR SCHEDULE IS MESSED UP, THAT'S ALL.
GUYS WHO WON'T SAY "NO" DIE YOUNG, Y'KNOW.
THIS IS NUTS. I NEED TO SORT IT OUT SOMEHOW...
WHERE DO I EVEN START?
SIGN: HAUNTED HOUSE
!
TAMAKO!
I BET SHE COULD GIVE ME LOGICAL ADVICE ON THIS!
TAMA...
TAMAKO! CAN YOU LOOK THIS OVER FOR ME?
I THINK MY CLUB'S GOING TO GO OVER BUDGET WITH OUR FESTIVAL CONTRIBUTION. COULD YOU MAYBE RE-RUN THE NUMBERS?
MINE TOO!
LET ME SEE.

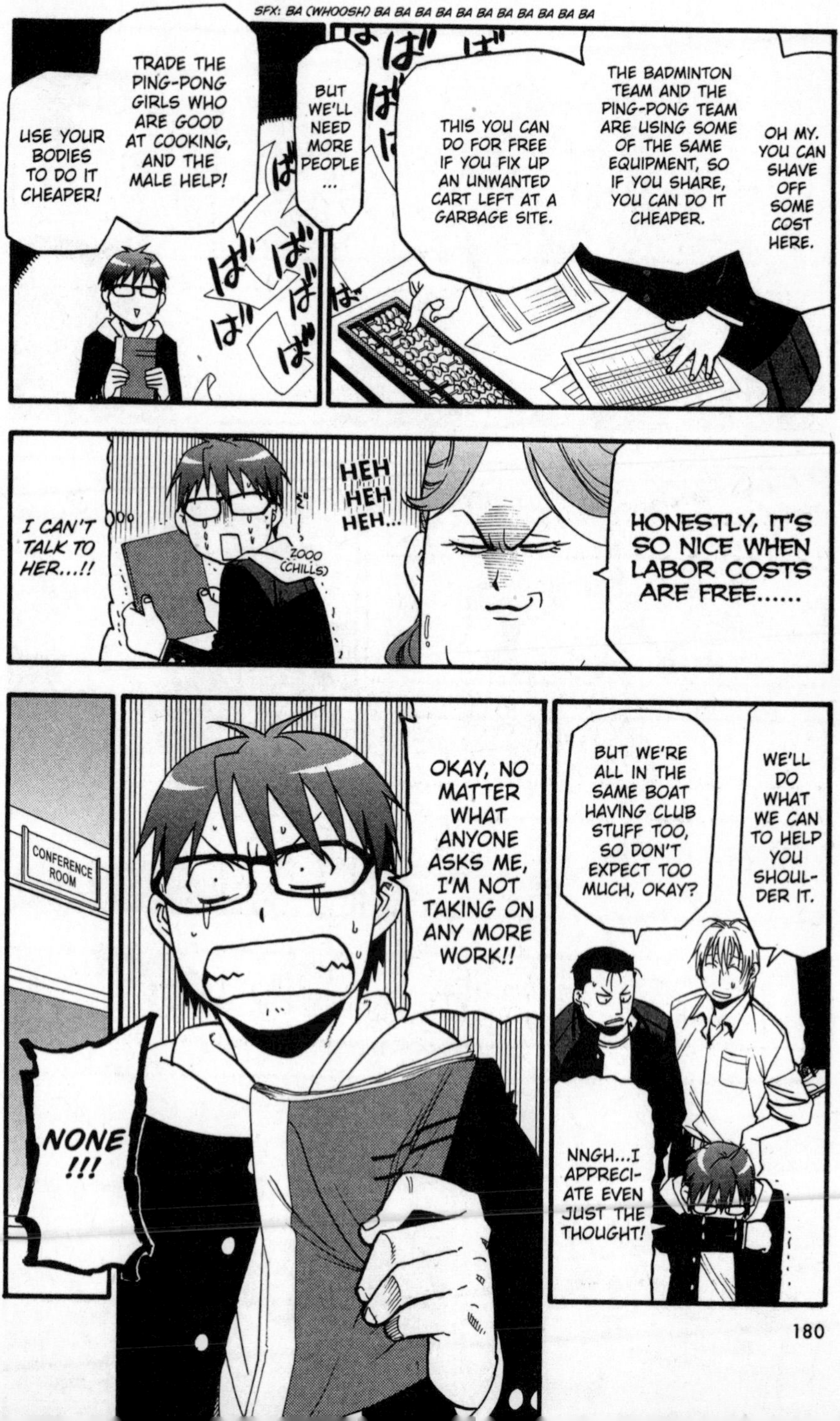
SFX: BA (WHOOSH) BA BA BA BA BA BA BA BA BA BA BA BA
OH MY. YOU CAN SHAVE OFF SOME COST HERE.
THE BADMINTON TEAM AND THE PING-PONG TEAM ARE USING SOME OF THE SAME EQUIPMENT, SO IF YOU SHARE, YOU CAN DO IT CHEAPER.
THIS YOU CAN DO FOR FREE IF YOU FIX UP AN UNWANTED CART LEFT AT A GARBAGE SITE.
BUT WE'LL NEED MORE PEOPLE...
TRADE THE PING-PONG GIRLS WHO ARE GOOD AT COOKING, AND THE MALE HELP!
USE YOUR BODIES TO DO IT CHEAPER!
HONESTLY, IT'S SO NICE WHEN LABOR COSTS ARE FREE......
HEH HEH HEH...
ZOOO (CHILLS)
I CAN'T TALK TO HER...!!
WE'LL DO WHAT WE CAN TO HELP YOU SHOULDER IT.
BUT WE'RE ALL IN THE SAME BOAT HAVING CLUB STUFF TOO, SO DON'T EXPECT TOO MUCH, OKAY?
NNGH...I APPRECIATE EVEN JUST THE THOUGHT!
OKAY, NO MATTER WHAT ANYONE ASKS ME, I'M NOT TAKING ON ANY MORE WORK!!
CONFERENCE ROOM
NONE!!!

WE'RE THE ONES WHO STARTED THE PIZZA-BAKING!
DAIRY SCIENCE
WELL, WE'RE THE ONES WHO REPAIRED IT!
AGRICULTURAL ENGINEERING
SILVICULTURE SCIENCE
IT'S IN OUR HANDS-ON AREA!
DO YOU THINK YOU CAN MAKE TOMATO SAUCE WITHOUT US?
FOOD SCIENCE
WHO DO YOU THINK GREW THOSE TOMATOES?
AGRICULTURAL SCIENCE

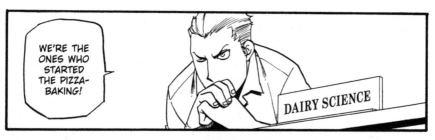

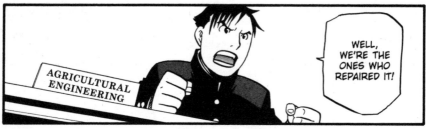

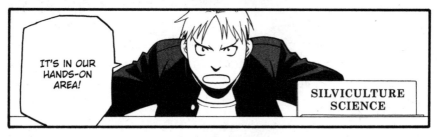

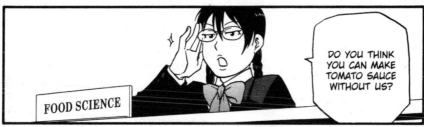

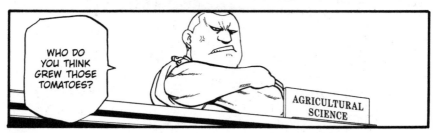

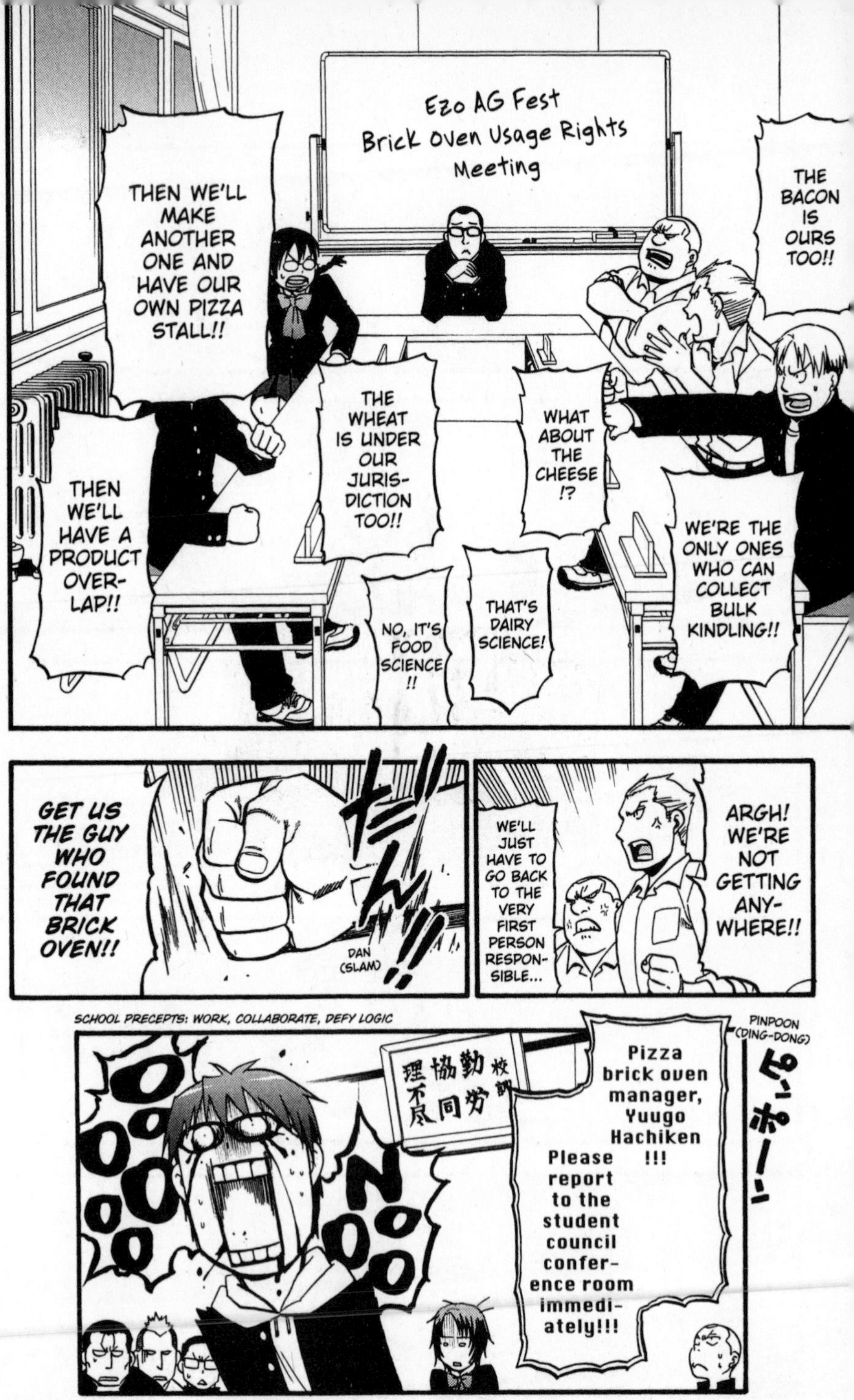
THE BACON IS OURS TOO!!
Ezo AG Fest Brick Oven Usage Rights Meeting
THEN WE'LL MAKE ANOTHER ONE AND HAVE OUR OWN PIZZA STALL!!
WE'RE THE ONLY ONES WHO CAN COLLECT BULK KINDLING!!
WHAT ABOUT THE CHEESE!?
THE WHEAT IS UNDER OUR JURIS-DICTION TOO!!
THEN WE'LL HAVE A PRODUCT OVER-LAP!!
THAT'S DAIRY SCIENCE!
NO, IT'S FOOD SCIENCE!!
ARGH! WE'RE NOT GETTING ANY-WHERE!!
WE'LL JUST HAVE TO GO BACK TO THE VERY FIRST PERSON RESPON-SIBLE...
DAN (SLAM)
GET US THE GUY WHO FOUND THAT BRICK OVEN!!
PINPOON (DING-DONG)
SCHOOL PRECEPTS: WORK, COLLABORATE, DEFY LOGIC
ピンポーン!!
Pizza brick oven manager, Yuugo Hachiken!!! Please report to the student council confer-ence room immedi-ately!!!
校訓 勤労 協同 理不尽
NOOOOOOOOOOOO

Silver Spoon

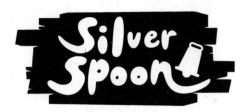

Recommending Riding

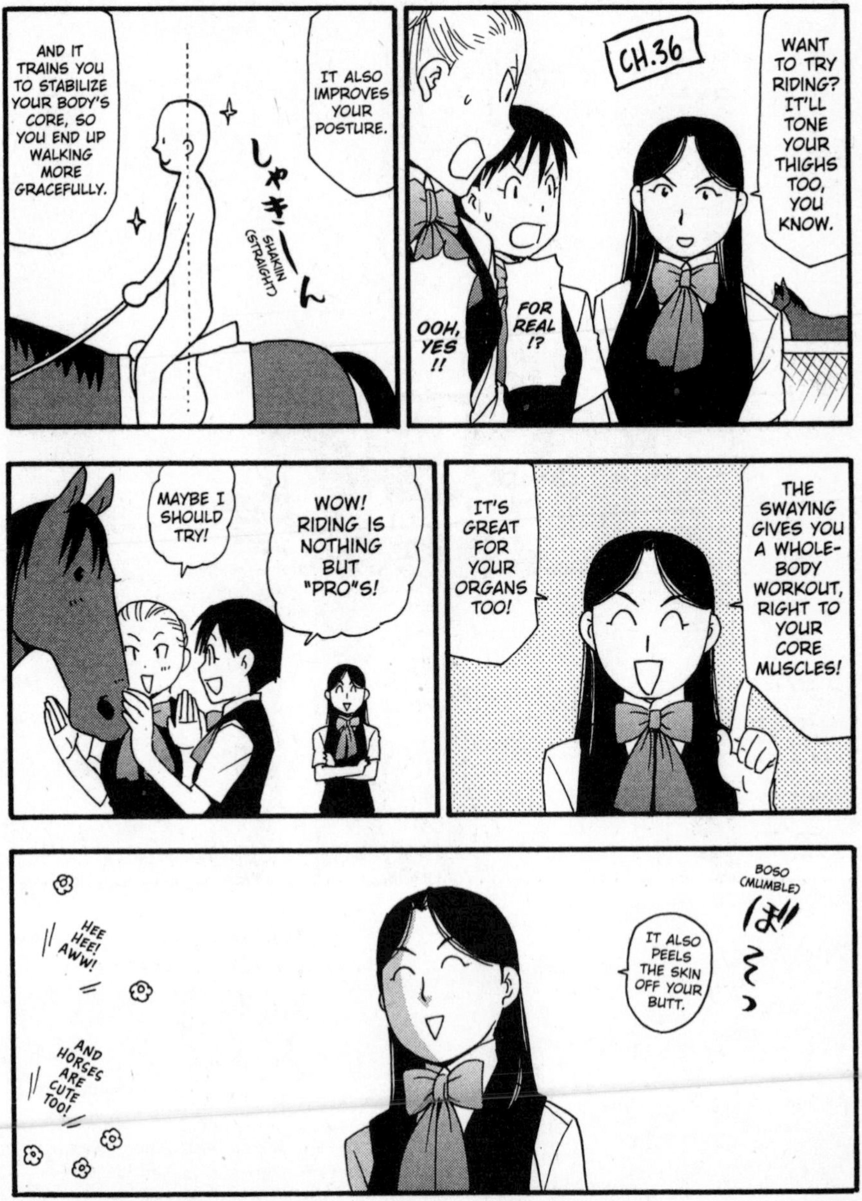
CH.36
WANT TO TRY RIDING? IT'LL TONE YOUR THIGHS TOO, YOU KNOW.
FOR REAL !?
OOH, YES !!
IT ALSO IMPROVES YOUR POSTURE.
しゃきーん
SHAKIIN (STRAIGHT)
AND IT TRAINS YOU TO STABILIZE YOUR BODY'S CORE, SO YOU END UP WALKING MORE GRACEFULLY.
THE SWAYING GIVES YOU A WHOLE-BODY WORKOUT, RIGHT TO YOUR CORE MUSCLES!
IT'S GREAT FOR YOUR ORGANS TOO!
WOW! RIDING IS NOTHING BUT "PRO"S!
MAYBE I SHOULD TRY!
BOSO (MUMBLE)
ぼそっ
IT ALSO PEELS THE SKIN OFF YOUR BUTT.
HEE HEE! AWW!
AND HORSES ARE CUTE TOO!

Cow Shed Diaries: Buying Hachiken's Glasses Chapter

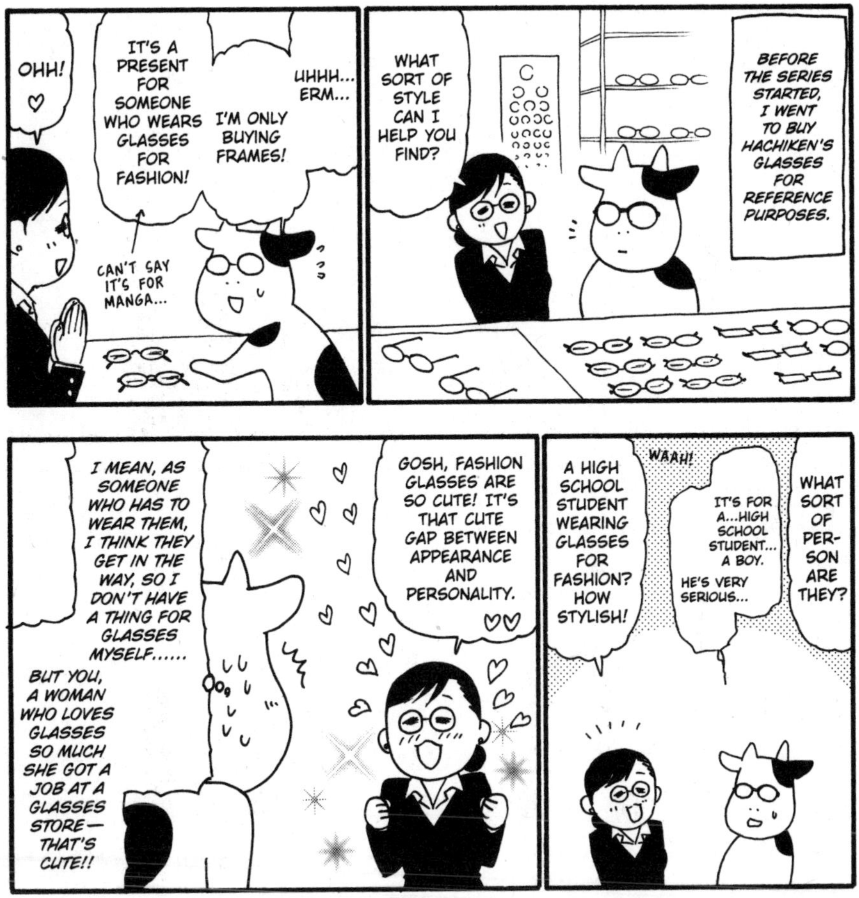
BEFORE THE SERIES STARTED, I WENT TO BUY HACHIKEN'S GLASSES FOR REFERENCE PURPOSES.
WHAT SORT OF STYLE CAN I HELP YOU FIND?
UHHH... ERM...
I'M ONLY BUYING FRAMES!
IT'S A PRESENT FOR SOMEONE WHO WEARS GLASSES FOR FASHION!
CAN'T SAY IT'S FOR MANGA...
OHH! ♡
WHAT SORT OF PERSON ARE THEY?
IT'S FOR A...HIGH SCHOOL STUDENT... A BOY.
HE'S VERY SERIOUS...
WAAH!
A HIGH SCHOOL STUDENT WEARING GLASSES FOR FASHION? HOW STYLISH!
GOSH, FASHION GLASSES ARE SO CUTE! IT'S THAT CUTE GAP BETWEEN APPEARANCE AND PERSONALITY. ♡♡
I MEAN, AS SOMEONE WHO HAS TO WEAR THEM, I THINK THEY GET IN THE WAY, SO I DON'T HAVE A THING FOR GLASSES MYSELF......
BUT YOU, A WOMAN WHO LOVES GLASSES SO MUCH SHE GOT A JOB AT A GLASSES STORE—THAT'S CUTE!!

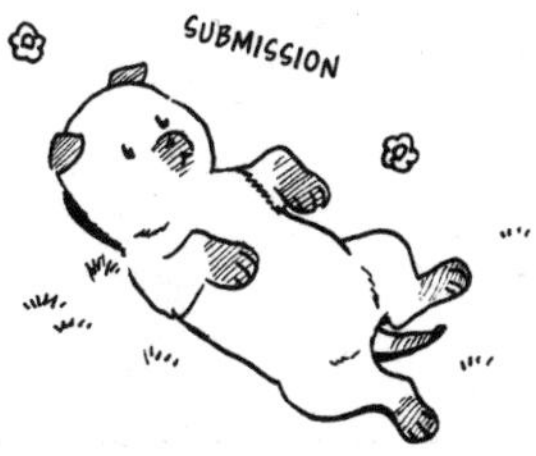
SUBMISSION

Silver Spoon 5!
Thanks so much for reading!

あらかわひろむ
Hiromu Arakawa

~ Special Thanks ~
All of my assistants,
Everyone who helped with collecting material, interviews, and consulting,
My editor, Takashi Tsubouchi,

AND YOU!!

NEXT......

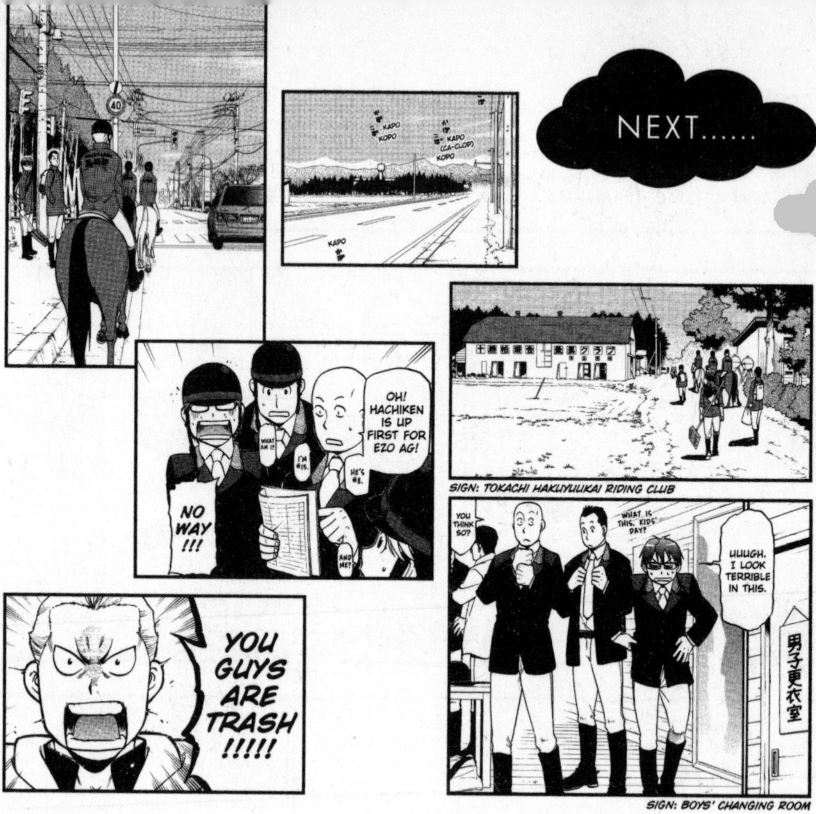
KAPO
KAPO (CA-CLOP) KOPO
KAPO KOPO
KAPO
SIGN: TOKACHI HAKUYUUKAI RIDING CLUB
OH! HACHIKEN IS UP FIRST FOR EZO AG!
HE'S #8.
I'M #15.
WHAT AM I?
NO WAY!!!
AND ME?
UUUGH. I LOOK TERRIBLE IN THIS.
男子更衣室
WHAT IS THIS, KIDS' DAY?
YOU THINK SO?
SIGN: BOYS' CHANGING ROOM
YOU GUYS ARE TRASH!!!!!

Even when you start something on a whim, the more you keep at it, the more ambitious you become: "I want to win." "I want to look cool riding." He can't help but think these things. The Ooezo Agricultural High School Equestrian Club Vice President Yuugo Hachiken's debut competition...

12/17/2019

Item(s) Checked Out

TITLE   Golden time. Vol. 1 /
BARCODE   33029106115918
DUE DATE   **01-07-20**

TITLE   Silver spoon. 5 /
BARCODE   33029106476476
DUE DATE   **01-07-20**

TITLE   Kaguya-sama : Love
BARCODE   33029106926876
DUE DATE   **01-07-20**

Total Items This Session: 3

Thank you for visiting the library!
Sacramento Public Library
www.saclibrary.org

Love your library?
Join the Friends!
www.saclibfriends.org/join
Visit our Book Den, too.

Terminal #   7

Hachi-ken-kun, riding Chest-nut.
HACHIKEN!!
GAH !!?
AKI MI-KA-GE!!
SO IT'S YOU !!!
THAT HURTS, YOU LITTLE...!
WAAAAAAAH!!
GUON (ZOOM)
PI (FWIP)
DON'T WORRY ABOUT ME.
DO (BOOM)
Hachiken-kun and Chestnut are off.

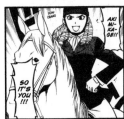

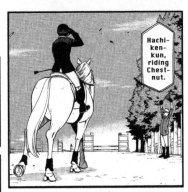

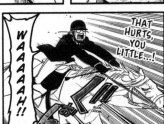

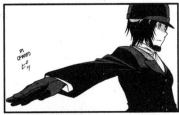

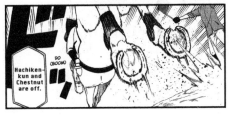

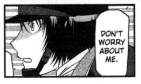

He may be good at exams, but it's the first sport meet of his life.

Silver Spoon Volume 6, coming December 2018!!

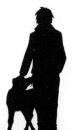

to be continued......

Silver Spoon

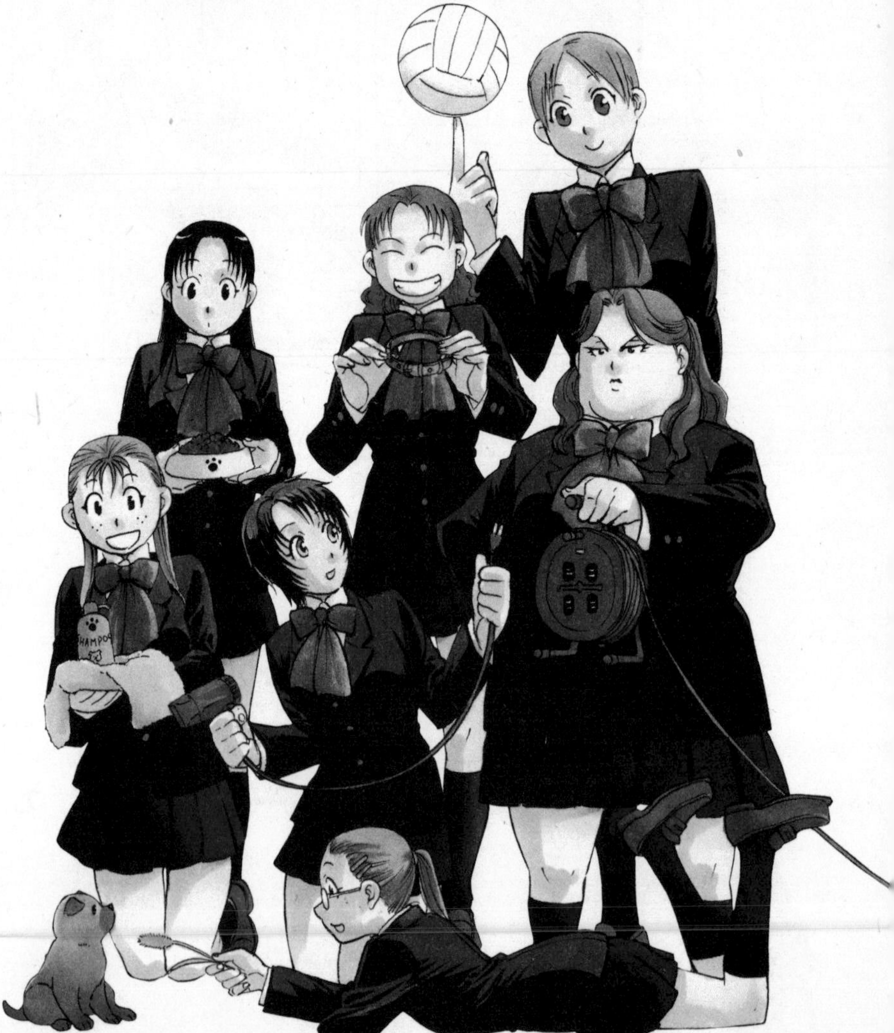

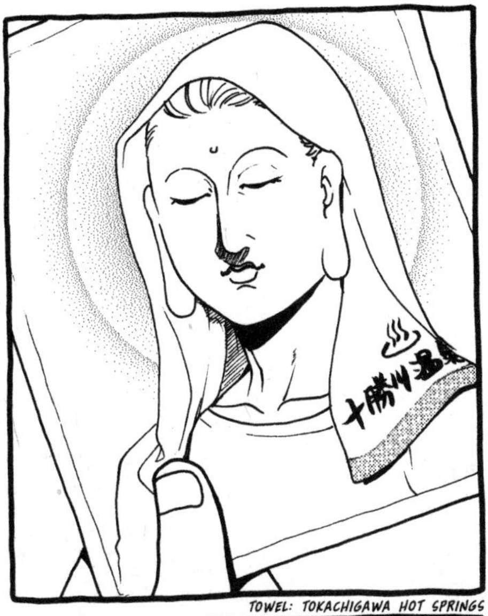
十勝川温泉

TOWEL: TOKACHIGAWA HOT SPRINGS

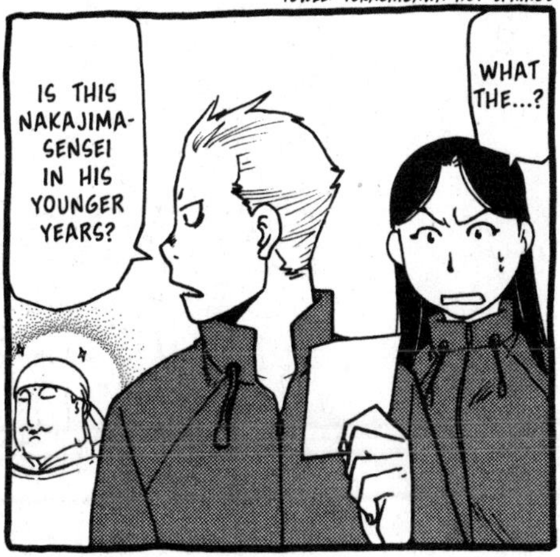
WHAT THE...?
IS THIS NAKAJIMA-SENSEI IN HIS YOUNGER YEARS?

Translation Notes

Common Honorifics

no honorific: Indicates familiarity or closeness; if used without permission or reason, addressing someone in this manner would constitute an insult.

-san: The Japanese equivalent of Mr./Mrs./Miss. If a situation calls for politeness, this is the fail-safe honorific.

-sama: Conveys great respect; may also indicate the social status of the speaker is lower than that of the addressee.

-kun: Used most often when referring to boys, this honorific indicates affection or familiarity. Occasionally used by older men among their peers, but it may also be used by anyone referring to a person of lower standing.

-chan: An affectionate honorific indicating familiarity used mostly in reference to girls; also used in reference to cute persons or animals of either gender.

-sensei: A respectful term for teachers, artists, or high-level professionals.

-niisan, nii-san, aniki, etc.: A term of endearment meaning "big brother" that may be more widely used to address any young man who is like a brother, regardless of whether he is related or not.

-neesan, nee-san, aneki, etc.: The female counterpart of the above, nee-san means "big sister."

Currency Conversion

While conversion rates fluctuate, an easy estimate for Japanese Yen conversion is ¥100 to 1 USD.

Page 66

Yakitori is skewered, grilled chicken and is a very popular festival food as it can be eaten without utensils.

Grilled offal (or *horumonyaki*) is another common festival food made from beef or pork organ meats. It is considered to be stamina building.

Page 67

Taiyaki is a cake filled with red bean paste and shaped like a fish. They are a popular sweet snack and best served warm. Like *yakitori*, they are a common food at many festivals.

Page 162

The "cringe sled" (*itasori*) is a play on "painful cars" (*itasha*)—cars that are decorated with fictional characters from anime, manga, or video games (especially pretty girls).

NPK48 is also a reference to AKB48, an idol group made up of forty-eight women that is named after otaku mecca Akihabara ("Akiba" for short, thus AKB).

The "48 Killer Moves" Nishikawa refers to are a group of wrestling moves taught to the titular character in the superhero wrestling manga *Kinnikuman* (published in the US as *Ultimate Muscle*).

Silver Spoon

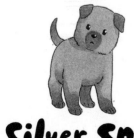

SACRAMENTO PUBLIC LIBRARY
828 "I" Street
Sacramento, CA 95814
11/18

Translation: Amanda Haley ✦ **Lettering: Abigail Blackman**

This book is a work of fiction. Names, characters, places, and incidents are the product of the author's imagination or are used fictitiously. Any resemblance to actual events, locales, or persons, living or dead, is coincidental.

GIN NO SAJI SILVER SPOON Vol. 5
by Hiromu ARAKAWA
© 2011 Hiromu ARAKAWA
All rights reserved.
Original Japanese edition published by SHOGAKUKAN.
English translation rights in the United States of America, Canada, the United Kingdom, Ireland, Australia and New Zealand arranged with SHOGAKUKAN through Tuttle-Mori Agency, Inc.

English translation © 2018 by Yen Press, LLC

Yen Press, LLC supports the right to free expression and the value of copyright. The purpose of copyright is to encourage writers and artists to produce the creative works that enrich our culture.

The scanning, uploading, and distribution of this book without permission is a theft of the author's intellectual property. If you would like permission to use material from the book (other than for review purposes), please contact the publisher. Thank you for your support of the author's rights.

Yen Press
1290 Avenue of the Americas
New York, NY 10104

Visit us at yenpress.com
facebook.com/yenpress
twitter.com/yenpress
yenpress.tumblr.com
instagram.com/yenpress

First Yen Press Edition: October 2018

Yen Press is an imprint of Yen Press, LLC.
The Yen Press name and logo are trademarks of Yen Press, LLC.

The publisher is not responsible for websites (or their content) that are not owned by the publisher.

Library of Congress Control Number: 2017959207

ISBN: 978-1-9753-2760-6

10 9 8 7 6 5 4 3 2 1

WOR

Printed in the United States of America